ISHIKAWA TAKUBOKU

OGIWARA SEISENSUI

TAKAMURA KŌTARŌ

MASAOKA SHIKI

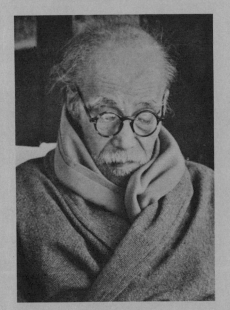

Modern Japanese Poets

AND THE NATURE OF LITERATURE

MAKOTO UEDA

Modern Japanese Poets

AND THE NATURE OF LITERATURE

STANFORD UNIVERSITY PRESS

STANFORD, CALIFORNIA

1983

Stanford University Press
Stanford, California
© 1983 by the Board of Trustees of the
Leland Stanford Junior University
Printed in the United States of America
ISBN 0-8047-1166-6   LC 82-60487

The photographs on the endpapers appear with
the kind permission of the following:
Masaoka Shiki, Yosano Akiko, Ishikawa Takuboku,
and Hagiwara Sakutarō, courtesy of the Museum of Modern
Japanese Literature; Miyazawa Kenji, from *Kōhon Miyazawa Kenji
zenshū* (Chikima Shobō), vol. 12, pt. 2; Takamura
Kōtarō, from *Takamura Kōtarō zenshū* (Chikuma Shobō), vol. 13;
Ogiwara Seisensui, from *Bashō kanshō* (Chōbunsha); and
Takahashi Shinkichi, from *Takahashi Shinkichi shishū* (Yayoi Shobō).

Preface

THIS IS A study of eight modern Japanese poets: Masaoka
Shiki, Yosano Akiko, Ishikawa Takuboku, Hagiwara Sakutarō, Miyazawa Kenji, Takamura Kōtarō, Ogiwara Seisensui, and
Takahashi Shinkichi. They have long commanded high respect
in their own country, and of late their works are also becoming
known to Western readers. Seven of the eight poets have had at
least one volume of poetry published in English translation, and
if the poems of Seisensui, the one exception, were collected from
the various English-language publications in which they have
been translated, they would more than make up a full-length
book. Altogether these poets' works represent the great bulk of
modern Japanese poetry available in English.

The study focuses on each poet's concept of poetry. Although
the poet may not have formulated a systematic poetic, since
verse writing is a self-conscious act (at least in its latter stages) he
or she must have had some ideas about what poetry is and about
its form, content, aim, and so on. An examination of those ideas
should provide useful clues for understanding the poet's work. I
have no intention of insisting that a poem should always be interpreted in the way its author wanted, but I do think any serious reader should pay some heed to the ideas about poetry
that informed it. Modern Japanese poetry has been little studied
from this angle, and I hope this book will help to fill the gap, as
my earlier book, *Modern Japanese Writers and the Nature of Literature* (Stanford: Stanford University Press, 1976) has done for
prose fiction.

To arrive at the eight poets' ideas on the nature of poetry, I have used their literary essays, critical reviews, personal correspondence, diaries, prefaces, postscripts, and other miscellaneous writings, as well as their poems. Some of these materials, bearing such titles as "Principles of Poetry" and "How to Write and Appreciate Haiku," are comprehensive expositions of a poetic. The great majority, however, are occasional pieces that reveal ideas about poetry in a more casual, indirect manner; I have tried to use such material only to the extent that its implications are consistent with the author's major poetic works. My foremost aim has been to elucidate each poet's ideas of poetry, not to criticize it. In view of the multitudinous (and often conflicting) poetic theories that exist in the West, I have decided to leave the latter type of study to other scholars who, unlike myself, feel a strong affinity with a specific theory.

As in my earlier book, I have assigned one chapter to each poet. The chapter is subdivided into five sections, each dealing with a major issue in literary criticism. The first centers on the question of the relationship between art and nature, between poetry as a work of art and the universe that surrounds it and supplies its subject matter. This is followed by a section on the creative process, the relationship between the poet and his artistic creation. Focus then shifts to the poem-reader relationship: the third section attempts to identify each poet's view of the nature of the emotional or aesthetic effect the poem produces in the reader's mind. The fourth section discusses intrinsic elements of the poem, such as form, structure, style, and vocabulary, with special emphasis on how the poet came to select a specific verse form as his main vehicle of expression. The chapter then concludes with a section probing the poet's ideas about the use of poetry. The last topic may seem a subset of the relationship between poem and reader; however, Japanese literary criticism has always discussed the use of poetry for the poet himself as well as for the reader, and therefore a separate section seemed in order.

For the benefit of those who are not familiar with the long tradition of Japanese verse, I have added a short Introduction out-lining its historical development and explaining various literary terms that recur in the chapters to follow. The book ends with a brief Conclusion that broadly sketches the general features of modern Japanese poetry and summarizes the contributions of our eight poets.

I feel some regret at not being able to discuss certain other poets, such as Shimazaki Tōson, Kitahara Hakushū, and Tani-kawa Shuntarō. But I had to draw the line somewhere. If a reader is provoked by my omissions or by my treatment of a poet, I hope he will go on to write his own book: there have been too few studies of modern Japanese poetry, and I shall be only too happy if this one serves to stimulate other scholars.

Several notes on more technical matters follow. The names of all Japanese writers in this book are given in the usual Japanese order, with the surname preceding the given name, *gagō* ("ele-gant name"), or *haigō* ("haiku name"). I have tried to refer to poets as they normally would be spoken of in Japan—Shiki, not Masaoka; Takuboku, not Ishikawa; and so on. For Sakutarō, Kotarō, and several others there seems to be no established prac-tice, so I have had to decide on a standard myself. All titles of Japanese poems and other publications appear in English trans-lation; those who wish to know the original titles should consult the index at the end of the book. The texts of haiku and tanka, which have no titles, are given in romanization in a section fol-lowing the text. For the benefit of those who read Japanese, source notes are also appended.

Although some excellent translations already exist, for the sake of uniformity all the translations in this book are my own. In translating a Japanese poem, I have tried to retain its original shape as much as possible. Of course it is impossible to translate every haiku or tanka in exactly 17 or 31 syllables, but I have at-tempted to render a seven-syllable line as somewhat longer in English than a five-syllable line. In free-style haiku, which has no fixed syllable pattern, my lineation is based on caesuras. I must confess, however, that through all those efforts I have once again been made painfully aware of the truism that the translator is an interpreter who in the process of translating a poem must focus on one aspect of its meaning at the expense of others. I therefore encourage my readers to consult other available translations. To make it easy to do so, I have appended a checklist of the eight poets' works that have been published in English translation.

My thanks are due to Stanford University for allowing me a year's leave to complete this book, and I am equally indebted to the Social Science Research Council, whose generous grant helped to support my research during the leave. The funds for the grant were provided by the National Endowment for the Humanities, the Ford Foundation, and the Japan–United States Friendship Commission. The commission, in cooperation with Osaka University, also helped to facilitate my research trip to Japan in the summer of 1980. Some of the materials I have used were difficult to obtain, and therefore I am especially grateful for the assistance of the staffs of East Asian collections at Stanford University's Hoover Institution, the University of California at Berkeley, the University of Chicago, the Library of Congress, Waseda University, and the University of Toronto. Some of my poetry translations have previously appeared elsewhere, and I thank *The Beloit Poetry Journal* and the University of Toronto Press for their permission to reprint poems they have published. Ms. Helen Tartar read the entire manuscript and offered me a countless number of helpful suggestions. Last, but not least, I am indebted to the members of my family, who made many sacrifices during the long period of my research and writing.

M.U.

Contents

Modern Japanese Poets

AND THE NATURE OF LITERATURE

Introduction

JAPAN OFFICIALLY entered the modern age in 1868, when with an imperial proclamation she asserted her resolve to westernize. Changes came quickly: a telegraph service opened, railway trains began to run, steamships set sail, and oil lamps and gaslight brightened the night. Braver folks started to eat beef, wear leather shoes, and go out with Western-style umbrellas (which they called "bat shades") on rainy days. The rapid westernization, however, did not impress at least one early visitor from Europe. Writing in 1880, the British philologist Basil Hall Chamberlain complained: "The Japanese, at no time given to idealism, have, during the last few years, attached themselves to the pursuit of the advantages of the material side of European civilization, with an eagerness amounting to disdain for everything poetical, or even literary, in any branch." The Victorian scholar, in the seventh year of his stay in Japan, was tired of the Japanese craze for Western technology.

As it turned out, Chamberlain spoke too rashly. Less than two years later, three professors at Tokyo University—the sociologist Toyama Chuzan (1848–1900), the botanist Yatabe Shōkon (1851–99), and the philosopher Inoue Sonken (1855–1944)— brought out a book introducing Western poetry to Japanese readers. Entitled *A Selection of New-Style Poems*, it presented verses by Shakespeare, Thomas Gray, Tennyson, Longfellow, Thomas Campbell, and other European poets in Japanese translation. Also included were a few examples of the professors' own poems written in the "new style," the style they used for translating Western verse. The anthology caused a tremendous stir among contemporary poets, and marked the beginning of a new era in Japanese poetry.

Chamberlain, however, had good grounds for predicting that poetry would change but slowly in modern Japan. In 1880, Japanese poets were working in just two major verse forms, neither of which had changed in outward shape for centuries. One, called tanka (or *waka*),[1] had five lines of 5, 7, 5, 7, and 7 syllables, for a total of 31 syllables. The other was haiku, an even shorter poem of 17 syllables, with the syllabic scheme 5–7–5. Despite the extreme brevity of these forms, there had been no serious attempt to invent a new verse form for a long time.

Of the two major forms, tanka had a considerably longer history. The two earliest known books in Japanese, *The Records of Ancient Matters* (711) and *The Chronicles of Japan* (720), include more than 80 poems written in 31 syllables. One of the poems was attributed to a brother of the mythological Sun Goddess, and this led some later scholars to claim a divine origin for the tanka form. By the time *The Collection of Ten Thousand Leaves* was compiled in the mid-eighth century, tanka was well on its way to becoming the dominant vehicle for lyrical expression in Japan. The massive anthology contained some 4,200 poems in that form, written by poets from all walks of life, ranging from emperors and princes to soldiers and peasants. The poems were on many subjects, including love, friendship, death, travel, scenic beauty, and the impermanence of human life. Their language was still unpolished, but its simplicity and artlessness had a seemingly effortless, natural quality envied by later, more self-conscious versifiers.

Tanka gained in elegance and refinement as the imperial court became the center of literary activities. From time to time the reigning emperor commissioned a poetry anthology, which

[1] Today the two terms are used interchangeably in Japan, although some scholars define waka as premodern poetry written in 31 syllables and tanka as its descendant in the modern period. To avoid confusion, the word "tanka" is employed throughout this book to designate a 31-syllable poem, modern or premodern.

set a standard for contemporary verse writing. *The Collection of Ancient and Modern Poems* (905), the first such anthology, was especially famous, and many generations of poets looked up to it as a model. It contained over 1,100 poems, almost all tanka, written by noblemen and noblewomen. The poems reflected the ideals of court culture, being aristocratic in theme, elegant in fancy, witty in tone, and dextrous in wording; however, their artfulness inevitably resulted in a loss of the simplicity and youthful vigor that had characterized earlier poetry. Contemporary taste was also affected by Buddhism, which had been introduced to Japan several centuries earlier. It induced many poets to cherish an aesthetic ideal called *aware*, an empathetic appreciation of the ephemeral beauty manifest in nature and human life. These features, with some modifications, were retained throughout the poetry of the Heian period (794–1185).

The trend to artistic refinement reached a peak in *The New Collection of Ancient and Modern Poems* (1205), the eighth imperial poetry anthology. All 1,978 poems it included were tanka, and the poets who wrote them had consciously cultivated a poetic identity, a distinctive sensibility or style to set their work apart from the tens of thousands of other poems that had by then been written in the 31-syllable form. Their poetic effects often relied on subtle rhetoric, hidden allusion, esoteric symbolism, and a delicate interplay of images, and they developed a more complex ambience, adding to elegance and *aware* elements of mystery, darkness, depth, and ambiguity to formulate a new aesthetic ideal they called *yūgen*. Seeking ever-greater refinement, they exploited virtually every literary device conceivable within the Heian cultural tradition, leaving little room for later innovation. Thirty-one-syllable poetry continued to be written in subsequent centuries, but it became stale and formulaic. Although some talented poets, such as Minamoto Sanetomo (1192–1219) and Tachibana Akemi (1812–68), tried to reinvigorate it, tanka never regained its former glory.

Although tanka was the dominant verse form, Japan was not without other poetic modes during those early centuries. *The*

Records of Ancient Matters, The Chronicles of Japan, and *The Collection of Ten Thousand Leaves* all contain longer poems, which usually consist of alternating five- and seven-syllable lines. Some were ritual poems, solemn in tone and formal in diction; others were lyrics that vented strong emotions in more personal language; still others were folk songs sung at feasts and festivities. The last evolved into *imayō,* or "modern-style songs," in the middle and late Heian period. A typical imayō consisted of four lines, each having twelve syllables, with a caesura after the seventh. The form, however, went out of fashion before it had a chance to mature as poetry.

Another poetic mode employed by early poets was *kanshi,* or poetry in Chinese. Ancient Japan imported much from the more advanced civilization of China, and people of the ruling class were expected to have a high competence in Chinese, including the ability to write verse in that language. The Japanese produced the best kanshi during the eighth and ninth centuries, before they grew more conscious of their national identity. The second—and final—flowering of the genre came in the fourteenth and fifteenth centuries, when a new sect of Chinese Buddhism, Zen, permeated Japanese culture and a great many kanshi were written by Zen monks living in mountain monasteries. Their writings were revered as *gozan bungaku,* or "literature of the Five Mountains," alluding to the five famous Zen temples in and around Kyoto.

However, kanshi remained poetry written in a foreign language, and it was not popular enough to take the place of tanka when the 31-syllable form began to decline after *The New Collection of Ancient and Modern Poems.* The verse form that came to the forefront of Japanese poetry in the fourteenth and fifteenth centuries was *renga,* or "linked verse." Originally renga had the same form as tanka, except that its first three lines (5−7−5) and last two lines (7−7) were composed by two different poets. In the Heian period tanka poets wrote it as a kind of game. Gradually, however, they became more serious. The form grew longer, too, as more than two poets began to participate. In this longer form, the first stanza, called *hokku* ("opening verse"), consisted of lines with five, seven, and five syllables and referred to the season of the year. It was followed by alternating stanzas of 7–7 and 5–7–5, which poets on the team kept contributing until the final stanza was completed. The number of stanzas varied. Normally a single renga was made up of either 36, 44, 50, 100, or 1,000 stanzas, although sometimes poets went on to write 10,000-stanza renga.

The poetic ideals of renga were generally those of *The New Collection of Ancient and Modern Poems*, the last great anthology of tanka. Yet because it was written by a team of poets, renga imposed a number of added rules and restrictions. For instance, each participant was expected to know how many times a specific image could be used in a linked poem. In a 100-stanza renga, an image like the morning sun or plum blossoms could appear only once; the summer moon or a wild goose, twice; cherry blossoms, three times; the snow, four times. In the sixteenth century, as a greater number of people became literate and began to show an interest in verse writing, there was a movement to popularize renga, freeing it from courtly ideals and intricate compositional regulations. The new type of linked poetry, called *haikai* ("humorous verse"), aimed to be more lighthearted, and sometimes even parodied the elegance and courtly refinement that were the main aesthetic goals of renga. In time, however, haikai too became more serious, and in the hands of the poet Matsuo Bashō (1644–94) it evolved into a major literary form. Bashō, a lifelong seeker after moral truth who conceived of poetry as a kind of religion, stressed the importance of spiritual discipline in writing haikai. His main poetic ideal, known as *sabi*, presumed a disciplined mind that would recognize the basic loneliness of man and, by calmly accepting it, elevate it to an ennobling aesthetic effect. Seeking to realize this ideal, he traveled far and wide within Japan, writing verse and keeping diaries along the way.

In his travel journals Bashō often cited hokku to mark lyrical moments of a journey. Some of these verses were originally composed to start off a haikai, but others seem to have been conceived with little or no expectation of being followed by other stanzas. After Bashō's time, such independent hokku came to be written more and more often. In order to distinguish them from ordinary hokku, I have decided to follow the present Japanese practice and call them "haiku" throughout this book, although the term was not widely used in premodern Japan. In my usage, a haiku consists of 17 syllables and includes a season word, as hokku does, but it differs from hokku in being a self-sufficient poem.

Haikai and haiku reached another high point with Yosa Buson (1716–83), a painter by profession. A consummate technician, Buson brought to his verse a painter's eye for form and color, along with an expansive imagination and a taste for the exotic, which at times led him to portray people and events remote in time or space. When he and his immediate followers were gone, however, poetry fell on hard times. Though Kobayashi Issa (1763–1827) wrote some powerful and intensely personal haiku, in his own lifetime he exerted little influence on the contemporary poetic scene. In the nineteenth century, haikai and haiku met the same fate as tanka. Although more people were writing poetry, most of their verses were trite in motif, hackneyed in diction, and lifeless in overall emotional appeal. In 1880, Chamberlain observed: "Ancient Japanese verses are now written just as our schoolboys write Latin verses."

The publication of *A Selection of New-Style Poems* was a timely stimulant to Japanese poetry in the late nineteenth century. Actually the "new style" was not strikingly new because its basic rhythm, the repetition of five- and seven-syllable lines, was that of traditional Japanese verse. Its vocabulary was pseudoclassical, too. Yet poems written in this style looked radically different from haiku and tanka, since they were longer and more open. They had broken free from the confines of 17 and 31 syllables, something that poets living in feudal Japan did not dare to do. Their themes also seemed fresh, since they encompassed more abstract intellectual materials. One of the original poems in the anthology, for example, was called "On the Principles of Sociology," a title unthinkable in traditional Japanese verse. From a literary point of view these poems left much to be desired, yet they opened a path for other innovators to follow. Indeed, a number of young poets did take that path. The most gifted was Shimazaki Tōson (1872–1943), who in 1897 published *A Collection of Young Herbs*, the first major collection of new-style poems. The form it explored was first known as *shintaishi* ("new-style poetry"), but as its newness wore off it came to be called *jiyūshi* ("free-style poetry"), or simply *shi*. Later poets who wrote in this form depended less and less on the 5–7 pattern, so that shi became virtually synonymous with "free verse."

The introduction of Western verse called attention to another major issue: the language of poetry. In 1880, Japanese poets were still writing verse in classical Japanese, the language of the Heian period, even though its vocabulary and grammar were considerably different from the language they used in daily conversation. When they discovered how close the idiom of Western poetry was to spoken language, these poets began to wonder whether they, too, should not be writing poems in a language less remote from daily life. The authors of *A Selection of New-Style Poems* had chosen to use a language very close to classical Japanese, despite their innovative form. For their followers, however, the choice was harder because later poets knew more about Western poetry and about the languages in which it was written.

The last decades of the nineteenth century, then, were a transitional period for Japanese poetry, a period when many issues were waiting to be settled. The foremost concerned poetic form. Tanka and haiku were still being written in great numbers, but poems in these forms suffered from mannerism as well as from close ties with premodern (and, in the public's eye, outmoded) culture. A new form inspired by Western poetry had been born, but it was still in its infancy. All three forms made use of a classical or pseudoclassical language, which was distinctly different from the vernacular. Japanese poetry was waiting for some talented reformers with fresh ideas who could resolve these issues. The wait did not last long. As we progress, we shall see how the efforts of the eight poets discussed in the following chapters contributed to modernizing Japanese poetry.

CHAPTER ONE

Masaoka Shiki

MASAOKA SHIKI (1867–1902) was the first major poet to appear in the formative years of modern Japanese verse. When his youthful ambition to become a statesman and help modernize Japanese society was foiled because of ill health, he made up his mind to modernize his country's poetry instead. Backed by a group of daring young poets, he vigorously worked to reform haiku and tanka, advocating a new set of poetic principles that he thought would be necessary in the coming age. Although these principles were not especially original, they were refreshingly innovative by contemporary standards and had a considerable effect on the generation of poets emerging at the time. If the value of a poetic theory can be measured by the quality of the poetry it has helped to produce, Shiki's would have to be rated very highly indeed. Above all, it was workable, and Shiki demonstrated this by writing verses himself. He was a teacher capable not only of lecturing on poetics but also of correcting specific aspects of a student's composition, and therein lay his greatest strength as a literary theorist.

Three Ways of Sketching from Life

Generalizations about Shiki's theory of poetry are difficult to make because it not only changed considerably in the course of his career, but also contained contradictions. Yet, on the relationship between art and nature, three ideas stand out. These are *shasei* ("sketches from life"), selective realism, and *makoto* ("truthfulness").

Of the three, shasei is the most famous, and has had the greatest effect on the practice of other poets. The idea was inspired in part by the realistic qualities Shiki saw in Western art, especially its attention to accurately observed perceptual detail and its claim to present the entire spectrum of experience. In the essay series "Six-Foot Sickbed," published less than three months before his death, Shiki stated that Western artists had valued shasei from early times, whereas the Japanese had neglected the principle. In advocating shasei, he emphasized the basics of realistic presentation: close and correct observation. A poet should, he felt, discipline himself to observe, not obtruding his thoughts or feelings and subordinating fanciful impulses to the simplest, most direct, and most common impressions of the things around him; he should express his observations in equally direct and simple language.

Shiki therefore inveighed against any tendency to idealize, saying in "Six-Foot Sickbed":

Even today 80 or 90 percent of all artists do not understand the value of shasei. Many of them advocate idealism both in poetry and in painting, and in their deficient knowledge they attack shasei as superficial. In reality, however, it is works based on idealism that are superficial, since they lack the variety of appeal possessed by works of shasei. I do not mean to imply that all idealistic works are mediocre, but an average work created on the basis of an ideal often is. Since ideals reflect a person's mind, they are apt to be unimaginative and trite unless the mind is that of a great genius.

A few lines later Shiki compared an idealistic artist to a man who tries to leap up to the roof of a house but falls into a pond below. "A work based on shasei may look plain and simple," he concluded, "yet it is seldom a complete failure." However, to reject idealism is not to reject imagination, the subjective coloring of experience, as we will see in discussing makoto below.

Shiki made shasei the basic principle of composition in his many essays intended to guide beginning poets. In "Haiku Wastebasket," for example, he likened an amateur versifier to a mother trying to help dress up her teenage daughter. More often than not the mother would put on too much face powder and select too gaudy a kimono, so that the daughter would end up looking either ridiculous or sickening. Decorative words chosen to emphasize the poet's emotional reaction or to heighten the effect of a scene were like the gaudy kimono and excess powder, but a composition that copied an actual scene with no verbal ornamentation would never be the worst kind of poem, even if it had other weaknesses. He then cited some dozen haiku that had made use of this principle and attained a marked success. Here are two such examples, the first by Bashō and the second by Tan Taigi (1709–71):[1]

> The wild sea:
> extending over Sado Isle,
> the River of Heaven.[2]

> Looking back, I see
> the barrier light up;
> mist at nightfall.

In "Letters to Tanka Poets," Shiki similarly quoted some tanka that he thought excelled because they objectively sketched nature. One example was this tanka by Fujiwara Sanesada (1139–91):[3]

> Through a break in the mist
> over the shore of Nago
> I gaze far out
> toward the billows' white
> splashing the sinking sun.

An island on the rough sea, a barrier in the mountains, and the sun setting into the ocean are presented with apparent objectivity, so that the beauty of the poem seems to emanate from the observed scene, not the poet's wording. For this reason, Shiki used these poems as fitting models for beginners in verse writing.

Such heavy emphasis on shasei had special pertinence in Shi-

[1] Tan Taigi was a friend of Buson. Fond of socializing, he was more skilled at writing haiku on human life than on nature.
[2] Sado is a small island off the northern coast of Japan, well known as a place of exile for prisoners in premodern times. The River of Heaven is the Milky Way, visualized as an immense river flowing through the sky.
[3] Fujiwara Sanesada was a well-known tanka poet in his lifetime, although his mundane interests apparently antagonized some of his fellow poets. He was fond of writing poems on seascapes, such as this one. It has been surmised that the shore of Nago was located near modern Osaka.

ki's time, when poetic composition was too often merely an intellectual exercise. Most haiku and tanka poets were in the habit of writing about imaginary scenes, stirred by a title such as "Plum Blossoms" or "Harvest Moon" and producing trite, emotionless poems. The practice of imagining a scene and writing a poem on it had a long history in Japan. Its origin dates back to the eighth century, and it gained wide popularity during the Heian period, when verse writing became a kind of game played at courtiers' gatherings. Poets amused themselves by writing verses on a given title and then comparing them, sometimes deciding winners and losers. This practice persisted throughout the centuries. Shasei was a revolt against it; moreover, by invoking the Western idea of realism shasei placed haiku and tanka in the context of world literature, thereby proving that these forms were not parochial or outmoded.

Yet intrinsically the principle of writing from direct observation was too simplistic, a tool for beginning students only. For more advanced writers, Shiki refined his theory by introducing the principle of selection. Students with some experience in shasei were to exercise choice in sketching nature. As he explained:

Shasei or realism means copying the subject as it is, but it necessarily involves a degree of selection and exclusion. . . . A writer sketching a landscape or an event should focus on its most beautiful or moving aspect. If he does this, the subject described will automatically begin to live its own life. It should be noted, however, that the most beautiful or moving aspect does not necessarily correspond to the most substantial or conspicuous or indispensable part of the subject. The aspect I speak of often lies in the shade, showing itself only partially in one's range of sight. A red camellia blooming in an ominously dark forest would strike one as exceedingly beautiful and attractive. In a case like that, a writer should sketch the scene focusing on the camellia. The flower does not have to be described in detail. It will deeply move the reader if the writer first describes the ominous darkness of the wood in some detail, then presents the camellia in the briefest words.

Although Shiki was talking about prose, the principle is equally applicable to verse. On its higher level, shasei is selective realism, the selection being made by the poet on the basis of his individual aesthetic sensibility. Each poet has his own taste, a personal predilection for a certain type of beauty. When he confronts a landscape, he should activate his aesthetic antenna and turn it toward the part of the landscape to which he is most attracted. A poem composed through this process will be more than a sketch from nature; it will be an externalization of the poet's sensibility, an expression of his aesthetic feelings, for by selecting a focus he cuts out a specific part of the landscape and frames it. That part of nature then has a center, a foreground, a background, and so forth. It will "begin to live its own life" because the poet has given his life to it.

Seen in this light, the poems cited by Shiki as models of shasei assume new significance. They are not just sketches from life, but each has a focus, its own "red camellia." The haiku by Bashō, for instance, concentrates on the tiny island of Sado, where many exiles from the capital lived out forlorn lives; it is set against the great expanses of the Milky Way above and the northern sea below. In Taigi's poem, the "red camellia" is the lighted barrier, and the "dark wood" the mountains at nightfall. A barrier was usually located at a mountain pass; it was also the point at which family and friends bade farewell to a departing traveler. As for Sanesada's tanka, the center of interest is the sun sinking in the waves. The clear image of the crimson sun gives a sharp focus to the otherwise hazy landscape of the seacoast folded in spring mist. In each instance the poet first selected a scene, then concentrated on certain aspects of the scene he had selected. To that extent, subjectivity is present in the poem.

Shiki seems to have thought that a student who had mastered the art of selective realism could increase the amount of subjectivity in his poetry if he saw fit. "At times," wrote Shiki, "the poet may even change the relative positions of things in an actual scene or subjectively replace a part of the scene by something that is not there. An actual scene is like a beautiful woman without makeup. She will not be free from imperfections, so that the artist must correct her eyebrows, put on rouge and powder, and dress her up in beautiful clothes." Shiki, who discouraged amateur versifiers from putting "makeup" on nature, here encouraged more advanced poets to do just that. He seems to have believed that an artist—a master artist—does not merely imitate nature but corrects her imperfections. Here an element of idealism modifies Shiki's basic commitment to realism: once he has established a basic truthfulness to things, an artist should also be truthful to his own wishes and ideals.

In order to correct nature's imperfections, the artist must have his own vision of how nature should be. Shiki was not blind to the pitfalls into which realistic poets sometimes fall. "Too realistic a poem," he once said, "is prone to be commonplace and lacking in surprise. . . . A poet too bent on realism tends to imprison his mind within the confines of the tiny world his eyes can see, forgetting about rare and fresh motifs that lie distant in time or space." It was from this angle that Shiki praised Buson's poetry. While recognizing objective beauty in Buson's works, Shiki was also fascinated by the poet-painter's fertile imagination. In his opinion, Buson was the only premodern haiku poet whose mind roamed freely between heaven and earth: he could "soar to the sky without wings and sink into the ocean without fins." The result was poetry rich in imaginative beauty:

> To Toba Palace
> five or six horsemen hurry . . .
> an autumn gale.

Toba Palace was an imperial villa located in the outskirts of Kyoto in the eleventh and twelfth centuries, a period when there were frequent uprisings in the area. This poem is intended to recreate a harsh mood as wartime breaks the elegant, aristocratic peace of the ancient capital. Shiki liked it well enough to try an imitation:

> Eleven horsemen, not
> for a moment turning their heads
> in the blizzard.

He wrote a number of other poems drawing on historical scenes, themes, or moods.

Shiki's view of the relationship between poetry and external reality was, then, a flexible one. Although it may look self-contradictory, from a pedagogic viewpoint it is coherent. He stressed the value of realistic representation for beginners, but for more advanced students recommended selective realism and allowed expert poets considerable freedom to choose between extremes of direct observation and imaginative creation. If he often appeared the champion of shasei, that was because he frequently addressed amateurs and beginning students, or established poets who relied overmuch on too meager an imagination.

Shiki's own practice reflected the broad range of his theory, for although he wrote more and more poems based on shasei as he grew older, the doctrine of realism was never strong enough to stifle his occasional fanciful impulse. For example, in the last year of his life, when he was a staunch advocate of shasei, he wrote these poems:

> Across the summer moor
> walks a traveler—on his back
> a *tengu* mask.

> At Akabane
> Village, an embankment
> covered with shoots of horsetail,
> so many my sister and I
> will never pick them all.

That these poems describe imaginary scenes is evident, since Shiki was confined to bed at the time he wrote them. A *tengu* is an imaginary monster with a fiery face and a long nose: the image of the grotesque mask adds an almost Gothic element to the otherwise normal haiku on a natural scene. The tanka is more realistic, because horsetail shoots were Shiki's favorite food, and his younger sister often went out to the fields to pick them. It presents an imaginary picture based on wishful thinking. Akabane Village was located near Tokyo, and one of his leading disciples, Kawahigashi Hekigodō (1873–1937), had gone there to collect horsetails shortly before Shiki wrote the poem.

However, in the Shiki canon non-shasei poems like these are in general inferior to realistic ones. Shiki gained his rank among the major poets of modern Japan through works based more directly on his actual life, especially on his last few years, spent in a losing battle with tuberculosis. At that time, his poetic sketches from life gained great vigor from the intensity of his

sensations, heightened by the knowledge of approaching death.
For example:

> The day I marked
> for a verse-writing party
> has come and gone. . . .
> Already beginning to fall,
> yellow mountain roses.

> For love and for hate
> I swat a fly and offer it
> to an ant.

> When I pour
> a nectarous wine
> into the vase
> the withered plumes of wisteria
> come back to life.

> New Year's calendar:
> during the month of May,
> a day for my death.

The first poem speaks Shiki's grief at not being able, because of
his illness, to hold the verse-writing parties that he used to enjoy.
The falling mountain roses, a popular subject in poetry, serve as
an apt image to suggest his drooping heart as well as his awareness that his life is likewise fading. In the second poem the poet
suggests his pent-up frustration, almost ready to explode. Jeal-
ous of a fly, which can move freely through space, he sympa-
thizes with an ant because, like himself, it can only crawl. In a fit
of anger he grabs a flyswatter, hits the fly, and gives it to the ant.
The third poem expresses a longing for regained vigor. Japanese gardeners say rice wine is good for plants, and the poet has
just seen proof with his own eyes. Unfortunately he has no such
wine to reinvigorate his own body. The fourth poem poignantly
suggests his awareness of approaching death. The month of
May frightens him because it is a season of luxuriant growth,
and anticipation of such overwhelming energy intimidates the
man struggling to cling to life.

These poems differ from those Shiki praised as embodiments
of shasei and selective realism. Whereas the poems by Bashō,

Taigi, and Sanesada cited earlier focus on the beauty of external nature, these works concentrate on internal, psychological reality. They can be called "sketches from life" only if "life" is interpreted to mean internal life-force, an invisible energy that keeps man living on, and they can be related to selective realism only if it means copying internal, rather than external, reality. Shiki had a different word to denote this principle: makoto.

Shiki borrowed the term "makoto" from the writings of a past tanka poet he much admired, Tachibana Akemi. In an essay entitled "Akemi's Poetry," he praised Akemi as a rare latter-day poet who tried to capture the spirit of the ancient poetry anthologized in *The Collection of Ten Thousand Leaves*. That spirit was makoto. "Makoto is the essence of Akemi's poetry," explained Shiki, "and that of *The Collection of Ten Thousand Leaves*. It should be the essence of all tanka. The principle I have been advocating—'copy reality as it is'—is nothing other than makoto." He then went on to observe how makoto was manifest in Akemi's works:

He [Akemi] sang of his impoverished life, of the things he believed in. He reminisced about his late parents and wrote poems envying those whose parents were still alive. He pondered the death of his child and composed poems recollecting how the little one used to hold his sleeves. . . . When he was happy he wrote happy poems; when he was angry he wrote angry poems. When birds sang he wrote poems about singing birds; when grasshoppers hopped he wrote poems about hopping grasshoppers. All this may sound so plain, but no other poet did what he did.

Makoto, then, is shasei directed toward internal reality. It is based on the same principle of direct observation, except that the object to be observed is the poet's own self. The poet is to experience his inner life as simply and sincerely as he is to observe nature, and he is to describe the experience in words as simple and direct as the ancient poets—so simple and direct that they seem ordinary.

Shiki further clarified his concept of makoto in an essay called "My Haiku," which traces the vicissitudes of his haiku poetic. In the initial phase he tried, he said, to present both subjective impressions and objective reality whenever he wrote haiku. Apparently he thought of subjective impressions and objective reality as two separate things, and felt composing haiku required a skillful blending of the two. Too frequently, however, he found decorative words, ornamental language, and self-conscious imaginings intruding, and soon he became tired of such haiku. Thereupon he strove to purge subjectivity from the poem, sketching objects unadorned and leaving readers to form their own impressions. But as time passed, he must have realized that absolute objectivity is impossible, that the process of selection necessary to isolate the poem's elements is rooted in the poet's individual aesthetic sensibility. In "Haiku Wastebasket," an essay series published a year after "My Haiku," he wrote, "Haiku expresses the poet's truthful [*makoto*] feelings. Even if he tries to distort them in the process of composition, truthful feelings are manifest somewhere in the poem." Shiki in his last years made a positive effort to focus on these "truthful feelings." With his characteristic terseness he described this shifting emphasis: "At first, I copied nature objectively. Later I became fond of copying humanity objectively." By "humanity" he must mean human nature and its manifestation in the form of emotions and feelings. Makoto is the truthfulness that enables the poet to copy such manifestations (and what lies underneath) "objectively," with no artifice interfering. It is a higher principle of selection—by being true to his own inner life, the poet is drawn to scenes, and within those scenes to objects, that express his inner life (and beyond it humanity) most directly. For example, in the last poem quoted, the calendar, and on it the month of May, are both simple, unadorned objects, yet in the poet's choosing to focus on them they come alive with his fear that in this most luxuriant of months he will die. Here we see makoto operating as shasei, a kind of shasei directed to internal reality.

Shiki died, however, before he had a chance to expound the principle of makoto very extensively. It is likely that he arrived at the principle from an intensive reading of ancient tanka, which he did fairly late in his career. Yet examples are sometimes more eloquent than theory, and lack of theoretical exposition is not to be equated with lack of importance. Unless in Shiki's poetic makoto carries as much weight as shasei and selective realism, there is no way to account for some of his best poetry.

The Poet as Traveler, on Foot and in Imagination

On January 8, 1900, the newspaper *Nippon* announced a tanka contest on the subject "forest." Shiki, the poetry editor for the paper, specified the contest rules. Rule number five was by far the longest, less a rule than a piece of advice for would-be contestants:

In writing a poem it will not do to borrow from classical tanka and use cliche phrases like "a legendary forest" or "a sacred forest." The poem would better depict a scene or express a feeling as actually seen or felt by a man passing through a forest. If you have the time to sit at a desk and read a book on tanka, you should instead pick up a cane and go for a leisurely walk along a path in the woods. When you are in the actual setting, look for some specific part of the landscape (such as a house, a village, a stream, a hill, a field, a tower, a bird, a paper kite, etc.) that you might combine with the forest in your poem. Observe also many other less conspicuous features of the forest (such as undergrowth, a grave mound, a small shrine, a temple, an animal, a watchman's hut, and so forth). When you think you have completely captured the "feel" of the forest, you can then return home. There you should begin composing many poems, bringing back the scenery in your mind's eye and focusing on one or another aspect of it. If you compose ten or fifteen poems this way, there will be at least one or two poems that are good. You are not likely to come up with a good poem if you write just one or two.

The passage illustrates Shiki's idea of the creative process in general, even though he was talking about tanka composition in particular.

The passage emphasizes observation: a poet who composes from books cannot do shasei. But Shiki wanted the sketching to be done at home rather than amid the actual setting. The time lapse was probably related to his idea of selective realism, since the poet needed time for the scene to settle, for certain aspects to select themselves out as the possible focus of a poem. The landscape had to be recollected in tranquillity.

Shiki recommended that an amateur poet follow these steps in composition because he saw at least two fatal defects often

emerge in poems not based on actual experience. The first was
falsification of fact. A poet writing of what he has not actually
experienced is in danger of creating an implausible scene. One
example cited by Shiki was the following tanka by Fujiwara
Norinaga:[4]

> A lodging I seek
> for the night is buried
> in spring mist. . . .
> From a warbler in the valley
> one call, no more.

The poem presents a tired traveler looking for a night's lodging
toward the end of day. The nearest village ahead, however, is
hidden in spring mist, and coming from it he hears only the single cry of a bush warbler. Shiki criticized the tanka, saying: "The
statement that the prospective lodging is in the mist implies a
scene viewed from a distance, but the fact that the poet has
heard a warbler's cry suggests his proximity to it. How could
such a false poem, which mixes up the far and the near, be expected to stir the reader's emotion?"

Another poem Shiki considered bad because contrary to fact
was the haiku:

> As I kneel
> in prayer, the waves fall silent—
> a shrine on the river.

The waves, he felt, could not have subsided so suddenly, and it
was unlikely that the poet stopped hearing them the moment he
knelt down. The opposite seemed truer to fact, so he suggested
revising the second line, changing the poem to something like:

> As I kneel
> in prayer, the waves sound—
> a shrine on the river.

Shiki thought this a better haiku because it was factually more
convincing.[5]

---

[4] Fujiwara Norinaga was a minor tanka poet of the eleventh century. According to legend, he considered this his finest poem.

[5] Shiki's criticism does not seem to be entirely fair. The original poem may be

The other weakness often found in poems not based on actual experience is a tendency to be bookish and overly intellectual. A tanka or haiku composed on an imagined scene is apt to appeal to the intellect rather than to emotion, which responds most directly to a scene one immediately feels to be truthful. Shiki was adamant in attacking this tendency, which he saw rampant in the practice of contemporary poets, and he distinguished his own haiku from others by the lack of it. "More than anything else," he said, "I want to appeal to emotion. They want to appeal to the intellect." He then cited a haiku by Tagawa Ōryū (1762–1845)[6] as a bad example:

> To the neighbor building
> a treasury, they did not come:
> the year's first swallows.

In the poem, all the families in the neighborhood have been waiting for swallows to return from the south to their homes in spring. The migrant birds do come back—except to a wealthy neighbor who is building a new warehouse. In Shiki's opinion, the poet deduced the birds' behavior from his own bookish ideas: a traditional Japanese poet liked to find beauty in poverty, and swallows, being poetic birds, must do the same.

In tanka, Shiki's targets were not only contemporary works but also some of the well-known classics, especially those in *The Collection of Ancient and Modern Poems*. He violently attacked this famous anthology, all the more because its poems had been extravagantly praised by his contemporaries as the ultimate models for tanka composition. He did not spare even the most celebrated poems, such as this one by Ōe Chisato:[7]

> Gazing at the moon
> I think of many things

---

interpreted as depicting a person so absorbed in his prayers that he stops hearing the sound of waves.

[6]Tagawa Ōryū, also called Hōrō, was a famous teacher of haiku who had students all over Japan. He published several books on the theory and practice of haiku writing.

[7]Ōe Chisato was a nobleman, poet, and Confucian scholar who lived about A.D. 900. He also wrote poems in Chinese.

> and my heart sinks
> although I know this autumn
> has not come to me alone.

Shiki felt that the last two lines were overintellectual. He said: "A poem is supposed to express emotion, but this one gives a reasoned explanation. Perhaps the poet did not know what poetry is." To make the poem more emotionally appealing, Shiki suggested that it be changed to:

> Gazing at the moon
> I think of many things
> and my heart sinks. . . .
> I feel as if this autumn
> had come to me and me alone.

He thought much contemporary poetry contained similar reasoned explanations and was therefore uninspiring.

It was to help cure this sort of intellectualization, as well as falsification of fact, that Shiki proposed shasei. Like a doctor urging his patient to exercise, Shiki urged his fellow poets to walk around and observe nature. His advice was sometimes quite detailed:

When you go out for shasei, do not take the train. That would be a waste of time. The best way is to walk—walk with a calm, undisturbed mind. It is better to wear straw sandals than shoes or wooden clogs, and you should dress in a kimono with a sedge hat and leggings rather than in Western clothes. You are urged to travel alone. You will not be able to get good haiku if you hurry and physically exhaust yourself.

Shiki had another piece of practical advice about destination. He felt that poets paid too much attention to places famous for scenic beauty or past history. He admitted that renowned places often provided good material for poetry because of their associations with the past, but pointed out that poems composed at such places tended to sound hackneyed. Even Bashō, he reminded aspiring poets, once confessed that he had not been able to write haiku on celebrated places like Mount Fuji or Mount Yoshino. Shiki therefore advised poets to pay more attention to lesser-known locales. "Such ordinary places," he said, "are more numerous, more varied, and less hackneyed." He did not say, but probably felt, that at a famous place on which many classical verses had already been written poets tended to falsify their feelings or intellectualize their emotional responses, seeking what they expected to feel rather than observing their true reactions.

Does not a poet who follows Shiki's suggestions end up producing a plain, unexciting poem? Verse composed at an ordinary place with a minimum of fictionalization or intellectualization is likely to look prosaic and banal, especially when the poet is an amateur. One beginning student, indeed, asked Shiki this very question. The student said he had often gone out to the fields with a notebook and tried to do shasei, but he always came up with a trite poem like:

> A bamboo thicket—
> inside, a camellia
> in full bloom.

Shiki's answer was twofold. He advised the student to pay attention to everything within sight, not just to conventional poetic subjects like camellias. "If you see dandelions, sing of dandelions," he suggested. "If you see starworts, sing of starworts. If you see a wheat field, sing of green wheat." He also admonished the student to try to introduce themes of his own. The camellia poem, Shiki thought, was too diffuse and lacked a new theme. "What you have stated in your poem," he wrote to the student, "can be condensed to just one line: 'camellia in a thicket.' You should use the remaining two for introducing other material and thereby make the poem more interesting."

Herein lies the second stage of the creative process as conceived by Shiki. In the first stage, a poet should go outside and observe life or nature; in the second, he should select material and theme in a way that will reveal his individuality. The manifestation of the poet's unique personality is what keeps the poem from becoming trite.

For this reason Shiki advised students to read extensively, an apparent contradiction to his insistence on shasei. In his opinion, an expert poet was a learned man. "It is most urgent," he said, "for a poet to be able to distinguish between the fresh and the hackneyed in haiku. The definition of a 'fresh' haiku will differ from one poet to another according to the degree of learning he has attained. The more poems he has studied, the more poems he will feel to be hackneyed." As for what to read, Shiki suggested for haiku poets the works of Buson, Bashō, and Bashō's leading disciples, even though he warned that Bashō's poems were not all good. He did not specify books for tanka poets, but the list would presumably include *The Collection of Ten Thousand Leaves* and the poems of its later admirers, such as Minamoto Sanetomo[8] and Tachibana Akemi. Shiki, however, wanted students not to confine their reading to classics written in their verse forms. He wanted students of haiku to know something about the poetics of tanka, and vice versa. Once he recommended that a student of haiku should familiarize himself with "first, tanka; second, Japanese prose; third, Japanese fiction, nō, and other forms of drama; fourth, Chinese literature; fifth, European and American literature." He further suggested that the student learn about painting, sculpture, architecture, and music, since all share many aesthetic principles with poetry.

The ideal poet as conceived by Shiki, then, is a learned person with refined artistic taste who can distinguish between the new and the stereotyped. Aided by his learning, he will have developed a unique personality, which manifests itself when he composes a poem. He will base his poem on shasei, but will focus on some new subject or look at an old subject in a new perspective. In the latter process he may make use of his imagination and depart from shasei, for a poet with a powerful imagination can, if he wishes, create a realistic scene without basing it on actual experience. A man who has traveled a great deal, not only physically but also in imagination, is the essence of the ideal poet as Shiki ultimately came to visualize him. One of the pieces of advice Shiki had for students in the last stage of their training was "You must combine realism and imagination, thereby producing

---

[8] Minamoto Sanetomo was attracted to primitive poetry because of its straightforward expression of powerful passion and tried to emulate it in some of his tanka. A shogun by virtue of his birth, he was assassinated at the age of 27, before he had time to realize his full potential as a poet.

great literature that is neither entirely realistic nor entirely imaginative."

Shiki, always a practitioner, once demonstrated this creative process quite specifically, describing it step by step in an essay entitled "My Moon Poem for a Contest." This essay reveals the secret of Shiki's craft as a haiku poet.

The occasion was a day in 1898 when Shiki was invited to contribute a poem to a haiku contest on the subject "the moon." Already bedridden, he set out to compose a poem while lying on his back. He wanted to write a realistic haiku, particularly since the contest judge was Hekigodō, to whom he had always stressed the importance of realism. Perhaps because of that desire, the first scene that came to mind was a plain, ordinary one—a road extending beside a forest in the moonlight, along an open field. He tried to focus on someone sauntering down the road, vainly attempting to glimpse the moon through the trees. The attempt did not succeed because the vision involved the lapse of too much time for a haiku. Thereupon Shiki's mind roamed to his own garden, where he had often watched the moon through the leaves of a large pasania tree. Recalling the familiar scene, he wrote:

> Somewhere in the leaves
> moonlight breaks and falls
> in myriad pieces.

After reciting this a couple of times, he realized that it was awful. So he abandoned it and went back, in his mind, to the road along the woods. This time he followed a trail into the forest and obtained this poem:

> Here and there
> the moonlight is seeping through:
> a trail under cedars.

When the poem was completed, however, its banality surprised him. He tried to write another haiku using the same setting, but when that attempt, too, ended in failure his mind left the woods and wandered to the edge of water.

There he visualized a small boat floating on an immense river, the waves reflecting the moonlight. Trying carefully not to use an unrealistic word like "unearthly," he wrote:

> Loaded with wine
> a boat is lazily adrift—
> lovers of the moon.

Although he was not quite content with the poem, Shiki was getting tired and almost decided to settle on it. Yet he was bothered by the thought that a haiku on the moon he had written spontaneously a few days before was better than this one, and he felt he had to try a bit longer. This time he imagined himself on a pavilion at the edge of the river. The opposite shore was invisible in the mist, except for a light that seemed to come from a house. It was high tide. The scene, however, could not be made into a haiku, as it seemed too much like a setting for a Chinese poem. When he saw a small boat coming out from among flowering reeds, he knew where he got the scene: it was from *Water Margin*, a Chinese novel he had read the previous year. He still let his fancy wander: the boat went out to midstream, the boatman began to sing a song—at that point Shiki realized he was getting too far from realism. So he imagined a messenger hurrying across the river on urgent business in the moonlight. But he just could not depict the scene in seventeen syllables. Again he returned to *Water Margin*, but in vain.

Still keeping the image of a pavilion overlooking the water, Shiki changed the setting to Japan. He imagined a group of students having a farewell party:

> At the seaside pavilion
> friends sorrowfully part
> this moonlit night.

However, he was not content, for the poem seemed a bit stale. He also did not like the friends' having a party inside while there was a beautiful moon outside. Therefore he changed the first line:

> On the wharf
> friends sorrowfully part
> this moonlit night.

Yet the poem seemed lacking in emotion. Accordingly he visualized a man and a woman parting on the wharf. The woman, without saying a word, stood close to the man. He too looked grief-stricken. He clasped her hand, then let it go and went aboard a barge. The woman remained on the pier, motionless. The scene soon crystallized into a haiku:

> On the wharf
> they sorrowfully part:
> a man and his wife.

Shiki then noticed that the poem did not have the moon in it. Without success he tried to move the setting to Mitsuhama, a seaport near his native town. Finally he settled on:

> They bid farewell—
> no one is drunk any more
> on the moonlit boat.

Shiki did not consider the poem a great success, but thought it at least without glaring faults.

The process through which this poem was written illustrates a number of Shiki's beliefs about poetic composition. Since he was bedridden, he could not do shasei in its strict sense, but he did try to base his poem on past experience. Rather than attempt to locate the moon in some renowned place, he tried to recall it shining on his garden in Tokyo or his boat at Mitsuhama. On the other hand, he was well aware of the traps into which realistic poems sometimes fall, and when his first attempts seemed trivial or stale, he shifted to imaginary scenes, such as those from *Water Margin*. He also endeavored to inject emotion by visualizing a farewell scene. It is noteworthy, however, that the parting scene, which originated in *Water Margin*, became more and more realistic as Shiki's revisions progressed. The final poem reflects, not the Chinese novel, but his past experience at Mitsuhama, where he bade farewell to his friends aboard the S.S. *Toyonaka* in 1883. A youngster of eighteen, he was departing for Tokyo, four hundred miles away. When the farewell festivities were over, the distance—no mean one in nineteenth-century Japan—weighed increasingly on the hearts of the one departing and those being left behind. Thus, in the process of finding and focusing emotion, Shiki did combine shasei and imagination.

The Sublime and the Plain

In his writings, Shiki was concerned less with the nature of the aesthetic effect than with its range. His concept of poetic beauty was considerably more inclusive than the traditional one: before his time, the average poet thought of beauty as characterized by elegance, grace, or exquisiteness, sometimes tinged with a sense of life's sadness, at other times blended with calm resignation. Shiki expanded the concept to include all kinds of effects, and comprehensiveness characterized his aesthetic. For instance, in attacking contemporary tanka poets he charged that they should prize not only "elegance" but also "the sublime," "the antique," "the novel," "the stately," and "the light." He mentioned still more possible effects in his discussion of haiku. Once, in classifying haiku, he referred to those that are: "vigorous," "genteel," "magnificent," "delicate," "shady," "exquisite," "mysterious," "lucid," "stately," "light," "novel," "plain," "complex," "simple," "serious," and "humorous." At another time he distinguished 24 styles of haiku and cited examples of each. Here are three of the new styles, with examples:

The ghostly:

Spring night: invisible
in the shade of a screen,
something breathes.

The picturesque:

There is a teahouse.
To the blossoming peach tree
he ties a white horse.

The sorrowful:

Long winter night:
when I think over the past
the wind begins to rise.

In the first haiku, something ghostly in the shade of a folding screen intrudes on the usual erotic mood of a spring night. In the second, the appeal is almost purely visual; the haiku is a painting composed in words. And in the third the wind is at once physical and metaphysical, suggesting the deep, almost cosmic sorrow of the poet.

Shiki's classification of poetic beauty was far from exhaustive or methodical; it was not intended to be. His chief aim was to show that poets can explore many types of aesthetic effects. More than anything else he disliked a stereotyped poem written with the sole aim of achieving one or another of the effects valued within the narrow confines of traditional Japanese aesthetics. In his view, a poet who would write such a poem had a mind like water in an abandoned well. He urged that the poet bail out all the stagnant water until the bottom was bare so that new, clear water could begin to seep in little by little. Possible sources of aesthetic pleasure were countless. "O poets," Shiki addressed his colleagues, "the universe is wide, and the material for poetry boundless. Why do you think there is no fitting material outside of the moon, dewdrops, singing insects, tear-soaked sleeves, friends, the fields, and leaves of grass?"

In his eagerness to extend the realm of poetic beauty, Shiki went so far as to discover—or rediscover—beauty in excrement. In an essay called "Haiku on Excrement," he demonstrated that the old masters produced beauty out of this unlikely material, citing 41 poems (most of them haiku) on feces, 18 on urine, 4 on farts, 24 on toilets, and 21 on loincloths. Here are three examples, composed by Buson, Chōha,[9] and Issa, respectively:

> Pink plum blossoms
> fallen on horse dung: they seem
> ready to flare up!

> The harvest moon
> shows a hare's droppings,
> clear as can be.

[9]Shimizu Chōha (1705–40), a merchant by profession, was also active as a haiku poet, and published several volumes of poetry by himself and his associates. In this particular poem, the poet is admiring the full moon during a stroll in the fields. The hare, usually a timid animal, apparently has come out of the bushes to enjoy the moon also.

> A wolf's dung—
> that's all there is, and yet
> how chilly I feel!

In these instances each poet beautified, or at least neutralized, his material by providing a proper setting, thereby creating something that can be called poetic. Because of the novelty of the subject, the effect is fresh and striking, if not beautiful.

At the conclusion of "Haiku on Excrement," Shiki made clear that he was not especially fond of using this sort of material for poetry; he only wanted to show how widely a poet might explore. In discussing the 24 styles of haiku, he did not specify which he preferred, yet despite his general evenhandedness, he seems to have harbored a predilection for the sublime and the plain. He especially admired the former in his younger days, and was more attracted to the latter in later years.

To designate sublime beauty, Shiki used different Japanese words, such as *yūsō* ("strength"), *yūkon* ("grandeur"), *sōdai* ("magnificence"), and *gōtō* ("valor"). (In Japanese, these words are very ambiguous; the English equivalents given here are only rough approximations that make no attempt to do justice to their full range of meaning.) Altogether, the sublime as conceived by Shiki seems to have combined the qualities connoted by such adjectives as "great," "magnificent," "spacious," "powerful," "violent," "courageous," and "masculine." Shiki once tried to suggest it by the images of a boundless ocean, turbulent waves, towering mountains, the spacious sky, a flood sweeping away villages, and two troops of enemy soldiers exchanging fire at close range. Elsewhere, among materials for haiku likely to produce sublime beauty he listed mountains in summer, a gust through green leaves, seasonal rain, pillars of cloud, lightning, the Milky Way, winter trees, and withered fields.

Specific poems Shiki cited as examples of the sublime include a haiku by Buson and a tanka by Sanetomo:

> Early summer rain:
> facing an immense river,
> a pair of houses.

> On the bracers
> of a samurai
> readying arrows
> hailstones spatter and roll—
> a bamboo field at Nasu.

In the haiku by Buson, the torrential rain of June continues without end, and the muddy water of the huge river, revealing the colossal power of nature, threatens to destroy the embankment at any minute. On the embankment stand two small houses, looking utterly helpless, yet trying somehow to survive. A similarly violent mood prevails in Sanetomo's tanka, although in this instance the violence is human as well as natural. The scene is a battlefield, where a warrior hiding in a bush hurriedly prepares for another skirmish. The harsh, masculine image of the armored warrior with his arrows is complemented by the mood of the natural setting, with spattering hailstones and the sharp blades of bamboo all around. The place, Nasu, also conjures up the image of a desolate wilderness.[10]

Shiki liked the sublime because it was fresh. Traditionally the Japanese had valued the opposite effect, elegance, and the result was an overabundance of elegant poems, with an inevitable decline in quality. As Shiki explained, "The type of beauty belonging to the highest kind of art and yet most lacking in Japanese literature is the sublime. Some is present in the poems of *The Collection of Ten Thousand Leaves* and earlier, but none can be found in the tanka composed since *The Collection of Ancient and Modern Poems*. (Sanetomo's poetry is the one exception.)" Shiki emulated, and urged other poets to emulate, the ancient poets represented in *The Collection of Ten Thousand Leaves*, who wrote from their own experience. Those poets were able to write sublime verse because they were motivated by deeply felt emotions; they did not try to adorn their language for the sake of an elegant appearance. Later poets merely tried to imitate classical

---

[10] Nasu was located in Musashino, the largest plain in Japan, extending north from what is now Tokyo. In Sanetomo's day it was inhabited by many wild animals. Some scholars interpret the poem as depicting hunters.

court poetry and ended up producing pseudoelegant poems that were trite and stereotyped, with no emotional appeal.

The effect of some of Shiki's more successful poems can be explained in terms of the sublime. Here are four examples:

> Hot spring in the mountains:
> high above the naked bathers
> the River of Heaven.

> Quietly it lies asleep:
> a hamlet, after all its
> lamplights are gone . . .
> Only the River of Heaven
> white above the bamboo grove.

> The wintry gust:
> they have left a temple bell
> by the roadside.

> New leaves on a tiny
> weed in my yard, and I think
> of heaven and earth
> limitlessly spacious,
> filled with spring green.

The first two poems share a common image, the Milky Way flowing in heaven. The image creates a sense of magnitude and eternity, which is further enhanced in the haiku by the addition of another grand image, the towering mountains. Amid the great expanse of the natural setting, human beings strip off their petty manners and customs. In the tanka, the villagers are all asleep. With not a single lamp burning, the stars in the sky sparkle even more brightly, looking ready to come down in a shower of light. In contrast, the bamboos below are dark and grow straight up, their stalks pointing toward the sky. Here is a communion of heaven and earth on a grand scale, approaching the sublime.

In the third poem the juxtaposition is more striking than harmonious. A huge black bell has been left by the roadside when the team of parish volunteers carrying it to their temple go to their night's lodging at the end of day. The bronze bell sits all alone, and the winter wind blows on it. The gust hits the bell so hard that it seems ready to begin ringing at any moment; yet it does not: silent and immobile, it looms in the growing dark.

The fourth poem starts on a smaller scale. The poet is ill and has been confined to bed; his yard is all of the outside world that he can see. Intently observing it as he does every day, he notices several new leaves on a familiar weed. Thereupon his imagination quickly expands: he visualizes the whole universe filled with verdant vegetation. The universe is all the more spacious, and the green all the fresher, because physically the poet is imprisoned.

If the last poem seems not quite as sublime as the other three, it shows the difficulty a bedridden poet has in writing a large-scale poem. To write such a poem he has to depend on his imagination, not on shasei. Whether for this reason or not, Shiki wrote fewer and fewer poems in the sublime vein as years went by. He became increasingly attracted to another type of beauty, plainness.

To designate this effect, Shiki employed such words as *heitan* ("flatness"), *heii* ("plainness"), *tanpaku* ("lightness"), and *jinjō* ("ordinariness"). Its connotations are more difficult to delineate than are those of the sublime. The concept of plain beauty seems to have originated, and is still used, in areas other than poetics. In painting it denotes a light layer of paint as opposed to a thick one; in cooking, the taste of light foods, such as salad, as opposed to that of heavy, greasy ones; in stylistics, plain, lucid language as opposed to elaborate, ornate diction; and in craftsmanship, simplicity and naturalness as opposed to complexity and artifice. When referring to a landscape, it implies a flat, smooth terrain as opposed to a rugged one.

Perhaps a couple of examples can better convey the meaning of plainness:

> Sowing wheat:
> branches of mulberry trees
> made into bundles.

> A road extends
> far into the distance

across the summer moor—
I have walked all morning
without meeting a soul.

The first poem, written by Shiki, depicts a familiar scene in some parts of rural Japan. Farmers are sowing wheat in a field where a few mulberry trees stand. The low-lying branches are in their way, so they have bundled them up with ropes (they do not want to cut them off, since they need the leaves to feed their silk-worms). There is neither a beautiful flower nor a striking incident in the haiku; it is a description of a common scene in plain language. A similar quality can be observed in the second poem, written by Hekigodō. The poet is walking along a road across a spacious moor on a summer day, without ever meeting a traveler coming from the other direction. That is all. According to Shiki, the poem is so plain that some readers may consider it commonplace, yet it has a certain freshness: a great many poets have sung about the loneliness of autumn, but few have noted that of a summer day.

On several occasions Shiki contrasted two or more poems on the same theme to show what he meant by plain beauty. For example, on March 20, 1898, he published in *Nippon* a tanka he had received from an amateur contributor:

In a village
among the mountains, a hedge
of flowering deutzia
just thin enough to let slip through
a cuckoo's low cry.

Shiki charged that the poem pretended to produce plain beauty but actually did not. He did not like the phrase "just thin enough to let slip through" because it was a forced conceit—no hedge is dense enough to shut out sound. The amateur poet apparently understood Shiki's point when he read the comment in the newspaper, for he immediately revised the poem and sent it to Shiki, who published it in the same paper two days later:

In a village
among the mountains, a hedge

> of flowering deutzia—
> under the evening moon
> a cuckoo's low cry.

Shiki liked the revised version better, remarking that it sounded more banal but less artificial.

From these examples, it can be gathered that plain beauty was an aesthetic manifestation of shasei, the faithful depiction of an ordinary place. If the depiction was based on actual observation, it would have a certain degree of novelty, since actual observation was personal and individual. The more individual the poet's personality, the more unique his observations, even of ordinary things. This uniqueness would show in his poem and would save the plain poem from being stereotyped.

Shiki's finest poems are plain in this sense:

> Ill on a winter day
> I have moisture wiped off
> the glass door by my bed—
> revealed on the other side,
> socks hanging from the clothesline.

> My nurse
> awaking from a nap
> swats a fly.

> Outside the glass door
> how bright the moonlight!
> A bank of white clouds
> extends far across the sky
> above a forest of trees.

> Blossoms have fallen
> and the water is flowing
> southwards.

The first two poems depict a trivial occurrence in the ailing poet's life. Shiki, utterly bored, has someone wipe the fog off the glass door near his bed. Through the cleared pane he sees no breathtaking sight—merely a few socks hanging from a clothesline. But even that is fresh to his eyes. There is an added poignancy in that he has no use for socks; he is too weak to stand on his feet. The next poem also describes a seemingly trivial occurrence. This time the season is summer. The day is hot and humid, as summer days usually are in Japan. Shiki's nurse, probably a young woman, is tired from her chores and dozes off while sitting by his bedside. The sick man, however, cannot sleep. When she awakes, their eyes meet. She is embarrassed, realizing that she has dozed in front of a young male patient. Without thinking, she grabs a flyswatter and swats a fly.

The next two poems are so plain and ordinary that they may seem trite. They are poems of pure shasei, describing common, familiar things—the moon, a forest, white clouds, blossoms, water. Yet in these ordinary scenes something mysterious and eternal is suggested. The bank of clouds trails far into the distance, the water flows toward the far south, and no one knows their destinations. In the process of observing nature, the poet senses an unknown force, manifest in phenomena such as these. Yet things simply follow their destiny without trying to solve the mystery. There is a tone of calm acceptance in both the tanka and the haiku; the haiku, in particular, is almost a Zen poem.

Shiki's famous deathbed poems convey a similar effect. He died in the early hours on September 19, 1902, two days after a full moon. On the morning of the previous day he had barely managed to jot down three haiku:

> Gourd vines flowering—
> mucus has stopped the throat
> of this Buddha.

> A gallon of mucus:
> liquid from the gourd vines
> is too late now.

> Two days ago
> we did not gather liquid
> from the gourd vines.

The season word in all three haiku is "gourd vines." Gourds, which were bleached and used as sponges, were a familiar sight around Japanese houses before the invention of the synthetic sponge. Their flowers are small, yellow, and unobtrusive. Shiki had the vines planted in front of his bedroom, not only because

‹

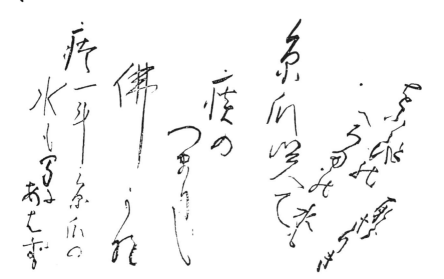

The manuscript of Shiki's deathbed haiku. From right to left:

Ototoi no	Two days ago
hechima no mizu mo	we did not gather liquid
torazariki	from the gourd vines.
Hechima saite	Gourd vines flowering—
tan no tsumarishi	mucus has stopped the throat
hotoke kana	of this Buddha.
Tan itto	A gallon of mucus:
hechima no mizu mo	liquid from the gourd vines
ma ni awazu	is too late now.

Reproduced from Fujikawa Chūji, *Masaoka Shiki*, by courtesy of San-kaidō.

they made good shade in summer but also because they produced a liquid that helped to clear his throat. The liquid was believed to be most effective medicinally when gathered on the night of the full moon. With such a plant for seasonal background, the poems produce no colorful or spectacular beauty, yet their effect is far from stale, because the poet who watches the familiar plant is dying. Mucus stops his throat, and he can hardly breathe. In spite of the pain, his mind is calm. He knows

his last hours have come and accepts the end quietly. Looking at
the situation with mental detachment, he calls himself a Buddha.
His life is behind him, as the day for getting liquid from the
vines is past and gone. Shiki, who advocated copying nature objectively, observed his own death dispassionately and distilled
what he saw in poems that produce a plain beauty.

Justification for Short Poems

Shiki's ideas of shasei, makoto, and selective realism do not explain his lifelong devotion to two traditional verse forms, haiku
and tanka, nor does his predilection for the sublime or the plain.
Indeed, longer literary forms might seem more suited to the
complexities of realistic representation, and an extended treatment more capable of producing a sense of magnitude and
power. Shouldn't Shiki have been attracted to write in prose or
in shi, a newer and freer verse form that imposed no restrictions
on length or lineation?

Shiki did have an interest in prose composition. He is considered the founder of a new prose genre called *shaseibun* (literally
"shasei prose"), short prose pieces objectively describing a scene
or incident that especially interests the writer. The piece has to
be true to fact, but the writer is free to select in order to focus his
presentation. Stylistically, the piece must be plain, lucid, and devoid of adornment. The new genre had a considerable effect on
the Japanese literary scene in the first decade of the twentieth
century, and many of Shiki's friends and disciples in poetry tried
their hands at it. Later, it developed into a type of autobiographical prose fiction and in its own way helped to promote realism in the modern Japanese novel. Shiki himself, however,
wrote only about a dozen shaseibun and penned no autobiographical novel. Although he did produce nine short stories, all
but one show little realism, and all are without much literary
merit. There is no doubt that Shiki's oeuvre as poet far outweighs his work as a writer of prose.

Shiki was interested in shi, too. When Tōson's *A Collection of
Young Herbs* appeared in 1897, in a review in *Nippon* Shiki said he

saw great potential in the new form. Even before Tōson's debut, when the success of the new poetic experiment was still very much in doubt, Shiki had defended the experimentalists by comparing them to military heroes who lost their lives for better times to come. Indeed, he once asserted that of all writers in contemporary Japanese literary genres, those writing shi had shown the most remarkable progress in modernization. He placed haiku poets next and tanka writers last.

Shiki's pessimism about haiku and tanka resulted in a shocking forecast. Since these verse forms have limited syllable counts, he speculated that one could calculate the maximum number of haiku or tanka that could possibly be composed. In his rough calculation, the last good haiku had already been written, and even if that were not true, haiku would surely exhaust its poetic potential by the end of the current Emperor's reign. Tanka, which has more syllables, theoretically would have a longer life expectancy, yet since it was more restricted in vocabulary, Shiki felt it had run out of energy in premodern times. When someone who noticed a recent trend of writing haiku in eighteen or nineteen syllables suggested that haiku might in time lengthen itself into a Western-style poem, Shiki agreed, saying he was not saddened by haiku's predicament because his loyalty was to literature in general, not to haiku alone.

That comment notwithstanding, as a poet Shiki was loyal to haiku and tanka throughout his career. He did write shi, 38 all told. These poems are interesting as experiments, especially because some attempt to use rhyme, a device previously unknown in Japanese poetry. Yet by and large they are devoid of poetic merit. Most are stereotyped in theme (as can be surmised from such titles as "My Father's Grave" and "Mourning the Death of the Empress Dowager"), monotonous in rhythm (based largely on a 7–5 pattern), and lacking in emotional appeal. Thirty-eight poems is not a large number in view of the fact that Shiki wrote some 2,300 tanka and 18,000 haiku in his lifetime.

Shiki's attachment to haiku and tanka may have been rooted in a traditional upbringing. Born into a former samurai family

in the nineteenth century, in early childhood he acquired a premodern education, which emphasized reading and writing traditional forms of poetry. As a young student he developed such
a passion for haiku and tanka that he indulged in writing them
when he should have been doing his schoolwork. "Charmed by
the demon of haiku," he recollected later, "I was helpless. I
failed the annual examinations in 1892." His illness, which lasted
much of his adult life, may also have contributed to his preference for short verse forms. One needs sheer physical endurance
to write a novel or a long shi, and Shiki did not have it.

In addition, Shiki felt that the Japanese people excelled in short
verse forms and therefore should try to cultivate them. He postu-
lated two reasons why short verse forms developed in Japan.
First, Japanese poetry had been reared within a self-contained
culture, where it had become a kind of sophisticated party game;
in such a situation, short poems function best. Second, Japanese
poetry concentrated on depicting natural landscapes rather than
communal events or personal feelings. Long literary forms better
served to depict events or sentiments, which tend to be complex,
but short forms sufficed to present landscapes. Nature, according
to Shiki, was simple to depict because it followed a regular course.
Cherries always bloom in spring; chrysanthemums in autumn.
People's lives are more irregular, he felt. To account for why Japanese poetry traditionally focused on nature, Shiki observed that
his country, because of her geographical isolation, had enjoyed
relative peace from ancient times and that his forefathers had no
strong cause to protest political, social, or religious injustice.
Furthermore, Japanese poets always had beautiful settings to inspire them. To recount his reasoning: Japanese poets were traditionally fond of writing poems on nature; nature poems were
relatively simple; and therefore short poetic forms developed in
Japan.

Personal preference aside, however, Shiki was receptive to all
verse forms. The most important consideration for him was that
the content fit the form. "In brief," he said, "various kinds of
verse forms should be allowed, each in the situation appropriate

to it. There is no reason for a poet to be restricted to 5–7 or 7–5 lines, nor need he try to create an unusual rhythm with extralong or extrashort lines. A fine poem will emerge when form matches feeling." Unknowingly, Shiki was advocating free verse, for it is in free verse that form aspires to mirror feelings exactly. One of Shiki's leading disciples, Hekigodō, later pursued this argument further and along with Ogiwara Seisensui became a prominent supporter of "free-style haiku."[11]

Shiki himself never conceived of haiku or tanka as unrestricted by syllable count, but he was quite generous in allowing extra syllables. He wrote, and encouraged others to write, haiku in 18 or more syllables and tanka in 32 or more syllables if a particular occasion warranted. When more conservative poets attacked this practice, he vehemently defended his stand on the ground that form should be determined by content. He also argued that the 17- and 31-syllable forms had been in existence for so many centuries that some variation would create refreshing effects. Moreover, the traditional 5–7 rhythm seemed to him so smooth, melodious, and elegant that he sometimes wanted to break away from it to produce something irregular. Being more anxious to write a fine poem than to write a haiku or tanka, he did not care if old-fashioned masters objected to his calling his extralong poems by those names. "When I write haiku," he explained, "I never direct my efforts toward writing a haiku. I direct them toward expressing my feelings. Whether the efforts will result in 17 syllables, 18 syllables, or more than 30 syllables is something I myself cannot predict."

Many of Shiki's haiku and tanka have extra syllables. Of the 920 haiku in one of the standard selections from his works, 155, or one out of every six, have 18 or more syllables. The proportion is even greater for tanka: of 544 poems included in *Bamboo Village Tanka*, 164 have more than 31 syllables. That is about 30 percent, a high ratio indeed. Most of the poems with an extra syllable or two are very successful. To take an example already cited:

[11] For more information on free-style haiku, see Chapter 7.

> For love and for hate
> I swat a fly and offer it
> to an ant.

The second line in the original consists of eight syllables instead of the usual seven. The extralong line helps to suggest the vehemence of the poet's frustration, as does the break it creates in the normal 5–7–5 rhythm, rendering the poem less melodious.

Another notable feature of Shiki's concept of form is a principle of internal harmony. He wanted a poem to place two or more images side by side in a way that creates an aesthetically pleasing impression. Because each person has his own sensibility, Shiki's principle of harmony is ultimately subjective, but he probably felt that Japanese poets, with their centuries-old cultural tradition, shared the same taste to a great degree. A poet's task, therefore, was to seek a new combination of images that most people would consider harmonious. Shiki thought the principle so important that once in a didactic tanka he placed it above even shasei:

> The most important
> is an arrangement of lines;
> next, comes
> shasei; and after that
> shasei over and over again.

Since the letter in which the poem appears was addressed to a student of tanka, "lines" must mean images; it is a term from painting applied to poetry, as is shasei itself. The principle is related to Shiki's idea of selective realism: if a poet makes his selection well, there will be a surprising yet harmonious arrangement of images in his poem, for the uniqueness of his personality will provide surprise, and the totality of his own person will create a link between otherwise disparate images.

Shiki demonstrated the principle in a number of specific examples. A haiku by Buson, already cited, was one of them:

> Pink plum blossoms
> fallen on horse dung: they seem
> ready to flare up!

Shiki explained that the principle of internal harmony was what gave the haiku poetic beauty despite its content. "Harmonious juxtaposition," he said, "is the only way to beautify dung." On another occasion he criticized this student haiku for lack of harmony among its images:

> In a pot, Chinese
> bellflowers begin to fade—
> misty rain.

Shiki felt that a pot, the misty rain, and fading Chinese bell-flowers did not harmonize. Bellflowers had stalks that were too hard and flowers that were too light in color to serve the poet's purpose. Shiki suggested that the pot be changed to a wooden bucket or that the bellflowers be changed to asters, pampas grass, cherry blossoms, or autumn leaves.

Although Shiki was the first to advocate internal harmony as a poetic principle, the method of juxtaposing images had been practiced in haiku long before his time. In fact, there is evidence that Bashō was already aware of the technique, and Shiki himself referred to it in "Elements of Haiku." It is definitely to Shiki's credit, however, that he advocated applying it to tanka. No poet before him had thought of using the haiku technique in tanka, since the two verse forms had evolved different poetics over the centuries, and a poet would specialize in one form or the other but not in both. Shiki wrote poetry in both forms, and saw nothing wrong with applying the technique of the one to the other. We have already seen his didactic poem urging a tanka student to use the haiku technique. In another instance, he criticized this tanka for lack of internal harmony:

> At a mountain village
> I take a leisurely walk
> under crimson leaves—
> for a while the autumn sun also
> glows in quiet happiness.

Shiki considered the crimson leaves out of harmony with the glowing sun. In his view, a balmy sun belonged to spring, not to autumn. "If you are going to allow the last two lines to go with crimson leaves," he carped, "you might as well allow them to go with chrysanthemums or bush clover or anything else in the world." The poet was woefully lacking in a sense of harmony, and that Shiki could not tolerate.

A number of tanka by Shiki center around haikulike internal harmony. For example:

> All alone, I watch
> spring depart from my garden:
> falling one by one
> and gathering on the water,
> petals from the mountain rose.

> On a peony
> looming in lamplight
> outside my window
> the rain of a spring night
> ceaselessly falls.

> The fleurs-de-lis
> have begun to bloom, and where
> my eyes cannot see
> spring prepares to depart
> the last year of my life.

In the first tanka, the fallen petals of a mountain rose match the poet's mourning for spring's departure, creating a sense of loss, evanescence, and loneliness. The mood is brighter and more colorful in the second poem, in which a peony, the lamplight, and the spring rain are cast together against the black background of night. The third poem embodies a sentiment similar to that of the first, but it is more poignant because the poet doubts he will live to see another spring. The fleur-de-lis is appropriate because its flower is white, the color of death. That these three tanka contain haikulike harmony is proven beyond a doubt by the fact that Shiki wrote a haiku using the same material:

> The mountain rose:
> all its yellow petals
> fallen on the water.

> From the hallway
> I stretch a lantern:
> a peony.

> The fleur-de-lis
> with one white bloom—
> spring at its close.

Being haiku, these are shorter, more imagistic, and less explanatory. The same internal harmony is present, yet because the poems include fewer verbs, the reader has to become more active and supply the connection between images himself. The poet has receded farther to the background, making more room for the reader's emotion. These poems stand as fine examples of the similarities and differences between tanka and haiku.

Finally, Shiki's concept of form is distinguished by what he called *rensaku*, or "sequential composition." This term refers to the practice of writing haiku or tanka in sequence, usually in such a way that the poems, although autonomous, take on additional significance when seen as a group. The practice was not unknown before Shiki's time, but seldom was it carried out with a conscious artistic aim. Shiki was the first to see a new poetic possibility in the technique; indeed, he seems to have invented the term *rensaku*. Although it does not figure prominently in his statements on theory, he practiced rensaku a number of times, with such successful results that he started a trend, especially among the tanka poets who looked to him for leadership.

Shiki's interest in rensaku seems to have had its beginnings in a pedagogic, rather than a poetic, motive. He taught that a student of haiku should compose as many poems as possible on a given subject and then choose the finest as his final product. Shiki did this himself, and at times he found it difficult to narrow down his choice to a single poem, especially when some of the draft poems expressed different aspects of the same subject. At such times, he would retain two or more poems and present them under a common title or headnote. A good example of this practice is recorded in his journal, *A Drop of Ink*. In the spring of 1901, one of Shiki's disciples presented him with three live carp in a tub. The gift was to help the bedridden teacher visualize spring visiting the spacious waters in the world outside. Overjoyed, Shiki began to write a haiku, with the tub by his bedside.

The task was not easy, however. "I rethought and rewrote time and again," he said of the experience, "until the number of poems I drafted reached ten. These were, and were not, ten separate poems. They were nothing more than ten attempts to express the same theme." In the end he retained the ten haiku, all describing carp in a tub on a spring day, but each with a slightly different nuance.

Shiki practiced sequential composition more deliberately in tanka. The fact that many of his tanka sequences consist of ten poems, a round number that was probably determined in advance, indicates the self-consciousness of his effort. The three finest examples are a sequence on pine trees, another on wisteria, and a third with the headnote "Forcing Myself to Take Up the Pen." The last is particularly famous and deserves quotation in full. It was composed one day in the late spring of 1901, when Shiki was especially aware of his approaching death:

> How sad it is,
> this parting with Sao,
> the vernal goddess!
> Spring will return, yet I
> shall not meet her again.

> The fleurs-de-lis
> have begun to bloom, and where
> my eyes cannot see
> spring prepares to depart
> the last year of my life.

> Eager to abate
> the pain of this sick man
> a peony
> unfolds its flowers—
> I gaze, heart aching.

> Evanescent
> is life on this earth—
> and so they too
> have fallen, yellow flowers
> of the mountain rose I love.

> Spring departs—for something
> to remember it by

I take a brush
and sketch a magnificent plume
of wisteria flowers.

I think
of building a trellis
for the moonflower—
until I begin to wonder
if my life will last till autumn.

Crimson rosebuds
have begun to swell, marking
the time of year
when my illness unfailingly
takes a turn for the worse.

My feet on a pair
of clogs, and my body leaning
on a cane
I used to trim the bush clover
in days long past.

The pine saplings'
green shoots are long, so
is this day—
as evening approaches,
my temperature climbs.

When will my illness
begin to abate? I do not
know, and yet
I have had my little garden
seeded with autumn flowers.

A single motif, the poet's confrontation with death, unites the
ten poems, and each presents a different aspect of it. The first
introduces the theme, indicating the poet's deeper appreciation
of nature's beauty because of his awareness of coming death. A
different plant appears in each of the subsequent poems, and as
the flower varies, so does the poet's response to death. The white
of a fleur-de-lis deepens his sense of approaching death. The
red of a tree peony is more soothing, and the poet allows himself
to indulge in grief. The yellow mountain rose, a fragile flower,
brings him a consolation more religious than aesthetic, and he
contemplates the evanescent nature of human and vegetable

life. The purple wisteria then suggests the possibility of salvation through art, and he takes up his painting brush. In the final analysis, however, art, a human creation, is no match for nature because man is mortal, whereas nature is cyclic. Thus in the sixth poem the poet, planning to build a trellis, comes to realize his own mortality. Appropriately, the flower he wants to support is white, the color of death. Nature, in its eternal cycle, now seems hostile, and the flower representing that aspect is a rose, which has thorns, as well as blood-colored flowers. The poet temporarily tries to escape into the past, into days when he was healthy enough to trim the flowers. In the ninth poem, however, nature takes its revenge: he runs a temperature, while youthful pine trees brimming with energy look on. Yet the poet does not lose hope, for only by hope can he keep himself alive. Thus in the last poem he has flower seeds sown for autumn. He may not live to see the flowers bloom, but even if he dies they will live on, and they are *his* flowers. He will live in them.

Through the device of rensaku, then, Shiki expressed a feeling too complex to formulate in 17 or 31 syllables, for no single tanka could successfully have traced the process through which his confrontation with death reached a resolution. Sequential composition brings haiku and tanka closer to Western poetry by enabling them to voice more complex and extended reflections. It also can be said to modernize these verse forms, for in allowing a topic to be presented under many aspects it is analogous to the presentation of multiple points of view typical of much modern art in the West. Although Shiki never said so, he may well have harbored a secret hope that rensaku could be a bridge between Japanese and Western poetry, as well as between modern and premodern verse. What started in a pedagogic motive came to have enormous potential as a poetic principle.

The Use of Poetry for a Dying Man

For Shiki, the usefulness of literature derives from the pleasure that it gives. Initially he saw this pleasure merely as recreative, but in his later years it began to take on greater importance, as an absorption in poetry came to provide him with the strength to remain calm and human in the face of suffering and eventual death. The charms of literature had caught him early in boyhood. As he related in an autobiographical essay, when he was a small child he was especially fond of listening to old stories. At around the age of nine he became an enthusiastic fan of the war tales told by professional storytellers, and soon he was reading popular novels that told of wars, such as *The Eight Dogs* and *The Romance of the Three Kingdoms*.[12] Another source of enjoyment for him was the novels serialized in the newspapers, and he could hardly wait for the paper delivery each day.

Shiki's imaginative flight to literature soon manifested itself in writing poetry, a practice encouraged by his traditional education. In elementary school he often scribbled tanka and showed them to his teacher, and in his late teens he amused himself by composing haiku "just like an average town sophisticate showing off a poem at blossom viewing." When Shiki entered college, the casual boyhood hobby developed into an addiction. *A Drop of Ink* describes him trying to concentrate on his studies but finding it impossible to resist an urge to write poetry:

Every time I managed to go over as much as twenty pages [of notes for a philosophy course] I became so bored and lethargic that I had to go out for a walk, carrying a pencil and a notebook. Outside it was a balmy day in late spring. Although the cherry blossoms had all fallen, pink clover was in full bloom along the lanes. I felt incomparable pleasure as I strolled along, looking for a possible inspiration for haiku. My illness was completely out of my mind. After about an hour I returned to resume study in my upstairs room, but by then I was physically too exhausted to begin studying right away. So I opened my notebook and tried to finish some haiku I had begun to compose during the walk. I was still too much a beginner to understand haiku properly, yet the pleasure of poetry is no less great for someone like that. When I was able to finish a haiku I was ecstatic; a mediocre poem seemed like a masterpiece.

[12] *The Eight Dogs*, a long novel by Takizawa Bakin (1767–1848), describes the adventures of eight superhuman samurai born of a marriage between a divine dog and a human princess. *The Romance of the Three Kingdoms*, by Lo Kuan-chung (fourteenth century), narrates the deeds of Chinese heroes in the Three Kingdoms period after the fall of the Han dynasty. It had long been a popular book with young readers in Japan.

Shiki did pass the examination, since the professor of philosophy was a generous teacher who never gave a failing mark. Other professors were not so kindly disposed, however, and Shiki failed in the following year.

Clearly, in this passage Shiki sets out a "play" theory of poetry. Philosophy is "study" or "work," an activity required of a college student as part of his duties. Poetry, on the other hand, is a hobby, a recreation. It takes the student's mind off his work; it leads him out of a cramped attic to the flowering fields bathed in the balmy spring sunshine.

The emphasis on enjoying natural beauty implied in the passage's spring setting characterized Shiki's play theory of art. "The men of the world," he once observed, "compete for prestige and wealth, suffer from passions and desires, and run around like madmen on a piece of land no larger than a man's palm. All this is alien to poets. They enjoy blossoms, admire the moon, and breathe clean air in a boundless space between heaven and earth." "Those who do not know how to appreciate beauty," he said at another time, "will lead a life of unhappiness. In contrast, those who can see beauty in painting and sculpture will be able to enjoy a reclusive life in the woods even while they live in the whirling dust of a metropolis. Those who enjoy the beauty of nature will experience the luxuries of a millionaire even if they are penniless." In these comments there remains a trace of premodern Japanese aesthetics, for in earlier times the ideal artist was thought to be a recluse who lived, actually or metaphorically, in the bosom of nature, far from the dust of the mundane world. "Nature," Shiki said, "knows neither good or evil nor filial piety or impiety." For Shiki, art was a special kind of play: an escape from the workaday world to a leisurely life in harmony with nature.

Shiki, however, seems to have been ambivalent about the value of art as play. At times he was unnecessarily modest. At the outset of "Haiku Wastebasket," for instance, he wrote: "If someone were to ask me in what way haiku is useful, I would answer that it is useless. . . . But I would not throw haiku away because of its uselessness, for what is useless is better than what is harmful." This modesty was probably his way of cautioning amateur poets who had extravagant expectations of poetry. As an established expert in the field, he often advised them not to abandon their occupations and to write poetry as a hobby. He urged: "Try to love your current line of work by reasoning that you are doing it in order to be able to spare time for your favorite hobby, haiku. If you are unwilling to try even this much, you are no true devotee of haiku."

At other times Shiki was quite firm in asserting the value of poetry. He usually started with the assumption that all men seek pleasure as the ultimate goal of life. To his way of thinking, there are two types of pleasure, positive and passive. Passive pleasure arises when pain is reduced or removed—when thirst is quenched, hunger satisfied, or illness cured. Statesmen, farmers, carpenters, physicians, and merchants are all engaged in helping to produce this kind of pleasure. But the other kind is different. "Positive pleasure," Shiki explained, "delights a man's mind and body in a more immediate way. It is the kind of enjoyment that frees a man from boredom, dissipates his melancholy, and refreshes his spirit." Art performs this second function. Usually people seek passive pleasure first, because it fulfills their minimum needs. Thus, according to Shiki, starving people never evolve a highly sophisticated art, but when they satisfy their basic needs they inevitably want positive pleasure. "Political or business undertakings merely provide the means of gaining pleasure," he wrote. "But literature and art bring forth pleasure itself, men's ultimate aim in life."

Shiki's diaries provide a concrete example of the usefulness of positive pleasure by revealing the irreplaceable moral support poetry provided during the years he was an invalid dying of tuberculosis. When he became unbearably bored, he could always turn to poetry. When he had a sleepless night (and he had many), he could draft haiku in his head. When an unseasonably hot spell tormented him, he could console himself by writing poems about it. When an overgrown pine tree in his garden bothered him, he could vent the frustration in tanka. He was quite honest when he said:

People praise me for my studiousness, but actually I read and write because I have this prolonged illness and do not know how to overcome boredom otherwise. Even those who will have nothing to do with books in normal life are said to become fond of reading novels and biographies, or even of composing amateurish tanka and haiku, when they suffer from a long illness. I have been living this way for so long that if for any reason someone should want me to abandon it he might as well sentence me to instant death.

We have already seen that Shiki wrote three haiku—and good ones, too—within 24 hours of his death. As two of the three poems imply, at the time his throat was stopped up with mucus, and he could hardly breathe. But it is clear why he made the desperate attempt to write them, his chest heaving hard, his hand shaking uncontrollably, and his energy all but exhausted. It was an assertion of humanity in the face of immutable fate. Although not a religious man, Shiki had an ultimate faith in art as the only way to confront death with courage and dignity. His last three haiku are unmistakable proof of the usefulness of poetry.

CHAPTER TWO

Yosano Akiko

A T NO TIME during her long literary career did Yosano Akiko (1878–1942) seek to reform poetry, as did Shiki and several other contemporary poets. "Unlike those gentlemen," she once explained, "I have never entertained a self-flattering, immodest ambition like starting a poetic reform." Nevertheless, she became one of the most influential tanka poets in modern Japan, with a reputation that matched Shiki's. She attained her fame and leadership almost solely by virtue of the poems she wrote. When her first book of tanka, *Tangled Hair*, was published in 1901, it shook the contemporary poetic scene because of its bold affirmation of sensual passion. Despite some older critics' detractions, it proved to have an irresistible appeal for the younger generation. As time gradually eroded the remnants of feudalism in Japanese society, Akiko's tanka and free verse came to seem prophetic of a bright new era soon to come, and before long she was a "queen" reigning over a countless number of young poets. Spurred on by their expectations, she continued to write innovative verse. In all, she produced 23 volumes of tanka and one volume of shi,[1] and both in quality and in quantity her poetry represents one of the highest literary achievements of her generation.

As a poet, Akiko was far more interested in self-expression than in "sketches from nature." She prized human passions and wanted to express them freely, unrestricted by the decorum of

---

[1] Four of these volumes were coauthored with other poets. Some contain prose pieces also.

contemporary society. The dominant theme of her poetry was romantic love, among the strongest of emotions. Unlike Shiki's oeuvre, which includes few love poems, her books of poetry are filled with pieces expressing her feelings toward her beloved. Her celebrated love affair with Yosano Hiroshi (1873–1935),[2] initially her tanka teacher and later her husband, supplied her with a rich source of inspiration for verse writing early in her career. After she married him, her struggles as a housewife and mother (she raised eleven children) stimulated, rather than stifled, her creative urge. They also led her to write a considerable number of essays calling for the improvement of women's status in society; some of her arguments anticipated the women's rights movements of the 1970's. Her social criticism, contained in both poetry and prose, was consistently humanistic. Whereas Shiki worried about the future of Japan as a modern state and tacitly supported her imperialistic policies, Akiko, seldom blinded by the fervent patriotism of her fellow countrymen, was far more concerned with the individual man and his welfare. One who reads the collected works of both Shiki and Akiko is astonished to discover how modern the latter was in her thought and sensibility, even though in age the two poets were only eleven years apart. Japanese poetry made a significant leap forward with the work of this remarkable poetess.

Poetry as Emotional Expression

Akiko published many essays on the art of poetry, mainly with the aim of giving guidance to young women who wanted to write tanka. Her two principal works in this area are *How to Compose Tanka* and its sequel, *Talks on Tanka*. In the former, under the heading "There Is No Such Thing as Shasei or Description of Nature in Tanka," she set forth her idea of the relationship between poetry and external reality:

[2] Yosano Hiroshi (pseudonym Tekkan) was a leader of the New Poetry Society, a group of young, radical poets intent on modernizing tanka. In 1899 he traveled to the Osaka area to seek more supporters for the movement, and it was there that he met Akiko. They were married in 1901.

Some poets seem to think there is a specific type of tanka to be categorized under "shasei" or "description of nature" as distinct from "expression of feelings." I do not agree. In my opinion, all tanka are lyrics expressing feelings. Some may refer to fruits or flowers or may sing of mountains or forests, but that does not necessarily make them sketches of natural objects or landscapes. Like love poems, they too express the poet's *jikkan* ["actual feelings"]. Jikkan are made to emerge by various stimuli, such as an event in life or the sight of natural objects or a landscape, yet in all cases they form the core of the subject matter to be treated in the poem. Hence every tanka ends up becoming a lyric.

To Shiki's selective realism, which advocated discovering one's true feelings through dispassionate observation of one's surroundings (the cycle from copying nature objectively through copying humanity objectively), Akiko opposed a stimulus-response theory of poetry. For her, the poem is the record of an emotional response—an acting out of individual impulses. As such, its course is powered by the inner drive of feeling and governed by the unique nature of each person's emotional life; its imagery need not directly reflect the exact scene or situation that serves as its immediate occasion. Thus Akiko's theory moves away from naturalistic depiction toward fantasy and vision, and away from concern with the objective stimulus that provokes creative endeavor to an emphasis on the outpouring of personal feeling, whether or not aroused by an external event.

Such an expressive theory of poetry was not new; it had been shared, with various modifications, by famous tanka poets from ancient times. Akiko reasserted it because she felt many contemporary tanka poets had swerved from that tradition. But she did not stop there: she went on to apply the same expressive view to all other verse forms, including haiku. Unlike tanka poets, writers of haiku had tended to sublimate emotions instead of expressing them outright, and we have seen how emphatic Shiki was about the principle of shasei in speaking to amateur haiku poets. In sharp contrast, Akiko took a firm stand against shasei, even in haiku. "Needless to say," she wrote, "haiku is a form of poetry. All poetry is emotional expression: its aim does not lie in narration, discussion, reportage, or communication. . . . All poems express poetic feelings and should therefore be termed lyrics." She was, of course, aware of the distinction between tanka and haiku in terms of expressive capacity. In order to make that distinction, she classified lyrics into two general categories, "active" and "passive." In her view, tanka are "active lyrics," which emerge when the poet vents emotion too powerful to contain. Many haiku, on the other hand, are "passive lyrics," which articulate the poet's response to the sight of a man, an animal, the moon, or a plant. In Akiko's opinion, some contemporary critics wrongly substituted the word "objective" for "passive" in this context, thereby misleading amateur poets into thinking that a haiku should objectively sketch something that lay outside of the poet. "The term 'shasei' has been used among haiku poets for many years," she continued. "But they are totally mistaken." This was a bold statement for Akiko, who was never known as a haiku poet, and it indicates how firmly she believed in the importance of emotional expression in all poetry.

As three of her aphorisms indicate, Akiko's expressive theory included all the arts:

Art lies deep in the painter's soul. It does not lie in the subject to be painted.

The artist does not live in nature. Rather, nature lives in the artist.

A work of art is an image of the self. It needs: first, the self; second, the self; third, the self; . . . absolutely, the self.

On another occasion her comment was more explanatory. "I do not like to see such terms as 'shasei' or 'description of nature' used in art," she wrote. "These words mislead the reader into thinking that the artist is subordinate to the subject matter. The artist is the principal in all cases. A work of art emerges only when the feelings in the artist's heart, stimulated by things in nature, focus in an image." Her vehement insistence is directed against a prevailing condemnation of individualism, and reflects her awareness of a strong trend toward realism in contemporary literature, a movement advocated by Shiki and his followers in traditional forms of verse.

Akiko's adamant opposition to shasei seems to have been connected with her desire to reach for a truth that lay beyond fact. She distinguished between the truth of art and that of science, identifying the latter as factual truth lying in external reality, the former as subjective truth hidden in the individual human heart. To her way of thinking, a poem that sketches nature merely copies fact, not truth. For example, she criticized these two tanka for being mere snapshots, reproductions of ordinary scenes as anyone could have perceived them:

> After rainfall
> sparkling rays of sunlight
> creep down along the trees,
> brightening a small garden
> where sweet oleanders bloom.

> Dusk has begun
> to settle on the highway
> buried in snow.
> The sunlight, gone from some hills,
> still lingers on others.

Akiko charged that these poems were boring because they differ in no way from unpolished prose passages recording scenes of nature. Their authors did not seem to understand the distinction between inner and outer truth. Like them, too many contemporary Japanese, she thought, took a wrong attitude when they read a poem or looked at a painting, even though they readily corrected that attitude when they went to see a nō or a kabuki play.

Thus the core of Akiko's poetic was jikkan, the feelings that a poet actually experiences at a given moment. As we have seen, she used the term to define the relationship between a tanka poet and external reality; it appears again and again in her discussions of poetry. The very first heading in *How to Compose Tanka* reads "It Is Jikkan That Becomes Tanka," and the book opens with the declaration, "My tanka are, almost exclusively, expressions of my jikkan." *Talks on Tanka* recapitulates the idea, asserting that her effort to articulate jikkan had remained unchanged from her younger days. Indeed, these two books on the art of composition can be read as explanations of what jikkan are and how they can be expressed in poetry. Akiko's third book of poetic criticism, *Lectures on Three Hundred Tanka*, does the same, using as specific examples 300 tanka of her own. "I took up my pen," she said in the preface, "mainly because I wanted to tell the reader what kind of jikkan it was that gave birth to each poem."

The word "jikkan" is written with two characters, one meaning "actual" and the other meaning "feeling(s)." In Akiko's view, poetry articulates not just feelings but actual feelings. She pointed out that the antonym of jikkan is *kyogi*, "falsehood." "By the word 'kyogi,'" she said, "I mean deliberately fabricating feelings that one does not actually possess." She felt that too many poets of her time fabricated poems because they wished to follow the example of famous masters or to join in fashionable literary movements. She repeatedly warned that jikkan exclude "arty" emotions already celebrated by many poets in the past; they are fresh feelings discovered by individuals for themselves. "The material for poetry," she said, "is feelings that have newness in them, feelings that have been discovered by each poet on a specific occasion."

From the denotation of "jikkan" Akiko excluded another type of feelings: ordinary, everyday ones. "What I mean by jikkan," she explained, "are a special type of excited feelings that belong to the realm of poetic emotion. These must enable the poet to transcend common sense, to experience an entirely new joy, sorrow, or other emotion, and to feel the soul stirred with extraordinary excitement." In her view, therefore, jikkan are more elevated, more intense, more excited feelings than those people routinely experience in their everyday lives. Ordinary feelings can be expressed in conversation, in letters, and in other forms of prose, but jikkan cannot be voiced in prose because they are too intense.

To show the kind of poem that embodied ordinary feelings rather than jikkan, Akiko once cited two tanka from the works

of Kagawa Kageki (1768–1843),[3] one of the most respected
tanka poets of the nineteenth century:

> There have been days
> when warblers failed to come
> and sing in our garden,
> yet no day has passed
> when I did not hear their song.

> It snows, darkening
> the vast expanse of sky . . .
> the mountains,
> so much closer to the sky,
> are first to whiten.

It is ironic that Kageki's poems are singled out for this dubious
honor, because in his day he was known as an advocate of poetry
that expressed truthful feelings. Indeed, these two tanka do vent
the poet's feelings: the first sings of his joy at being in the country and hearing warblers every day; the second, of his wonder-
ment at the workings of nature, which metamorphose earth and
sky. But, to Akiko's taste, these emotions are insufficiently individualized to make good poetry. Since they are little different
from what anyone would feel out in the countryside on a balmy
day in spring or a snowy day in winter, Akiko considered them
"commonplace feelings," unworthy of a poet's attention. She
said she was tempted to ask Kageki why he had uttered such useless words. "Perhaps," she complained, "this poet thought that
any commonplace emotion could be made into a tanka if he
could verbalize it in the 5–7–5–7–7 pattern."

Akiko offered plenty of examples of what a poem of jikkan is
like. In *How to Compose Tanka*, for instance, is a section entitled
"Jikkan as It Is Manifest in My Tanka," in which she quoted 50
of her own poems. The first was:

> On spring's white fabric
> spread between heaven and earth

[3]Kagawa Kageki was the founder of the Keien school of tanka, which remained influential in Akiko's youth. Part of her antagonism toward Kageki
seems to lie in the fact that many conservative poets who disapproved of her
tanka were from the Keien school.

there falls, like gold dust,
the sound of young maidens
hitting a shuttlecock.

Akiko explained, "Here is the jikkan I had while listening to the sound of battledore and shuttlecock being played by young girls one day in the New Year's season. Because it was the New Year, I had the illusion that the universe was a pure, white silk fabric, and when I heard young girls happily playing the seasonal game I felt as though the sound of the shuttlecock were falling like gold dust on the fabric. It sounded pure, graceful, and beautiful."

Another tanka Akiko quoted as embodying jikkan is about her happy married life:

In a tower
beautifully painted in gold
I have been asleep
for a whole decade,
this woman of dreams.

Akiko commented, "I am a person peacefully asleep in a tower of beautiful gold, transcending for years the world's good and evil. This is another poem of fantasy, not of fact. But the fantasy accurately represents the mental state I am in when I let myself indulge in the ecstasy of love. It is the jikkan I have as I live a life of love."

The third example is a free-verse poem entitled "One Day":

In the sunlight of a day in March,
the wisteria's purple creeping into my study,
the white of Hikaru's face,
the red of Nanase's sash,
the amber of a tablecloth,
all are full of life and warmth . . .
Only a branch of *higan* cherry in a vase[1]
and myself are pale and cold.
Like a still life I live, because
you have been gone for so long.

[1] Hikaru and Nanase are the names of Akiko's children. A *higan* cherry (*Prunus miquieliana*, or equinoctial cherry) blooms around the time of the vernal equinox.

Akiko had a lengthy comment on this poem, beginning with the explanation "I jotted down this poem out of my jikkan one day when my husband was traveling in Europe." She continued to say that her jikkan spontaneously flowed out in words at the time, and all she did was put it down in the order it came out. She never changed the wording later, fearing that her attempt to polish might impair the freshness of the jikkan.

These three examples from Akiko's own poetry reveal in specific terms what she meant by jikkan. The emotions appear ordinary if they are described using abstract terms such as "love," "loneliness," or "appreciation of beauty." But they have been individualized; none merely embodies a universal pattern of feeling. Not all people who are in love feel that they are sleeping in a tower beautifully painted in gold; no one else has felt that spring is a huge piece of white silk fabric extending into an infinite distance, and that a shuttlecock sounds like tiny particles of gold falling onto that fabric. It is not merely that similes and metaphors are individualized. Because jikkan are individualized feelings, they automatically take on individualized forms; feeling and expression are one.

In Akiko's view, then, a poet must be a strong individual, who will not fall into stereotyped thoughts or feelings; a poet who lacks a strongly personal sensibility has less capacity for jikkan. Indeed, Akiko asserted that only those who recognize the importance of individuality can succeed in grasping the ultimate truth for which every poet must strive. She wrote:

In actual human life each individual forms a new class all his or her own, like a new plant that has emerged through mutation. Among individuals there are a great many differences, since all lead their lives with different aims and in different styles. The human psyche differs from one person to another, just as fingerprints do. Different persons use the same word "love," but each person's love differs in density, intensity, and color, far more so than plumes of wisteria differ in length. That is the "truth" in human life.

Akiko here seems to imply that this subjective "truth" lies in a direct experience of individual being, unmediated by intellectual stances or predetermined moral, aesthetic, or perceptual categories. All those intervening forms are based on groupings that deny the fundamental fact that, finally, no two things are exactly the same. She valued jikkan as a means of access to the inner truth, this pure experience of being; they provided the only way to reach the most basic fact of one's existence.

Akiko, of course, believed in an objective, generalized truth as well. To her, however, that type of truth is the proper object of study for scholars and scientists. It is grasped through the intellect, in operations that ignore differences among individual beings. Scholars and scientists address collective man, not individual men. For an individual, therefore, their studies have only a secondary importance. "The raison d'être of a scholar's theory," Akiko observed, "lies merely in that it can provide reference material for a person on a specific occasion." Science shows in universal terms how man normally conducts himself; poetry reveals how particular people behave on specific occasions.

Another reason Akiko thought less highly of objective, abstract truth was that the intellect, in its process of abstraction, destroys the immediacy of experience. She explained:

A person who resorts to the intellect may attain a measure of success in systematizing various experiences of love and in making them into a philosophy of love, a history of love, a critique of love, an ethics of love, and so forth. A product thus made may partly touch on the truth about love, but largely it will be removed from the initial experience and will no longer be empirical love. . . . Intellect may enable us to understand love, but in no way can it make us feel or experience love in its immediacy. For this reason, since ancient times no one has tried to learn about the definition of love or the morality of love before he goes out to experience love.

Since poetry depends on the abstracting power of intellect less than do philosophy, history, and ethics, it can present more directly the vitality of experience.

As the two passages cited above suggest, although in principle Akiko maintained that all jikkan can be made into poems, in practice she seems to have been partial to romantic love as material for poetry. This tendency may have been encouraged by biographical factors, for just a few months after she started writing tanka as a young girl, she fell in love with a man—Yosano Hiroshi—for the first time in her life. The feeling of love dominated her daily existence, and as she recalled in *Talks on Tanka*, "Tanka served as the best expression of my love. It became an inseparable part of my life. . . . I can honestly say that my love gained its fullest expression by means of tanka, and that my tanka suddenly made progress by means of love."

Many of her finest poems concern romantic love. Here are three examples from *Tangled Hair*:

> Pressing my breasts
> with both hands, I gently kick
> the door to mystery . . .
> A flower opens there, how
> brightly crimson it is!

> My small young fingers
> dissolving white color
> hesitate a moment:
> cold in the evening twilight,
> a magnolia blossom.

> The clear spring
> inside me spurted, overflowed
> and became muddy.
> You are a child of sin
> and so am I.

With colorful and sensual images the first tanka boldly expresses the joy of first love as experienced by a young woman. The second poem is more subdued: it portrays a maiden preparing to sketch a white magnolia. Her hand dissolving the paint pauses a moment; because her heart harbors burning—and probably sinful—love, the white of the magnolia looks too pure for her. The third tanka more directly depicts the poet's feelings of guilt: her maiden love, initially as pure as clear water, has gained in sensuality as it intensified. Her guilty feeling increases when she considers the fact that her lover is a married man.[5]

[5] At the time Hiroshi was married to his second wife, Hayashi Takino. The poem was written a few months before their divorce in 1901.

The cover design of the first edition of *Tangled Hair* suggested Akiko's idea of poetry. It showed a young woman's face with abundant black hair hanging in tangles alongside. The design itself was shaped like a heart, pierced by an arrow; in the wound several flowers were blooming. Poems are flowers of the heart, which bloom when it is pierced by the poignant emotion of love.

Akiko repeatedly stressed the importance of one other aspect of jikkan in poetic composition: she insisted that when she talked of "actual feelings" she included fantasy or, to borrow her favorite word, "vision." Indeed, Akiko's assertion that the jikkan at the core of good poems are not the stereotyped feelings of everyday life might be extended to argue that the farther a feeling is removed from routine reality the more personal—and hence poetic—it becomes. In *How to Compose Tanka*, Akiko explained the matter more moderately, saying that jikkan include memories of the past, experiences in the present, and hopes for the future, as well as fantasies and visions that are not likely to be realized. Although some people might consider the last only futile imaginings, Akiko thought fantasies part of "actual feelings" as long as they honestly represent inner wishes. Her predilection for fantasy is even more pronounced in *Talks on Tanka*. In a section entitled "I Consider Visionary Jikkan the Glory of Life," she attacked contemporary realists, calling them "pseudo-jikkanist poets" who did not understand the true value of vision. Indeed, she made vision the raison d'être of all the arts. "Art can claim its usefulness for both society and the individual," she wrote, "because it can symbolically present a vision hitherto unknown to men, thereby suggesting a spirit or mode by which they can enter on a new life." Visionary jikkan belong to one of the highest types of emotion because of their prophetic function.

It was in this sense that Akiko wanted to call herself an "idealist" and a "romantic." By those terms she meant that she was bent on pursuing visionary jikkan, which would enable her to dream of another reality. Some of her most appealing poems show a measure of success in that attempt, for example:

The cover of the first edition of Yosano Akiko's *Tangled Hair*. Reprinted from Satake Toshihiko, *Zenshaku midaregami kenkyū*, by courtesy of Yū-hōdō.

A peony in my hair
is set afire, the ocean
burns in flames—
the dream of a woman, her thoughts
hopelessly entangled.

This evening's rowboat
carrying a monk I love
took longer to return.
Which lotus flowers, the red
or the white, attracted him more?

Many curse poems
I have scribbled and thrown away—
picking up one of
those manuscripts, I trap
a black butterfly.

The first tanka is admittedly a dream, the vision of a woman in distress whose passion would inflame the whole ocean. The second poem presents a visionary love affair, presumably between a woman and a young Buddhist monk. The monk has gone on an excursion through a lotus pond (a Buddhist symbol of the world), and the woman, left behind, wonders whether the red lotus (sensual love) or the white one (religion) so attracted his heart that it delayed the return of his boat. In the third tanka, the poet imagines catching a symbolic black butterfly with a scrap of paper. Frustrated for some reason (in discussing the poem, Akiko mentioned the gloomy atmosphere of her parents' home and the conservative norms of society in her younger days), she thinks that she has finally pinned down the cause by repeatedly venting her emotion in poems, even though they may be imperfect from an artistic point of view. In all three cases the poet's jikkan are expressed in the form of a fantasy—a flaming sea, a lotus pond, and a black butterfly. The tanka about a golden tower quoted earlier falls into the same category, and similar examples abound in Akiko's books of poetry. *The Falling Star's Path*, in particular, has many such poems, including 54 tanka in which the poet visualizes herself in the world of *The Tale of Genji*.

To summarize, Akiko's view of the relationship between art and external reality was characterized by a strong assertion of the artist's expressive capacity. She looked down upon shasei because she thought it assigned a passive role to the artist. For her, a work of art should above all be an expression of powerful emotion, an embodiment of jikkan, and in her poetic every poem worthy of the name is a lyric that sings out what lies in the poet's heart. Of all the jikkan that can provide material for poetry, Akiko seemed most to value romantic love and what she called "vision," dreams or fantasies that present an altered reality, one that can embody the heart's inmost urges. Her own poetry excelled in expressing these two emotions.

How a Molten Ball Is Cast

As a practicing poet, Akiko often spoke of the process through which a poem comes into being. In general, she seems to have recognized four stages in the creative process. In *How to Compose Tanka* she called them "jikkan," "combustion," "leap," and "finished work." In her view, a poet first has an "actual feeling," which heats up in him to the point of explosion. That explosion throws out a molten ball, which cools into a finished work of poetry.

What Akiko meant by jikkan has already been discussed. A jikkan can be any feeling—love or grief or admiration of beauty—provided that it is a genuine feeling, a fresh feeling from one's actual life that has not yet hardened into an abstract concept. Jikkan include fantasies as well as recollections. Akiko did not know why they initially occurred, and simply said that they emerged spontaneously. She did, however, distinguish two types of jikkan according to the presence or absence of external stimulus. "Positive jikkan" emerge by themselves in the poet's mind, whereas "passive jikkan" appear when the poet is stimulated by an external event, like seeing a beautiful moon or a busy street in town.

For attaining a state of mind conducive to jikkan, Akiko recommended travel. "When a flower blooms beautifully in the poet's own garden," she said, "he is apt to feel that it is beautiful merely in an ordinary way, since he is used to the sight. It will not lead him to a discovery, a new discovery that excites him powerfully enough to result in a poem. But when he sees a flower or a mountain or a river while traveling—especially if he is visiting a place for the first time—his poetic feelings will be stimulated." Here Akiko concurred with Shiki, presumably because she was talking mainly about passive jikkan, the type that often provided a source for haiku. On inducing a state of mind conducive to positive jikkan she said little, although she did cite instances of various attempts made by famous Japanese poets of the past. Priest Saigyō (1118–90), for example, would walk around his house reciting verses whenever he wanted to compose a poem. Izumi Shikibu (eleventh century) always pondered a poem with her head covered; she put her face into her sleeve when she had to compose in the presence of other poets. Fujiwara Teika (1162–1241) would dress himself in formal costume, sit in the central room of his house, and gaze far into the southern sky when he composed a tanka.[6] In citing these and other episodes, Akiko seemed to imply that different poets have different ways of creating a poetic state of mind.

Akiko also had something to say about what a poet might do if such attempts to induce jikkan should fail. She suggested a method to force jikkan to come, one she practiced herself. If she was with verse-writing friends, she would play a kind of game. The participants would decide on a clue word, such as "death," "to swim," or "smoke," and then they would compete in writing poems that made use of the word. In her experience, when she did this the key word sometimes awakened a jikkan asleep in the depths of her mind. If she was alone, she would play the game herself, jotting down a number of words at random as they passed through her mind. If she was fortunate, one of the words

[6] Saigyō and Teika were two outstanding poets whose works appear in *The New Collection of Ancient and Modern Poems*. Izumi Shikibu, author of *The Diary of Izumi Shikibu*, was a talented poetess of the Heian period. The working habits mentioned here are more legendary than historical.

would administer an almost electric shock, inducing a jikkan to leap out. At that instant she would begin composing a poem. The first couple of poems would center on the clue word, but then she would let the jikkan freely express itself, whether or not the expression included the key word.

"Combustion," the second phase of the creative process, is an intensification of jikkan in the poet's mind. "When I say I have a 'combustion,'" Akiko explained, "I mean there is a brisk boiling of jikkan, the emotion moving me with such great force that it impresses a clear form on my consciousness." Her words point toward a state of mind so agitated that an emotion is on the brink of bursting out. The emotion has to be powerful: otherwise it will not lead to a combustion, or will not cause a major combustion. When a poem is composed out of a small or imperfect combustion, it is a "draft piece" in Akiko's terms and should be distinguished from "finished work." She saw a use for draft pieces, however. In the process of writing many such pieces, she sometimes hit upon a jikkan that caused a great combustion, resulting in a genuine work of art. It was partly because of this possibility, she explained, that she wrote so many poems, even risking some critics' charge that she wrote poetry for money.

For a jikkan to cause a combustion, the passage of time is required. An emotion that emerges in the poet's mind will increase in intensity with time, finally coming to the point of explosion. Akiko once compared the process to pregnancy and childbirth: a poem that comes out of an imperfect combustion is like a baby delivered prematurely by an operation. Her metaphor of boiling water seems to suggest the same point: it takes time for the water to come to a boil. A poet should let his jikkan alone for a while to see if a poem has truly been conceived or, to change the metaphor, he should wait for the jikkan to reach the boiling point.

When the emotion finally goes through combustion, there comes a stage Akiko called the "leap." The two stages are actually two sides of the same coin, because there can be no leap without combustion. According to Akiko, the leap is the externalization of the jikkan burning inside: some jikkan are too strong to be contained. She had several explanations for why strong jikkan seek expression. At the most elementary level, she attributed the urge to a kind of instinct possessed by all living beings: she thought warblers, larks, and canaries sang, and cranes, penguins, and dogs "danced" because of an instinct to express their feelings. Because people also have this instinct, they weep when they are sad and dance when they are ecstatic. When their feelings are more complex or delicate, they write poetry.

On several occasions Akiko illustrated this instinct by referring to the time when she first began to write poetry. In *Talks on Tanka*, for instance, she recalled that she had been an avid reader of novels and plays but had held a rather contemptuous opinion of poetry until she was around twenty years of age. "But then," she continues, "all of a sudden I discovered an instinct newly manifesting itself within me. It was a sweet and yet maddening, agonizing instinct, like a force that makes a flower bud swell." She had fallen in love. As her passion intensified, the instinctual force pressed upon her. She had a dire need to relieve the tension by some means, a means more eloquent than ordinary speech. Fortunately, help was near at hand. "Suddenly," she said, "tanka appeared before me to fill the need."

In analyzing the human instinct for self-expression, Akiko conceived of a "possessive impulse" and a "creative impulse." The terms were Bertrand Russell's, but she viewed their functions somewhat differently. She thought that there were two types of possessive impulse, and that both could give rise to the creative impulse. The first was a spiritual type, which made a person want to possess all or part of the outside world by means of imagination. Such a person wishes to own part of external reality by recording impressions of it in poetry; alternatively, the person may create a private universe through idealistic vision and thereby become its sole owner. According to Akiko, from such wishes can emerge the creative impulse, an urge to create something, love it, and possess it. In Akiko's view, there was also a second type of possessive impulse, a more material kind, which could spark the creative impulse more indirectly. A person with the second type of impulse wants to possess material wealth. Most people cannot satisfy this wish, however, whereupon frustrations emerge. Some of the frustrations become sources for poetry, often resulting in poems of social protest or of sadness at the poet's powerlessness.

One other motive for self-expression, or leap, as conceived by Akiko was the desire for communication. She thought that a person normally wants to share feelings with others, despite the fact that those feelings are peculiar to each individual. "A person cannot," she asserted, "be completely satisfied when he or she is the only one experiencing an emotion." In her opinion, a person who enjoys loneliness has been forced to assume that attitude after being rejected by society, since under ordinary circumstances anyone would want to enjoy happiness or share grief with others. In the process of communication an emotional leap occurs, joy or sorrow being externalized in the form of art or literature.

When the leap is ready to be distilled in the language of poetry, the creative process enters its fourth and final phase, the "finished work." Akiko thought this stage, too, was largely spontaneous. "Language is a jikkan dancing," she said. "So long as a jikkan burns itself fully and is filled with energy for a leap, a poetic form will emerge easily and naturally." She then compared jikkan in this phase to flowing water:

To use a simile, jikkan is like gushing water. Water has within itself a potential for new forms: it can become a mountain stream, a pond, a large river, a lake, or a sea. Likewise, jikkan has in itself a demand for one or another verse form, such as the poem with a 5–7 or 7–5 pattern, the free-style poem with indefinite line length, or the tanka. The poet need only be quick in sensing the demand. If the jikkan has the rhythm of tanka, the poet need only let it take the tanka form.

In Akiko's opinion, then, not the poet but the poem (or "prepoem") chooses the verse form. For her, emotion and expression were one, and the process of their coming together was not to be disturbed by the meddling intellect, with its reflections and second thoughts. As we have seen, Akiko did not dare to change a word in her poem "One Day" for fear of impairing her original jikkan.

Nonetheless, Akiko did admit that in some cases the last stage of the creative process is not so simple or spontaneous. She could complete the stage in no time when her jikkan was extraordinarily powerful, but on other occasions she had difficulty choosing the right words. In such cases she would jot down words, erase them, and try other words, repeating the process until the paper was black. She would have a particularly hard time with tanka, because tanka was such a short verse form. She would take pains, she said, to choose evocative words, ones that would give the impression of "fragrance arising from a flower" or "the mountain haze dyed in the morning sun." Choosing the right word became extremely important in creating the correct emotional nuance, and she deplored the stand of some contemporary poets who insisted on "artless art" and did not pay enough attention to the craft of verse writing.

For the same reason, Akiko approved teachers' usual practice of correcting their students' poems. She often did this herself after she became famous. When correcting a poem, she tried to empathize and to compose the poem with the poet. Understandably, a poem with powerful underlying jikkan made her job easier, sometimes giving her the kind of pleasure she felt when she was writing her own poems. Most hopeless were poems lacking in jikkan: she usually left them untouched. When the material seemed usable, however, at times she wrote her own poem on the same topic and showed it to the poet for the sake of contrast.

The shi entitled "Memories" provides an example of Akiko's verse-writing process.

> As I stroke my daughter's hair
> memories of home pass through my mind.
> Things about mother, my late sister, an aunt,
> this and that, all trivial things—
> For a while I am in a shower of golden rain.

Yosano Akiko

In an article called "How to Write Shi," she explained the circumstances:

> I wrote this poem five or six years ago. One day, when I was combing my little daughter's hair, my mind somehow wandered back to my home in Izumi Province where, as a small child, I lived with my mother and older sister. The sister was now dead. I also remembered how my aunt had been in those days. As I recalled all those little things one after another, I forgot the worries of my daily life and felt a pleasure like that of standing in a golden shower.
>
> Since my jikkan at that time had a colloquial mood, it spontaneously came out in colloquial language. First, the opening line floated up in a pattern of 5–7–5. As soon as I became aware of it, the remaining lines followed in no time, each with the same 5–7–5 rhythm. I had had no advance plan for making the verse form as it came out. It was simply that my jikkan of that occasion spun out naturally into a 5–7–5 rhythm.

Akiko did not spell out the four phases of the creative process, but they are all there. She first had a jikkan, a recollection of her childhood days. It was a passive one, a jikkan stimulated by the sight and feel of her daughter's hair. The emotion went through a combustion as her thoughts about her birthplace intensified and clearly separated themselves from the worries of mundane life. Then there came a leap, which externalized the emotion. Conspicuous in her explanation is a repetition of words indicating the spontaneity of her self-expression. Finally, the external rhythm, in this case the 5–7–5 pattern, was established, more through the demand of the jikkan than through the poet's design. Presumably her emotion was strong enough that she had little trouble in selecting words during the final phase of composition.

To summarize, Akiko's concept of the creative process is distinguished by its emphasis on the power and spontaneity of jikkan. A poet remains a passive agent throughout most of the process. One cannot force a jikkan to come, but must wait until, largely by chance, it forms itself in the mind. Then the poet must continue to wait for the jikkan to burn and to explode. Even in the final stage of composition, it is the jikkan, not the poet's conscious mind, that chooses the verse form through which it expresses itself.

Such being the case, one begins to wonder if there is anything a poet can do to become an expert. Akiko, who always wanted more women to write poetry, answered that question on various occasions. Her most detailed answer appears in *How to Compose Tanka*, in which she made five suggestions to amateur poets, advising that they sharpen their senses, enrich their emotions, have a vital interest in society, commune with nature, and read good books. These suggestions convey her ideas about the qualifications of a poet.

The first two of the five suggestions are necessary corollaries to Akiko's jikkan-oriented idea of poetry. In order to acquire strong jikkan, a poet must be equipped with sharp senses and a capacity for rich emotions. According to Akiko, a person with ordinary visual awareness perceives snow to be white and cherry blossoms to be pink, and nothing more. But someone with sharper senses notes a delicate shade of purple in snow or cherry blossoms in the daylight. Akiko thought a poet must be like the second person. Here is an example she cited from her own work to show a poet's high sensitivity:

> More ephemeral
> than a faint voice
> from afar:
> a bindweed flower
> blooming in the verdant grass.

Here Akiko did not see a bindweed flower as being merely whitish; she felt it had a color like a faint voice coming from a distance. Her sharp sensitivity individualized the feeling. Akiko advised would-be poets to try to develop this kind of sensitivity by conscious effort. "We . . . must consciously focus our attention on things," she said. "We must touch them directly through our fresh senses, without depending on the sensitivity of other poets, ancient or modern." In the same way, she taught that amateur poets should enrich their capacity to feel a strong emotion once it is stirred by the senses. A great poet always has a great capacity to cultivate emotion and to make it grow within the mind. The larger the combustion chamber, the bigger the fire that can burn inside it.

Akiko admonished that a poet should be actively interested in society because she believed someone isolated from society is limited in experience and knowledge of human reality, and therefore is apt to be limited in depth and scope of emotional capacity. "Poets must enrich their thoughts," she said. "In order to do so, they need to taste multitudes of human feelings by throwing themselves on the turbulent waves of the world. That will provide constant stimuli to the heart and keep it fresh." Akiko's fifth item of advice, recommending that a beginning poet read many books, may have been made for a similar reason, since books enable us to experience vicariously things we cannot in actuality. Akiko deplored the practice of many contemporary tanka poets who read nothing but books on tanka, and of many haiku poets who read nothing but books on haiku. She urged poets to read all kinds of books, not only on literature but also on religion, philosophy, and science, thereby enlarging the scope of their knowledge and emotional capacity.

Akiko's recommendation that a poet commune with nature had the same motive: to enrich emotional experience. In our lives, she said, we frequently come in contact with the sea, the mountains, trees, and flowers, and our emotions are stirred by the sight of these and other things in nature. She also pointed out that a person familiar with nature can express emotion metaphorically or symbolically through natural images. She then cited a number of tanka on nature, many of which used nature as a means of expressing the poet's inner feelings. For instance, here is a tanka by Chino Masako (1880–1946),[7] which Akiko cited as an example:

> White plum blossoms,
> like a scent rising
> from the hair
> of my corpse—how lonesome
> and how dear they seem!

[7] Chino Masako (maiden name Masuda) was a member of the New Poetry Society. She was a good friend of Akiko's, and the two joined with a third woman poet to coauthor a book of tanka in 1905. Later Masako became a professor at the Japan Women's College.

The poem is about plum blossoms, but it also expresses the feelings of the lonely poet obsessed with death.

If Akiko's five suggestions for amateur poets have any weak link, it is this advice about communing with nature. Though Akiko offered it sincerely, in the light of her own practice, the comment she made on another occasion is more convincing: "It is not that I do not love nature. I, too, think a wild chrysanthemum is lovely. But the pleasure of picking seasonal flowers in the wild every year is no match for the joy of seeing the steady growth of many children whom I have nursed at my breast."

An Aesthetic for an Individualist

Akiko did not concern herself overmuch with issues of literary criticism because she thought the prime beneficiary of verse writing was the poet, not the reader, and that the poet was to vent jikkan regardless of whether or not there was any other reader. She once said that a poet who showed poems to others for critical commentary was swerving from the main purpose of writing poetry. In the same article, entitled "The Essence of Poetry," she declared:

Of all the arts, I believe poetry is the one that most begins and ends with the maker. As I conceive the essence of poetry, poets freely express what they feel or what they want to say, without thinking of readers, spectators, or audience in advance. They are at once author, reader, and critic. Poets do their work for the pleasure of self-expression, like a little child that naturally sings out whatever it likes to say.

Later in the article Akiko defined poetry as "a monologic art."

Underlying her lack of enthusiasm for literary criticism was her high regard for individuality, both in the poet and in the reader. She felt that the jikkan embodied in a poem was an emotion peculiar to the poet, one most attractive to the poet. Whether it is also attractive to the reader depends upon a similarity in taste between poet and reader, and the same reader may want a different type of art on different occasions. Since both poet and reader are unique individuals, there is no common meeting ground that can provide a basis for literary or art criticism. From another angle, this means tolerance for all kinds of literary approaches. "Depending on the critic's individuality," Akiko said, "various types of criticism could be invented." She disliked critics who were attached to one kind of approach and considered it the only right one; leftist critics were among her targets in this regard. She was also unhappy with classicist critics who read her tanka according to the standard of *The Collection of Ten Thousand Leaves* or *The Collection of Ancient and Modern Poems*.

On the whole, Akiko seems to have favored impressionistic criticism. In an article entitled "Criticism Is Taste," she wrote:

In my opinion, there is no way to evaluate a work of art except through the instincts of the individual spectator. Reflecting on my own experience, I must say that all I feel when confronted by a work of painting or poetry or sculpture is a sheer intuitive sense telling me it is "interesting" or "uninteresting," "good" or "not good." To put it more directly, my critical approval or disapproval depends on whether or not I am struck by surprise at that instant and say "Ah!" in admiration.

Later in the same article Akiko further probed these intuitive likes and dislikes until she reached "love." She thought taste was a manifestation of a love that each individual held deep within. As a person instinctively loves certain people and dislikes others, so that person has spontaneous likes or dislikes for certain works of art. Someone who intuitively loves a poem will proceed to find something good or interesting in it. "One who wants to evaluate a work of art," Akiko suggested, "should first of all try to love it. One should confront a work of art through one's own likes and dislikes."

On several occasions, Akiko made clear what her personal likes and dislikes were. Her comments differ somewhat in implication, but one that appears in *How to Compose Tanka* is perhaps the most representative. There she said that she liked tanka whose jikkan had five characteristic elements: "truth" (*shinjitsu*), "uniqueness" (*tokushu*), "freshness" (*seishin*), "excellence" (*yūshū*), and "beauty" (*bi*).

By "truth" Akiko meant truthfulness to one's own feelings, a central element of jikkan. She applied the word "truth" in describing many of her early tanka. For example, in later years she apparently felt that the poems collected in *Tangled Hair* were largely immature, and when she compiled an anthology of her own poetry in 1925 she selected only one out of the 399 poems that appeared in her first book of tanka. Still, she felt that those immature poems did have the quality of truth in them, by virtue of having been true to the life she was leading at the time. She cited these three in that connection:

> Without ever touching
> the warm, youthful blood
> under this soft skin
> you lecture on the Way. . . .
> Are you not lonely?

> Head lying on my arm,
> I had been asleep, when a hair
> by my ear broke:
> one twang of the koto
> in my dream on a spring night.

> From where you live
> you can look up and see
> what lies inside my heart:
> myriad bits of amber cloud
> in the sky of a spring evening.

For the later Akiko there was perhaps a bit too much narcissism in the first poem, a bit too much girlish fancy in the second, and a bit too much sentimentalism in the third; she felt embarrassed by them. Nevertheless, she was confident that they embodied what was true of her life of that time.

"Uniqueness," the second of Akiko's five elements, stems from her high regard for jikkan: jikkan are unique because each poet has a different sensibility. A good poem, which derives its power from the force of jikkan, is likewise unique. Akiko once illustrated this quality by contrasting five tanka on warblers that she thought showed uniqueness with this tanka by Kageki cited earlier:

> There have been days
> when warblers failed to come

and sing in our garden,
yet no day has passed
when I did not hear their song.

This poem lacked unique feeling, she said. One of the tanka she opposed to it was by Kitahara Hakushū (1885–1942):[8]

Cherry petals fall
on the rusting steel plates
of a ship. . . .
In the fragrant evening
sunlight, a warbler sings.

Akiko asserted that this tanka embodied a jikkan the poet experienced one spring evening at a seaside or riverside. She did not explain further, but it is likely that she saw as unique the juxtaposition of a warbler's song and a broken boat showing its rusted bottom: a premodern poet would never have placed such an ugly man-made object in the center of a vernal natural scene. There is something new about the poem, some modern sensibility that is lacking in traditional poems on warblers. Akiko called it a unique sentiment, "so unique and appealing that the poet had to articulate it in verse."

The aesthetic quality Akiko called "freshness" is closely related to uniqueness. A poem embodying a unique jikkan usually creates a fresh impression on the reader. To force a distinction between the two, freshness seems to place more stress on freedom from conventional aesthetic ideals. Akiko particularly emphasized the importance of freshness in tanka, because the 31-syllable form had an age-old history and it was easy for an inexpert poet to fall into stereotypes. In order to illustrate what she meant by a fresh tanka, in *How to Compose Tanka* she cited a poem by Mori Ōgai (1862–1922):[9]

[8] Kitahara Hakushū was a member of the New Poetry Society as a young man. His tanka display the influence of French Symbolist poetry. In addition to tanka, he wrote shi, popular lyrics, and children's songs, and eventually attained a popularity rare among symbolist poets.

[9] Mori Ōgai, a physician, a bureaucrat, and one of the most prominent novelists of modern Japan, tried his hand at tanka, too. He associated with members of the New Poetry Society and at times published his poems in their magazine.

Your heart remains
just as unsettled, like
the wavering
of a cosmos flower
after the bee is gone.

According to Akiko, the poem attempts to describe a woman's mind beginning to regain calm after an outburst of anger toward the poet. Apparently Akiko felt that this kind of psychological description was rare in traditional Japanese poetry. Of this and four other tanka cited with it, she said: "Every one of these poems is fresh and novel in conception, in expression, and in technique. This type of tanka had never existed in Japanese poetry before, and we must conclude that these came to be through the individuality of each poet." In another article, "How to Write and Appreciate Tanka," Akiko also emphasized the modernity of this and 24 other tanka by contemporary poets, saying that they differed significantly from classical poems found in *The Collection of Ten Thousand Leaves* and *The Collection of Ancient and Modern Poems*. She thought they were modern tanka made of "entirely new emotions conceived by modern men."

Although by and large Akiko refrained from applying the terms "uniqueness" and "freshness" directly to her own poetry, she must have recognized these qualities in the poems she cited under the heading "Modern Tanka" in the article "How to Write and Appreciate Tanka," a section intended to show the reader what modern tanka, as distinct from classical tanka, were like. Here are three examples:

The aster
has flowered, its
pale purple
like the color of smoke
rising from my reveries.

A flock of crows
utterly motionless
turn into pieces
of charcoal, as the flames
from the falling sun subside.

Covering
the whole distance between
the sun in the sky
and me, jubilantly flies
a crimson butterfly.

In the first tanka, the height of the tall aster stalk and the pale
purple of the flower suggest the poet's longing for a distant land
or person. The second poem is striking in its contrast of red and
black as well as in its comparison of a crow to charcoal. The third
praises the colorful beauty of an admiral butterfly, but it also indicates the burning passion of the poet, which, she imagines, at-
tracts the butterfly, a messenger from the sun. Each poem can be
said to show "uniqueness" or "freshness" because of the way in
which the poet's jikkan manifests itself. Its images, too, are fresh,
since asters, crows, and admiral butterflies had seldom appeared
in classical Japanese tanka, those in *The Collection of Ten Thousand
Leaves* and *The Collection of Ancient and Modern Poems* included.
They distinctly belong to the realm of modern tanka.

The final two elements in Akiko's literary aesthetic, "excellence" and "beauty," are difficult to define. She herself gave no
explanation of the former term, which seems to denote a general value judgment, nor did she use it in her critical commentaries on specific poems. Like Shiki, who usually specified a connotation for the equally comprehensive "beauty" by adding such
adjectives as "sublime" and "plain" when he used the term in his
critical essays, Akiko often used "beauty" in combination with
other words. For instance, she described the mood of the following haiku by Buson as "charming and beautiful," considering it
one of the most lovely of his works:

At the sight of
green plums, she knits her eyebrows:
a beautiful woman.

Akiko's praise of the haiku is striking because it is not among the
better-known poems of Buson. A little-known poem by Akiko
herself, one that she thought presented a "beautiful" jikkan, was
this tanka:

> Like a fresh
> passion of love springing up
> from the heart,
> resplendently rises
> a red-leafed amaranth.

Explaining the poem, she commented: "A supreme beauty emerges from the image of the amaranth, with its leaves tinted crimson, growing vigorously up toward the sky. It is like the flaming heart of a person experiencing first love."

Even though Akiko's concept of beauty was in general an all-encompassing one, the amaranth poem suggests where her preference lay. She liked bright, colorful, vigorous images. The subdued ambience cherished by premodern Japanese poets had little appeal for her. As the poems quoted in this chapter testify, her favorite colors were red and gold; she also liked purple, a color associated with Heian culture, in whose creation women played a vital role. In poetry, she preferred such forceful natural phenomena as storms, waves, and fires. Among plants, she liked those that grew vigorously and bloomed gorgeously. Yet, as has been noted, for poetic material she liked the human world even better, and consequently sometimes she expressed even the beauty of nature in terms of human life, describing a red-leafed amaranth by an allusion to passionate love, and depicting an aster by comparison to a woman's musing.

Sing Out Everything in One Breath

"With one arm missing," Akiko once wrote, "the Venus de Milo is a complete statue, a great statue." The aphorism was meant to indicate the insignificance of artistic form in comparison with what the form embodies. In Akiko's poetic, form is subordinate to jikkan. It is not imposed on jikkan; the jikkan spontaneously flows out in a certain form, like gushing water that in time becomes a pond or a mountain stream. It is the force and beauty of the water that matter most, not the shape it happens to take.

Under the rubric of poetry, Akiko included more forms than

contemporary scholars would normally have allowed. Categorizing Japanese poetry, she once mentioned nine forms: the "long poem," tanka, sedōka, the "half poem," renga, haiku, the "new-style poem," the prose poem, and the popular song.[10] Sedōka and the half poem had seldom been considered independent or viable verse forms, and the new-style poem and the prose poem were still in their infancy at the time. Her inclusion of popular songs, too, is unusual.

Akiko herself, however, was primarily a tanka poet. She wrote an immense number of tanka in her lifetime: it is estimated that she produced as many as fifty thousand. She did write shi, and some very good ones too, but her output in that form totals fewer than seven hundred poems. As for haiku, she once said that she often experienced sentiments that could only find outlet in the 17-syllable form; but there is no evidence that she seriously tried to write haiku, nor is there evidence that she attempted to explore any of the other six verse forms on her list. There seem to be at least four reasons why Akiko, although she held such a permissive view on verse forms, concentrated so heavily on tanka in actual practice.

The first and most straightforward explanation given by Akiko is that the 31-syllable form is profoundly rooted in traditional Japanese culture, of which she was a part. "The rhythm based on the 5–7 pattern," she said, "has been vibrating in the pulse and breath of the Japanese people for several thousand years. It has been the rhythm of our lives since the time of our ancestors. Accordingly, we get used to it and learn to like it in no time. And when our jikkan reach the stage of combustion, they come leaping out in phrases that inherently contain the tanka rhythm." In other words, Akiko thought that the mind of a Japanese, especially one educated in the traditional mode, was culturally oriented in such a way that powerful emotions would naturally

---

[10]The long poem, consisting of an indefinite number of lines with the 5–7 pattern, and the sedōka, a poem with lines of 5–7–7–5–7–7, appear mostly in *The Collection of Ten Thousand Leaves*. The half-poem is a verse that looks like one half of a sedōka, and it is often complemented by a half-poem written by another poet.

burst out in the tanka form. In Akiko's own case, at least, her excited emotion flowed out in phrases of thirty-odd syllables as smoothly as "yarn loosened from a spool." The fixed-verse form was no restriction, and to her, both haiku and tanka seemed like free verse because they spontaneously expressed the poet's emotion. Akiko's explanation is valid for her own specific case, since as an avid reader, she had from childhood been steeped in classical Japanese literature, in which the dominant mode of poetic expression was tanka. Although attracted to the freedom and individualism offered by Western society, she was deeply Japanese in her literary orientation.

Second, Akiko seems to have been especially partial to tanka because it is a predetermined verse form. On one occasion she compared a fixed verse form to a tensely drawn string that gives forth a sound when touched by the wind. Just as the wind would pass silently by if no string were hung in the air, so an excited emotion would wordlessly subside if there were no 5−7−5−7−7 pattern waiting to receive it. On another occasion she compared the form to a box that traps smoke. Because she had this box in her heart, she was able to scoop up her emotion and present it to herself and to the reader; otherwise the emotion would fade away like smoke disappearing into the sky. The tanka form, in other words, provided her with a ready-made tool with which to arrest her emotions, and since childhood she had used the tool so often that it had become part of her.

Third, Akiko's predilection for the tanka form may be related to her emphasis on jikkan. In her view, the kind of jikkan that becomes material for poetry has to be powerful, and no powerful feeling lasts for long.

> Since my songs are short
> people think I left out words.
> There was nothing to omit in my songs—
> what more can I add now?
> My heart is not a fish endowed with gills:
> it sings out everything in one breath.

In this poem, entitled "My Songs," Akiko compares a poet's heart impregnated with jikkan to a swimmer submerged in water. As the swimmer dives into the water, so the poet sinks into the inner world of the heart for a few moments of intense emotion and, coming up, lets out the experience in a single breath. The swimmer's period of submersion in water is physiologically limited, and so is the poet's period of submersion in the heart. Therefore, for beginners Akiko advocated short free verse, meaning poems of five to ten lines. She warned that in order to write a long poem one must have an appropriately fertile jikkan, which was hard to come by. For Akiko, tanka was like a five-line free-verse poem: it was a form through which she could sing out everything in a single breath.

Finally, Akiko's liking for the tanka form and its brevity of expression seems grounded in a fascination with process. The passage that shows this best appears in one of her miscellaneous notes:

All processes fascinate me. I am especially attracted to a process that is so complex as to look chaotic at a glance. A conclusion or ending usually emerges according to one's expectations, seldom making one's heart leap, and moral stories, which consist merely of conclusions, do not appeal to young people for that reason. The longest process of all is human life. How foolish it is to attempt to put a conclusion to a process that continues endlessly! For this reason, I like the writings of all skeptics. The art best suited to my nature is one that displays a random fragment ripped out of the process that is called human life.

Akiko did not specify what that art was, but presumably she meant 31-syllable poetry. Tanka is a partial or inconclusive art in that its brevity makes it impossible to have a beginning, a middle, and an end. It is a poem with a middle only; its beginning lies in the poet's actual experience, and its end, if any, has to be sought in the reader's mind. It is a piece of life captured verbally, a little chunk of the endless, orderless continuum called life.

Unlike later modernizing poets, who associated a concern for process with writing poetry in the spoken language, Akiko did not favor the use of colloquial Japanese in tanka. Although she sometimes wrote free verse in the spoken language, especially in her later years she insisted on the use of classical Japanese for tanka, arguing that the rhythm of tanka was peculiar to the classical language. Since neither the grammar nor the feel of the spoken language matched the rhythm of tanka, a colloquial tanka seemed to her as incongruous as liqueur served in a Japanese tea bowl. This was a question not only of poetic language but also of jikkan. In Akiko's opinion, a genuine tanka poet conceives jikkan in the rhythm of the classical language; invariably that was the case with her. If she felt her jikkan had the rhythm of colloquial Japanese, she expressed it in a poetic form other than tanka, such as shi.

Perhaps Akiko felt that the grammatical units of modern Japanese did not break up into five and seven syllables as readily as did those of classical Japanese. In explaining why modern Japanese did not harmonize with the tanka form, she referred to the fact that the spoken language, because of its specific particles and auxiliary verbs, generally has longer phrases. "I believe," she said, "that the spoken language is too verbose to be condensed into 31 syllables." In addition, she felt that the colloquial language was more crude, less refined, and less elegant than the classical; as a result, one who wrote tanka in the spoken language resembled an architect who wanted to erect a beautiful structure but ended up building a crude barrack because of the material he used. Thus Akiko, who approved of free verse, firmly opposed free-style tanka and free-style haiku. To demonstrate how unpoetic a free-style tanka was, she once rewrote four of her own tanka in colloquial Japanese and compared them slightingly with the originals.

Although she advocated the use of classical Japanese in tanka, Akiko disapproved of modern poets' borrowing archaic vocabulary from *The Collection of Ten Thousand Leaves*. She was well aware of the virtues of the ancient poems, which were traditionally considered to represent the kind of poetry that is most expressive of powerful feelings, but she felt that the language used in them was no longer alive in the twentieth century. According to her, latter-day poets who used archaic words were "antique lovers" who tried to cover up their lack of originality with outdated diction. She made an exception for Tachibana Akemi, Shiki's idol, but unlike Shiki she approved of Akemi's tanka because in her opinion his archaic vocabulary was a means of unleashing his vehement dislike of the contemporary age.

Since less than two centuries separate the languages of the Nara *Collection of Ten Thousand Leaves* and the Heian *Collection of Ancient and Modern Poems*, Akiko's emphatic distinction between classical and antique language seems puzzling and somewhat arbitrary. Its most likely explanation may be biographical: not only had she been immersed since girlhood in the classics of the Heian period, but she had undertaken a complete translation into modern Japanese of the most massive masterpiece of them all, *The Tale of Genji*. Thus the language of the Heian period—standard classical Japanese—was very much alive in her life, whereas the language of the earlier period was much less familiar.

Another issue that loomed large in Akiko's thoughts about poetic form concerns what she loosely called "symbolism." The term had been in popular use since the introduction of French Symbolist poetry to Japan during the first decade of the twentieth century, but Akiko used it as a general conceptual term to designate the technique of symbolizing emotion through external objects that has been used in all the arts of both East and West. Apparently she was attracted to symbolic poetry because, by opening up semantic space for multiple meanings, the symbol allows more room for the operation of individual emotion or imagination—in both poet and reader. As she said, "A true masterpiece of art is like a garden occupying the maximum space available. Any number of visitors can stroll, play, or meditate in it. Symbolic art provides plenty of room for empathy. All masterpieces are works of symbolic art."

The best exposition of Akiko's ideas on symbolic tanka appears in a section of *Talks on Tanka*:

What do I mean by "symbolic"? By that word I refer to a case in which the author, in attempting to express emotion, mentions one thing in a way that suggests many others. Emotion is profound and delicate, distant and formless, intricate and indistinguishable. It cannot be depicted by common, expository language. Therefore a poet uses a special language that by mentioning a fraction of his emotion suggests the whole of it. In this type of language, being grammatically correct is not enough. The language must have elements of music as well as a special complexion that appropriately represents the shades of the author's emotion.

Here Akiko seems to have been making a basic distinction between poetic and scientific language. In scientific description, language is designed to denote as restricted a referent as possible in order to attain maximum objectivity. The language of poetry moves a long way toward the other pole. Because poets aim to present emotions that are private and personal, they must go beyond the accepted use of words and suggest a meaning too subjective to be defined through verbal exposition. They must exploit to the maximum the nuances of denotation and connotation, the play of presence and absence in what is referred to and what is left unsaid, and the nonsemantic elements in the word and its context, such as sight and sound. The language of symbolism, as expounded by Akiko, is poetic language in its extreme.

Akiko classified symbolic poetry into two types. Characteristic of the first type was a poem that has two levels of meaning, the surface level expressing the main emotion and the subsurface level suggesting the subordinate one. A couple of examples Akiko cited will better explain her idea. One was a tanka by her husband, Hiroshi:

> Stark naked
> the little baby flails and kicks
> in an overhand crawl,
> determined to meet the challenges of life
> at just one year of age.

The main emotion expressed here is the poet's admiration of the vigor of a baby that seems ready to confront any number of adventures waiting for him in the years to come. The lively movements of his arms and legs on the floor look like those of a brave swimmer daring turbulent waves in the ocean. As Akiko interprets the poem, however, beneath this surface meaning is symbolically suggested the poet's own attitude toward life; he views it as a spacious ocean and man as an adventurer who tries to navigate across it to a far-off destination.

Such a double meaning is also present in the following tanka by Akiko herself:

> A chrysanthemum
> has flowered, its face
> forlorn and white
> like a thought that coldly
> lies within my heart.

On its surface the poem describes a chrysanthemum blooming in late autumn, its whiteness and purity creating an impression of chill beauty. But underneath the tanka suggests the loneliness of the poet gazing at the chrysanthemum, for the white flower is an apt symbol of her heart. Akiko observed that almost all her tanka belonged to this category of symbolic poetry.

The second type of symbolic poetry conceived by Akiko comprised poems in which the main and subordinate emotions are one. Such a poem does not have two levels of meaning; rather, its single level of meaning is complex and all-inclusive. Using the vocabulary of Zen Buddhism, Akiko explained: "In this second type of poetry the one and the many are merged, the particular entirely embodying the universal." She cited several Buddhist and Taoist episodes to explain this type of symbolism. One was the Zen account of Buddha's sermon on Vulture Peak. Asked to teach the Law, Buddha did not say a word, but simply showed a flower to the audience, turning it in his fingers. Among the multitude of people who saw the symbol, only his disciple Kāshyapa understood the message and smiled. In Akiko's view, a tanka belonging to the second type of symbolic poetry must be like that flower, and its ideal reader must be like Kāshyapa. It does not express a specific feeling; rather, it suggests a comprehensive imaginary reality that envelops both the poet's self and the world that surrounds it. Its central image would symbolize not just a happy or a sad feeling but the entire complex of thoughts and emotions unified through the poet's perspective. It would be a pointer directing the reader toward the poet's personal universe, whether religious, metaphysical, or mystical.

Akiko quoted eight poems to clarify what she meant. One was a tanka by her husband, Hiroshi:

> Along the slant
> of a billow about to break
> on the bright
> blue ocean, a pair
> of white seagulls slide away.

Akiko commented that the two seagulls enjoying their play on the beautiful sea represent the poet's dream of a joyous life of peace, beauty, and love. The seascape, in her opinion, symbolized all of reality as reflected in the poet's mental landscape. A second example is from her own poetry:

> Out of black ice
> in the land of shadows
> it comes flying
> to me, to enfold me
> in its wings: a bat.

Here the poem does not pretend to describe nature, but presents an inner landscape that is externalized by way of symbolic images. The central image, a bat, bodies forth what Akiko explained as "a cold, melancholy sorrow that sneaks into my heart from time to time." In these instances, the seagulls and the bat are more metaphysical than metaphorical; they are the key that opens the door to the poet's private, esoteric world. In such poems as these Akiko seems to be moving toward Western symbolist poetry.

Akiko was in fact attracted to French Symbolist poetry, and on occasion she referred to it in her explanation of symbolism, citing comments made by such poets as Théophile Gautier and Henri de Regnier. But she had some reservations, the main one being that, in comparison with symbolic poems in the Japanese tradition, French Symbolist poems seemed artificially composed and lacking in vigor. However, Akiko felt that a poet who immersed himself in French poetry might subconsciously be inspired to write a fine symbolist poem.

Symbolic poems of the second type conceived by Akiko are

often difficult to understand because they employ symbols that
are private and personal. Much of the difficulty of Western symbolist poetry lies in this use of private symbols, and the same may
be said of the type of tanka advocated by Akiko. She was well
aware of the problem, and conceded that when a poem's symbol
was too personal a reader might not experience exactly the same
vision as the author. But she thought this was all right as long as
the reader could approximate the poet's vision. Indeed, she recognized a positive value in a difficult poem: in the process of trying to understand the poem, the reader's creative imagination
was stimulated and he felt the pleasure of being a poet. After
calling the poem "a beautiful mystery," she said, "Each reader
will endeavor to unravel the mystery by exercising his intuitive
power. He will not passively let the poet guide him; rather, he
will take the initiative and work creatively in his mind. Herein
lies one of the reasons why the second type of symbolic poetry is
valuable." In other words, this type of poetry makes the reader
an active participant rather than a passive recipient.

Akiko was the first major poet to talk about symbols in tanka.
By doing so she confirmed that the classical Japanese verse form
was not as obsolete as some detractors made it seem, and that it
could be discussed in the same terms as French Symbolist poetry.
She helped her fellow poets to realize that tanka could be a
daringly modern verse form.

Toward a Humanistic Ideal

Akiko's ideas about the usefulness of poetry are characterized
by a preoccupation with the poet rather than with the reader.
She seemed to believe that poetry is more useful for those who
write it than for those who read it. Verse writing was for her a
manifestation of a basic human impulse; it satisfies an expressive
instinct and thereby brings people the pleasure of purgation, a
pleasant feeling of relief that follows moments of physical tension. Akiko speculated that this type of pleasure lies at the origin
of all the arts. Thus, in her view, verse writing satisfies basic human physiological needs.

On the basis of that assumption, Akiko pointed out other functions poetry could perform for the poet. She argued, for instance, that poetry was a path to self-understanding. To borrow her metaphor, trying to peer into one's own feelings is more difficult than trying to look at one's own eyebrows, but the difficulty can be solved by writing poetry. Furthermore, when others comment on the inner thoughts thus expressed, the poet can learn about the level of his (or her) spiritual life and be stimulated to raise it. If the poem gains the sympathy of many readers, the poet will gain a momentary relief in this life laden with struggle and loneliness. Akiko said she herself enjoyed much pleasure of this kind when she began writing poetry. Born in a family that she considered old-fashioned and oppressive, she successfully sought escape in tanka. "I gained triple freedom all at once," she recalled, "in love, in morality, and in art." Here she seems to imply that the act of verse writing, by calling attention to one's inmost feelings, helps awaken a person to individuality and freedom.

Verse writing thus assumes an educational value. Akiko was eager to convince contemporary educators of that value and to induce more young people to write poetry. In an essay entitled "Humanistic Education," she bitterly attacked the government's educational policy, which aimed to make boys into skilled professionals and girls into obedient housewives. She pointed out that music was not on the curriculum for boys in the advanced grades. It was available for girls, but the music taught consisted predominantly of songs from the feudal age that presumed the lower status of women. In art classes students were taught to copy model paintings printed in textbooks. Akiko was especially incensed at the fact that teachers of Japanese taught language, and not literature. "No literature is being taught in a course labeled Japanese language and literature," she fumed. "This is just as outrageous as a flower shop that does not sell flowers." For her, the two main sources of energy that kept human life going were love and creation in the broadest sense, yet these were completely absent from the philosophy of elementary and secondary education in modern Japan. As a consequence, she felt her

country produced only male and female slaves, the former subservient to their professions and the latter subservient to their
parents, husbands, or children. Each individual sorely needed to
assert himself, and, in Akiko's opinion, one of the best ways to
create opportunities for doing so was to give children a chance
to write poetry and prose. By means of creative writing children
could freely create what they loved, and could freely love what
they had created. Love and creation are at the core of human
nature, and literature, by allowing those instincts free play, enriches one's humanity. Verse writing, like other creative activities, is an essential part of humanistic education. Akiko's essay,
published in 1920, anticipated events in Japanese education by
nearly thirty years, for the government began to stress the Western idea of liberal arts education only in the late 1940's.

What was true of schoolchildren was, of course, true of adults
too. In Akiko's view, all people benefit from writing poetry because it enriches their daily lives, which are by and large spent in
the monotonous repetition of routine activities. Because verse
writing is creative, it breaks the monotony and provides the
pleasure of contributing, by whatever tiny amount, to the progress of civilization. The work of farmers, seamstresses, and other
laborers does the same, but artists make a greater contribution
because art is a purer form of creation. "This may be dogmatic
of me," Akiko once observed, "but if human life could be compared to a building, I believe learning and art would occupy the
highest floor." Her pride in being an artist is reflected in one of
her few tanka on poetry:

> On a palace
> being built since the beginning
> of history
> I too hammer in
> a nail of gold.

The various uses of poetry for the poet conceived by Akiko
can also apply to the reader, albeit to a lesser extent. According
to her, the reader of poetry, although generally a person whose
expressive instinct is not as intense as a poet's, is likewise able to

gain the pleasure of purgation by reciting a poem composed by someone else. Reading a poem that vents a feeling like one's own serves as a proxy for expressing the emotion oneself. A boatman, a soldier, or a factory worker who recites a favorite poem or sings a song gains a moment of relief from his labor. And, of course, reading poetry has its value as humanistic education. "A person who reads a work of art rooted deep in life," Akiko wrote, "will become aware of a high, broad, and great self, forgetting a low, narrow, and small self."

In Akiko's opinion, however, the usefulness of poetry for the reader is different in at least one respect from its usefulness for the poet. A good work of poetry, indeed of any art, has prophetic implications:

Man cannot predict the future of art. But art can predict the future of man. The artist, living in the world of *Sein* ["is"], fervently wishes to live in the world of *Sollen* ["ought to be"]. Through his wisdom he senses the spirit and mode of man's future life and suggests these in his works. Art is a great dynamic force that changes life for the better; it also provides symbols pointing toward the possibility of an ideal life in the future.

Here Akiko conceives of the artist as a prophet who can see things ordinary people cannot, a concept that explains her fondness for jikkan that present a vision rather than a slice of ordinary life. In Akiko's view, the reader of poetry is given images of a future life that would otherwise be impossible to foresee. Provided with an ideal to strive for, the reader is supplied with the courage to live for the future, and with an invitation to reflect on his present life and to improve it. In this respect, Akiko's idea of the function of poetry approached religion. Indeed, one of her aphorisms was: "Those who live in art have no need for a god, for through art they come in contact with symbolic representation of the future possibilities of humanity—of a being that constantly changes and develops." A lofty view of poetry, but one appropriate to Akiko the humanist.

CHAPTER THREE

Ishikawa Takuboku

SINCE HIS DEATH, Ishikawa Takuboku (1886–1912) has gained great fame as a poet, attracting many followers and admirers in succeeding generations. More books and articles have probably been written about him than about any other modern poet. His popularity, however, seems to depend less on his poetry than on the life that produced it. Takuboku's poems—many of them tanka—often sound trite or sentimental, or seem facile, when they are read as autonomous works of art. More appealing are the diaries that he kept intermittently from 1902 on, which honestly trace the vicissitudes of his restless mind. His life was a dramatic one, sprinkled with incidents that seem stranger than fiction. He had many failings: it is easy to accuse him of being irresponsible, overdependent, self-indulgent, emotionally unstable, or given to self-aggrandizement. Yet he was also brilliant, dynamic, and unremittingly honest with himself. He had explosive passions and a penchant for action, and seldom hesitated to do what he believed to be right. Seen against such a biographical background, his poems begin to breathe. They are a vital part of his life rather than independent works of art. For a tanka poet, the distance between life and art is usually short; for Takuboku, it hardly existed at all.

It has often been said that Takuboku began his literary career as a romantic poet, turned into a naturalistic writer, and died a socialist. In his early teens he was a dreamer who longed to escape from contemporary society, but soon external circumstances dragged him deeper into the mundane world. When he discovered the many injustices in society, he began wanting to reform it. His poetry records these changing attitudes, and his concept of poetry likewise changed. In adolescence he harbored excessive expectations of poetry, which gradually faded as he grew older. Disillusioned, he became increasingly critical of poetry, sometimes even feeling a sadistic pleasure in deliberately derailing it from its traditional track. Poems were "sad toys," playthings for those who had failed in life. No major poet in Japan had reached such a conclusion before, and therein lies the significance of Takuboku's view of poetry.

A Heavenly Messenger Trapped on Earth

Takuboku published his first book of verse, entitled *Longing*, in 1905. It included 77 poems, all written in the shi form, their images and idioms much like those of the leading poets of the day, including Yosano Akiko, for whom the young Takuboku had great respect. The reactions of contemporary reviewers were mixed. Some praised the poems' youthful exuberance, flamboyant vocabulary, and precocious artistry; others condemned their pedantry, imitativeness, and self-indulgence. Today the collection is largely neglected, having been eclipsed by Takuboku's highly esteemed later volumes of verse; nevertheless, the book is a valuable document, for a number of its poems reveal Takuboku's early view of poetry in varying degree. The poem called "In Seclusion" is typical:

> Leaning against a gigantic dead oak
> I stand in the graveyard on a hill.
> There, remote from the voices of men,
> my world floats in the evening dusk.
>
> With sturdy wings of longing
> I soar high in search of heaven's light.
> Fresh flowers emerge from somewhere
> to cover my chest.
>
> The men of old rest peacefully
> deep under moss.
> So does my world, where a divine soul
> blooms in the white mist of dawn.

When I inhale the fragrant air
my expanding chest turns translucent with light.
When my sleeve touches a flower,
there sounds a faint song of love.

Oh, the earth is in the grip of raging night,
a black fog crawling all over its surface!
Amidst all, my breath rises to heaven
and my heart rejoices in a fleeting vision.

Here is the image of the ideal poet as seventeen-year-old Takuboku conceived him.[1] A poet is endowed with a special ability to
glimpse heaven's light, an ability derived from the strength of
his aspiration to transcendent beauty. Because of that aspiration
he is alienated from the rest of humanity, but his reward is a vision of heaven.

Using different metaphors, Takuboku reiterated this lofty
view of poetry in other poems and prose pieces written during
his early phase. In a poem called "The Sunken Bell," for example, the poet ecstatically listens to the faint, mysterious sound of
a huge bell that God the Creator threw into the ocean ages ago.
In another poem, entitled "The Boat of Life," he is a sailor
searching for a pearl in the ocean, confident that his search is
God's will. In "Secret," he witnesses a stream of light flowing
from a divine fountain unseen by ordinary men for the last eight
thousand years. An entry in Takuboku's diary for March 8,
1906, states the view forthrightly: "Art is the product of the divine nature in man, of his power to create. It is the voice echoing
the very instant when man's heart approaches the inmost being
of the universe."

It is more difficult to find Takuboku's view of poetry in his
tanka, because the 31-syllable form tends more toward lyricism.
The young Takuboku was dazzled by the sensual love poetry of
Akiko, and like many other amateurs of the day he tried to emulate her whenever he composed in 31 syllables. Nevertheless, the
poet who wrote "In Seclusion" is undoubtedly present in some
of his tanka:

[1] Takuboku wrote the poem on January 12, 1904, more than a year before the
publication of *Longing*.

Did you not see it?
In a far corner of the sky
toward which the beautiful clouds
all go drifting—
a land of the heart's desire.

Feeling certain
God has whispered something
in my ear,
I wander along the way
to a place I know not where.

Up there, amid
the dazzling light in the clouds,
Five Continents of Poetry—
Let the sound of a whip
awaken the sleeping child!

Again the image of the poet as a seer—or a hearer—is recurrent. He is endowed with an extraordinary sensitivity that enables him to communicate with a realm beyond the earth.

The main weakness of this view of poetry lies in its failure to specify the nature of the vision the poet sees. Takuboku said little about the world yonder, save to imply that it was beautiful and desirable. Although he spoke of God, what he meant by the word is vague; he did not seem to be referring to Christianity, Shintoism, or Buddhism in particular. Although he probably conceived of God as a metaphysical being who reigned over the cosmos, the vocabulary presenting his concept is more sensuous than metaphysical. The title of Takuboku's book is appropriate in an ironic sense: in it there is a great deal of longing, and that is all. What the poet longed for seems to have remained inaccessible; he had to wander along the way—to a place he did not exactly know where.

Takuboku's involvement with poetry began early, for his father, a Zen priest, was an amateur tanka poet. Some of his friends at middle school wrote poetry, too, and competed with one another in getting their works accepted by magazines. The magazine they admired most was *The Morning Star*, edited by Yosano Hiroshi and filled with the work of young poets dreaming of a beautiful, far-off land. Encouraged by his schoolmates, Takuboku began to write verses and soon managed to have them published, first in campus magazines and then elsewhere. In 1902, *The Morning Star* printed one of his poems for the first time, pleasing Takuboku no end. He made up his mind to become a poet at around this time. Dropping out of middle school in his senior year, he left his home in Iwate Prefecture and went to Tokyo, where he joined the New Poetry Society headed by the Yosanos. His poetic ambition was fated not to be satisfied at this time, however, despite the Yosanos' friendship and patronage, for he soon fell ill and had to return to his native village. Back home, he fell passionately in love with his middle-school sweetheart, Horiai Setsuko, whom he married in 1905.

Takuboku was not able to sustain for very long the idealistic view of poetry he developed in his youth. Just before the publication of *Longing*, his father was excommunicated by the hierarchy of his Zen sect on the charge of failing to pay dues levied on his temple. The elder Ishikawa, an outcast priest at age 46, had no prospect of employment, and suddenly responsibility for supporting the family fell onto the shoulders of his only son. Another dependent was added when Takuboku's daughter Kyōko was born in 1906. The long and bitter struggle for survival that ensued not only changed Takuboku's life but affected his idea of poetry.

At first, Takuboku became a substitute teacher at an elementary school in his native village. He was dismissed one year later, however, when he joined a student strike against the principal of the school. Then he went to Hokkaido, the northernmost main island of Japan, where he wandered restlessly from place to place, often leaving his family behind. One job followed another in rapid succession: he was a magazine editor, a Chamber of Commerce employee, a substitute teacher, a proofreader, a newspaper reporter. His intense personality always polarized coworkers who came into direct contact with him. Those who recognized a poet in Takuboku were irresistibly attracted to him and were ready to forgive occasional impulsive actions, but others felt intimidated, and often unfortunate clashes resulted.

Takuboku became painfully aware, through those experiences, that he could be happy only in the realm of literature. In the spring of 1908 he left Hokkaido and moved to Tokyo, determined to devote his life to creative writing. That determination notwithstanding, he had to take a nonliterary job to support himself and his dependents when his efforts to sell his writings failed miserably. The job, that of a proofreader, was neither intellectually stimulating nor financially rewarding, and his frustrations in the mundane sphere continued. Added to them were domestic worries: the frequent illnesses of his little daughter, discord between his mother and his wife, and the latter's absence from home for a short while. He did continue to write poems, mostly tanka, which he managed to collect and publish under the title *A Handful of Sand* in 1910. But his attitude toward poetry had changed noticeably during this period of continued hardship.

Takuboku's changing attitude toward literature was suggested in various writings at this time. In his diary entry for January 29, 1907, for example, he expressed disillusion with his former ideals:

Poems written by the New Poetry Society and other schools of poets neither interest me nor impress me these days. I keep wondering what the reason could be. . . . Could it be because my heart has become rough and prosaic? More likely it is because poetry has plummeted from heaven to earth in my mind, because it has transformed itself from a melodious recitation in an auditorium to a chat in a shabby little room. I think of prose fiction day after day. I really must write a story.

A comment Takuboku made in 1908 reveals the poet's parallel fall into experience and sets out the specific realities he had come to consider the most appropriate material for poetry. In an essay called "A Branch on the Desk," he observed that every person initially believes in his own capabilities, but when some painful experience forces him to realize his limitations, he concedes his defeat by nature and mutters to himself, "Whatever will be will be." Takuboku continued:

However, nothing could sound as disgraceful as these words to a person who has had a profound confidence in himself and has prided himself on his dignity as an individual. Often, therefore, these words turn into a desperate wailing. Yet at other times, when a person carefully reconsiders them, he may conclude that defeat by nature is really a process by which to make that undefeatable power his own.

Although here Takuboku did not mention literature, he was talking about basic attitudes toward life that he thought should be the concern of all thinkers, including poets and novelists. According to him, these attitudes result in two types of literature. One is the "desperate wailing" of a person who has empirically learned human limitations; the other is a revelation of nature's forces, which, although intimidating, may benefit a person who can identify with them. The first mode is more lyrical, the second more naturalistic; both feature a man defeated by external forces. The proud poet confident in his extraordinary sensitivity is gone.

These two views of literature are embodied in *A Handful of Sand*, although the poems in that volume, being tanka, show the lyrical mode more clearly than the naturalistic. Several of Takuboku's most celebrated works can be cited as examples:

> The autumn sky, boundlessly vast and vacant,
> is too desolate.
> Let a crow or something fly!

> On a beach of white sand at a tiny eastern island,
> tears streaming from my eyes,
> I play with a crab.

> Though I work
> and work, my life is no easier.
> I stare at my hands.

The first poem, written in 1908, presents no alienated poet longing for a transcendent realm lying beyond the beautiful clouds of the evening. Instead, the poet wants earthly company, such as a crow or another familiar, not at all beautiful, bird. The second tanka, composed in the same year, makes clear that the poet is not a proud member of an elect group, but an agonized dropout from the mainstream of life crying on a lonely beach, his sole companion a small, helpless crab. The third poem, composed in 1910, also presents a desperate wailing, the wailing of a man who labors day in and day out without being able to ease the hardship of life. All three tanka are written in three lines instead of the usual five.

Takuboku's lyrical wailing can also be observed in some of his shi. Although his production in this genre markedly decreased after the publication of *Longing*, he did continue to write shi and planned to publish a collection in 1908. The short proem he wrote for this abortive collection expresses his new view of poetry, and can serve as a preface to all the lyrics he wrote after *Longing*:

> Sing out, when an everlasting struggle
> makes your tired joints ache,
> when a bitter grief almost overwhelms you,
> when your ailing child is on the verge of death,
> when you see your mother's image in a beggar,
> or when you are helplessly bored with your love.
> Gaze at the wordless sky
> and sing out, when those times arrive,
> O my starving friends!

Takuboku's poems were the outcries of a man suffering from the sorrow of life in this world.

Takuboku's naturalistic impulse is more pronounced in his prose fiction. He began writing stories in 1906, and wrote them with renewed fervor after his arrival in Tokyo in 1908, thereby fulfilling the desire expressed in his diary one year earlier. "The Funeral Procession," one of his earliest stories, describes how the indifferent workings of death destroy the transcendent happiness of two insane lovers. "Two Streaks of Blood" also tells of death indiscriminately closing in on a lovely little girl and a dirty begger woman. In "The Plague" the destructive force is dysentery, which attacks a village of peasants, and in "The Window of a Clinic" it is internal, the dark impulses of a newspaper reporter. Sinister forces become more numerous and complex in the longest of Takuboku's works in prose fiction, *The Birds*, which tells of the loves, griefs, and jealousies that envelop the residents of a rural town. In all these stories, the protagonists either passively surrender to fate or, after recognizing the inevitability of the surrender, begin leading lives of depravity.

Despite such naturalistic overtones, Takuboku's prose fiction was not well accepted in contemporary literary circles. Although early naturalist writers in Japan had tried to emulate the writings of Flaubert and Zola, by the time Takuboku turned to prose fiction in earnest the Japanese naturalistic novel had come to be an autobiographical genre in which the hero, closely modeled on the novelist, confessed his innermost impulses honestly and without verbal adornment. Takuboku was aware of the trend, but he was by nature too self-conscious to reveal his naked self in his stories, and preferred to depict dark impersonal forces manifesting themselves in characters distinctly different from himself. To contemporary readers used to confessional novels, his attitude seemed cowardly and dishonest. Moreover, his stories were often technically defective: the plot was weak, the theme was unclear, the characters were not fully developed, or the narrative viewpoint was not consistent. Sometimes he was not objective enough: he was either too sympathetic or too unsympathetic toward his characters. At other times his escapist impulse got the better of him, and he beautified his setting. In general, there was too much emotion and too little impartial observation.

His failure to become a successful novelist disheartened Takuboku, not only because it revealed his lack of talent in that genre, but also because it confirmed his failure to earn a livelihood through creative writing. And he needed income even more urgently than before. In the fall of 1910 his wife gave birth to their second child, who died three weeks later. Takuboku himself suffered from ill health, but he did not consult a doctor for fear of the expense. When he finally sought medical help early in 1911, he was ordered hospitalized immediately for a severe case of chronic peritonitis. After surgery and a 40-day stay in the hospital, he was able to go home, but in his weakened condition he could not resist the onslaught of tuberculosis. Professionally, he was having difficulty with the publishers through whom he and his friend had planned to start a new magazine. Domestically, he had a running quarrel with Setsuko, and at one time he even announced that he was divorcing her. She stayed on, but Takuboku severed relationships with her parents, as well as with one of his closest friends, who had tried to intervene on her behalf. Then his wife fell ill with bronchitis. His mother began to spit blood, too, apparently because of tuberculosis. No longer able to bear the unending crisis and tension, his aging father left home. Takuboku's own illness steadily worsened, but he refused to enter a hospital. Finally, his mother died in the spring of 1912. His own death followed one month later.

The dark days of Takuboku's last years brought another significant change in his attitude toward poetry. Part of this can be viewed as a transference of his naturalistic impulse from prose fiction to verse: having failed as a novelist, he tried to do in poetry what he could not do in prose. His new stance is expressed in the essay "Various Kinds of Poetry," written in 1910. There he remarked, tongue in cheek, that he envied a poet who did not possess "a mind that must scrutinize everything he does or says or contemplates throughout the very process of his doing or saying or contemplating, a mind that must challenge every problem squarely and reach its inmost core, or a mind that every day discovers many irrationalities and contradictions in himself and in the world, each discovery in turn intensifying further the irrationalities and contradictions in his life." Takuboku clearly wanted to become a poet who *did* have such a mind, one who scrutinized the forces operating in himself and in society. This is the type of naturalism he wanted to attain in his prose fiction, except that it places more emphasis on the mind of the writer himself. It is a more subjective, personal naturalism.

The same attitude can be detected in the most celebrated of Takuboku's critical writings, "Poems to Eat," a short autobiographical essay published in 1909 that traces his growth as a poet. Its opening section is filled with negative rhetoric, vehemently rejecting the stance of Takuboku's younger days. He describes his early poetry as made of fantasies, childish music, a tiny intermingling of religious (or pseudoreligious) elements, and stereotyped sensibility. He then reveals how he became disillusioned with poetry during his days of struggle in Hokkaido. The latter part of the essay is an exposition of his newly discovered poetic, whose essence can be seen in the excerpts below.

At this stage in his life, Takuboku defined the poet as follows:

A true poet must be as resolute as a statesman in reforming himself and in putting his philosophy into practice. He must be as singleminded as a businessman in giving a focus to his life. He must be as clearheaded as a scientist, and as straightforward as a primitive. He must have all these qualities and thereby make a calm, honest report on the changes of his psyche as they happen from one moment to the next, describing them without a word of adornment or falsehood.

In a corollary to the first definition, he defined poetry:

Poetry must not be the so-called poetry. It must be a detailed report of changes that take place in a man's emotional life (I cannot think of a better word); it must be an honest diary. Hence, it must be fragmentary—it must not have unity. (Poetry with unity, namely philosophical literature, will turn into prose fiction when it takes an inductive form; into drama when it takes a deductive form. True poetry is related to fiction and drama in the same way daily reports of receipts and disbursements are related to a monthly or yearly balance sheet of accounts.) Furthermore, unlike a minister gathering material for his sermon or a streetwalker looking for a certain kind of man, a poet must never have a preconceived purpose.

The essay concludes with an appeal to his fellow poets, urging them not to be too imitative of Western poetry but to look intently at their own lives. "Have you not forgotten to stand with your two feet on the ground?" he asked.

In a sense, "Poems to Eat" expresses an idea of poetry to which Takuboku had unconsciously subscribed from the beginning, for if the essay's central thesis is an equation of poem and diary, he had been a diarist all along. Even as a teenage poet who gazed longingly at the sky, he sang about himself rather than about the sky. He was a diarist in the literal sense from an early age, too: his earliest surviving diary dates to the autumn of 1902, when he was sixteen; his last ends on February 20, 1912, a few weeks before his death. The surviving diaries cover much of the intervening ten years, the entire span of his literary career. The most moving of them all is known as *The Rōmaji Diary*, a diary of 1909 written in romanized Japanese because Takuboku did not want his wife and others to read the private thoughts he set down there. Clearly superior to any of his works in prose fiction, it provides ironic testimony that he was temperamentally less suited to be the novelist he wished to become than to be an author of diaries, which he wished to hide.

The Rōmaji Diary is a fine work of literature because it gives "a detailed report of changes that take place in a man's emotional life," the very quality Takuboku sought in poetry. It and the other diaries are sprinkled with poems, both tanka and shi, expressing the kind of psychological changes that cannot well be expressed in prose. For example, here is an entry dated August 21, 1911:

I wrote seventeen tanka and sent them to Maeda Yūgure, editor of *Poetry*, at night.[2]
　The morning was so cool that I was almost sure autumn had arrived.
　　　Vaguely I felt
　　　a shrinking in my lungs, and I awoke.
　　　Near-autumn morning.
My wife is slowly getting better.

In this instance, the poem has become part of the diary, both literally and metaphorically.

One weakness inherent in this theory of composition is that the poem sometimes becomes so much a part of the author's diary that it loses its appeal to readers unfamiliar with the details of his life. To the poet, all his autobiographical poems are valuable because they are directly related to his personal life; however, unless they embody an experience rooted in universal human reality, they lose the means of relating themselves to readers. Unfortunately, some of Takuboku's later poems fall into this category: they have a measure of appeal to those who are thoroughly familiar with his biography, but they mean little to others. The fault lies less with the poems themselves than with Takuboku's poetic, his equation of poem and diary.

Takuboku himself was aware of this weakness. In a letter to a friend he once said: "At present I write tanka almost exclusively in the same frame of mind as I would have when keeping a diary. I suppose there are well- and ill-written diaries, depending

[2]*Poetry* was a tanka magazine founded by Maeda Yūgure (1883–1951) in April 1911; Yūgure had solicited a submission from Takuboku. The seventeen tanka were published in the magazine in September.

upon the author's literary craftsmanship. But the merit of a diary should have nothing to do with the author's skill in writing. Indeed, a diary is valuable to no one but its author." Here Takuboku concedes that poetry is valuable to no one but the poet, that the value of poetry is entirely personal.

Such an admission implies a devaluation of poetry in relation to all other human activities. Takuboku recognized this. In an essay written in 1910, he compared a man of letters to a planner without the ability, opportunity, or financial resources to carry out his plans. He even compared literary composition to masturbation. In another short essay, bluntly called "Devaluation of Literature," he concluded:

True, the distance between literature and actual life has narrowed. But even if the former should try to approach the latter with barbaric courage, there would always be a space between them. Literature can never provide the tension-filled sense of reality that actual life can. That is the very nature of literature. In creating a literary work, the author must of necessity take himself out of real-life activities and assume an observer's standpoint. And the work thus created is a finished—that is, transfixed—product, regardless of the skill of its creator. Accordingly, the impact of literature on our lives is always indirect. All literary works, whether or not they treat contemporary affairs, affect our lives only in the way that bygone historical events do, because they are transfixed objects.

Takuboku's comparison of literature to history is appropriate, because a diary is history on a personal scale. He could not be content with being a diarist or historian, with being removed from the mainstream of actual, everyday life. Ultimately, literature seemed too passive to him. He had learned from bitter experience how ineffectual it was in the real world, and he wanted to be more active, to become part of a force that directly participated in changing society.

Given such a pragmatic view of literature, it seemed that the only way poetry could play a positive role was by becoming overtly ideological in the service of a political movement. When poetry incites the masses to social reform, it can be said to have made a positive contribution to actual change. Takuboku's view of poetry seems to have been moving in this direction in his last years, especially after he became attracted to socialism in around 1910. In a long New Year's greeting to a fellow poet that year, he wrote:

To my present way of thinking, a poet in the conventional sense is as useful as a toymaker or a clown. I believe there is all the justification in the world for literature's being journalistic in the broad sense of the term. I believe a literary work must be a concrete explanation of the author's *critical thought*, thought that emerges when he views life or the contemporary age in the light of his (practical) philosophy (the aggregate of his conscious life).

The word "journalism" has a wide range of connotations in Japanese, referring not only to the reporting of actual happenings but also to interpretative and critical commentary on those happenings and on the trend of the times in general. By adding the phrase "in the broad sense of the term," Takuboku emphasized the latter meaning. It is not enough, he implied, that a literary work report on changes that take place in a man's emotional life; it has to report and comment on changes that happen in the outside world. In other words, Takuboku meant that literature has to be social criticism and deal with contemporary problems, ultimately leading to social reform. In order for it to serve in this capacity, the writer has to hold a political or social philosophy— Takuboku called it a "practical philosophy"—by which to judge the state of affairs in his time. As for what that philosophy might be, Takuboku indicated that it must be an all-inclusive set of principles—the "aggregate"—unifying different parts of the writer's conscious life. It has to address itself not only to the part of himself that stands by and observes, but also to the part that eats, drinks, and struggles in the physical world. Indeed, it has to respond to the practical needs of the masses.

What Takuboku meant by "journalistic" is further clarified in some of the poems he wrote in his last years. The best examples are a series of free-verse poems written in 1911. The first, called "After an Endless Debate," begins:

In our reading, in our debates
and in the sparkle in our eyes
we are not inferior to the Russian youths of fifty years ago.
We debate what is to be done.

But none of us strikes the table with a clenched fist
and cries out, "V Narod!"

"The Russian youths of fifty years ago" are a group of student radicals who tried to incite peasants to rise against tsarism in the 1870's. Their motto—"V Narod!" ("To the people!")—showed their determination to mingle with working-class people and thereby generate a prime moving force for a proletarian revolution. Takuboku here compares his own group with these students and deplores the fact that no one among them is willing to take the lead in the movement about which they constantly read and debate. The last two lines of the quotation recur as a refrain in each of the remaining three stanzas of the poem. The repeated lament is an expression of hope for the emergence of an activist leader; thus, because it addresses a present political need, the poem is "practical."

Other pieces in the same series, such as "A Spoonful of Cocoa" and "Intense Debate," have similarly overt political overtones. But Takuboku's leftist poems are not limited to free verse. Some of the tanka he wrote in his last years fall into this category, as the following three examples testify:

The Russian name Borodin,[3]
  for some reason,
frequently comes to mind today.

My friend seems saddened and so does my wife—
  Even in sickness I keep
  talking of revolution.

The anguish of a terrorist
which seemed rather remote
draws close of late.

These appear in *Sad Toys*, the last collection of Takuboku's tanka, published posthumously in 1912.

The poems with socialist overtones, however, are only a small portion of Takuboku's later poetry. Of the 194 tanka that consti-

[3] Borodin was an alias of Peter Alekseevich Kropotkin (1842–1921), the Russian anarchist and revolutionary. Although his books had been banned in Japan, Takuboku apparently had access to them.

tute *Sad Toys*, no more than a dozen overtly suggest his leftist beliefs. At least two reasons may explain this scarcity. One has to do with the nature of Takuboku's socialist beliefs. His socialism was more personal than political or philosophical, and therein lay its weakness, as well as its strength. It was an empirical belief deduced from a series of tragic experiences in actual life. When he discovered that no matter how hard he worked he was unable to support his family, he had to conclude that something was wrong with the existing capitalist society. On the other hand, he was not a systematic thinker who could, after sustained thought, arrive at a series of possible solutions for current social problems. Nor was he a political activist who could, through some drastic action, incite fellow workers to social reform if not to revolution. Socialism was a general direction in which his personal frustrations found an outlet. His belief in it was utterly sincere, but tended to be more emotional than ideological, more anarchist than Marxist.

That fact leads to the second possible explanation of why Takuboku did not write more political poems. He knew that poetry was of secondary value, that it was "masturbation"; yet he had to continue writing it because he had feelings too intense to contain. His dilemma was that of the poet who comes to hold a contemptuous view of poetry. He once confessed to a friend: "For me, the day I write tanka is an unhappy day. It is a completely wasted day, a day when I could find satisfaction nowhere except in gazing at my naked self of the moment. As you know, I am a poet at present. Frankly, however, I want to become the kind of person who has no need to write tanka." His unhappiness with being a poet sometimes made him take a sadistic attitude toward poetry. In fact, his abusive use of poetry began when he failed to become a successful novelist. He told of his changing attitude then: "A husband who has lost a quarrel with his wife sometimes finds pleasure in giving a bad time to his child. I discovered that kind of pleasure in willfully abusing the tanka form." The same attitude is suggested in another of his metaphors for tanka, "sad toys." For Takuboku, poems became toys to which he would return whenever he was frustrated by his struggles in adult life; he could take out his frustrations on his toys.

Takuboku's last poetry collection, to which his friends posthumously gave the title *Sad Toys*, contains numerous tanka showing that attitude—so numerous, indeed, as to overshadow his leftist poems almost completely. Here are three of the more famous poems in the anthology:

> When I breathe
> something sounds in my chest.
> A sound lonelier than the autumn gust!

> Forgetting my illness for a moment
> I try to bellow like a cow—
> before my wife and child come home.

> A white dog passes by the garden.
> Turning to my wife
> I propose buying a dog.

In the first poem the autumn wind, a favorite poetic image in traditional tanka, is associated with the sound of a tubercular patient's breathing. The association is an abuse of the tanka convention, because premodern poets always recognized a lonely beauty in the sound of the wind and juxtaposed it with some beautifully poetic natural object. The second poem reduces the tanka form to a comic level, until the reader reaches the last line and learns that the poet can play the clown only because the pressure of family responsibility is momentarily lifted from his mind. The third poem, which on the surface depicts a peaceful family scene, has a chillingly mocking tone for a reader who knows that not only did the poet have no money to buy a dog but that there was nothing for the ailing poet and his tired wife to talk about; the white dog merely gave him a chance to try to break the awkward silence. Takuboku, who wanted to reach a state of mind where he had no need to write poetry, never succeeded in that attempt. He was aware of his failure, and as a result a mixture of self-pity and self-contempt underlies his lyricism. He ended as a masochistic lyricist, a poet who tortured both himself and his form.

In conclusion, throughout his short and eventful career Takuboku consistently wanted to depict in his poetry fluid inner reality, the changes that occurred within his mind. Never greatly interested in external nature, he always sang of himself, depicting a vision of the self that constantly changed. At first he conceived of himself as a divine messenger from heaven, and accordingly he described the joys, hopes, and ecstasies of being a poet, the ethereal landscapes that were his inner reality at the time. Frustrations in his outer life quickly changed those landscapes, however. He came to see more shadows than sunlight, and subsequently he began to sing of the things that cast the darkest shadows. But singing did not remove the shadows, and he became increasingly aware of the powerlessness of poetry. He made an effort to restore its strength by absorbing the destructive energy of a revolutionary. Yet basically he remained a man of longing. Just as he longed to reach the far-off land of the Creator in his younger days, so he dreamed of a proletarian paradise that was to come after a wholesale destruction of the existing social order. When he tired of dreaming, he vented his impatience with himself by writing self-depreciating poems, or pitied his circumstances and wrote sentimental poems, or did a mixture of the two. He was a diarist in verse who was at times too dreamy, at times too wide awake. His poetry is a record of both those occasions, and as such it is intensely personal, honest, and alive.

Three Types of Creative Process

On the morning of May 24, 1908, Takuboku was awakened in his lodgings in Tokyo at around half-past six by an unexpected visitor, a young woman friend who seemed rapidly to be falling in love with him. She was on her usual morning stroll and stopped by on the spur of the moment. When he got up, an express letter arrived from his home in Hokkaido reporting that his little daughter Kyōko was in a coma. Takuboku became extremely worried, but could do nothing except pray for her quick recovery. After the woman left, he wrote a letter to his wife and then visited a friend to vent his worries about his daughter. At his friend's house, he tried to convince himself that Kyōko would not die. Returning to his lodgings, he began to compose some shi. Until the previous day he had been writing a story, "The Window of a Clinic," but he felt that "this is not a day to write prose fiction." By three o'clock in the afternoon he had written eight poems, all the time feeling as if "his heart were being ripped open." He sent seven of the poems to Yosano Hiroshi for possible publication in *The Morning Star*.

The episode illustrates one type of creative process through which Takuboku wrote poetry: a specific occasion so agitated him that he had to relieve his mind in one way or another. He went to visit his friend to vent his feelings, but that was not enough to calm his mind. He had to express his feelings in writing—not in prose fiction but in verse. For Takuboku, verse writing was the spontaneous outburst of an agonized mind, the agony being brought on by some painful external event. One is reminded of his lines "Sing out . . . when your ailing child is on the verge of death." This day was precisely such an occasion.

But even in this simple theory of verse writing cause and effect are not directly related. None of the eight poems overtly involves his ailing daughter or the young woman who visited him early that morning. Here is one of them, entitled "Murderous Intent":

> "What made you dare
> to murder that woman?"
> So asking, the judge
> solemnly rose from his seat.

> With the pale face of a criminal,
> I cried, "Red ink . . . oh!"
> and knelt down, trembling all over.
> "When I saw her white skirt
> suddenly spattered with red ink."

The poem seems to be concerned with the mystery of the impulses that make a man do strange things without a motive. But how is it related to the day's events, which presumably inspired Takuboku to write it? Nothing is explicit, except that the poet's mind has been assailed by a murderous intent and that he feels guilty about it.

The relationship between Takuboku's life and his poetry is generally more straightforward in tanka. An example has already been cited, the tanka about "a shrinking in my lungs," which he wrote one day in the late summer of 1911. In that instance an event in his life directly resulted in a tanka, the poem expressing his feelings as they were. Such examples are numerous. To give another, Takuboku was introduced to a young man one afternoon in 1911 by a friend. The youth was interested in creative writing, but at the time was doing secretarial work for a politician. Takuboku liked the man and talked with him until dark. When the two visitors finally took their leave, Takuboku suddenly felt exhausted. After supper he went to bed for a short rest. At around nine he got up and wrote a tanka:

> To a man younger than me
> I talked big for half a day
> and how weary this mind is!

Here the external stimulus and the resultant poem are in a direct relation of cause and effect. One might say the relation is too direct to make the poem a good one, although the poet's self-derision saves it from being trite.

On the other hand, Takuboku produced a number of poems without an external stimulus directly exciting the creative impulse. In this second type of creative process, what he called "inspiration" (kyō) visited him from time to time, apparently without warning. For example, a diary entry for September 1, 1908, records: "After going to bed, I was visited by an inspiration. This had not occurred for a long time, for several years in fact. By around 2:00 A.M. I had written a draft of 'The Blue House' and some ten other shi." Except for eating lunch with an old friend, nothing much had happened that day, nothing to explain the Muse's visit that particular night. The same can be said of a similar occasion, June 24, 1908. Takuboku then wrote in his diary:

I began writing tanka after going to bed last night. The inspiration became so intense with the passage of time that I did not get to sleep at all. At dawn I took a stroll through the graveyard of Honmyōji Temple. I felt incomparably refreshed. After that inspiration still kept its grip on me, and by 11:00 A.M. I had written more than 120 tanka.

Again nothing extraordinary had happened the previous day. He did have some freshly cut flowers in his bedroom, so the smell of white lilies filled the air. The next day he bought a red lily, and again he had a productive night. "My head was filled with poetry," he wrote in his diary. "Everything I saw, everything I heard, all became tanka. By 2:00 A.M. that night I had written 141 of them. Some forty of these were about my parents. I was crying when I wrote them."

All these poems are recorded in his notebook. Here are three examples composed on the night of June 25:

Just for fun
I put Mother on my back
yet she weighed so
little, I began crying
and could not walk three steps.

For no reason
I left my home
and for no reason
I returned: this I have done
five times already.

Whenever my father
back home coughs,
here I cough, too—
so imagining, I lie
sick in bed.

None of the three poems can be directly connected to the day's events. Indeed, they are marked by their imaginative nature. The first tanka certainly has no roots in Takuboku's actual life: his parents were living far away in Hokkaido at the time. The second may seem more reflective than imaginative, but it should be noted that Takuboku was actually in Tokyo. In the third tanka he imagines a mysterious bond between himself and his father that makes the two cough simultaneously.

In the second type of creative process, then, Takuboku was more imaginative and meditative. Because no immediate external stimulus attracted his attention, his mind turned inward and probed its own depths, digging up memories of past events such as those at his home, or hidden desires such as a longing for reunion with parents. Not restricted by external events, the poet's mind was allowed freer play.

Takuboku also composed a considerable number of tanka by a third method: *kakai*, or a tanka-writing session. Takuboku, always in want of company, evidently enjoyed a chance to be with other poets, and when he was invited to a kakai seldom refused. Many of the gatherings he attended were sponsored by Mori Ōgai or the Yosanos. His diary entry for August 29, 1908, describes one of the longer kakai in which he participated:

In the evening I went to Sendagaya.[4] The Chinos were there. Yoshii, Hirano, and Kitahara arrived, too. Yamashiro was fat like a Dharma doll.[5] Watanabe somewhat resembled Iwasaki of Hokkaido. Ōnuki looked like Okayama Gekka of Morioka. There were more than ten people, counting the Yosanos.

Each of us was to produce one hundred tanka, using certain key words we had agreed upon. We set to our task when the clock struck eight. I felt in an inspired mood.

At 8:00 A.M. everyone was asked to stop writing. I was the fastest composer, having completed my assignment at around six. By noon we finished making clean copies of our poems, and we began ranking them at around one. But the task was a painstaking one because there were 1,300 poems in all, more than the entire volume of *The Collection of Ancient and Modern Poems*! Selected poems were read out in the evening. The session was finally over at eight, precisely 24 hours after it had begun. My poems received fairly good appraisals.

After some chatting, I took leave at a little after nine. My head was blank, and my body could not keep itself steady. I felt good, however.

His diary does not list the one hundred tanka he wrote at the kakai, but his notebook does. These two were typical:

> A puddle
> floating the sunset sky
> and a piece
> of crimson cord
> after an autumn rainfall.

[4]The Yosanos lived in the Sendagaya section of Tokyo. Yoshii Isamu (1886–1960), Hirano Banri (1885–1947), and Kitahara Hakushū, as well as Chino Masako and her husband Shōshō (1883–1946), all mentioned in the ensuing passage, later attained considerable poetic fame. All were members of the New Poetry Society at this time. Little is known about the others Takuboku mentions.

[5]A popular Japanese doll said to be modeled on Bodhidharma, the first patriarch of Zen. It portrays a stocky man with no hands or legs.

The autumn sky
boundlessly vast
and vacant,
resembling the mind
of an awakened man.

These tanka seem more conventional in form, imagery, and diction than those cited earlier; indeed, they resemble Akiko's poems in their striking juxtaposition of images from nature and from human life. One wonders whether her presence and the fact that they were written in her house did not affect Takuboku's work.

The third type of creative process may seem to contradict Takuboku's general identification of poem with diary. Kakai is an artificial way of writing a poem: the participant begins composing at a prescribed time, using certain predetermined words, in front of fellow poets who are to read and appraise his work later. Regardless of whether he is in the mood or not, the participant has to produce a certain number of tanka within a limited number of hours. On the other hand, kakai has its merits. It stimulates a poet by putting him under pressure, giving him key words, and exposing him to other poets at work. Although the presence of fellow poets may somewhat restrain the free play of his individuality, it may also lead him to explore poetic possibilities he has not thought of before. Most valuable is the fact that his poems are read and evaluated by other poets immediately after their composition. In general, he may enjoy the party atmosphere, with drinks, refreshments, and small talk. These positive factors had made kakai an age-old tradition in Japan. Shiki, who insisted on shasei, and Akiko, who valued jikkan, both were fond of kakai and actively participated in it, even though they knew it was not quite consistent with their poetic principles. Takuboku did the same.

For Takuboku, the creative process often did not end when he finished the initial writing. Although most of his poems give the impression of having been written spontaneously, he was a conscientious, painstaking versifier who reworked poems un-

til he was completely satisfied. He often revised poems on re-
publication, a practice that is especially noticeable in the poems
collected in *A Handful of Sand*. For example, the first of the two
autumn tanka cited above was published in two different magazines during October 1908. On both occasions, the poem appeared in the way Takuboku originally wrote it at the Yosanos'.
But when he included it in *A Handful of Sand*, he changed it into
the three-line form in which all the other tanka in the anthology
are written:

> A puddle
> floating the sunset sky and a piece of crimson cord
> after an autumn rainfall.

No word has been changed, but the bold new form adds something refreshing to the conventional imagery of the poem. The
second tanka, on the autumn sky, suffered a more drastic change
when it was anthologized. The revised poem has already been
quoted:

> The autumn sky, boundlessly vast and vacant,
> is too desolate.
> Let a crow or something fly!

Takuboku completely revised the last two lines of the poem, introducing the image of a crow. As a result, the poem became
more contemporary both in its verse form and in its emotional
effect, bringing to the forefront the loneliness of a modern man.
    As a final example of Takuboku's revisions, here are three dif-
ferent versions of the same tanka:

> A: For no reason
>   I left my home
>   and for no reason
>   I returned: this I have done
>   five times already.

> B: For no reason
>   I left my native province
>   and for no reason
>   I returned: this I have done
>   five times already.

C: For no reason I left my home
     and for no reason I returned—though
     my friend laughs at this habit of mine!

As we have seen, Takuboku composed Version A on the night of
June 25, 1908. Version B appeared in the July issue of *The Morning Star*, and it is not clear whether the revision was made by
Takuboku or by the editor of the magazine, Yosano Hiroshi.
The change from "home" to "province" seems to have the effect
of transforming a young libertine who thinks nothing of leaving
his parents into an ambitious youngster repeatedly trying to explore his career potential in far-off places. Version C was published in *A Handful of Sand* in 1910. There is no doubt that the
change was made by Takuboku this time, and it is a significant
one. In the first two versions, the poem focused on the restless
nature of a man who could not be confined at home; the last version emphasizes the loneliness of the man, whose basic nature
cannot be understood even by his friend.

Some poems in *Sad Toys* show marks of revision, too. A good
example is the following tanka, which Takuboku originally
wrote while lying in a hospital bed in March 1911:

A: Loneliness without end!
     This day, when I close my eyes
     and endure the pain in my chest.

B: How late the doctor's round!
     This day, when I close my eyes
     and silently endure the pain in my chest.

C: How late the doctor's round!
     Placing my hand on the aching chest
       I tightly close my eyes.

Takuboku published Version A in a magazine in April 1911.
When he copied it down in a notebook for his second tanka collection some time later, he made the revisions that appear in
Version B. Still later, he crossed out the second and third lines
and added new ones, thereby making Version C, which is now
included in *Sad Toys*. The revisions show a definite improve-

ment. In all three versions the central theme is the loneliness of
the hospitalized poet, but whereas the first version spells this
emotion out in words, the final version leaves it unsaid, the silence enhancing its poignancy.

Because Takuboku left so many records of his revisions (or
rather, his admirers have been so careful to preserve them), a
student is tempted to compare different drafts of his poems in
an effort to arrive at the secret of his craft. But such a method
does not easily lead to conclusions, for the examples are far too
diverse. Each time Takuboku revised, he was thinking of im-
proving a given poem, not of general poetic principles. Still, if
one were allowed to make one grand generalization about his
tanka revisions, it would be that his poems became more modern
and experimental in form and content each time he reworked
them. When he initially composed a tanka at a kakai or on a similar occasion, he was restricted to some degree by the long tradition of tanka, and even when he composed a poem alone, he had
to take into consideration the fact that it was likely to be sent to
the editors of a traditional tanka magazine for publication. He
felt no such restrictions when he made the final revisions for his
own tanka collections. Indeed, on those occasions he must have
tried to show his individuality by breaking away from the orthodox tradition. This is demonstrated by the fact that all of his
later tanka were written in the unconventional three-line form.
Traditional tanka poets had never attempted to create poetic
effects by manipulating line length, but in his tanka Takuboku
began to emphasize the appearance of the poem on the page,
in much the same way as did Anglo-American poetry in the
twentieth century. When the conventional line length and therefore the rhythm was changed, the traditional poetic sensibility
changed, too.

A Wind Loaded with Needles

Like Akiko, Takuboku felt poetry served those who wrote it
far more than those who read it. On rare occasions, however, he
did contemplate the relationship between poetry and the reader.

On March 8, 1906, for example, he pondered the comparative merits of art and education and wrote in his diary:

To make a comparison, what practical education does is like visiting someone's home with a gift, whereas what art does is like inviting someone to dinner and then giving him a souvenir when he leaves. This souvenir can be "beauty." Or it can be "problems," or "thought," or "human life," or *kokoro* ["the heart"], or "truth." All these are at once beautiful and true.

Though Takuboku has used the word "art," there is no doubt that poetry was foremost in his mind. The passage proposes that poetry first entertains the reader and then gives him something of educational value.

Among the six effects mentioned in the passage, "beauty" and "truth" are too comprehensive to mean much. All good poems are beautiful and true, as Takuboku himself implies in the last sentence. Beauty and truth constitute general effects, which are modified by specific elements of the poet's individuality. For Takuboku, there existed four such specific elements: "problems," "thought," "human life," and kokoro. These four qualities defined the kind of beauty and truth he preferred, especially in his mature years.

Of these four qualities, kokoro is the easiest to understand in light of Takuboku's poetic. By that word he meant the poet's honest heart, what lay in the innermost part of his mind. In Takuboku's opinion, a good poem conveys the poet's heart to the reader; the honesty of his confession strikes the reader with a sense of beauty and truth. The idea is an extension of Takuboku's concept of the verse-writing process, his feeling that poetry was a diary, a record of the changes in his mind at various moments of his life. Indeed, he once defined poetry as "the voice of the heart," and on another occasion taught an amateur poet that tanka should "sing out what he truly felt, what he truly thought." A poem thus created should impress the reader with the truthfulness of the poet's thinking and feeling, the integrity of his kokoro. For Takuboku, that was the beauty of poetry.

Takuboku recorded in his diary an interesting example of a magazine editor's tampering that impaired "the voice of the heart." On July 10, 1908, receiving a new issue of *The Morning Star*, he was pleased to see that 114 of his tanka adorned its pages, but dismayed to discover that some of the poems had been changed by the editor, Yosano Hiroshi, without his knowledge. In the corrected poems, he felt, "my emotion had been falsified." Here is one of Takuboku's originals, followed by the editor's revision:

> At long last
> I have managed to climb
> a wall of steel
> to its very top—only to find
> night beginning to fall.

> At long last
> I have managed to climb
> a wall of steel
> to its very top—then I see
> the fog is completely gone.

The original poem reflects the melancholy of a man who has worked hard for an ambitious goal and has finally attained it, only to discover that his days are numbered. Hiroshi's revision drastically changes this, transforming the poem into the success story of a hard-working young man. Such optimism was utterly alien to Takuboku at the time; it was definitely not "the voice of the heart."

Takuboku's idea of kokoro seems close to Akiko's concept of jikkan. He was an ardent admirer of Akiko in his teens, and at times he used the term "jikkan" in discussing the beauty of tanka. It appears, however, that as time passed he became increasingly disillusioned with the kind of beauty her tanka produce. "Mrs. Yosano's poetry is skillfully written," he observed, "but it is completely lacking in vigor." Below are two examples from a group of Akiko's tanka he specifically criticized:

> Is it crimson
> or is it green or blue?
> I cannot tell
> the color of the halo
> adorning you I love.

Worms have settled
and eaten away the walls,
the pillars and all.
Such is the house I live in
because of this heart of mine.

Takuboku felt these poems showed too much artifice, which reduced the amount of jikkan conveyed to the reader. Takuboku's point becomes clearer when one reads a tanka by his friend, Toki Aika (1885–1980), which he thought did have jikkan:

On the bricks lying at a fire-site
I make water—thereupon a deep sense
of approaching autumn.

When this poem was published, a reviewer attacked it and its author. On hearing of the unfavorable review, Takuboku counterattacked, saying, "I wonder why the critic could not approve of this penetrating jikkan." To him, the reviewer seemed to be a narrow-minded reactionary who appraised tanka strictly by the age-old conventional standards. The image of a man pissing on bricks at the site of a fire was inelegant and unpoetic to a traditional critic, but to Takuboku the anarchist it appealed with a poignant jikkan. The kokoro he wanted in verse was not that of a dreamy maiden in love, but that of an ordinary citizen engaged in the petty routines of daily life.

To be interpreted in the same light is another of the souvenirs that Takuboku thought a poet gave the reader: "problems." By "problems" he meant social and moral questions that bother common people, extraliterary issues that are dominant concerns in contemporary life. As we have seen, he said that literature should be "journalistic" in the broad sense of the term; that is, poetry should comment on current problems and should invite the reader to think seriously about them. "A literary artist," he said on another occasion, "used to confine himself in a room, jot down whatever he liked, and enjoy a leisurely time all by himself. Those days are past. Now everyone must be a member of society and engage in a great deal of struggle." Takuboku thought poetry should impart a sense of that struggle, as well as of its causes.

Problem-oriented poetry abounds in Takuboku's later work. One example is a short poem in free verse entitled "Afternoon in My Study":

> I do not like this nation's women.
>
> On the rough surface of a page
> of a Western book I am reading
> the red wine I have accidentally spilled
> spreads much too slowly, and my heart sinks.
>
> I do not like this nation's women.

The poem was written on June 15, 1911, shortly after Takuboku had a violent quarrel with his wife. Therefore, when he wrote "this nation's women" he was probably thinking of Setsuko, who seemed to him too feudalistic and backward. In that sense, the poem was "the voice of the heart," which aired his personal feelings. But when he transformed Setsuko into "this nation's women," he transformed a domestic problem into a national social problem. Japanese women in general seemed much too slow to absorb the new thoughts contained in Western books, and he wanted this poem to make his reader aware of the problem.

Takuboku wrote similar poems in the tanka form, too. Here are two tanka treating the problem of the backwardness of Japanese women:

> A woman
> straining to follow my words. . . .
> As I watch, my heart aches.
>
> How spiritless
> these women of Japan!
> I shout at them on a night of autumn rain.

Because tanka are more lyrical than shi, in these instances the social problem that is the theme is less clearly defined. The first tanka, in particular, seems confessional in nature. Yet beneath the surface is an element of social criticism, for the word "woman" refers to all women as well as to Setsuko. In the second poem, the generalization is clearer, even though biographical critics tend to see Setsuko in "these women of Japan."

Takuboku dealt with many other social problems in his poetry, such as poverty, the current marriage system, left-wing movements, terrorism, political corruption, and the dehumanization of urban life. Behind these poems lies the image of a sensitive young man deeply troubled by the state of affairs in contemporary society, and the sincerity and passion with which he confronts the issues provide the appeal of the poems.

Not only do these problem-oriented poems make the reader aware of contemporary social conditions, but they often suggest ways to improve those conditions. Such suggestions must be what Takuboku had in mind when he mentioned "thought" as one of the souvenirs the poet gives the reader. Thought is ideology, philosophy, a scheme by which to view society and the human condition. We have already heard Takuboku say that literature must be criticism of life, that an author must view the contemporary age in the light of his "practical philosophy." In Takuboku's view, it is not enough for a poet to be a newscaster; he must be a social critic and thinker who works toward reform through his poetry. In his later years Takuboku criticized his initial mentor, Yosano Hiroshi, for that reason. "Mr. Yosano's poetry," he charged, "never makes progress until he receives some external stimulus. This happens because he hardly has any thoughts of his own."

Takuboku himself made an attempt to write ideological poems in his last years. The direct result was a series of free-verse poems beginning with "After an Endless Debate," which we discussed earlier. Other poems in the sequence have similar political implications. The best-known is "A Spoonful of Cocoa":

> I can feel a terrorist's
> sorrow:
> a forlorn heart
> unable to discern action from word,
> a heart deprived of words
> and speaking through action,

a heart hurling itself at a foe.
It is the sorrow of every sincere, dedicated man.

After an endless debate
I sip a spoonful of cocoa that has become cold
and in its slightly bitter taste
I feel a terrorist's
deep sorrow.

The background of this poem, which was written in 1911, is the plot of a group of Japanese left-wing activists who wanted to bring about a revolution by assassinating Emperor Meiji (1852–1912). The plot was discovered prematurely, and the conspirators were promptly executed. Takuboku, who showed a great deal of interest in the incident, revealed his sympathy for the activists in this poem. Yet the poem is more lyrical than philosophical: it is the terrorist's heart rather than his brains that Takuboku tries to enter.

In the final analysis, most of Takuboku's poems deal less with a specific political ideology than with current human conditions in general and with human suffering under those conditions. They are criticisms of life in that they make the reader aware of existing human reality. This awareness must be what Takuboku meant when he cited "human life" as one of the souvenirs the reader receives. Those who read a poem are exposed to a slice of human reality to which they would otherwise have been strangers, or of which they had only an imperfect understanding.

The life that a poem imparts to readers is human life, not poetic life, for to the later Takuboku poetic life meant little more than a dreamer's fancy. He wanted readers of poetry to hear a man's voice, not a poet's voice. Once he was very much impressed by the poems of Takamura Kōtarō[6] and said he felt as if his heart were being buffeted by a strong wind blowing sharp needles. "Clever poems, poems that merely appeal to the reader's curiosity, poems that look as if they were on display at a dry goods store"—so he referred to the typical poems of his time. "If

[6]Takamura Kōtarō, to whom Chapter 6 is devoted, wrote tanka as a member of the New Poetry Society in his youth. Here, however, Takuboku is referring to his free verse.

these are really a poet's poems, then the wind from a valley loaded with sharp needles is a man's voice. And, in my opinion, a man is greater than a poet." He admired Kōtarō for being more man than poet, for living rather than dreaming.

In a similar vein, Takuboku once criticized the novelist Tayama Katai (1871–1930)[7] for being too much a man of letters. The criticism was all the more shocking because Katai was Japan's leading naturalistic writer and had tried assiduously to shun elements of fancy in his prose fiction. Takuboku wrote of him:

> He is preoccupied with the idea of being a man of letters, so much so that he tends to neglect probing into the relation between human life and Mr. Tayama himself, a naked man apart from his literary profession. I am sure this is the case. For Mr. Tayama literature has become too professional. Normally a man both lives and observes. Doesn't Mr. Tayama too frequently take an observer's attitude, drawing a line between himself and human life?

The contrast here is between living and observing. To Takuboku, Katai seemed to be too much attached to the latter.

Takuboku created a dilemma for himself when he insisted that poetry should convey the voice of a man who lives rather than that of a poet who observes, for poetry can never replace life. Takuboku wanted a poem to convey the voice of an activist, but an activist must become a poet—an observer—in order to write a poem. A person who wishes to be moved by human life in poetry might as well enter the actual world and participate in life's activities himself, for as Takuboku observed, an actual incident will move him far more directly than could an incident described in literature. Takuboku sought beauty and truth in poetry, but the kind of beauty and truth he sought can be found more readily in actual life.

The Poem Must Be Fragmentary

Takuboku's view of poetic form is characterized by an insistence on structurelessness: he wanted a poem to be fragmentary.

---

[7] Katai published one of his major works of naturalism, *The Country Teacher*, in October 1909. Takuboku's critical essay was written the following month.

As we have seen, he felt that poetry with unity turned into prose fiction when it took an inductive form, and into drama when it took a deductive form. In other words, a novelist or a playwright sets to work with a premeditated purpose, whereas a poet should spontaneously express his feelings of the moment. Takuboku's conclusion, then, was that a poem should have little or no structure because it lacks a preconceived message to provide a focus.

Such a notion of poetic structure—or its lack—may seem to contradict Takuboku's idea that poetry should convey, among other things, thought. If Takuboku wanted thought in literature, should he not have wanted to write a well-structured philosophical poem, which, in his view, was another way to name a novel, a short story, or a play? Indeed, he once decided to abandon poetry in favor of prose fiction because "poetry . . . is small-scale, and unable to sing out the true, deep emotions of modern man." Yet that determination did not last long. His justification for resuming verse writing was:

One hour consists of 60 minutes, each of which in turn consists of 60 seconds. It is an accumulated total of continuous parts, the total showing itself only at the very end. What is wrong with singing out fragmentary thoughts one after another as they float up fragmentarily in the mind?

In other words, poetry expresses fragmentary thoughts, whereas a novel or a play expounds more systematic thoughts. For that reason the latter needs an internal structure, and the former does not.

In theory, then, Takuboku argued for short free verse. But in practice he took up tanka, destroyed some of its conventions, and brought it closer to free verse. He had a liberal attitude toward syllable count, not strictly restricting it to 31 syllables. "A poet should try to use the language closest to the speech of his time," he said, "and if that language does not easily lend itself to a 31-syllable poem, he should write a tanka that has more than 31 syllables." He was also intent on breaking up the conventional rhythm of tanka. He felt that the 5–7–5–7–7 pattern was based on the rhythms of premodern Japanese and therefore had little meaning for tanka written in the modern vernacular. "What used to be a five-syllable unit now consists of six syllables, and a seven-syllable phrase of former days has now added another syllable," he said. "Not only that, a word unit of five or seven syllables can be further divided into units of two, five, or four syllables. There is plenty of room for tanka to increase its rhythmical complexity." The logical conclusion of this argument is that each tanka has a rhythm of its own and therefore should be written with its own arrangement of lines rather than in the uniform 5–7–5–7–7 format.

Takuboku, then, was arguing for a "tanka" of 30 to 35 syllables with varying length and arrangement of lines. It sounds as if he would have allowed a tanka of, say, 34 syllables, written in four lines. In the actual writing of tanka, however, he was more conventional. Every poem in his two tanka collections is written in three lines, with a total of roughly 31 syllables. Line lengths differ from poem to poem, but each line is usually a variation on the 5–7 pattern. In *A Handful of Sand*, for example, there are six basic forms:

$$5-7 \: / \: 5 \: / \: 7-7$$
$$5-7-5 \: / \: 7 \: / \: 7$$
$$5 \: / \: 7-5 \: / \: 7-7$$
$$5-7 \: / \: 5-7 \: / \: 7$$
$$5 \: / \: 7-5-7 \: / \: 7$$
$$5 \: / \: 7 \: / \: 5-7-7$$

On rare occasions there appears a variation, such as 5–4 / 3–5–7 / 7 or 5 / 7–5–4 / 3–7. But the underlying rhythm of even these is the 5–7 pattern.

The chief merit of these unique tanka forms lies in their shock effect. On the printed page they look like free verse, and no reader would think of appraising them by the standard of *The Collection of Ancient and Modern Poems*. One might recall Akiko's complaint about her poems being judged by the criteria of premodern Japanese poetics. Takuboku's tanka, being printed in an unconventional format, convey a sense of modernity, of being cut off from the past. To take an example already cited:

> A puddle
> floating the sunset sky
> and a piece
> of crimson cord
> after an autumn rainfall.

> A puddle
> floating the sunset sky and a piece of crimson cord
> after an autumn rainfall.

The first version, published in *The Morning Star*, is an undistinguished tanka with conventional imagery and diction. The revised version, which appears in *A Handful of Sand*, visually breaks the convention with its extralong second line. In it, the reader has the illusion that the poem before him is not a tanka but a Western-style imagist poem.

After the publication of *A Handful of Sand*, Takuboku extended his visual innovations by indenting lines and adding punctuation.[8] The result was a further break with the conventional tanka format and a closer approach to free verse. Several examples have been cited earlier; here are two more from *Sad Toys*:

> Today, too, I feel pain in the chest.
>   If I am to die
>   I wish to die in my hometown.

> The color of the fresh lettuce leaves
>   so pleased me,
>   I picked up my chopsticks, and yet—

In the first tanka, physical pain is in the forefront of the ailing poet's consciousness. That pain sinks deep into his mind, where he secretly longs to visit his hometown to die. The dislocation created by indenting the second and third lines suggests that his longing for home lies in that deeper layer in his mind, in a different part of his consciousness. Likewise, in the second tanka the beautiful salad bowl is in the forefront of the poet's mind as he takes up his chopsticks, but his pleasure is deep within, and

---

[8] Conventionally, neither tanka nor haiku use punctuation. Because of the nature of the English language, translators usually add it, as I have done in this book.

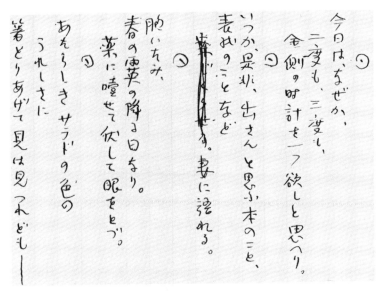

A page from Takuboku's tanka notebook, showing poems later published in *Sad Toys*. The poem at the extreme left is:

Atarashiki sarado no iro no	The color of the fresh lettuce leaves
ureshisa ni	so pleased me,
hashi toriagete mi wa mitsu-	I picked up my chopsticks,
redomo—	and yet—

Reproduced from *Nikuhitsuban kanashiki gangu* (Shomotsu Tenbōsha).

the centrality of that feeling is indicated by the central positioning of the word "pleased" in the tanka. Unfortunately, in this instance that deeply felt pleasure is not directly related to appetite. The poet is too sick to have a good appetite, and despite his pleasure at seeing the salad he has to put down the chopsticks. The indescribable feeling of that instant—disappointment, sadness, anger, irritation—is suggested by the dash that ends the poem.

All the experimental innovations Takuboku devised were visual;[9] aurally, his tanka are not strikingly new. Yet it should be

[9] Takuboku and his friend Toki Aika were the two leading pioneers in writing tanka for the eye. Aika was even more experimental than Takuboku: in 1910 he shocked contemporary readers by publishing a book of tanka written entirely in romanization.

remembered that Japanese poetry was becoming increasingly visual in Takuboku's day because of rapid progress in the publishing industry. Even though kakai was still held from time to time, by and large people read rather than heard tanka. There were no such things as public poetry readings, and Takuboku fully expected his readers to see his tanka on the printed page. If his tanka produced a visual impression resembling that of free verse, he felt his aim had largely been attained, that he was indeed writing modern tanka.

Since Takuboku in his mature years wrote tanka that visually resemble free verse, one wonders why he did not abandon the tanka form altogether and try to write more poems in the modern genre. Although he did write shi, they are greatly outnumbered by his tanka. In the absence of his own explanation we can only speculate, but one of the main reasons may have been an almost sadistic wish to jeer at the age-old verse form. Having failed to be a successful novelist or a good wage earner, the later Takuboku had within him a thwarted, destructive kind of energy. To express his frustration, he seems to have needed a verse form he could torture, and tanka, revered for a millennium, served the purpose well. Takuboku's use of tanka is somewhat similar to senryū, a satirical verse form with a 5–7–5 pattern. There is no specific reason for satirical verse to be written in seventeen syllables, but senryū poets like that form because it has the effect of parodying haiku. Takuboku, tortured by emotions within himself, found in tanka a fitting form on which to inflict them.

The same conflicting impulses may account in part for the fact that Takuboku used classical Japanese in practically all of his works in tanka, a practice surprising in a leftist poet who did not hesitate to write tanka with socialist overtones. Takuboku advocated using spoken Japanese in verse writing, arguing that the use of classical Japanese in modern poetry always involved falsifying the poet's true emotion to some degree. In his opinion, a poet who does not feel satisfied unless he employs classical words has in his heart something vain, evasive, and dishonest. "Surely it is a kind of cowardice," Takuboku declared. According to him, such a poet is also guilty of arrogance because he secretly harbors an unjustified conviction that poetry is valuable jewelry and that a poet is better than the man on the street. Takuboku did use colloquial Japanese in some of his later shi, and he did so convincingly. All the poems collected in *Longing* were written in classical Japanese, but in 1909 Takuboku began writing shi in the vernacular. The few pieces that resulted from his first experiment more than satisfied him. It is interesting to note, however, that he reverted to classical Japanese in writing his last shi, a celebrated group that includes such poems as "After an Endless Debate," "A Spoonful of Cocoa," and "Afternoon in My Study." In these poems, however, there is a strange harmony between radical themes and the classical language in which they are presented, for such modern-sounding words as "airplanes," "terrorists," and "V Narod" blend well into Takuboku's classical vocabulary. The secret seems to lie in his success in modernizing the classical language, so to speak. He has stripped his diction of all decorative words, so that his language has none of the "valuable jewelry" that often impairs poetry written in classical Japanese.

Although he never was forced to do so, Takuboku might have defended the use of classical Japanese in his later tanka on two grounds. Of one group of tanka, he might have said that classical words placed a poem in the long tradition of tanka and created an ironic tension between it and the tradition. Classical words, which evoke associations with premodern life, are juxtaposed with the emotion embodied in the poem, which is often strikingly modern. Of the other group of tanka, Takuboku might have said that he had modernized the classical language sufficiently to include the vocabulary of modern Japanese life without seeming strained. In these poems, he carefully avoided the pretty, decorative words often employed by traditional poets. In short, classical Japanese was a double-edged weapon: he used its undesirable aspects for ironic purposes, and he changed the others to suit his own aims.

A tanka Takuboku wrote toward the end of his life will serve as a fitting conclusion to this discussion of his ideas on poetic form. The poem, written in 1911, is included in *Sad Toys*:

> Accidentally breaking a teacup
> I ponder the pleasure of breaking
> this morning, too.

The implications are political and social, pointing toward a secret hope for a revolution that would completely destroy the current order of society. But Takuboku must have felt the same kind of pleasure when he broke the current tanka norms. He preferred writing poetry in the tanka form, rather than in free verse, so that he could taste the pleasure of breaking the tradition.

Better Than Crying

It will suffice merely to summarize Takuboku's view on the use of poetry, since much has been said about it in the preceding pages. His view changed considerably with time, as his concept of poetry changed. When he was in his teens, the capabilities of poetry seemed almost limitless. That idealistic view had to be modified as he grew older, but he still saw an educational value in literature. In the last years of his life, however, he came to denounce poetry as of little practical use—being no better than a toy. This drastic change in attitude took place within a span of only about ten years.

In his student days, Takuboku felt that poetry was useful as revelation, that it was a message from God the Creator telling of realms that normally lie beyond the range of sight. With the passage of time, however, he became more realistic. In 1906, one year after the publication of *Longing*, he still held that "art is close to God," but he emphasized a pragmatic value of poetry, saying "The poet is a teacher of mankind." In this modified view, poetry was one of the best means of educating people. Formal school education, Takuboku thought, gave lifeless knowledge, which became vital only when delivered by a true educator. In contrast, poetry (and art in general) has within itself life, in addition to knowledge. Because poetry is full of life, even children who do not want to go to school will flock to it. To use a comparison cited earlier, schooling is like visiting a man's home and giving him a gift, whereas art invites him to dinner and then gives him a souvenir. Poetry entertains and edifies.

These souvenirs, however, can be given by novels and short stories as well. Indeed, prose fiction may serve the purpose better because, with an entertaining plot, it can have a more popular appeal than poetry. Thus Takuboku turned to writing stories, and his inclination to depreciate poetry increased. When he failed as a novelist and his domestic and financial woes multiplied, he became firmly convinced of the uselessness of literature as a whole. To him, poetry no longer seemed education; it looked like a game. And a poet no longer seemed a teacher; he resembled a toymaker or a clown.

Takuboku came to consider poetry useless both for the poet and for the reader because he believed it could not change external reality. Writing poems can give a momentary relief from the strains of daily life, but can do nothing to eliminate the cause of those strains. He brought home this point in "Various Kinds of Poetry," in which he wrote about an amateur poet who had sent tanka to a newspaper of which he was the poetry editor. After reading this young poet's work, he mused:

There were a great many missing words in these poems, perhaps because the poet had drafted the manuscript on a day when he had such urgent business or such a happy event that he was beside himself. I am sure that was the case. But if there should exist the kind of poet I visualized from these poems [i.e., a man suffering from dire circumstances], and if that poet should voice the kind of agony expressed in these poems, how would other people who heard him respond? I thought of many possible responses coming from various people. All of them made sense. Yet all the stirring remarks, words of encouragement, and expressions of sympathy—would these change the circumstances of the unfortunate young man even by a tiny bit?

Clearly Takuboku saw in this young man an image of his own past. He himself had been in wretched circumstances, had written poems to vent his misery, and had gained many words of encouragement from his readers; yet all that changed nothing in the actual conditions of his life, where he needed help most urgently. Poetry had failed him.

Thus Takuboku's later writings are sprinkled with remarks disparaging poetry because of its uselessness. He said that poetry was a toy, a game, clowning, masturbation. In the same vein, he compared poetry to smoking. "Poetry is no more useful than a cigarette," he wrote to a friend. Another phrase he often applied to poetry was "after work." He wrote, "I intend to call my next tanka collection (if it can be published) *After Work*. After work! Good enough, isn't it? It [poetry] is something we can do without. The value and significance of all literature is like that, I think." He implies that poetry is play, recreation, something not absolutely essential to human existence, something one might do after other important things have been taken care of.

His basic criticism notwithstanding, in his later years Takuboku did envision two minor uses for poetry. One was its journalistic function, its role in reflecting and criticizing contemporary affairs. If impregnated with an appropriate ideology, poetry can incite people to social reform, or even to revolution. But Takuboku, although he recognized that use, did not take full advantage of it, for he was too much a lyrical poet to be a political activist. The other use of poetry he perceived, and did take advantage of, was its cathartic function. For him poetry was no more than play, but on rough days he needed play to relieve his tension. Wailing did not help his plight, but it at least brought a little solace. He made this point well in "Better Than Crying," a free-verse poem about a dream in which a wretched, drunken woman sings a song. The last stanza of the poem is:

> "Why do you sing so?" I asked her
> in the dream.
> She answered
> with a drunkard's rosy smile,
> "Because it is better than crying."

Since Takuboku was not drunk, his singing was even sadder.

CHAPTER FOUR

Hagiwara Sakutarō

H AGIWARA SAKUTARŌ (1886–1942) is generally considered the most original of the poets who helped perfect the art of free-style poetry in modern Japan. Shi existed before him: Shiki, Akiko, and Takuboku, along with many other poets, tried their hands at that new verse form. But in two respects Sakutarō's contribution outweighs that of anyone else. First, his consummate skill with words demonstrated that modern spoken Japanese could be used for verse writing in an artistically satisfying way. Takuboku and some others had made use of the vernacular in their works, but their diction was little different from that of everyday speech. With Sakutarō, modern Japanese became a poetic language for the first time. Second, he was the first Japanese poet to write successful poems about the existential despair of a modern intellectual. Born into a wealthy physician's family, he never experienced the financial struggles Takuboku confronted. Yet his extraordinary sensitivity and resulting personal conflicts led him to harbor grave misgivings about the meaning of human existence, eventually driving him to a helpless sense of loneliness, melancholy, and despair. Modern pessimism, rooted in Nietzsche and Schopenhauer, blossomed in Japan in the poetry of Hagiwara Sakutarō.

Sakutarō's three major books of poetry, *Howling at the Moon* (1917), *The Blue Cat* (1923),[1] and *The Ice Land* (1934), had an im-

---

[1] Sakutarō published two editions of *The Blue Cat*, the first in 1923 and the second and definitive in 1936. Unless otherwise noted, I refer to the definitive edition.

mense impact on the Japanese poetic scene. He was equally known to his contemporaries as a literary theorist through many books of essays and aphorisms that promulgated his idea of poetry. The pivotal work among his theoretical writings, *Principles of Poetry*, took ten hard years to write: it is difficult to think of any other major Japanese poet who would have spent so long writing a book on literary theory. Sakutarō was also an indefatigable debater who never shied away from literary controversies, as well as a perceptive reader who put forward imaginative interpretations of classical tanka and haiku. Consequently, one who studies his poetic has to cope with a massive amount of material. In the following pages, I shall be able only to touch on the highlights of his concept of poetry.

Poetry as the Expression of Nostalgia

A poem is a poem less on account of its form than on account of a certain spirit it embodies: this is one of the basic ideas Sakutarō took great pains to explain to amateur poets who sought guidance from him. He felt a need to emphasize the truism because much contemporary poetry, as he saw it, was distinguished from prose only by its syllabic patterns. Therefore, in his *Principles of Poetry* he chose to expound the inner spirit of poetry at length before answering questions on poetic form. What identifies poetry as poetry, he kept insisting, is ultimately *shiseishin*, a poetic spirit that can manifest itself in a variety of other forms, albeit to a lesser degree. He recognized that spirit not only in such other literary genres as the novel and drama but also in ethics, religion, and even natural science. According to him, the Christian Bible and the Confucian *Analects*, Plato's philosophy and Lao-tzu's ethics, all contain shiseishin and thereby move the hearts of those who read them. However, he found the purest manifestation of shiseishin in poetry, especially in lyric poetry. He stressed that without it poetry would lose its raison d'être.

To find out what that all-important poetic spirit is like, one can do no better than to read Sakutarō's aphorisms, collectively entitled "Characteristics of Shiseishin." There are eight in all:

1. Poetry soars *above reality*. Hence shiseishin is essentially romantic.
2. Poetry seeks ideals. Hence shiseishin is essentially subjective.
3. Poetry corrects language. Hence shiseishin is essentially rhetorical in intent.
4. Poetry demands form. Hence shiseishin is essentially normative.
5. Poetry ranks beauty higher than truth. Hence shiseishin is essentially aesthetic.
6. Poetry criticizes reality. Hence shiseishin is essentially pedagogic.
7. Poetry dreams of a transcendental world. Hence shiseishin is essentially metaphysical.
8. Poetry demands the noble and the rare. Hence shiseishin is essentially aristocratic (antidemocratic).

These aphorisms point to the core of Sakutarō's thoughts about the nature of poetry. In the following pages they will be examined in the light of his other writings, beginning with the statements that concern the relationship between poetry and reality.

The first of the aphorisms is that "poetry soars *above reality*." (Sakutarō italicized the last two words for emphasis.) The point is related to the sixth aphorism, which states that poetry criticizes reality. In both instances the word "reality" refers to ordinary physical reality, the routine existence of an average person in the everyday world. The first question to be asked, then, is what Sakutarō thought prompted a poet to flee reality. Does any element of physical reality repel shiseishin?

Unlike Takuboku, Sakutarō seems to have found the main cause of the poet's flight not in the contemporary social order but in the poetic temperament. In his opinion, it is because he has a poetic temperament that the poet finds falsehood, corruption, and ugliness in the physical world and feels an urge to abandon it for the world of Ideas. "Such a poetic temperament is entirely due to fate," Sakutarō said. "It is an inborn disposition, a heaven-given nature, which is not humanly changeable. A poet is born, not made; his fate has been sealed from the outset."

How Sakutarō came to hold such a deterministic view of his own character is a question difficult to answer. In his early teens he seems already to have been a confirmed pessimist. He once recalled how as a middle-school student he used to listen to his classmates tell their dreams of becoming statesmen, scholars, or military officers, while he alone was not able to hold any rosy hopes for the future. Of course, youthful disillusionment has not been uncommon in any century or in any country, but young Sakutarō's was not a passing phase, and his disillusion was directed at the very fact of his own existence.

Such existential despair soon found an outlet in verse writing. A look at one of Sakutarō's poems from *Howling at the Moon* will help define the nature of his feelings:

Dangerous Walk

When spring arrived
I had rubber soles attached to my new shoes
so that no footstep would be audible
however rough a sidewalk I might walk on.
I am carrying plenty of breakables,
a dangerous venture in the extreme.
Now it is time to begin my walk.
Be still, every one of you.
Be still, please!
I am worried, so very worried.
No matter what may happen
don't look at my misshapen feet.
There is no way out for me.
Like a sick balloonist
I keep tottering, staggering,
forever in this exasperating place.

The poem presents the image of a person in a grave predicament who places the blame on himself rather than on society or the people around him. He feels that he is crippled, and he is extremely self-conscious. His body is a cracked receptacle carrying many breakable things; it is fragile enough to shatter at the faintest sound of a footstep. He is like a balloonist in his wish to leave the earth, yet he is sick. All he can do is totter about, his body emaciated and his mind exasperated, in a place that has no exit.

Howling at the Moon is filled with poems portraying this kind of person, a man plagued with shiseishin. "An Ailing Face at the Bottom of the Earth" depicts a sick man whose ghostly face looms in the subterranean darkness. "Hanging in Heaven" presents a suicide who tearfully hangs himself from a heavenly pine tree. "An Alcoholic's Death" describes a murdered alcoholic

"Ennui," an illustration by Tanaka Kyōkichi for the first edition of *Howling at the Moon*. Many poems in the collection suggest that something essential and vital in the poet's being is ailing or decomposing. Reproduced from *Hagiwara Sakutarō zenshū* (Chikuma Shobō), Vol. I.

whose body is rotting. In other poems the man possessed by shiseishin has been transformed into an animal or a plant. In "Dawn," for example, he appears as a deformed dog howling at the moon, and in "Rotting Clam" he is transformed into a clam whose insides have begun to decompose. His pained consciousness is metamorphosed into a delicate stem of grass in "The Stem of Grass," into a dying chrysanthemum in "Chrysanthemum Turning Sour," and into wintry bamboo plants in two poems entitled "Bamboos." Images and metaphors differ, but common to all these poems is the poet's agonized awareness that something essential and vital within his being is deformed, ailing, or decomposing. Although the word "sin" is used in some poems, the root of evil is more physiological than religious or moral. There is something seriously wrong with the poet's basic life-force, the hidden energy that should keep his roots alive.

When Sakutarō said poetry criticizes reality and soars above it, he meant that poetry gives expression to the inner life of a man who, because of his acute awareness of a spiritual ailment, is forever at odds with normal human existence and feels an urge to flee it if at all possible. The actual world looks superficial and false to him because it is insensitive to his need. It often does not understand that for a man with a poetic temperament living in itself is painful.

The next question to be answered concerns the destination of the poet's flight. A poet soars above reality, but to where? The second of Sakutarō's aphorisms answers that question, but only in a very general way: "Poetry seeks ideals." One of Sakutarō's most direct statements about the nature of these ideals appears in *Principles of Poetry*. After observing that all poets have been idealistic seekers, he wrote, "In my opinion, what they sought was some Platonic Idea, which they could never hope to attain in actual life. They had been gripped by a nostalgia for the eternal homeland of their souls—for an existence projected by their longing." The remark contains two key words that Sakutarō used time and again throughout his essays: "Ideas" and "nostalgia." The former, which he borrowed directly from the Greek, had Platonic overtones, as in this quotation. Sakutarō used it to refer to a higher order of existence, of which the physical world is but a shadow. There is, he believed, an archetypal world beyond this one, to which people with shiseishin long to soar. That longing is "nostalgia," for the Platonic world of Ideas is the ultimate homeland of the human soul. According to him, an ordinary person longs for his physical home; a poet, for his metaphysical home.

Despite this dualistic world view, Sakutarō stressed that poets seek Ideas not with the intellect but through emotion and sensation. To make the concept clearer, he proposed using the Chinese character *meng* ("dream"), with a pronunciation "idea" written beside it. A philosopher constructs a world of Ideas through discursive reason, but a poet dreams it as objects that are tangible, although they transcend physical reality. Hence the seventh of Sakutarō's aphorisms, "Poetry dreams of a transcendental world." The poet's yearning for a higher order of reality must be rooted deep in the unconscious, since his loathing of human existence is physiological; it is an instinctive impulse. "This is probably akin to the instinctive way in which certain creatures are attracted to light," Sakutarō speculated. "It is *eros*, the longing of a human soul instinctively flying toward a certain being." He once gave form to this longing in a short poem:

Moonlit Night

Flapping large heavy wings
what feeble hearts they have!
On a night when the moon is as bright as a gaselier
watch the swarm of white creatures flowing.
Watch their calm direction.
Watch the suffocating emotion those creatures have.
On a night when the moon is like a bright gaselier
what a doleful flight of moths!

Through the images of the moths, the light, and the moon, this poem presents the soul possessed by shiseishin drawn upward by instinctive attraction. The moths must be drawn to an earthly light, but the only "gaselier" that appears in the poem is a description of the moon. Thus the poet not only recognizes in the moths an image for himself, but by seeing the moon as like a lamp, he places himself in the same relation to it as the moths are to the lesser light. He notes its surface similarity in size, shape, and brightness, but the fact that he makes the comparison reveals a deeper similarity, this time between himself and the moths—like them, he feels an instinctive attraction to light.

In an essay written many years later and entitled "The Moon and Shiseishin," Sakutarō identified a physical instinct as the source of the moon's attractiveness. Referring to the habits of certain fish and insects that are instinctively drawn to light, he remarked, "All those creatures perhaps sense their existential homeland, the very origin of their lives, when they see a beautifully burning light. The phenomenon belongs to the primeval mystery of life shared by all creatures." Such arts as poetry and music, he believed, probe into that mystery through the artist's preempirical memories. In another essay written about the same time, he wrote: "In poets' consciousness there reside a priori memories handed down from the ancestors through millions of years. In those memories they find themselves to be cave dwellers, or shellfish eaters, or apes, or (going back further) birds or beasts or reptiles."

It is unlikely that Sakutarō knew about Jung when he wrote "Moonlit Night," but these later essays outline a concept close to Jung's idea of the unconscious. However, unlike Jung, for whom the collective unconscious contained archetypal forms that organize human behavior, Sakutarō saw the "collective unconscious" primarily as a reservoir of subtle and complex sensations, sensations that at their deepest level are at the boundaries not only of human consciousness, but also of human being—they phase off into an empathy for the evolutionary origins of our consciousness in other forms of life. For him, a poet's nostalgia arises from his contact with these sensations; their attraction for him may resemble the numinous quality Jung ascribed to symbols that externalize the archetype. Through attention to these deep-seated sensations, the poet hopes to reach the source of his being.

A number of poems dealing with the sensation of preempirical memory are collected in *The Blue Cat*. In a number of them, the sensations provide a basis for empathic identification with animals, and the poem is written through the eyes of a horse, a cat, a bat, a cock, or a crab. In a particularly fine example, Sakutarō instead imagines his way back to Adam, who as the first man is the very boundary between human and nonhuman being, the point at which human consciousness becomes itself:

Most Primitive Emotion

Deep in a jungle
gigantic rubber trees grow
like ghostly elephants' ears.
Shadowy figures crawl on the marsh,
one on the heels of another: ferns, reptiles,
snakes, lizards, newts, frogs, salamanders, and so on.

During his melancholy longing at midday
what did Adam recollect?
Primeval emotion is like a cloud,
like infinitely sweet love.
It floats on the other side of memory
far beyond my reach.

Being the first man, Adam has no personal recollections as subsequent mortals know them. Instead he has only the urge to remember, sparked by a vague sense of something beyond his reach, some primal and prior being he cannot quite touch. Because he cannot identify those forms below consciousness, they are "like a cloud." May they be the sensations of that vaguely evolutionary line of shadowy figures crawling "one on the heels of another"? Adam himself cannot know; he can only feel an unaccountably sweet, ineffable nostalgia, the tantalizing, fascinating attraction of something we almost remember but cannot quite touch.

At other times, the metaphysical homeland Sakutarō glimpsed developed itself quite differently. However, the visions he presents in the following two poems are linked to that of "Most Primitive Emotion" by the feeling that infuses them, an emotion Sakutarō termed "romantic nostalgia" in commenting on the first:

Skyscape

Run, softly creaking wagon,
along the faintly glimmering sea
and far away from the flowing wheat.
Run, softly creaking wagon.
Through a skyscape luminous with fish and birds
and through buildings windowed blue,
run, softly creaking wagon.

Elegant Appetite

Walking through a pine grove,
I saw a cheery-looking café.
Too far from the city streets
for anyone to come and visit:
there the café was, hidden in the grove of memories and
    dreams.
A maiden, lovingly bashful,
brought me a special dish as refreshing as dawn.
Casually I picked up a fork
and ate omelet, fried food, and such.
A white cloud floated in the sky,
and I had a very elegant appetite.

The worlds of these poems are displaced, not in evolutionary time, but through dreamlike images. The setting continually reminds us of its distance from practical reality: the wagon is a vehicle nonexistent in Japan, and the cafe is "hidden in the grove of memories and dreams." Moreover, Sakutarō uses figurative language that emphasizes the ideational nature of these places by combining disjunctive things rather than similar ones—employing synaesthesia in "softly creaking wagon" and illogical conjunctions in "a skyscape luminous with fish and birds" and "a special dish as refreshing as dawn." The connections that unite these images are the emotive processes of the mind itself, not resemblances noted in the physical world. It is thus, perhaps, that they flee external reality as perceived and approach another, more congenial homeland of the soul.

Interestingly enough, in all three poems things Western join the objects of dream and of projected preempirical memory. The poet found himself to be Adam rather than any hero in Japanese mythology; he rode in a Western wagon rather than in a

Hagiwara Sakutarō 147

Japanese oxcart; and he used a fork rather than chopsticks to satisfy his elegant appetite. How could Sakutarō's nostalgia be directed toward Europe? Two possible answers can be given. First, Sakutarō's nostalgia seems to exist at the boundaries of the ordinary consciousness centered on everyday life, so it feeds on the unfamiliarity of dream or of distance in space or time. The West, being remote, thus provided an apt focus for poetic energy. In this respect Sakutarō admired what he called the "childlike romanticism" of his Meiji forefathers, who had an insatiable passion for Western civilization. In his nostalgia, he may have longed to share with them that pure passion. Second, Sakutarō probably wanted his world of Ideas to be a synthesis of both East and West. For him, preempirical memory must have encompassed all of Western, as well as Eastern, history.

To sum up, then, in Sakutarō's view a poet is an existentially deformed man who dreams of returning to a complete self existing on another level of reality. The spirit of poetry, shiseishin, must therefore be subjective and idealistic; it must be "romantic" in that sense. The poet aims to achieve and present a vision, either a painful vision based on his own crippled existence or a sweet vision based on his longing, his subtle attunement to deeper impulses and sensations neglected in a normal life. Either way, the vision does not and should not present physical reality as it is. "The difference between photography and painting," Sakutarō once said, "is that the former contains all reality and no falsehood, whereas the latter presents reality by depicting falsehood. Of course, literature is painting and not photography."

Sakutarō once categorized romantic poets in two groups by examining whether they were more concerned with search or with defiance. He called the first type of poets "adventurers," for they sought adventure in an unknown land. Sakutarō thought many French poets belonged to this category, citing Baudelaire, Rimbaud, Valéry, and Cocteau, as well as Poe. He called the second type of poets "sentimentalists"; these were misfits who because they sought lofty ideals always were angered by the world in which they actually lived. His examples included Goethe,

Heine, Verlaine, Dehmel, Rilke, Nietzsche, and Novalis, and he observed that this type was more common in Germany.

Sakutarō himself appears to have changed from the first type of poet into the second as he grew older. When he wrote the poems collected in *Howling at the Moon* and *The Blue Cat*, he was largely an adventurer who sought every opportunity to roam in a visionary land. But in his last book of verse, *The Ice Land*, he was more of a sentimentalist angry with the actual world. Describing his frame of mind at the time, he wrote, "I was angered by everything. I never stopped feeling like shouting at the top of my voice." That suppressed shouting found its way into his poetry, as in this example from *The Ice Land*, composed when Sakutarō's wife left him and their two young children:

Returning to My Parents' Home
In the winter of 1929 I was separated from my wife and
went back to my native town with my two children.

The train pushes forth against a gale
toward my native town.
Awakening from sleep, all alone by the window,
I hear the steam whistle scream in the dark
and see flames brighten the plain.
Have the Kōzuke mountains come within our sight?
In the pale light of the night train
the motherless children sob in their sleep.
Furtively, all measures my gloom.
What homeland am I heading for,
this refugee from the capital?
My past leads to the valley of solitude,
and my future to the shore of despair.
How gravelike this life is!
With my strength long gone,
I am too weary to live out the melancholy days.
How can I return to my native town
and stand alone by the Toné River again?
The train pushes forth across the wilderness
toward the desolate shore of Nature's will—
only to intensify my rage.

This poem is considerably different from the ones cited earlier. The sentiments it contains are more directly related to the actual situation, that of a man deserted by his wife, and they are ex-

Hagiwara Sakutarō 149

pressed through more realistic images, including two actual places. Inevitably, there is a degree of fictionalization,[2] yet here the poet definitely lives in the same sphere as the man on the street. He despairs of that life, but he is there. Japanese critics have long argued about which type of poetry is of higher value. Those who favor *Howling at the Moon* and *The Blue Cat* have charged that the poems in *The Ice Land* are limited in their visualization of basic human existence, and that they represent a marked decline in Sakutarō's imaginative power. On the other hand, critics who prefer his later poetry have replied that Sakutarō was an escapist in his early works and that only in *The Ice Land* did he face reality with total honesty. It is impossible to determine which of the two appraisals is correct, for the judgment is ultimately personal and depends on whether one sees reality in the daily existence of an average man or in a transcendental sphere of which this life is only a shadow.

In terms of Sakutarō's own poetic, however, the poems in *Howling at the Moon* and *The Blue Cat* seem closer to the ideal. As we have seen, he felt that poetry should soar above reality, trying to present a visionary world by "metaphysical" means—that is, by using metaphors and symbols that distance or distort the objects within the poem, dissolving their ties with reality as it is ordinarily perceived. He did say that poetry should criticize reality, but he added that the criticism should be done in a "pedagogic" way; negative criticism alone would not suffice. Elsewhere in his writings he observed that the criticism of contemporary society belongs more to the realm of prose than to that of poetry. He implied this, for instance, in a brief aphoristic passage called "Poetry and Prose":

Life consists of two kinds of time: nighttime and daytime, dream and reality, subconscious life and conscious life. Hence literature is divided into two categories, too. Poetry deals with images floating in a dream at night; prose, with conscious perceptions of reality in the daytime. In its own dreamlike manner, which ignores reason or grammar formulated

[2] Sakutarō and his two daughters returned to his native town by train in July 1929. In the poem he changed the season to winter.

by common sense, poetry gives expression to the essence of the poet's self, which appears and disappears in the twilight zone of consciousness. Ideally speaking, a person can attain complete self-expression only when he works in both types of literature (poetry and prose), the one articulating his subconscious being and the other his conscious life.

The poems in *The Ice Land* seem to embody conscious perceptions of reality rather than images floating in a dream. "Returning to My Parents' Home," for example, presents the poet's acute awareness of the sad situation facing him at the time. The autobiographical notes he added to it and to some other poems in the same volume embed his poetic material in a flow of prosaic circumstance like that depicted in a novel, a diary, or an autobiographical essay—one could even imagine these poems being written in prose. Such explanations indicate a move away from the pure, dreamlike poetry he advocated; no such notes appear in *Howling at the Moon* or *The Blue Cat*.

After the publication of *The Ice Land*, Sakutarō wrote essays, aphorisms, and prose poems, but almost no poetry in verse. According to him, poetry was to soar above reality, and in his later years he had lost his wings. "At the Zoo," one of the poems in *The Ice Land*, ends with these lines:

> Now as autumn nightfall approaches
> the wind rages over the deserted road,
> yet I cannot soar away like a bird
> across the endless expanse of solitude.

Inspiration, Liquefaction, and Correction

Sakutarō's *Principles of Poetry*, comprehensive though it is, says little about the process through which a poem comes into being. Apparently he had planned to treat the question, for he scribbled notes about it at some length in a notebook he used in preparing the book. These jottings even have a title, "Two Types of Creative Psyche," which suggests that he intended to make them into a chapter of the book. The title refers to a classification of artists into two general types: inspirational artists, like Mozart and Poe, who create their works through lightning flashes of inspiration, and laborious artists, like Rodin, who produce art through long, sustained effort. The chapter was never written, however, and Sakutarō stopped just when he seemed ready to enter a serious discussion of the creative mind. When hints on the subject are gathered together from among his other writings, they suggest that he thought of the creative process in three stages: inspiration, expression, and correction. They indicate, moreover, that he may have been unable to write systematically about the creative process because in his own case a crucial part of both inspiration and expression took place in the subconscious mind. He himself did not fully know how he wrote a poem.

Sakutarō repeatedly wrote about the unpredictable way in which creative inspiration is born. In his experience, inspiration would occur without forewarning, in a way he himself could not explain. It was like "a spark that flares up and dies in an instant," or was "something mysteriously vague and itchy billowing up from within the mind." At one time he was inclined to explain it as "divine inspiration"; at another he preferred to relate it to "physiological anomaly." The passage that comes closest to describing it appears in a notebook dated in or around 1914, at the beginning of the fertile period that produced *Howling at the Moon*. Using physiological metaphors, there he vividly traced the way a poem took root in his mind:

Some while ago a strange, unidentifiable light was conceived within me. It has slowly begun to move about. But because the walls are thick, it cannot break through. That is agonizing in the extreme—the suffocating pain before childbirth. Every day I scribble incomprehensible things on a piece of paper. Finally it looks as if the Sentimental Nirvana were approaching. The heaven and the earth are so radiant they dazzle my eyes. The September sun is covered with thick clouds. There is a halo around everything I see. What joy! What excruciating pain! I can't breathe. This is too much!

In an article called "How to Write Poetry," Sakutarō once speculated about possible means of inducing such inspiration. His main suggestion echoes the physiological emphasis in the passage just quoted; it was to bring about "physiological anomaly" in one way or another, so that the normal pattern of thinking would be drastically changed. He referred, half in jest, to various experimenters in the past who tried to attain inspiration by taking opium, fasting, or shaking their heads to the frenzied rhythm of delirational music. The most practical method, he wryly commented, was to utterly exhaust the body by excessive drinking, debauchery, lack of sleep, or some other act detrimental to one's health. At the conclusion of the article, however, he stated that of course he himself had never written a poem by such means. In his opinion, true poetic inspiration visits, not a poet who takes opium for its sake, but a poet who has to take opium because he cannot stand reality otherwise. Opium, alcohol, and sleeplessness are at most catalysts. "A poem should naturally seep up from the bottom of the poet's soul," said Sakutarō. "It should be neither devised by intellect nor aroused by opium or any other artificial means." To quote another of his articles, the ideal poet, temperamentally unfit for the world, is "a romantic in the broad sense of the word, a man who by his inborn nature possesses his own subjective Ideas."

According to Sakutarō, poetic inspiration also has an aesthetic, and hence impractical, component: what a poet conceives through inspiration is not an ordinary sensation directly related to practical affairs. Sakutarō once called such ordinary sensations jikkan, inviting protests from those accustomed to the definition of the term given by Yosano Akiko and her associates. In defense he clarified his terminology, saying that in his usage jikkan was a feeling restricted by practical concerns, whereas its opposite, bikan ("aesthetic feeling"), aspired to transcend the utilitarian sphere.

After it is conceived by inspiration, a poetic sentiment needs to be given verbal expression. Sakutarō once gave the name "liquefaction" to this phase of the creative process. "Verse writing," he said, "is an art by which the poet, using rhythm, liquefies the subject or material he has acquired through experience." He continued, "In liquefaction, all matter loses the forms it had when it was solid. It is for this reason that poetic expressions have vague, mysterious beauty: all actual experience has been transformed into images. A literary work that still retains raw experience in its solid form cannot be called poetry." He was implying that poetic expression is the ordinary process of verbalization plus two additional factors. First, a sentiment or experience conceived in the poet's mind must be transformed into "images." Second, it must be accompanied by rhythm. If a work lacks these two elements, it is a prose piece instead of a poem.

Sakutarō's term "images" (he used the English word in the quotation cited above) must refer to symbols—that is, to images that imaginatively expand beyond their exact denotation. Otherwise they could not have "vague, mysterious beauty." Why the poet must use images in this expanded sense is explained in *Principles of Poetry*, where Sakutarō distinguishes between two types of artistic expression. One is "description," an attempt to delineate the external form of an object; this method is employed more often by painters, novelists, and writers of realistic drama. The other method, often used by poets, musicians, and opera-writers, is *jōshō*, a word Sakutarō coined by joining the two words *jō* ("emotion") and *shō* ("image"). Even when poets and musicians depict an external object in their work, their depiction is so subjective, he felt, that the outlines of the object become blurred. The object is transformed into an image that produces vague, mysterious beauty; solid matter is "liquefied."

Sakutarō attributed the necessity of rhythm in poetic expression to the intensity of the sentiment to be expressed. "When a man's sentiment is heightened," he said, "his language forgets its expository function; his words automatically become a kind of exclamation. It is for this reason that the language of poetry has musical tones and rhythms, and allows no prosaic description." To support his point, he cited primitive poetry and children's songs. Poems of all races at the dawn of civilization, he pointed out, had clearly recognizable rhythms, and so do the songs that today's children spontaneously sing at play. He did not know exactly why heightened language should be rhythmical, but he speculated that this might be due to man's "aesthetic instinct."

According to Sakutarō, every intensified sentiment contains

a rhythm in itself, and a poem resulting from the sentiment should approximate that rhythm. As will be discussed in more detail later, this is the basis of his defense of free verse. When expression is completed, there follows the third phase of the creative process, "correction." Either rhythm or imagery can be corrected. "As soon as you finish writing a line, read it aloud and see if it sounds pleasant to your ear," Sakutarō advised beginning poets. "Next," he added, "be wary of a word's connotative function." Every correction, of course, should be made so that the initial inspiration is approximated more closely.

Sakutarō advised that a good deal of caution be used when undertaking correction long after the original composition of a poem. In an article entitled "On Revising One's Own Poems," he argued that a poem can be reworked and improved long after its initial writing only when the poet's shiseishin remains the same throughout the intervening time. He felt that too often a poet changes temperamentally as he grows older; he then attempts to improve his earlier work and ends up changing it for the worse. As examples of such unfortunate reworking, Sakutarō cited several poets he otherwise admired, including Yosano Akiko, who later detested and tried to revise the tanka of her youth. He felt that the only major poet in contemporary Japan who was discreet in this respect was Shimazaki Tōson.

How did Sakutarō himself write poems? To answer the question, we shall trace his creative process in two specific instances. The first resulted in the poem "The Corpse of a Cat"; the second, in "Howling Dog."

"The Corpse of a Cat" was first published in a magazine in 1924, during a period that Sakutarō later recalled as "the most depressing rainy season of my life." A man well over thirty with no job, he had been living a miserable life at his parents' home. Marital problems intensified his depression, for by the arrangement of his parents he had married a woman he hardly knew. According to his own description of his life with her, no love, understanding, or delicate sentiment was communicated between them; they were merely male and female, connected by sensual

desire, living together under the feudalistic family system. To
make the situation worse, children were born to them. Sakutarō
was mentally too exhausted to take any positive action; he would
simply lie sprawled on a sofa, dreaming of his dead sweetheart.
In his vision the dead woman, dressed in pink, roamed a graveyard on spring nights. He dreamed of his body dissolving to
nothing, whereupon his soul would go out to embrace her tearfully by the graves. The vision eventually crystallized into a
poem:

The Corpse of a Cat

In a spongy landscape
it is big and swollen, soaking wet.
No living creature is around
except a strangely sad waterwheel crying.
In the hazy shade of a willow
I see my sweet love waiting.
A thin shawl wrapping her body
and a lovely, vaporous garment trailing behind,
she wanders silent as a ghost.
Oh, Ura![3] Lonely woman!
"Darling, you are always late."
Possessing neither a past nor a future,
we have disappeared from *things real.* . . .
Ura!
In this odd landscape
please bury the corpse of the muddy cat.

Sakutarō left a later comment on the poem, in which he explained in detail several of its images:

Ura was my Ligeia. And the whole of my family life was "The Fall of the
House of Usher." Possessing neither a past nor a future, it had disappeared from "things real"; it was an unlucky, cursed, nihilistic existence—an existence like that of the House of Usher. That unlucky, ugly
existence is symbolized in the corpse of a muddy cat. "Ura! Don't touch
it with your hand!" So I always cried out in my dream, trembling with
an instinctive fear.

The note reveals the stages of inspiration and expression in
Sakutarō's creative process. He was inspired by a dream, or a series of dreams, during a time when he felt he could not bear his

[3] A Japanese word meaning "seacoast."

daily life. Through shiseishin, both his life and his longing were imaginatively removed from "things real" into a distorted and heightened realm, conceived in terms of exotic Western analogues. There, in the course of expression the poetic spirit "liquefied" the material of actual experience. The forms of longing condensed into the single figure "Ura," whose name suggests both the beauty and the loneliness of a remote seacoast. She was originally a young woman whom Sakutarō admired, but she was dead, purified by memory and transformed into a symbol of ideal love.[1] The opposite forms, the repugnant experiences of his married life, took shape in the image of the dead and muddy cat, projected into the visionary landscape. In the poem's final wish, Sakutarō beseeches the image of desire to bury that of reality and to free him from its burden.

At the stage of correction, Sakutarō made only one significant change in the poem. When he republished it in 1928, 1929, 1936, and 1939, he made almost no internal revisions (except for minor changes in punctuation and spacing), but in the 1936 version he added a subtitle, "To a Woman Called Ula." This meant that the name of the woman, which appears twice in the body of the poem, has to be read "Ula" also, even though the Japanese language has no liquid consonant "l." After making the revision, Sakutarō emphasized the importance of this aural effect. As he explained, "The poem's motif is embodied mainly in the sound of the name 'Ula.' A reader who is sensitive enough to the sound to catch its musical sentiment will be able to grasp the poem's main theme clearly. A reader whose sensitivity falls short of that will not be able to understand the general meaning of the poem." The motif is "a musical image of nostalgia like a wind coming from a desolate graveyard." *Ura* ("Seacoast") already evokes a sense of beauty and loneliness; the sound "Ula" may create such a "musical image" because the substitution of the consonant "l," which does not exist in Japanese, makes the name sound even more otherworldly to Japanese ears. "Ula"

---

[1] The woman's name was Baba Naka; Sakutarō nicknamed her Elena. She died in 1917 at the age of 27.

may also evoke associations of Ulalume and the nocturnal world of Poe's poetry to which Sakutarō referred in his note. In any event, Sakutarō must have been absolutely certain that "Ula" was better than "Ura," because he was extremely cautious about revising a poem after a considerable length of time, and twelve years had elapsed between the first publication of the poem and the addition of the subtitle.

Sakutarō was, of course, less cautious about revision while he was still in the process of composing a poem. Probably he made more than one draft before he initially published "The Corpse of a Cat" in 1924, although the drafts have not been preserved. Our next example, "Howling Dog," focuses on revisions he made during the initial process of composition.

We do not know what specifically motivated Sakutarō to write this poem. Its origins apparently date back to 1914, when he was an especially ardent admirer of Nietzsche, so the image of a howling dog may have originated in a similar image in *Thus Spake Zarathustra.*[5] At any rate, a vision of a dog came to him one day in late 1914, and he tried to record it in his notebook:

> On a moonlit night
> a dog
> runs round a willow tree.
> The dog has sensed something.
> His soul glows luminously
> like fluorescent light.

Soon after writing this down, he went about transforming it into a better poem. His notebook shows that he changed a number of words until he settled on this second draft:

Dog

On a moonlit night
a dog runs round { a willow tree.
                  { a tombstone in the graveyard.
The dog howls at the distant center of this globe.
He has sensed his master's safe hidden deep in the impene-
    trable earth,

[5] The image of a howling dog appears in Chapter 46, "The Vision and the Enigma."

a safe filled with nephrites and noctilucent stones.
The howling dog has a soul that glows white, its heart radi-
ating fluorescence through the body.
The pale dog struggles to dig the hard surface of the earth
with his forepaws,
a dog who has clearly sensed something that faintly stirs in
the far, far netherworld.
The dog, wailing and sick, struggles to dig up something he
has sighted on a moonlit night.

This is quite a substantial elaboration on the initial image of a
dog running around a willow tree. The flash of inspiration being
over, Sakutarō seems to have begun to grope for the meaning of
the insight, using intellect as well as emotion. In the main, he appears to have tried to see what it was that the dog in his initial
inspiration had sensed, and subsequently he introduced a safe
loaded with nephrites and other luminous stones. This and similar elaborations transform the impressionistic poem of the first
draft into the metaphysical poem of the second.

The poem went through further extensive revisions. It was
first published in the February 1915 issue of the magazine *Poetry*
in the following form:

Howling Dog

On a moonlit night, a dog runs round a tombstone in the
graveyard,
The dog howls at the distant center of this globe.
For he has sensed his master's safe hidden deep in the impenetrable earth, a safe he knows is filled with nephrites
and noctilucent stones.
The howling dog has a soul that glows white, his heart ra-
diating fluorescence through the body.
This pale dog struggles to dig the hard surface of the earth
with his forepaws, for he has sensed something that faintly
stirs in the far, far netherworld.
The howling dog, wailing and sick, struggles to dig up something he has clearly sighted in the graveyard on a moonlit
night.

The howls are poetry.
You, a loyal, sensitive, and yet utterly lonesome dog! You
keep howling, until you are shot by your callous neighbor
or until you starve to death, telling of mystery to your
last breath.
The howling dog is the poet on a pale moonlit night.

Here the willow tree is completely gone. Apparently Sakutarō decided to write another poem centering on that image; entitled "About a Willow Tree," it was published in the same issue of *Poetry* as was "Howling Dog." A more significant change is the addition of another stanza, in which Sakutarō identifies the dog as a poet and the dog's howl as poetry. It is as if he had a firmer grasp of the import of his initial inspiration. The identification clarifies considerably the meaning of the poem, but at the same time it limits that meaning, too.

Revisions were not as extensive in the fourth version of the poem, but they were no less significant:

Howling Dog

On a moonlit night, a dog roams the graveyard.
The dog howls at the distant center of this globe.
For he has sensed a safe hidden deep in the impenetrable earth,
a safe he knows is filled with nephrites and noctilucent stones.
The howling dog has a soul that whitely glows and radiates fluorescence from his heart.
This pale dog struggles to dig the hard surface of the earth with his forepaws,
for he has sensed something that faintly stirs in the far, far netherworld.
The howling dog, grieving and frenzied, struggles to dig up something he has clearly sighted in the graveyard on a sorrowful moonlit night.

The howling dog is man.
You, a loyal, sensitive, yet utterly lonesome dog!
You keep howling until you are shot by a neighbor who has a sick child.
The howling dog is man on a pale moonlit night.

Sakutarō decided to change "the poet" to "man." This significantly broadens the implications of the poem, which then portrays the plight not just of the poet but of all men possessed by shiseishin. Sakutarō was satisfied with this version and did not revise the poem any more in subsequent publications, except for slight changes in punctuation.

The process by which "Howling Dog" developed reveals the passivity of the poet in the initial stage of verse writing, as well as his positive efforts in subsequent stages. A subconscious flash of insight occurs, and he himself does not understand its full meaning at the time. He can only jot down the vision. As he contemplates it, he gradually comes to understand its significance. The vision, intuitively perceived, is now studied in his mind, both intellectually and emotionally. Expression helps the study, for words clarify thoughts. Through many drafts, in a conscious, deliberate effort, the poet then carries out the process of fully understanding his thought as he transforms it into words.

Sakutarō eloquently summed up this process in a letter he wrote to a friend in March 1917, shortly after the publication of *Howling at the Moon*:

> I am practically blind to my own poem at the time of its creation. I do not know what I am singing about. The thoughts or emotions I harbor in my mind, or what I am trying to write, all are beyond my comprehension. I simply pick up a rhythm flowing at the bottom of my heart and follow it automatically. At the time of creating a poem, therefore, I am half-conscious, merely an automated machine. Even after completing the poem, I am often unable to grasp the core of thought or emotion embodied in it. Hence, I feel I am not entitled to talk about my poem immediately after its composition. But, strangely enough, as time passes (say, a few months or a year) I come to clearly understand the core of the poem's thought without effort on my part.

Beauty Aspires to a Body

Sakutarō was more deeply concerned with the issues of literary criticism than were most other contemporary poets. He wrote many articles both expounding his idea of poetry and explicating poems written by other poets, and he published two books of practical criticism, *Masterpieces of Tanka on Love* and *Yosa Buson: A Poet of Nostalgia*, which offered his interpretations of selected tanka and haiku. Although he never published a similar book on shi, his critical comments on free-style poems frequently appeared in literary magazines. He was a regular columnist for several magazines at one time or another, and when asked also lectured on such topics as "The Appreciation and Interpretation of Poetry."

Sakutarō was one of the first Japanese critics to recognize multiple levels of meaning in a poem and to conceive positive significance in a meaning not consciously intended by the poet. This was so because he was aware of the poet's passivity in the initial stage of the creative process. "In all cases the best interpreter of a poem is not the poet but the reader," he conceded. "The poet is like a sleepwalker; he is not cognizant of what he has written." The main responsibility for interpretation lies not with the poet but with the reader. Of course, readers' literary sensibilities differ, allowing for widely different interpretations of the same poem. Sakutarō once compared this variation to two people listening to the same piano piece by Chopin: one listener might hear in the music the patter of rain, whereas another might associate it with a series of gunshots. Sakutarō's conclusion about reading poetry was that there was no right or wrong interpretation, that there were merely "shallow" and "profound" ones.

The principal question, then, is what makes an interpretation shallow or profound. Sakutarō mentioned three criteria: a correct understanding of vocabulary, empathy, and a grasp of the poetic sentiment. As for the first, each word has a history of usage in literature, and the profundity of an interpretation depends upon the extent to which the reader is aware of that history as well as upon the degree of appropriateness with which he identifies a specific use in a given poem. The second and third criteria also seem to refer to an understanding of what is appropriate in a given poem: an interpretation is profound, Sakutarō implies, in proportion to the degree to which it empathizes with the poetic sentiment embodied in the poem. But what is meant by "poetic sentiment"? The original Japanese word is *shijō, shi* meaning "poem" and *jō* meaning "sentiment," "emotion," or "heart." *Shijō* comes close to the meaning of shiseishin except that it refers to a sentiment particularized in the context of a given poem. In other words, shiseishin is the spirit of poetry; shijō, the spirit of a specific poem. Sakutarō suggests that an interpretation is profound when it is based on a reader's empathy with shijō, and thus with the shiseishin lying beneath. When the reader fails to empathize, his reading will be superficial.

Because shiseishin is critical of reality and longs for a transcendental world, the poetic sentiment manifest in an individual
poem tends to be idealistic in its implications, too. A critic wishing to come up with a profound interpretation of a poem will
need to empathize with that idealistic mood. In the following
two instances, Sakutarō the critic operates on that principle.
The first example centers on a haiku by Buson:

> When we join our palms
> together and scoop it, how
> muddy the water grows!

Premodern annotators gave a didactic interpretation to the
poem. In their view, this haiku teaches that an act that is blameless when done by one man may become complicated or even
corrupt ("muddy") when he is joined by others. Sakutarō would
not want to say this interpretation was wrong, but he had a totally different one. As he saw it, the haiku embodied Buson's
nostalgia for childhood: the aging poet fondly remembered a
bygone day in spring when he and a little girl played together by
a stream. Clearly Sakutarō's reading is based on empathy with
Buson's heart, which he believed often yearned for the idyllic,
innocent world of his happy childhood.

The next instance is also a haiku, this one by Chiyo (1703–75):

> The piercing wind:
> in the screen, there still remain
> holes poked by a finger.

Sakutarō referred to two extant readings of the poem. According to the first explication, the haiku concerns the sorrow of poverty: the poet is too poor to have her sliding screens repaired,
and consequently the cold wind comes in through the holes. In
contrast, the second interpretation sees the poet as mourning
over her lost child. The child, once so vivacious and mischievous,
is dead and gone, leaving only the holes he made in the screens
with his fingers. Sakutarō sided with the second interpretation,
empathizing with the mother who longed for a nonexistent
being. To him, the first reading seemed superficial because that
empathy was lacking.

Sakutarō used the principle of empathy as the main criterion throughout both his critical commentaries and his books of practical criticism. Two examples from *Masterpieces of Tanka on Love* demonstrate how it applies to tanka. The first is an anonymous poem included in *The Collection of Ancient and Modern Poems*:

> When evening comes
> I gaze at the banner-shaped clouds
> and think of things
> as my heart yearns for a woman
> living in the distant sky.

Of this tanka, Sakutarō wrote, "Evening clouds, shaped like banners, hang in the sky over the distant horizon. His beloved lives in the place where the doleful sun sinks, across far-off mountains and cities that loom as if in a dreamland. His love is a piece of music: it is a nostalgic melody played to the lonely evening sky. A person in love is a philosopher whose soul calls to an ideal existence, an Idea that lies at the end of space and time." The originality of this explication appears when it is compared to the usual interpretation, which takes the woman to be a noble lady who far outranks the poet. In his reading, Sakutarō made a real woman into an ideal one.

Sakutarō gave an even more imaginative interpretation to a group of tanka on the sea included in *The Collection of Ten Thousand Leaves*. Although they are not love poems, he was so attracted to them that he decided to include them in his book. Here is one of the seven poems he cited:

> As I stand and gaze
> from the shore of Sahika
> in Kii Province,
> lights on the fishermen's boats
> flicker amid the waves.

The poem is little more than a fragment from a traveler's diary. At a certain coastal town one evening, the traveler went out to the shore and watched the lights of fishing boats on the sea; the scene was so beautiful he wrote a tanka. But Sakutarō, commenting on this and six other undistinguished tanka on the sea, observed:

Sea poems in *The Collection of Ten Thousand Leaves* all create a mysteriously solemn music, sounding like a boundless ocean that lies in the
distance. They lead us to a vague feeling of nostalgia, the kind we feel
when we put a seashell to our ear and hear the sound of the ocean. In
my opinion, those ancient people expressed such nostalgia in their
poems on the sea because they had inherited memories from their ancestors who migrated from the continent across the sea. The nostalgia
stemmed from their recollections of the distant homeland they had
never seen.

This is an ingenious interpretation. At work is Sakutarō's idea
that true poetic nostalgia reaches after sensations at the bounds
of consciousness, sensations sparked by the underlying forms
of archetypal Ideas or by the inchoate stirrings of inherited
memory.

As a critic, Sakutarō awarded high acclaim to poems that he
thought showed ample nostalgia. For that reason he considered
Buson the greatest of all haiku poets, although he respected
Bashō, too. Among classical tanka poets, he especially favored
Priest Saigyō (1118–90) and Princess Shikishi (?–1201). At the
other end of the scale, he disliked the haiku of Shiki and his followers, since he thought they did nothing but copy physical reality. And he did not like poetry written by novelists, such as Ihara
Saikaku (1642–93) and Ozaki Kōyō (1867–1903), because again
he thought they were more concerned with actual rather than
transcendental reality. He praised Takuboku for his "wanderer's
nostalgia," but condemned other contemporary tanka poets for
having lost true shiseishin. Possibly the most brutal attack in
Sakutarō's critical writings is directed at *One Hundred Best Tanka
of the Shōwa Period*, a widely publicized collection of 31-syllable
poems by leading contemporary poets. "Their signboards say
'Shasei-ism' and 'Empathic Observation of Reality,' sounding as if
they were following some profound poetic principles," he wrote.
"But in practice they are no different from a modish photographer who, showing off his expensive Leica, takes many pictures
of an unimpressive landscape and boasts of his photographic
skill."

In retaliation, Sakutarō was attacked by other critics and scholars, to whom his critical comments seemed highly idiosyncratic.

His book on Buson was especially controversial, because Buson had never before been considered "a poet of nostalgia." An example will illustrate the nature of the controversy:

> White plum blossoms . . .
> Who was it? Since olden days,
> outside the fence.

In his book on Buson, Sakutarō took the plum blossoms to symbolize a lover. According to him, as a sensitive young boy Buson felt as though a maiden, beautiful and pure as white blossoms, were standing outside his fence, and that feeling still remained in his memory after a great many years. "On a spring day," Sakutarō wrote, "he felt nostalgia for a spiritual homeland existing somewhere in the universe, and he longed for the eternal soulmate he had never seen."

In his review of the book, the haiku poet Itō Gessō (1899–1946) declared that Sakutarō had completely misread the poem. In Gessō's reading, Buson was simply looking at white plum blossoms and wondering who had built the fence near the tree. Buson felt uncomfortable about the tree's being *outside* the fence, and that uneasiness became the motive for writing the haiku. Reading Gessō's interpretation, Sakutarō was astounded. When he responded to the review in an essay entitled "On Interpreting Haiku," he did not insist on the superiority of his own reading, but he clearly had little sympathy with Gessō's interpretation.

Which interpretation is more valid? Sakutarō's identification of plum blossoms with an adolescent lover is imaginative and poetic, but there is simply too little internal evidence to support it. If Buson intended the poem to mean what Sakutarō said, he would have included some small hint to indicate that the blossoms stood for a maiden. Gessō's interpretation, on the other hand, seems too prosaic. It makes Buson into an amateur gardener who is curious about the position of the fence in relation to the tree. An explication that is at once poetic and faithful to the wording of the poem might take the haiku as expressing Buson's curiosity about the origin of the plum tree. Gazing at the beautifully blossoming tree, Buson wondered who had planted it outside the fence. He probably thought the tree had grown there by itself, for the owner of the house would have planted it *inside* the fence. In any event, while at the scene Buson must have mused on his own past—his home, his boyhood, and perhaps his adolescent love—for white plum blossoms, one of the most familiar flowers for Japanese children, lead one to recollect one's childhood. To that extent, Sakutarō had a point.

Thus although Sakutarō advocated empathizing with the sentiment of a poem, too often he sought nostalgia, the poetic spirit of longing for an ideal world, in any poem on which he commented. Intent on finding that spirit, he at times stretched the meaning of a word or phrase, or read too much into a poem. Yet if a poem was by an idealistic poet, Sakutarō's imaginative insight reached deep into its core. More through empathy than through analysis, he grasped the aspiration lurking almost imperceptibly in the poem. Controversial as it was, his book on Buson helped awaken Japanese scholars, who had been inclined to rely too much on historical and biographical criticism.

In the final analysis, for Sakutarō the beauty of poetry is equivalent to the beauty of nostalgia. One of his most haunting statements of that belief, fundamental to both his own verse writing and his criticism of others' work, is an aphorism entitled "Beauty." "Beauty does not own a body," he wrote. "It is for this reason that every beautiful thing—a piece of music, a poem, a landscape—is as sad as romantic love. Beauty is nostalgia for a body it does not own."

Versification in a Rhythmless Language

Foremost among the hints about Sakutarō's idea of poetic form included in the previous discussion is the aphorism "Poetry demands form. Hence shiseishin is essentially normative." By seeking a form beyond the raw material of experience and feeling, the medium of poetry echoes the poet's spiritual search, inspired by shiseishin, for a homeland of the soul beyond the flux of life in the everyday world. Like a Platonic Idea, form could be conceived as an ideal shape, a norm that the poet discovers underlying its contingent manifestation in the things that actually surround him. However, in his writings on poetic form Sakutarō takes another course. He concentrates not on the shaping power of poetry but on rhythm, the element that dissolves discreet objects and words in the flow of sound and feeling that constitutes the whole. His idea of form, like his critical emphasis, is thus governed by nostalgia—not by an attempt to define and communicate metaphysical truth, but by an urge to sing out the yearning that impels the poet to seek sensuous experience of that truth in vision and waking dream.

Sakutarō's concept of rhythm is a complex and sometimes confusing one. He used the term many times in his critical writings, not always in the same sense. His most coherent statement on the topic is an article entitled "On Rhythm," in which he attempted to clarify the concept for others, as well as for himself. There he distinguished between two kinds of rhythm, one in a narrow and the other in a broad sense. According to his definition, rhythm in the narrow sense is "a flow of melodies," a temporal movement of sounds that produces an intended emotional effect. It is the prime formative element of music. Applied to language, it designates a regulated flow of accents, beats, and other phonetic elements. As for rhythm in the broad sense, Sakutarō termed it variously "emotive rhythm," "metaphysical rhythm," and "shapeless rhythm." This rhythm resides in all things beautiful—whether painting or sculpture or scenic landscapes—and stirs the spectator's mind to soar toward the higher world. It does not have to be aural; it can be an arrangement of colors, forms, or any other sensory stimulants that produce an aesthetic response. When used in reference to language, it denotes a flow of verbal nuances. To simplify terminology, I will call the former "auditory rhythm" and the latter "emotive rhythm" in the following pages. Sakutarō concluded that much of the confusion in the current use of the word "rhythm" was caused by an inability to distinguish between the two.

In Sakutarō's opinion, a syllabic pattern did not constitute a rhythm in the narrow sense. Thus the Japanese language, which has no accentual stress, must be considered lacking in auditory rhythm; if auditory rhythm is a prerequisite of verse, then Japanese can be a vehicle for prose but not for verse. This logic led Sakutarō to conclude that all Japanese poetry had been written in a rhythmless language—prose. As he said, "Japanese poetry is totally different from the poetry of other countries. . . . In Japan, there is no such thing as verse in the true sense of the term."

Sakutarō felt that past Japanese poets, because their language lacked auditory rhythm, were forced to explore and to utilize emotive rhythm. According to him, the rhythm in tanka and haiku is largely of this type. "Frankly, I must say," he once wrote, "that of the total emotional impact of a Japanese poem, 70 percent is derived from nuance and 30 percent from rhythm." By "rhythm" he meant auditory rhythm: he thought that in classical Japanese poetry 70 percent of the rhythm was emotive, and only 30 percent auditory. Among the examples he offered to demonstrate his point was the following:

Inazuma ga	Lightning
tōku no sora de	in the distant sky
hikatteru	flashes.

Sakutarō rightly observed that this is neither haiku nor poetry, even though it has the 5–7–5 pattern. As far as he was concerned, it was a plain prose sentence. In order to make it into a haiku, he suggested the following change:

Inazuma ya	Lightning:
tōku no sora no	in the distant sky,
usuakari	a faint flash.

The main difference, he explained, was the particle *ya*, which creates a caesura. The verbal flow temporarily stops at the end of the first line, making it possible for the following words to rise to an emotional height and refresh the mood. Sakutarō stressed that the effect is attained psychologically, not through any aural quality.

This example illustrates Sakutarō's point conveniently, but it is not a good haiku, as he knew. His favorite examples were poems by Bashō and Princess Shikishi. Here are two of them, the first a haiku by Bashō:

Araumi ya   The wild sea:
Sado ni yokotau   extending over Sado Isle,
amanogawa   the River of Heaven.

Sakutarō remarked, "The sublime effect created by this poem does not come from its auditory rhythm. Aurally it is a monstrous-sounding poem, consisting of all even-toned words. Nevertheless it has an extraordinary appeal because in it the reader tastes the nuances of such words as *araumi ya* ('the wild sea') and *yokotau* ('extending'). To put it another way, here verbal nuance has been substituted for rhythm, serving the same function." He probably was referring to the artful sequence and interplay of the delicate shades of meaning implied in the individual words that constitute the poem. The word *araumi*, for instance, does not mean just a sea that has become wild because of a storm; it implies a sea that has been wild for eons because of its geographic location. The nuance complements the sense of permanence evoked by the images of Sado Island and the Milky Way. *Yokotau*, literally "horizontally lying," makes one think of a long bridge extending from the seashore to the distant island and beyond. It is as if the heart of the poet standing on the shore went out to an infinite distance where the sky and the sea merged.

The second example is a tanka by Princess Shikishi:

Show me the way,
Wind, through the eightfold waves
of this markless sea.
My rowboat is astray, not
knowing which way you blow.

This is a love poem, the wind symbolizing a man whose feelings toward the poetess are painfully ambivalent. Sakutarō, as usual, found nostalgia in the poem—in a woman desperately attracted to a lover who lived far beyond the ocean. He felt that the nostalgia was presented entirely through the music of words, and analyzed that music: "The music played here is not the kind that is heard through the ear. It is complex music that emerges through a combination of meanings embodied in different semantic units. After all, music in poetry is nothing other than a symphony unifying all elements of the language (tones, moods, associations, colors, thoughts, and so on)." The parenthetical comment reveals the nonauditory linguistic elements that Sakutarō felt constituted emotive rhythm.

Despite his emphasis on emotive rhythm, Sakutarō did not completely rule out auditory rhythm in Japanese poetry. Having been interested in music since childhood, he sometimes went out of his way to seek musical qualities in Japanese poems. In articles such as "Rhythm in Tanka" and "Musical Qualities in Bashō's Haiku," he attempted to show how auditory rhythm helps to enhance the poetic effects of certain tanka and haiku. *Masterpieces of Tanka on Love, Yosa Buson: A Poet of Nostalgia*, and other critical works on classical Japanese poetry also are distinguished by attention to such qualities as rhyme, alliteration, and repetition of consonants or vowels—qualities that many traditional critics ignore. Sakutarō sometimes romanized a tanka or haiku to show more clearly what he thought was a deliberate arrangement of vowels and consonants. Some of his discoveries were quite original and represent definite contributions to Japanese literary scholarship.

Sakutarō believed that tanka had more potential for auditory rhythm than did haiku. With characteristic hyperbole he once asserted, "The difference between tanka and haiku can be compared to the contrast between the Dionysian and the Apollonian in poetry. Whereas shiseishin in tanka is sentimental and passionate and makes one feel a flaming fire, haiku has observant, wisdom-filled eyes that gaze at its subject calmly and discover what lies in the depths of nature." The perception of this difference led him to conclude, "Tanka and haiku, therefore, differ from each other as music and painting or romanticism and realism differ." Tanka is more lyrical and melodious, whereas haiku tends to be imagistic and to create visual comparisons or contrasts. Haiku is at its best when it tries to catch a momentary insight into the mystery of nature; tanka takes advantage of its greater length to vent the poet's overflowing emotion.

It is no wonder that Sakutarō, who yearned for auditory rhythm in poetry, chose to write tanka rather than haiku in his youth. Nevertheless, he stopped writing tanka and devoted his creative energy to free verse. In the end he gave up attempts to write in the traditional verse forms altogether. He had many reasons for doing so.

One was his increasingly skeptical attitude toward syllabic pattern as a device for creating rhythm. He came to feel that the 17- or 31-syllable form was only a superficial outer shell and that the true form resided in the inner emotive rhythm of the poem. If the syllabic pattern had little to do with the rhythm of the poem, it might as well be abandoned. Sakutarō demonstrated that the true rhythm of tanka or haiku was created not through syllabic pattern but through an arrangement of other linguistic factors. As we have seen, he observed that rhythm is created by the particle *ya* in the haiku

Inazuma ya	Lightning:
tōku no sora no	in the distant sky,
usuakari	a faint flash.

He then wrote two free-verse lines that he thought were rhythmically better than the haiku:

Inazuma su	Lightning flashes—
sora no tōki ni mie	in the distant sky.
Sora no tōki ni hikari	Flashing far in the sky,
inazuma su	lightning.

Sakutarō indicated that in these lines *su* and the *ri* in *hikari* create caesuras. These words spotlight the inner rhythm of the lines, obscured in the haiku by the outer rhythm of 5–7–5. Consequently, for Sakutarō the free-verse lines (although otherwise not markedly superior) created "clearer impressions" than did the haiku. Some of that clarity may have derived from the lines' fresh and modern sound, their freedom from traditional values.

Another reason for Sakutarō's rejection of tanka and haiku was the fixed lengths of these forms. The fact that they do not allow a poet to write a long poem disturbed him. Pondering why the Japanese had written almost no long poems, he found the answer in the nature of the language: syllabic patterns, the prime auditory element in Japanese poetry, would be too monotonous in a long poem. Tanka, in his view, was the longest possible verse form in Japanese that could effectively avoid monotony. "Try adding to tanka one more 5–7 line," he challenged. "Tension will be gone, and the reader will find the rhythm monotonous and dull." It would be the same, he continued, if a poet used a 6–4 or an 8–4 pattern. The only solution would be to mix 7–5, 6–4, 8–5, and other syllabic patterns in a single poem, which would be the same as writing a poem in prose. Thus he arrived at a paradoxical conclusion: "In Japanese, the more prosaic the language is, the closer it approaches verse." Free verse, written in a mixture of various syllabic patterns— that is, in prose—seemed freer from monotony and hence more poetically rhythmical than tanka and haiku.

A more extrinsic social factor made Sakutarō lean toward free verse, too. He was keenly aware of the rapid Westernization taking place in all phases of Japanese life, and he found tanka and haiku incapable of adequately serving the emotional needs of a twentieth-century Japanese. He explained, "Whether or not we like the West, the fact remains that Japan is being Westernized today. We have been educated at Western-style schools where Western science, Western music, and other such subjects are taught. The books we read are all Western thoughts translated into Japanese. . . . Naturally our tastes and sentiments are becoming Westernized. That is a fact of life in contemporary Japan." In his opinion, the Westernization of Japanese poetry was socially inevitable. And, unlike Shiki, he felt tanka and haiku were too much a part of the Japanese cultural tradition to be Westernized. Undoubtedly referring to Shiki and his followers, he remarked, "Some may insist that from tanka and haiku we can inherit just verse forms and replace the traditional content with the sentiments of our new age. In all the arts, however, form reflects content. If today's poetic sentiments are not traditional ones, which they are not, there must necessarily be a new form to express them." By "a new form" he meant shi. A verse form invented for translating European poems into Japanese, shi was the form most suitable for articulating the Westernized sentiments of a modern Japanese poet. Without it, Sakutarō thought, the vital sentiments of modern Japanese life could not be expressed.

Sakutarō was disturbed by the comments of foreign visitors who did not seem to understand that fact. Once he was irritated at a lecture given by Georges Bonneau, an eminent French specialist on Japan, who praised classical Japanese poetry highly and criticized recent Japanese efforts to emulate Western poetry. He likened Bonneau's remark to a comment by Jean Cocteau, who wondered why the Japanese came to substitute Western-style clothes for their beautiful kimonos in modern times. In Sakutarō's view, these foreigners did not understand the realities of contemporary Japanese life. "They are tourists," he said. "They are not residents of today's Japan."

The final and possibly the most important factor that contributed to Sakutarō's choice of free verse over tanka and haiku as his main poetic medium was the nature of his nostalgic impulse. He felt classical verse forms were too much a part of traditional Japan to allow a poet to soar toward the far-off land of his heart's desire. Sakutarō was attracted to Western-style shi, not only because the West represented the future of Japan, but also because Western poetry reflected a more dynamic culture. He explained:

The literary writings that we call poetry derive their basic spirit from "struggles with routine life." Poe and Baudelaire are obvious cases, but the spirit of all Western poetry lies in a hatred of "the routine" and in a longing for unrealistic Ideas and dreams. All poets are symbolists or transcendentalists or surrealists or romanticists or some other "-ists"; that is to say, they are all believers in some doctrine that rejects routine daily life. In contrast, all tanka and haiku derive their spirit from "conformity to routine life." Haiku in particular finds its subject matter in the familiar things of everyday life, such as an insect singing in the garden and the sound of water boiling in a teakettle. Such poeticizing of ordinary life presumes enjoyment of daily routine; underneath it lies an optimistic view of life native to Orientals. It is no wonder that in an age of anxiety like ours such a poetry of elegant beauty and leisurely pleasure has begun to bore readers.

Sakutarō was expressing a feeling shared by many progressively minded Japanese poets of his day. A poet who wrote haiku or tanka automatically placed his work against the background of the classical tradition—at least, that was how readers treated it. One may recall Akiko's plea that her tanka not be read in the light of the classical tradition; she had reason for her complaint. Sakutarō, feeling as she did, wanted to place his poetry outside the classical tradition altogether. In free verse, his nostalgic impulse could be expressed without being constrained by the practice of previous poets.

Yet the choice of free verse for his medium posed a serious challenge. Shi was still an experimental form, with a number of problems yet to be solved. The biggest of these was language. Sakutarō did not want to use classical Japanese, since he felt its expressive capacity was limited to the sentiments of premodern Japan. Modern spoken Japanese, on the other hand, was largely a practical language lacking in artistic maturity. Because it had not been used in literature for long, it had not developed a capacity to express complex psychological reality or delicate shades of meaning. Sakutarō said he even had difficulty finding a proper word for the personal pronoun "you" when writing a love poem in modern Japanese. Adding to the problem was the paucity of auditory rhythm, a deficiency that was greater in the modern language. Classical Japanese poets, knowing the weakness, did their best to improve the language and had succeeded to a degree, but no one had even made the attempt for modern Japanese, which was not yet half a century old. In terms of aural effects, classical Japanese was more resilient, more sonorous, simpler, and crisper, whereas its modern descendant seemed prosaic, slack, heavy, and pedestrian in comparison. Yet most twentieth-century poets were not even aware of the risk involved in using modern Japanese. The result was depressing. "I have read hundreds of free-verse poems written by today's poets," Sakutarō observed, "but I have yet to meet a poem that creates a rhythm so beautiful as to entice me to recite it aloud."

Sakutarō did recognize a small number of poets who were painfully conscious of the problem and trying to find a solution. Some of them were writers of what he termed "impressionistic prose"; they saw no possibility of creating auditory rhythm in modern Japanese and had abandoned any effort to do so in their free verse. Like haiku poets of the past, they turned their attention to creating imagistic, associational, and nonauditory poetry: their poems were to be seen, not to be read aloud. Other poets tried to find another route to a solution. Although well aware of the auditory poverty of modern Japanese, they still tried to make its musical qualities work in their poetry. The actual works of poetry by this second group were quite experimental and were not as successful as those written by the first.

In his own work, Sakutarō synthesized the efforts of both groups. In his first volume of poetry, he was primarily a member of the first one. "Most of my poems collected in *Howling at the Moon* have no charm from the viewpoint of rhythmical beauty," he himself observed. In the poems collected in *The Blue Cat*, on the other hand, he attempted to incorporate rhythmical charm as well. As we have seen, he thought 70 percent of the rhythm in Japanese was nonauditory and 30 percent auditory; he wanted to make the best of that 30 percent. In an essay appended to the first edition of *The Blue Cat*, he explained the rhythm of his free verse: "I make a comprehensive use of all the attributes of words —tone, tempo, nuance, mood, idea—as well as auditory rhythm. I try to create a symphony with words." In other words, he tried to synthesize auditory and emotive rhythms to enhance the total effect of a poem. He succeeded in that effort to a remarkable degree.

How Sakutarō did so can best be seen through actual examples, such as this poem from *The Blue Cat*:

Littoral Zone

I have strayed into a littoral zone
where horses and camels roam in the lonely sunlight.
There is neither a market
nor any other place to sell my blanket.
Without a single store
lonely tents line up on the sand.
How could I pass at such an hour!
Like dreadful weapons of the natives
curses hang all over.

The scenery grows dim and dark
as a weird gale whirls the sand.
I don't see any signboard,
and even if I could trade, that wouldn't help me much.
I would rather be a tired, lazy man
lying face up on the white sand.
Then I would go and seek a passionate love affair
with a dark-skinned girl.

As he tells us in his explication, Sakutarō wanted to write a "heart-rending lyric that incites nostalgia." He tried to do so through the music of words. "For that one purpose," he explained, "I used words as pliantly and as lyrically as possible, like the steel spring of a musical clock automatically unwinding." He deliberately repeated negative conjunctives, such as "neither" (*naishi*), "not able to" (*dekiwashinai*), and "without" (*naku*), which he thought had lazy, weary tones. He also made frequent use of tentative verb forms, such as "would go" (*ikō*), "would do" (*shiyō*), and "would be" (*iyō*) because he thought these words aurally created a feeling of indecisiveness, inaction, and ennui. He was fond of such words as "then" (*sōshite*), "like" (*yōni*), and "is there not?" (*aru de wa naika*), as they seemed to sound soft and lyrical to the ear. These sound effects were employed to create an auditory rhythm that resulted in a nostalgic mood. When that rhythm was combined with the image of a desolate littoral zone, there emerged an emotive rhythm appropriate to the meaning of the poem.

In effect, in "Littoral Zone" and other pieces in *The Blue Cat* Sakutarō added musical qualities to otherwise imagist poems. Other poets had written similar poems, but seldom had they paid such deliberate attention to the aural values of the modern Japanese words they used. Fortunately for Sakutarō, the slack, pedestrian, and "dull" rhythm of spoken Japanese matched the mood of ennui he wanted to create in the poems of *The Blue Cat*. He consciously looked for such words as *naishi* and *yōni* and used them so that not only their connotations but also their aural effects contributed to the impact of the poem. In this respect he was daringly experimental and, when successful, brilliantly original. Below are two more examples of how he expanded the poetic potential of modern spoken Japanese.

One is his use of the word "like" (*yōni*), a word that frequently appears in *The Blue Cat*. In ordinary speech it is a connective indicating a simile. Sakutarō felt the word sounded mysteriously soft and ambiguous, and he exploited that nuance poetically. For instance, in one of his poems he wanted to say:

> A quail, flapping its wings,
> flits over the tall wild roses.
> Likewise my heart
> wanders over the grassy wilderness.

He was able to cut the length of the section in half by a special use of *yōni*:

> Watakushi wa uzura no yōni habataki nagara
> sōshite take no takai noibara no ue o tobimawatta.

> Flapping my wings like a quail
> I flit over the tall wild roses.

The Japanese syntax is looser than the English, so that in the original there is more ambiguity as to who, the poet or the bird, is flitting over the moor. The conjunctive *yōni*, in bridging the two possible levels of meaning, blurs the borderline between the subjective and the objective, which is precisely what Sakutarō wanted. No one before him had used the modern Japanese word in this way.

An even more striking feature of Sakutarō's poetic language is onomatopoeia, which he used often in *The Blue Cat* as a way of bringing more aural elements into poetry. Fearing the intrusion of conventional associations, he consistently avoided using traditional Japanese onomatopoetic words, but invented new ones more appropriate to the moods of his poems. In a poem entitled "Cats," for instance, he had two felines meow *owaa* and *ogyaa*; the uncanny babylike meowing enhances the sick, weary, yet somehow erotic atmosphere of a spring night. In another poem, "Clock," he described the tolling of a clock in a dream, which he wanted to sound mysterious and dreamy, as if coming from an infinite distance. The result was the coinage *jibo-an-jan*. Similar inventions include *bumu bumu* for a fly's buzz, *tefu tefu* for a butterfly's flutter, *doobon doobon* for the firing of a cannon, *nowoaaru towoaaru yawaa* for a dog's bark, and *zushiri batari dotari batari* for the footsteps of marching soldiers. His personal favorite was *Too-Te-Cūr Too-Ru-Mour*[6] for a rooster's crow, which appears in one of the finest poems in *The Blue Cat*:

Rooster

Near daybreak
a rooster crows outside the houses.
That long, quivering cry—
it is Mother calling from the lonely countryside.
Too-Te-Cūr Too-Ru-Mour Too-Ru-Mour.

In the morning's cold bed
my soul flaps its wings.
A peek through the storm door's crack:
the outside is beginning to brighten.
Yet, near daybreak
a sorrow slips into my bed.
Over the hazy treetops
it is the rooster calling from the distant countryside.
Too-Te-Cūr Too-Ru-Mour Too-Ru-Mour.

My love!
My love!
In the shade of cold screens at twilight
I sense the faint scent of a chrysanthemum,
like the scent of an ailing soul,
the faint scent of a white chrysanthemum decaying.
My love!
My love!

Near daybreak
my heart wanders in the shade of a graveyard.
Oh, someone is calling me! How exasperating!
I can't stand this pale pink air.
Love!
Mother!
Come at once and turn off the light.
I hear the roar of a typhoon far out at the corner of the
    earth.
Too-Te-Cūr Too-Ru-Mour Too-Ru-Mour.

[6]This is Sakutarō's own romanization. The standard romanization would be *towotekuu toworumou.*

Sakutarō explained that in this poem he tried to put into words a mixture of frustration, sorrow, gloom, and other "sour" sentiments that many modern men feel as they lie awake in bed in the twilight of dawn. His aim being what it was, he felt the ordinary Japanese cock-crow, *kokekokkō*, would not fit the poem. To his ear, the repetition of the consonant "k" sounded too strong. He wanted the crow to sound more "quiet, doleful, distant, and suggestive." To produce that effect he chose to rely on "t" and eventually came up with *Too-Te-Cūr Too-Ru-Mour.*

Through Sakutarō's efforts, the language of Japanese poetry became auditory to an unprecedented degree. More than anyone else, he was aware of the limitations of modern spoken Japanese as a poetic language, yet he managed to use its aural effects most skillfully. In that respect the poems collected in *The Blue Cat* provide examples of the ultimate poetic potential of spoken Japanese.

Yet Sakutarō had to resort to classical Japanese when he began writing the poems for *The Ice Land.* He did not like doing so; indeed, he called the move a "shameful retreat." But he felt he had no alternative, because in *The Ice Land* he wanted to vent intense anger and hatred, and the rhythm of modern Japanese was too lax and weak for the purpose. In his previous volumes of poetry he wanted to articulate boredom and gloom, for which spoken Japanese provided an apt vehicle. Now needing to express intense anger, he had to return to classical Japanese, which sounds more sonorous and resolute, crisp and strong. He also liked the Chinese flavor of classical Japanese, with its many assimilated and contracted sounds.

Sakutarō's use of classical Japanese in *The Ice Land* was quite successful; as noted before, some critics consider it to be his best book of poetry. Still, to his last days Sakutarō seems to have been unhappy about the question of poetic language. His essay on the language of *The Ice Land*, written six years before his death, ends on a sad note: "After desperate attempts to discover a new language for Japanese poetry, I ended up returning to the age-old literary language. In doing so I abandoned my cultural mission

as a poet. I have aged. May new poets emerge and open a new
road, a road I failed to build in my time!"

A Pacesetter of Culture

Although much of his own poetry consists of lyrics that sing
out personal feelings and visions with no reference to current
social or political issues, Sakutarō's thoughts on the use of poetry
are distinguished by a strong belief in its social function. It was
not that he did not recognize the personal usefulness of poetry:
in the preface to *Howling at the Moon* he compared poetry to
a young maiden's consoling hand, and such comments on the
pleasures of verse writing are scattered throughout his work.
But there is no doubt that he wanted to see the prime function
of poetry in the much wider context of human history and civilization. That social function forms the major theme of a collection of essays entitled *The Poet's Mission*.

What is the poet's mission? In brief, Sakutarō's answer in his
essays was that a poet serves society as a "journalist." He explained, "A journalist's prime mission lies not merely in reporting news but in enlightening contemporaries with his pen, scru-
tinizing new cultural trends and taking leadership as a 'guide of
the public.' Likewise, a poet's mission goes beyond being a mere
versifier. Poets in the correct sense of the word are those who set
the trend of the times through their criticism of contemporary
civilization. 'Poet' and 'journalist,' in the words' most basic senses,
are synonymous." In his view, Goethe, Byron, and Victor Hugo
were journalists who heralded the intellectual current of their
time, Romanticism, whereas the Parnassians helped to guide
their age toward naturalism. In modern Japan, he considered
Akiko and Takuboku to be two outstanding examples of true
journalists. Akiko's romantic tanka, he felt, suggested the future
direction of the spirit of the age, whereas Takuboku's poetry
gave full expression to the despair and the revolutionary spirit
of contemporary young men who were born too late to live under the old morality and too soon to establish a new one. Unfortunately, journalism had fallen into the hands of profit-seeking

publishers in Sakutarō's own time, and poets were driven into hiding by commercial journalists. "Japanese poets are unfortunate," he observed. "But even more unfortunate are those men of letters who are being led not by poets but by businessmen." Sakutarō thought a poet could be a true leader of contemporary society because he believed poetry deeply affected the human mind. "Politics changes social institutions, and art changes human sentiments," he once said. "But social institutions are founded on human sentiments. Hence politics is a means for attaining the end of art, and not vice versa." Social and natural sciences affect the human psyche, too, but Sakutarō placed poetry above them. "As a rule, man's thought processes follow certain phases," he explained. "At first a vague vision emerges, then a more concrete idea follows, and finally a theoretical vindication is devised. The vague vision in the first phase is poetry, and the vindication in the last phase is science." He made the same point elsewhere in *The Poet's Mission*. "A poet intuitively feels truth," he said. "Whereas a philosopher *thinks*, a poet *feels*. And in all cases *feeling* precedes *thinking*." One is reminded of how Sakutarō, in writing a poem, first conceived a vision and then went on to elaborate it consciously.

The idea that feeling precedes thinking led Sakutarō to make another set of rankings. He felt a poet was more a forerunner of new culture than was an essayist or a novelist because poetry depended more on feeling. "If I compare culture to a mountain," he said, "poetry is located at its very summit, essays and criticism are perched halfway to the top, and prose fiction lies at its foot, adjacent to the plain where the general public resides. In the name 'PEN Club,' the order is poet-essayist-novelist, too." Despite the joke about PEN, he was serious about his list. In his view, a novelist can never be as purely subjective as a poet because he must mingle with the general public and depict the realities of contemporary society. A poet is different because, as Sakutarō said in his aphorism, "Poetry demands the noble and the rare. Hence shiseishin is essentially aristocratic (antidemocratic)." In his opinion, haiku and tanka are more like prose fiction in this respect; he thought these two traditional verse forms represented "conformity to routine life." In spite of Akiko's and Takuboku's innovations, many modern tanka and haiku derived their inspiration from traditional Japanese sentiments, taking their material from the familiar things of daily life. To Sakutarō, the poets who wrote these poems seemed to be leading the public back to premodern Japan, not toward the new, Westernized Japan of the future. They were people of feeling rather than thought, but their feelings were behind, not ahead of, the present age.

Ultimately, Sakutarō saw the use of poetry in its prophetic capacity. A poet can become a prophet because he is by nature a dreamer who, with his shiseishin, always tries to soar ahead of his age and civilization. Sakutarō wrote, "The best artist is also the best teacher of the public. The best teacher always has within him the most fervent longing for ideal beauty; he is by nature a poet. . . . By definition, a poet is a romantic, a man who has dreams. For that reason he is a pacesetter of culture and a leader of the public." Here is his syllogism: to be a good teacher one must be a prophet; a poet is by nature a prophet; therefore a poet is a good teacher.

Sakutarō's conception of the use of poetry contains a paradox, however. He used poetry's idealistic nature as grounds for claiming that it can be the best means of edifying the masses, but idealism often alienates the masses, as he indicated when he said shiseishin was antidemocratic. How can poetry be a pacesetter of culture when the general reading public is alienated from it? Sakutarō tended to blame the commercialism of his time for the diminished role of poetry in society. Writing well before the age of television, he predicted that the public would be increasingly attracted to visual communications media, neglecting the more painstaking method of reading. "What will become of literature in the future?" he asked. "In all likelihood literature will not die out. But from now on it will no longer enjoy the kind of prevalence and popularity it has had in the past. Literary works will retreat to a quiet room in the library where books on science and other scholarly subjects are shelved, and they will be sought only by a small group of select readers." Sakutarō fervently believed in the edifying power of poetry, but he also knew that in actuality the public would not take advantage of it. Thus his concept of the social usefulness of poetry turned into a dream, into wishful thinking not firmly grounded in social reality. He was a dreamer even in his conception of the use of poetry.

CHAPTER FIVE

Miyazawa Kenji

S ECLUDED FROM THE mainstream of modern Japanese verse, Miyazawa Kenji (1896–1933) was almost totally unknown as a poet during his lifetime. He published few poems in magazines of nationwide literary reputation, and for his one published book of poetry and single collection of children's stories he shouldered all publication costs himself. After his death, however, his works soon gained a large following of people from all walks of life. Six different periodicals have been founded by different groups exclusively to study his works. Although literary critics still find it difficult to place him in the history of modern Japanese poetry, his faithful readers could not care less, nor could his posthumous publishers. Five different editions of his complete works have been published, the latest matched in its comprehensiveness only by Sakutarō's among modern poets.

The charms of Kenji's poetry are manifold: his high idealism, his intensely ethical life, his unique cosmic vision, his agrarianism, his religious faith, and his rich and colorful vocabulary. But ultimately they are all based in a dedicated effort to unify the heterogeneous elements of modern life into a single, coherent whole. Kenji stood in solitary opposition to all the other major poets of his time, who as modern intellectuals suffered one or another kind of dichotomy within the self. By training he was an agricultural chemist, and he considered it his heaven-sent work to mingle with farmers in the open fields and to give them expert advice on soil conditioning. He was also a devout Buddhist of the Hokke sect who wanted to propagate the teaching of the Lotus Sutra as widely as possible. He was a man of science, religion, and poetry; yet his mental energy was of such a centripetal nature that he could unify them all. Furthermore, that mental energy was not satisfied until it took a physical form in daily life. Kenji was a whole man, and therein lies the basic charm of his poetry.

In Search of the Galaxy Within

Kenji wrote many works directly or indirectly touching on the nature of literature. A story called "The Dragon and the Poet," for instance, presents his concept of poetry in the form of a Buddhist parable; several fairy tales, such as "Grape Juice" and "A Night in the Oak Grove," reveal what he thought of the origin of poetry, music, and dance; and an aphoristic essay entitled "Agrarian Art: An Outline" sums up the idea of art he came to conceive in his later years. Most significant of all, however, is the prefatory poem to *Spring and Asura*,[1] the only collection of verse published during his lifetime. Here he directly addressed his prospective readers and explained his concept of poetry, which he knew was radically different from the prevailing ones. He wanted a reader to digest his preface before venturing into the anthology, and we too shall begin our discussion with this poem.

The poem, appropriately called "Proem," consists of five stanzas. The first reads:

> The phenomenon called I
> is a blue light
> coming from the temporary, organic AC lamp
> (a synthesis of all transparent spirits).
> With the landscape and with everybody
> it incessantly blinks
> yet never stops glowing:
> a light
> from the karmic AC lamp
> (the light remains, the lamp vanishes).

The stanza metaphorically defines a poet: he is a light shining out across, or rather with, the landscape. But that light is from an AC lamp, a lamp whose constant glowing is in fact an inces-

---

[1] Published in 1924. "Asura" was originally used in ancient India to designate certain nature gods, but different sects of Hinduism and Buddhism later gave it

sant blinking, although so little time elapses between each blink that we are not aware of the light's other truth, the darkness.

Despite its imagery from modern technology, the stanza portrays the poet from a Buddhist perspective. Both the significance of the karmic AC lamp and its Buddhist background are made clearer in one of Kenji's fantasies for children, "A Night on the Galactic Railway."[2] In the story, young Giovanni is grieving over the disappearance of his schoolmate Campanella. At that point, a pale-faced man appears, wearing a large black hat and carrying a dictionary. After telling the boy how knowledge of history and geography changes through the ages (an impermanence not unlike what Giovanni has just experienced in the loss of his friend), the scholar raises one finger and then lowers it. In the next instant,

> Giovanni saw that he and his thoughts, along with the train, the scholar, the Milky Way, and all else, glowed brightly, faded out, glowed again, faded again, and when one of the lights glowed there spread out the whole wide world with all its history, but when it faded there was nothing but empty darkness. The blinking grew faster and faster, until everything was back as before.

Giovanni's vision seems a comprehensive view of fundamental reality. As he himself, his thoughts, his surroundings, and all of human history in turn glow, then fade to empty darkness, they come to be like the AC lamp. In faster and faster alternation, he sees both the fundamental emptiness underlying all phenomena and the transitory existence of himself and all the world fuse into samsara, the stream of appearances comprising repeated births and deaths that is reality as we ordinarily know it, "everything . . . back as before." Giovanni's vision reveals the unity of phenomenal world and empty darkness in the ongoing process of constant transformation or change.

To return to the "Proem," the "temporary, organic AC lamp"

---

widely different meanings. In Mahayana Buddhism, asura are believed to be demons ranking between humans and beasts.

[2] This episode is included in what appears to be the first draft of the story. It may have been cut in later versions, but the author's intent cannot be ascertained because no definitive draft exists.

seems a comparable vision of a reality that is at once plenum and void. It is explicitly linked to the Buddhist concept of karma, the accumulation of deeds, intentions, and events that continually works itself out through the cycles of cosmic history and thus powers the revolutions of samsara. Yet the poet's spiritual essence (at one with all other "transparent spirits" in the absolute mind that contains and creates all beings), although it at present seems determined by the organic lamp of the karmic world, is finally independent of samsara in the absolute mind that forms its ultimate reality, along with that of all other creatures: "the light remains, the lamp vanishes."

In the second stanza and throughout the rest of the poem, Kenji gives his own twist to this Buddhistic image of self and world in the manner in which he conceives of its realization in time and in his poetry. He continues:

> These have come from a period of 22 months
> that I feel lies in the direction of the past.
> By bringing paper and mineral ink together
> (it blinks with me
> and is felt simultaneously by everybody)
> I have preserved until now
> each chain of shade and light
> in these imagery sketches.

The key phrase here for describing Kenji's poetry is "imagery sketches," a phrase Kenji considered important enough to print as a subtitle on the cover of *Spring and Asura*. He deliberately avoided using the term "poems," since he felt his sketches were different from ordinary poems. In a letter to a friend he wrote, "What I have published in *Spring and Asura*, what I have written between then and now, all of those are definitely not poetry. They are no more than rough sketches of images I have drawn on various occasions in preparation for a certain project in psychology, which I would very much like to complete, although I do not have time to undertake a full-scale study." What Kenji called "imagery sketches," then, differ from ordinary poetry in two ways. First, they are not finished products but rough drafts, and since they have not yet received the poet's finishing touches, they are closer to the immediate thoughts and sensations in his mind. Second, Kenji's imagery sketches, besides recording what lies in his mind, also duplicate what lies in the minds of everyone else. His presupposition is that the imagery sketches he draws portray what is common to the human race in general, since like all people he is but a transitory creation out of the pure and absolute mind that is true reality.

This second point is elaborated in the third stanza, since Kenji apparently felt a need for further explanation:

> From these, men and the galaxy and asura and sea urchins
> as they eat cosmic dust or breathe air or seawater
> may each think up a fresh cosmology,
> but ultimately all is a mental landscape.
> These scenes, clearly recorded,
> are the records of scenes as they were.
> If they show the void, it is the void as it was
> and is shared to some degree by all people.
> (For everything is within me, within my inner everybody
> and likewise within everybody else.)

The stanza's first line reminds us that although the Milky Way and sea urchins possess different habits and follow different life cycles, they are one with men in being manifestations of the cosmic mind, the primal reality of the cosmos. Kenji's sketches are not, then, depictions of external objects as observed by the poet but records of internal images and sensations that reflect this greater mind. There is no borderline between the subjective and the objective, nor is there a division between man and inanimate things. Imagery sketches are the records of this nondivisive consciousness.

The fourth stanza, a long one, reintroduces the element of time:

> However, it is theoretically conceivable
> that these seemingly accurate verbal records
> made amid the piles of massive, bright time
> in the alluvial epoch of the Cenozoic era
> have already changed their structures and qualities
> in what to them is a momentary blink
>   (or asura's one billion years)
> and yet neither my printers nor I

have noticed the change.
For we sense our own emotion
and see a landscape or a person
only through the faculties common to us all.
Likewise, what we know as records or history or geology
probably is, with all its numerous data,
nothing more than what we feel
   (within the karmic limits of time and space).
Perhaps in two thousand years
a new geology proper to that age
will unearth plenty of proper evidence for the past.
Everyone may think two thousand years ago
a transparent peacock filled the blue sky.
New bachelors of science may excavate splendid fossils
from the ice nitrogen zone
glittering at the top layer of the atmosphere
or discover gigantic footprints
of an invisible man
in the Cretaceous sandstone.

The time referred to is cosmic time, hence the use of many geological terms. Human life, which is part of the life of the universe, must be measured against cosmic time, as both geologists imply and Buddhists say it should be. Seen in this perspective, imagery sketches are extremely fleeting things, as evanescent as a blink of light. Nevertheless, they are made by a man who has transcended human time, who is well aware of the limits of human faculties. They are significant, and insignificant, for those reasons.

The fifth and final stanza consists of just three lines, which cryptically bring the poem to its conclusion:

All these problems
inherent in the nature of imagery and time
will be pursued within the fourth dimension.

"The fourth dimension" is one of Kenji's favorite phrases; in "Agrarian Art" and elsewhere he repeatedly used it to describe his artistic ideal. In art, the "fourth dimension," which Kenji roughly associated with time, is the source of fluidity, an ability to change through time as reality does. As he said in "Agrarian Art": "The four-dimensional sense adds fluidity to a static art." Kenji must have considered an awareness of time and temporal change to be the basis of that fluidity, for he also said, "The huge drama of human life moves along the axis of time and creates an everlasting, four-dimensional art." Thus, in being imagery sketches the 73 verses in *Spring and Asura* are the tentative records of a man who was clearly aware of the fleeting nature of his vision. Ordinary poems are three-dimensional: they are snapshots of nature, portraits of people, depictions of sentiments, and the like. On the other hand, Kenji's verbal sketches are four-dimensional, since they are aware of their own change through time.

To summarize, Kenji's concept of poetic mimesis as expressed in the "Proem" is characterized by two features. First, the reality represented in poetry is conceived neither as external reality mirrored in the poet's mind nor as internal reality expressed through metaphors, but as cosmic reality rooted in a Buddhist vision of the ultimate unity of all creatures in being manifestations of an absolute and all-pervading consciousness. Second, the reality thus represented is four-dimensional in the sense that it is not a framed picture or a piece of finished sculpture but a slice of infinite space and time.

Kenji reiterated his idea of cosmic reality in other writings. It appears, for instance, in a letter to his brother, in which he wrote, "When I forget my existence in the wind and the light, when I feel the world has turned into my garden, or when I am entranced to think that the entire galaxy is myself, how happy I feel!" Once he expressed such happiness in a short lyric called "A Grove and Thoughts":

> Look! You see?
> Over there, drenched in the fog,
> there is a small mushroom-shaped grove.
> That is the place where
> my thoughts
> swiftly drift
> and one by one
> dissolve.
> Butterburs are flowering everywhere.

The communion between man and his surroundings is not a one-way street. The grove, and all other beings on earth, respond to the poet in turn. So Kenji implied when he said in a note, "I am interested in the clouds and the wind not only for their scenic beauty, but because they provide a source of new strength for man, an endless source of strength." In the preface to his collection of children's stories, *The Restaurant of Many Orders*, Kenji recalled, "I received all these stories of mine from the rainbow and the moonlight as I was in the woods, on the fields, or alongside the railway. Honestly, I could not help feeling these things when I passed near the green oak forest in the evening all by myself, or when I stood shivering in the mountain wind of November." In some of his stories he cited examples of a poem's emerging from a cosmic awareness shared by all things. In "Grape Juice," for instance, a youngster named Seisaku hears a song coming from afar, but he cannot tell whether the singer is the sky, the wind, or a little child standing in the field; apparently it is something within all three. In "A Night in the Oak Grove," Seisaku ventures into the woods, from which a song is coming, and he finds that oak trees, owls, and a human painter all sing similar songs. In "A Spring Day at Ihatove School of Agriculture," a song is sung by the sun in the sky, and the author has even provided its melody in musical notation. To a person who can hear, poetry comes from all things in the universe, as they all share in the cosmic mind.

The relationship of poetry and this cosmic awareness is reiterated in the story "The Dragon and the Poet," where it is connected with the idea that there is a progressive trend in cosmic history. The story outlines how a budding poet named Surdatta wins a decisive victory over a poet of great reputation, Alta, at a song contest. Surdatta himself does not know how he composed his winning song; all he remembers is that he seems to have heard it in his sleep one windy day when he dozed off on a headland. But the older Alta knows the creative process better and explains it to the younger poet in a song of his own:

> No sooner have the wind sung and the clouds echoed and
>   the waves resounded
> than you sing their song, Surdatta.
> You are a prophet who envisions

a model of truth and beauty for tomorrow's world
after which the stars yearn and the land shapes itself
and who eventually makes the world become so.
You are an architect, Surdatta.

Here again is the idea that a song—or a poem—expresses an impulse or an awareness shared by the wind and the clouds as well as the poet, and here too is the idea that the world and all it contains are constantly changing through time. But Kenji also suggests that the changing cosmos has a direction and purpose, and that the change is for the better. The poet, in singing out the cosmic mind, conveys a sense of progress.

In Kenji's view the purpose thus expressed is that of universal reality, not the individual poet. In an advertisement he wrote for *The Restaurant of Many Orders* he said, "These stories are designed to provide materials for building a new, better world. But that world is entirely a development of this world, a ceaseless, wondrous development unknown to me. Definitely it is not a sooty, misshapen utopia." In his opinion, most utopian stories are products of authors' individual imaginings, reflecting their personal idiosyncrasies. But the stories collected in *The Restaurant of Many Orders* are based on the cosmic mind, and hence on the cosmic will at work to perfect the world.

The clearest expression of Kenji's idea of cosmic will appears in what seems to be a draft of a letter to an unidentified acquaintance:

There is one problem I can never pass over. Is there such a thing as cosmic will deigning to lead all living things to true happiness? Or is the world something incidental and sightless? If confronted by this choice between what is known as religious faith and what is known as science, I would by all means select the former. The universe has a great many stages of consciousness, and the final one is endeavoring to lead all living things away from all delusions and toward ultimate happiness.

Kenji, an avid reader of the Lotus Sutra, may have associated the highest stage of universal consciousness with the compassionate bodhisattva, who strives to lead all beings to the pure bliss of the Buddha's Paradise, "away from all delusions and toward ultimate happiness." Here he sees a similar ideal embodied, not in a specific religious figure, but in the movement of cosmic history as a whole.

Kenji does not seem to have believed that poetry always reflects universal consciousness in its last stage of supreme happiness. By and large, his own poetry reflects various prior stages. The title of his anthology, *Spring and Asura*, is symbolic; "spring," denoting the most beautiful time of the year, alludes to the last and highest stage, whereas "asura" refers to one of the lower phases. (In Mahayana Buddhism, an asura is a demonlike creature suffering from such delusive passions as arrogance, suspicion, and jealousy in one of the four spheres occupying the space between heaven and hell.) In "Spring and Asura," the title poem of the collection, Kenji described himself as such a creature, tears streaming from his eyes, who restlessly roams the idyllic countryside on a radiant April day. The poem's speaker is aware of universal consciousness, but he has not yet reached its final stage.

Three representative poems pin down more exactly Kenji's idea of mimesis. I will start with a simple one:

> *Politicians (Opus 1053)*
> Over there, and here too
> everybody wants to make a fuss
> and get treated to a drink.
>   Fern leaves and the clouds.
>   The world is so cold and dark.
> But before long
> those fellows will
> rot
> and flow away in the rain,
> leaving only the silent green ferns behind.
> "That happened in the coal age of man,"
> Some transparent geologist will record.

This is not among the best of Kenji's poems. The satire is too simple, and a facile, escapist attitude is implied. Nonetheless, the poem clearly shows the nature of his cosmic awareness, since it regards reality from a standpoint that transcends human time and recognizes a slow progress on the universal scale. The human perspective and resulting anger presented in the first three

lines are replaced by a cosmic perspective as the poem progresses, and the anger is thereby sublimated.

The next poem is more famous and more complex. I shall
quote its longer version:[3]

Flower of Karma

Over the moisture of night forlornly blending with the wind
and above a black grove of pines and willows
the sky is filled with dark petals of karma.
Having recorded the names of gods
I shiver violently with cold.
Oh someone, come and assure me
that there will arrive a radiant world
where millions of great men are born
and live together without defiling one another!
A heron is crying in the distance.
Will it stand on the cold marshland
throughout the night, its red eyes burning?
As dewdrops fall from pine trees
a few lonely clusters of stars
emerge afresh from the western clouds.
By coincidence a pair
join their rays to form a yellow plume,
while the rest, a large bushy shadow,
show an obscure white shape.

Here again the imperfections of human reality are implied, and
they are viewed from the standpoint of a poet who can identify
the gods. Transcending the limits of human time, he envisions
the great accumulated mass of actions past, present, and future
spread out like petals across the night sky, and in it he recognizes
the force determining the course of people's lives. But, in contrast to "Politicians," in this poem the poet is not sure whether
time will eventually bring forth a radiant world. By chance a person may attain luminous harmony with others, as a few of the
stars do, after coming out of the clouds of suspicion. Yet most
of mankind may be like the heron that keeps crying throughout the night. A sense of a higher level of consciousness is still
present in the poem, but there is no longer certainty of cosmic
progress.

[3] What seems to be Kenji's final draft consists of only the first five lines.

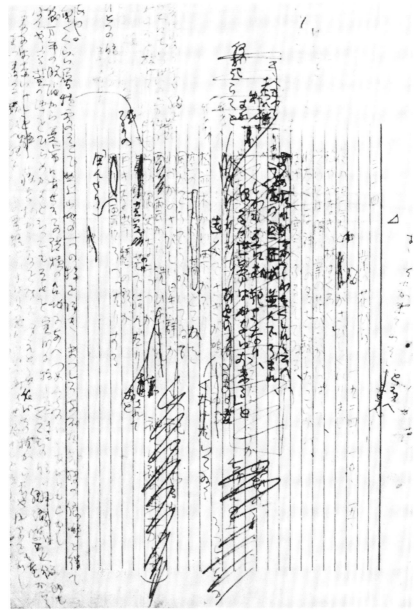

The manuscript of Kenji's "Flower of Karma." Reproduced from *Kōhon Miyazawa Kenji zenshū* (Chikuma Shobō), Vol. III.

Kenji must have wondered about the ways of overcoming such doubts. His answer is implied in some of his later poems, such as this one:

Opus 1063

These are modest fences like the Ainu's.
Yes,
the mulberry tree by their house
was stripped down to the letter Y
and yet they could not make a living.
Last April
the water was black in the rice paddies
as eddies of dark air
incessantly fell from the sky
and crows
noisily flew by.
It makes me wonder.
Though the field is full of sharp-edged gravel
and overgrown with horsetails and mugworts
they till it, those women clothed in black,
while rearing their babies,
patching together the rags from older children,
cooking, doing duties for the village,
shouldering the whole family's discontents and desires,
with no more than a handful of coarse food
and six hours' sleep nightly all the year round.
They also clear a bamboo grove
and make an acre of farmland
in exchange for eight yen's worth of fertilizer.
In this area
if they sow two bushels of buckwheat they harvest four.
It makes me wonder:
Aren't these people
comparable to those modern heroes—
the many revolutionaries chained in prisons
or the many artists starved by their luck?

Again, in the final lines a broad perspective of time and history forms the background for the comparison of peasant women to reformers and artists from a standpoint that transcends current, imperfect human reality. Yet the dominant emotion is admiration for those women courageously battling against adverse natural and human circumstances. They are farming in northeastern Japan, where neither the climate nor the soil is favorable, and

their attempts to raise silkworms on mulberry leaves, or to cultivate rice in the paddies, all too often end in disaster because of
circumstances beyond their control. Their fields have such poor
soil that only the sturdiest of weeds, horsetail and mugwort, can
grow, yet they are too poor to afford much fertilizer. Still they
keep working hard to improve their farms and to change their
lives by even a tiny bit. For them, it does not matter whether the
world is changing for the better or for the worse; they try to
make a positive contribution in a small way. In that sense they
can be compared to revolutionaries who endeavor to reform society and to artists who envision a model of truth and beauty for
a future world.

Here Kenji's concept of poetry merges with agrarianism. For
him, ideal poetry unifies theory and practice, dream and reality,
the imaginative capacity to conceive an ideal and the physical energy to work toward it: a farmer is an artist, and an artist should
be a farmer. His "Agrarian Art" begins:

> We are all farmers, with a rigorous schedule and exhaust-
>   ing work.
> We seek the way to a more radiant, vital life.
> Among our forefathers there were some who did so.
> Scientists' proofs, mendicants' tests, and our intuitions all
>   form a common base for our discussion.
> No one person can attain happiness until the entire world
>   does.
> Self-awareness evolves in stages: first the individual, then
>   the community, and then the society and the universe.
> Isn't this the way the ancient sages trod and preached?
> The new age points toward a world with a single conscious-
>   ness, a single living thing.
> To live a righteous and sturdy life we must become aware
>   of, and respond to, the galaxy within us.
> Let us seek happiness for the world. Such seeking is itself
>   the way.

Here is Kenji's ultimate poetic, which has been absorbed into
something larger than poetics. Natural science, which provides
objective proof, religion, which provides human test cases, and
poetry, which provides intuitive insight, are brought together to

contribute to progress at personal, global, and cosmic levels.
Kenji's poetic gains its identity by losing it.

All Poems Are Tentative

  To the north of the city of Morioka in northeastern Japan is a
plain known as Ippongi. One fine day Kenji walked across it,
and the experience resulted in this poem:

Ippongi Plain

Suddenly the pine grove brightens
and opens a field before me, showing
an endless expanse of dead grass aflame in the sun
and a row of hydro poles, with white insulators, gently
extending almost as far as the city of Bering.
The sky of clear ocean blue
and cleansed human wishes—
Larches regain their youth
and I hallucinate the call of a transparent lark.
Green Nanashigure Hills
rise and fall in my mental landscape too.
A cluster of willow trees
are the willows along the Volga.
Hiding in the heavenly malachite bowl,
clay-colored Yakushi Peak points harsh and sharp.
Snow in the crater contours its wrinkles
and Kurakake's sensitive ridges
let nebulae rise toward the blue sky.
  (Say, Oak,
   is your nickname really
   Mountain Tobacco Tree?)
What a blessing
to stroll for half a day
on the grass, under such a bright canopy!
To obtain it, I would be willing to be crucified.
Isn't it like a rendezvous?
  (Say, Mountain Tobacco Tree,
   if you keep doing that awkward dance
   you may be mistaken for a futurist.)
I am the beloved of the woods and fields.
When I make my way through the reeds
green messages, coyly folded,
slip into my pockets.
When I walk in a shady forest
crescent-shaped lipmarks
cover my elbows and trousers.

The poem reveals an early stage of the verse-writing process as conceived by Kenji, even though its persona cannot, of course, be considered identical with Kenji himself. It begins in a sudden brightening, as a landscape unexpectedly appears beyond the dark woods. The poet emerges and surveys the scene, and as he does so ordinary external reality, such as the line of hydro poles, begins to be transformed in his act of perceiving it. This transformation becomes in effect hallucination, visual and aural, for the city of Bering is imaginary and not even the lark's invisible call, let alone its body, is actually transparent. As his physical eyes sight the Nanashigure Hills in the north of Ippongi Plain, the eyes of his imagination glimpse Siberian hills that he has never seen.

In the second half of the poem, he communicates with trees and plants. Using human language, he addresses an oak tree, which happens to be shaped like an object in a futurist painting. Nature seems to respond to him, too: reeds slip their messages into his pockets as he passes, and trees, helped by the sun, print their kisses on his clothes. As he perceives the things around him, he at once transforms and communes with them: in the act of seeing the shadows of pine needles as the marks of lips or the blades of reeds as messages, he shares with these fellow beings, both in their eternal flux and in a cosmic awareness, the ecstasy of a fine day.

For Kenji, then, the first step in verse writing is to submerge oneself in one's surroundings, particularly natural surroundings. "Communicate with the wind, and obtain energy from the clouds" was his advice to would-be agrarian poets. He seems to have thought that such oneness must be attained on a preconscious level, presumably because the conscious mind makes distinctions between different objects. "Unless it flows out of the subconscious," he said, "what you have is frequently powerless or false." The young poet Surdatta in "The Dragon and the Poet," who sings out the song of the wind, the clouds, and the waves, conceives the song in his sleep and does not himself know how he arrived at it; he has communed with all things while unconscious. A similar experience is told by the narrator of "The First Deer Dance":

Then, from between the bright, frizzled clouds in the western sky, the evening sun shed its crimson rays aslant on the moss-covered plain, making plumes of pampas grass waver like white flames. Exhausted, I fell asleep there. Then the rustling wind gradually began to sound like human words, eventually telling me about the true spirit of the deer dance, which is still performed in the Kitakami mountains and plains.

In Kenji's view, a storyteller, like a poet, is a medium: he does not speak his own thoughts, but allows the cosmic mind to speak through him.

However, the poet must immediately record his visions in words; otherwise his memory of the experience will fade away. Kenji habitually kept a notebook with him, whether at home or outdoors, in which he jotted down whatever came to mind. Some of his notebooks have been preserved, and they give clues to the second stage in his creative process.

We have, for instance, a notebook with a black leather cover that Kenji used around 1928. He wrote down all kinds of things in it: names, dates, a study schedule, mathematical formulas, and letters of the English alphabet. On two of its pages he scrawled in a hurried hand:

> already
> I am a feverish
>   forlorn salt lake
> along the shore
>   many miles of
>   jet-black
> lepidodendron
>   groves extend
> must I
>   until the reptiles
> change into birds
>   keep
>   oozing up?

Without other evidence, there is no way of knowing the exact circumstances that prompted Kenji to scribble these words. The contents of the note suggest that while lying sick with fever he had a dream or vision in which he became a salt lake in prehistoric times. Immediately afterwards, he jotted down these fragmentary words. Kenji seems to have wanted to polish his wording almost as soon as he had finished initially setting it down. Using the same pencil, he erased the word "already" and changed "I am" to "I have turned into." Then, some time later, he copied the jotting in another notebook, making revisions as he did so. There it reads:

> Now my chest
> has turned into a feverish, forlorn salt lake.
> Along the shore, miles and miles of
> jet-black lepidodendron groves extend.
> And I wonder: Must I
> until the reptiles change into birds
> keep lying like this?

After copying this version, Kenji inserted the word "still" between "lying" and "like this" in the last line.

The third draft is written on a sheet of manuscript paper, and the handwriting is much neater, although the poem still shows the traces of revision:

> Now my chest
> is a feverish, forlorn salt lake
> on whose shore, for full five hundred miles,
> a jet-black lepidodendron grove extends
> and I wonder —must I
> until the reptiles change into some birdlike form
> keep lying
> still?

Kenji apparently intended to publish this version. He placed the manuscript among other poems he wrote around this time, inserted them all into a binder, and put on the cover a label reading "During an Illness," a collective title for all the poems.

The first of these three drafts is like a personal note, syntactically looser and semantically more vague than the other two. The second version tries to focus the images more sharply. Thus "already I am" is revised to "my chest has turned," and "oozing up" is changed to "lying like this" and then to "lying still like this." The third draft continues the process. The vague "miles and miles" turns into a more precise phrase, "five hundred miles"; the personal "lying like this" is transformed into "lying still," explaining to the reader what "like this" means. The changes of "has turned" to "is" and of "birds" to "some birdlike form" are probably intended to emphasize the slowness of evolutionary time. "Is" expresses the length of time the poet experiences that state, for the change is so slow he does not experience it as change; "some birdlike form" emphasizes the many stages of evolutionary development—the reptiles turn, not to birds, but to some lower form gradually developing toward a bird. The third version expresses the poet's original experience in a way that is easier for the reader to understand.

In another example of Kenji's verse-writing process, the initial note is even more fragmentary:

```
child eating a melon while walking
                    sun resides on the castle field
                                              bird
        mother gathers plumes of pampas grass     pine grove
```

The note, scrawled in light pencil on a page of a notebook, gives the date as August 1918. Other evidence shows that at this time Kenji was working as an assistant to a professor at a local agricultural school who had been commissioned by the county government to do soil research on farms in the area. When he made the note, Kenji was probably on a field trip to a farm. Having poetic inspiration but no time to compose a poem, he jotted down the essence of his impressions in his notebook.

Some time later he drafted a poem from the jotting. The earliest surviving version is written in pencil on a sheet of manuscript paper:

> Over a manifold pine grove
> a flock of birds swiftly passes,
> and off the mountains in the clear wind
> white clouds of autumn coil.

> The child with a black snow-skirt
> eats a melon,
> and the mother, gathering red plumes
> of pampas grass, walks across the field.

It seems that Kenji, on completing this draft, crossed out the initial note in red ink. He crossed out this first draft, too, when he came up with a new version. The second draft is written on the back of the paper on which the first appears:

> A child with a black snow-skirt
> eats a melon, walking:
> off the mountains in the clear wind
> white clouds of autumn coil.
>
> Doesn't she want a melon herself?
> The young mother of the child,
> absorbed in gathering red plumes
> of pampas grass, comes across the field.

Kenji further revised the poem and eventually published it in a local women's magazine on November 15, 1932. The published version was entitled "Mother." It retained the first stanza intact, but changed the second to:

> Doesn't she want a melon herself?
> The mother, still young in age,
> amuses herself by gathering red plumes
> of pampas grass as she crosses the field.

Apparently the poem was a favorite of Kenji's, for he placed it at the very beginning of *One Hundred Poems in Classical Japanese*, a poetry anthology he compiled in August 1933.[1] The version in the anthology is virtually the same as that published in the magazine.

The three drafts of the poem "Mother" reveal something of Kenji's art in polishing a poem. One can gather from the initial note, fragmentary as it is, that the core of the poet's experience was contemplation of a scene: a child eating a melon and a young mother plucking pampas plumes in a wide expanse of landscape that included the sun, a field, birds, and a pine grove. The first draft tries to capture the communion with the scene the poet seems to have felt, but it is not successful because there is too wide a gap between the two stanzas. The first stanza is merely a landscape sketch, with no suggestion of correspon-

[1] Kenji died before he had time to arrange for its publication.

dence between man and nature. The second draft corrects the situation by placing a child in the center of the landscape: both the child's snow-skirt and the coiling clouds anticipate the coming winter. The new second stanza is linked more closely with the first through its revised first line, which makes the mother similar to the child by implying that she might want a melon, too. We cannot tell whether she does or not, however, for she is "absorbed," caught up in communion with another aspect of the landscape. In the third draft, Kenji chose to emphasize the new link by making the mother still more childlike. He revised the stanza's second line to place stronger emphasis on her youthfulness and changed "absorbed" to "amuses herself"—her action in picking the plumes becomes like a child's play. This final version presents a happy vision of the two walking across the autumn field, their gaiety and self-absorption dispelling any hint of melancholy in the signs of coming cold.

The second stage in Kenji's creative process, as illustrated in these two examples, may not seem significantly different from what other poets do at a similar stage in their verse writing: he attempted to clarify his initial inspiration and to communicate it more fully. Kenji was different, however, in that for him there was no such thing as a finished poem. His clearest statement of this point appears on the cover of *One Hundred Poems in Classical Japanese*, where he wrote, "I regard the current revision as the definitive version at that particular time." The statement is dated August 22, 1933, just one month before his death. Kenji undoubtedly knew he was dying, and he did not know how much more time he had to revise the poems intended for the anthology. That did not bother him, however, because he considered each poem's current version to be the final draft *at that time*, and he wanted to convey this belief to his family and to others who would take care of the manuscripts after his death. Indeed, many of his manuscripts show the marks of continual revision up to his final days.

The belief that no poem is ever final can be seen at work in *Spring and Asura*, too. Kenji personally oversaw this anthology's publication, occasionally even helping the publisher with details of printing. When the book appeared he was quite pleased with it and gave copies to a number of his friends and acquaintances. Yet he went on revising the poems after publication, just as he had before it. In at least three surviving copies of *Spring and Asura*, Kenji wrote down postpublication revisions. The first copy includes some three hundred amendments; the second, approximately ninety; and the third, ten. To be sure, many poets want to revise poems after publication, but how many would take the trouble to revise an anthology in four hundred places if they had no plans to publish a second edition? Kenji thought the poems printed in *Spring and Asura* were merely "the definitive version at that particular time," the time of publication. They continued to metamorphose after publication, just as they had before it.

Kenji's unique conception of the creative process is related to his idea that art is four-dimensional. In his view, art has to be fluid, for human life—and the life of everything else—flows along the axis of time. A poem has to move along that axis, too, even after it is printed, and even after its author is dead. The verse-writing process has to be open-ended because the poem itself exists in time and people "rewrite" it whenever they read it. Toward the end of "Agrarian Art" Kenji declared, "An eternal incompletion is itself a completion." That idea applies to the creative process, too.

We Create New Beauty

In "Agrarian Art," Kenji made some strong statements about aesthetic beauty. Deploring the corruption of art and religion in modern times, he said:

Nowadays, men of religion and art monopolize the sale of truth, goodness, and beauty.
We cannot afford these, nor do we need them.
Now we must start along a new, authentic path and create beauty of our own.

. . .

Of course, agrarian art will have beauty as its essence, too.
We create new beauty. Aesthetics keeps moving on.
It will expand boundlessly until the very word "beauty" perishes.

These statements indicate that Kenji was dissatisfied with the aesthetic effects created by contemporary works of art. No doubt he saw these works as becoming progressively isolated from the lives of ordinary people; yet their creators claimed truth, goodness, and beauty as their own elite and exclusive property. He had no use for such art or for the rarefied productions of a modernist avant-garde. Instead, his goal was to infuse life and art with a single spiritual awareness—a single understanding, acceptance, and grateful fulfillment of man's place in the universe. In life, this would take the form of a simple and selfless dedication to one's work and one's fellow human beings; in art, it would take the form of a new beauty, whose connection with life would grow until finally the two would become indistinguishable, and the very concept of beauty as a separate phenomenon would disappear.

Kenji seems to have had ideas about the new kind of beauty he wanted agrarian art to create, but he had not formulated them well enough to commit them to writing. Apparently he discussed the subject publicly around the time he wrote "Agrarian Art." One of his comments was recorded by a young man who in February 1926 heard Kenji give a lecture entitled "Agrarian Art: An Introduction." According to him, Kenji wrote the main points of the lecture on the blackboard but discouraged the audience from copying them down, saying that his thoughts had not yet been finalized. Of aesthetic effects, he wrote, "Features of poetry in the new age: it must be sound (hope, determination to progress, resistance to corruption, emphasis on being social and productive)." The comment, fragmentary though it is, points toward Kenji's concept of the "new beauty" he urged his fellow agrarians to create in the years to come. In a word, the new beauty yields the impression of being "sound," and its ingredients are aspiration, will to progress, hatred of wrongdoing, and a positive contribution to society. The connotations of these terms become clearer in the context of Kenji's other comments and his poems touching on the subject.

It is easy to see that a poem expressing hope produces a sound, healthy impression. Contemporary Japanese free verse, dominated by a school of which Hagiwara Sakutarō was a leader, must have seemed misguided to Kenji, as it frequently embodied aspects of modern pessimism. Kenji would have no part of this. He chose to believe in a cosmic will that would eventually direct all living things to true happiness, and he felt verse composed by a poet of the new age should reflect that optimism. Indeed, when Kenji was asked where such a poet should start, he answered, "First of all, hold a great hope for the world."

Kenji's poem "Snow on Kurakake" embodies such hope:

> All I can depend on
> is the snow draping Kurakake.
> Since the fields and the woods
> are either fuzzy or dusky,
> though it is a snowdrift
> as blurry as yeast,
> I hang my last faint hope
> on the snow covering Mount Kurakake.
> (An old-fashioned faith)

Kurakake is a high mountain located near Kenji's hometown, but it was also part of his mental landscape. As Kenji looked around, people looked "fuzzy" or "dusky," with pallid faces and a gloomy appearance. He could see no ideology, religion, or art in contemporary Japan that promised salvation; the only encouraging sight was a mountain towering in the distance, capped with pure, white snow. The mountain was remote, but he could hang his hope on nothing else. Such a state of mind seemed to him to be the kind of faith cherished by people of older times, when religion was a more important part of life. The poem, despite its largely dark imagery, does leave a positive, wholesome impression because of the poet's refusal to lose hope in a hopeless world.

The second ingredient of soundness, "determination to progress," can be considered an extension of hope or a restatement of it in more practical terms. It is not enough to stand by and hope; one must work actively to realize one's aspirations. As we have seen, Kenji urged his readers, "We seek the way to a more radiant, vital life" and "Let us seek happiness for the world." Elsewhere in "Agrarian Art" he called out to his fellow farmers, "Oh, friends, let us join our righteous forces together and transform all our farms and all our lives into a magnificent, four-dimensional art." Of course, in Kenji's view determination to progress should not be an individual assertion but part of the cosmic will. Yet as he realized later in life, one cannot identify oneself with that will without making an effort to do so.

Many of Kenji's literary works embody such a determination. One of his finest stories for children, "A Biography of Guskobudori," is a good example, as it traces the life of a man who devoted his life to helping others. Also belonging to this category are some of the finest poems of his later period, such as "Rice-Farming Episode" and "The Gentle Breeze Fills the Valley." Here I will cite "To My Students," a poem drafted in 1926 or 1927, when Kenji had just resigned from a teaching position at Hanamaki School of Agriculture.

> Dear students:
> When the dark blue horizon swells upward
> do you feel like submerging yourselves in it?
> You must become the many-shaped
> mountains on the horizon.
>
> Don't you feel this
> transparent clean wind
> coming from your wondrous new world?
>
> With a black flower called *sakinohaka*[5]
> a revolution will soon be here.
> It is a ray of light sent to us,
> a southerly wind already decided on.

[5] A word coined by Kenji. According to one theory, *sakinoha* was derived from components of the Chinese character *pao*, which means "violent" or "sudden"; *ka*, from the character *li*, which means "force."

Do you want to endure a slave's life
and keep serving an age that leads you by force?
No, you must create a new, stalwart age.
The universe is ceaselessly changed by us.
You must go a step further
than using up all the energies of nature
like the tide and the wind;
you must try to form a new nature.

Copernicus of the new age:
set this galaxy free
from the oppressive law of gravity.

Marx of the new age:
reform this world that moves on blind impulse
and give it a splendid, beautiful system.

Darwin of the new age:
board the *Challenger* of Oriental meditation
and reach the space beyond the galaxy.
From there, send us a purer, deeper, more accurate
geology and a revised biology.

All that labor on the farm
performed as if driven by an impulse:
through a cool and transparent analysis
elevate it, together with
its dark blue shadow,
to the level of dance.

New poets:
obtain new, transparent energy
from the clouds, from the light, from the storms
and suggest to man and the universe the shapes they are
    to take.[6]

In bidding farewell to his students, Kenji described in lucid terms what he wanted them to do in the coming years. Underlying the poem is his optimistic view of cosmic progress, but he also urged his students to work actively to create a better age. "The universe," he declared, "is ceaselessly changed by us." The piece is filled with his confidence in human capabilities, and as a result it produces the kind of positive, vigorous impression he wanted from a poem.

[6] Kenji left the manuscript in a very rough state. This translation represents one of several possible ways to reconstruct the poem out of his scribbles.

Now it is easy to understand why "resistance to corruption" was the third ingredient of poetic beauty as conceived by Kenji. "Corruption" probably included all the political, social, and moral evils that seemed to him to obstruct the progress of mankind. He wanted poetry to criticize those evils. "Religion, after tiring itself out, has been replaced by modern science, but science is cold and dark," he said. "Art, having gone away from us, has degraded itself." In his view, contemporary religion and art had lost the critical spirit they should have. He wanted poetry, his type of poetry, never to follow suit.

Resistance to corruption is more directly manifest in Kenji's stories for children than in his poetry. For example, "Oppel and the Elephant," describing how an agricultural entrepreneur takes advantage of a gentle elephant, attacks the capitalist exploitation of labor; "The Spider, the Slug, and the Raccoon," which recounts the destinies of three graduates from a school in the woods, criticizes modern laissez-faire society and its educational philosophy; and "The Restaurant of Many Orders," in which two game hunters from the city narrowly escape being served up at a dinner table in a wildcat's restaurant, satirizes the aggressive, warlike civilization of modern industrialized countries. Kenji did not write such overtly satirical works in verse; yet, as we have seen, such poems as "Politicians" do contain elements of social satire.

Another example embodying social criticism is the following untitled poem, of which I will cite only the opening section:

> Two or three more times
> I must glare at Kōsuke.
> In the shrill wind blowing off the mountain snow
> he ordered all the villagers to come out
> and had them cut cedars, chestnut trees, and whatnot
> to erect two poles amid the willows on the canal's edge
> and three more along a cliff shaded by the grove—
> those unneeded hydro poles
> for unneeded electric light.
> Now, to thank the electricians
> he says we'll have a celebration.
> He says we'll drink in the grove;

he says all the dignitaries are invited;
he says I'm one of them too.
What! I'm not like you.
Rambling about in a group all day,
you say this hole isn't deep enough or that pole looks
    slanted
as if you were performing an important service
when in fact you are just loafing.
I'm not one of you.

The poem so far is a fierce invective against Kōsuke, a representative of an electric company, and against the kind of civilization he stands for. In the rest of the poem, however, the attack is blunted as the poet becomes more reflective and thinks of his own imperfections. In general, Kenji seems to have been too self-conscious and too gentle-natured to write bitingly satirical poems. His spirit of criticism was more constructive than destructive.

Indeed, being constructive was the fourth element of sound, wholesome poetry as envisioned by Kenji. His term for it was "emphasis on being social and productive." In the same lecture he referred to "true poetry," saying, "It must be the prime energy for production, capable of helping one to recover one's strength and complete one's labor." "Agrarian Art" contains such statements as "Set your gray labor aflame by means of art" and "It [agrarian art] always affirms actual life and tries to heighten or deepen it." There he also said, "No one person can attain happiness until the entire world does." Evidently Kenji believed that all people, including poets, should be directly concerned with the welfare of society and should work constructively to improve it. In his view, therefore, poetry should inspire all workers toward the aim of ultimately bringing about an ideal society. In other words, sound poetry should concern itself with social issues and should incite its readers to productive action.

At this point Kenji's poetic seems to approach that of socialism. Indeed, "To My Students" includes lines suggesting his belief in a coming revolution. "Oppel and the Elephant" also appears to support a proletarian revolution, and in another of his stories, "The Polano Plaza," some laborers who have been ex-

ploited by a shrewd capitalist finally succeed in setting up a cooperative factory of their own. However, in the context of all his
writings such works are in the minority. As Kenji himself wrote
in a letter, "Our age must as a matter of course move toward proletarian literature, but my writings somehow do not clearly follow
that course." His idea of revolution and social reform was too
idealistic and dreamy to motivate the kind of social criticism socialist critics would want. On the other hand, that dreamy idealism helped keep his poetry from becoming propaganda.

Examples of poems that try to be social and productive are
more abundant in Kenji's later poetry. "Opus 1063," in praise of
peasant women, is a good example; another shows Kenji himself
as a farmer:

> *Clearing the Wild Land (Opus 1017)*
> When we at last finished clearing
> all the thorn bushes
> the sun was shining brightly
> and the sky was hollow and dark.
> Taichi, Chūsaku, and I
> felt like dropping on the bamboo grass
> and sleeping like logs.
> The stream carried nine tons of needles a second;
> a large flock of herons flew toward the east.

Taichi and Chūsaku are typical names of farmers, and the poem
portrays Kenji toiling side by side with them and sharing their
hard work and fatigue. The sturdy thorns indicate the poor
quality of the soil, as well as the difficulty of clearing it. Yet the
three are not discouraged, and by sheer hard work they complete the project. The poem calls to mind one of Kenji's remarks
in "Agrarian Art": "We are all farmers," he said, "with a rigorous
schedule and exhausting work."

One of the most famous poems in modern Japan, written by
Kenji, falls into the same category. It is untitled and was written
only 22 months before his death:[7]

---

[7] The poem is sometimes called "November 3," but that is not a title, being
instead the date of its composition in 1933.

Neither rain
nor wind
nor snow nor summer's heat
will affect his robust body.
Free of anger
and desire
he will always keep a calm smile.
A quart of brown rice, miso
and some vegetables will be his daily food.
In all things
he will not think of himself
but will observe, hear, and understand well
and will not forget.
Living in a small, reed-thatched hut
under pine trees in the field,
he will go to tend
a sick child in the east
or carry a bundle of rice plants
for a tired mother in the west
or try to dispel the fear
of a dying man in the south
or stop a trivial quarrel or lawsuit
of people in the north.
He will shed tears if a drought comes
and trudge disconsolately if the summer is cold.
Called a bum by all
he will be praised by no one
and will bother no one.
I should like to become
such a man.

The poem has attracted a great deal of attention because it is
believed to represent the image of an ideal man Kenji held in his
last years. Because of its intense idealism and lucid diction, it has
been a staple of Japanese textbooks for many years, but of late it
has become an object of controversy. The militarist government
advocated a similar self-abnegating spirituality in its propaganda
during the war years, and this has been the basis for some critics'
disparaging remarks. Kenji's ideal man takes too passive an attitude, others say, when he does nothing more than shed tears in a
time of drought and trudge disconsolately in a cold summer.
Those critics, however, overlook Kenji's basic stand as a man of
morality and religion. The reform he had in mind was more reli-

gious and moral than political and social, and the social reform he talked of was of a nonviolent nature. He would rather be a bum who was praised by no one than a revolutionary hero who hurt others in the course of attaining a worthy aim. He would do everything within his power to help others, but he knew some things were beyond his control, and when they happened he would grieve with other victims. Whether or not such an attitude is too passive is a matter of opinion; from Kenji's own point of view, the poem's implications are sufficiently "social" and "productive."

The foregoing examples show how various ingredients in Kenji's poetry contribute to a "sound" emotional effect. It must be conceded, however, that many of his poems do not produce such an effect. "Spring and Asura" and many of his elegies for his sister, for example, although they are not morbid like many of Hagiwara Sakutarō's poems, show anxiety, irritation, or grief. "Flower of Karma" and the untitled poem beginning "Now my chest," both already cited, are cases in point. To quote another example:

Opus 1087

What a coward I am!
Because those rice plants were beaten down by the rain at
    dawn
I have been working with abandon
to help drown my woe.
Yet again
the black death
floats up in the west.
Last spring,
wasn't that radiant love itself?

This is a poem not of hope but of lost hope. The poet, an expert in soil conditioning, had advised farmers on fertilizing farms in the spring and had been delighted to see the rice plants growing well. Then a rainstorm came one morning in late August, beating down all the plants and ruining any hope for a good harvest. The poem implies no determination to progress, no resistance to corruption, no positive desire to make a contribution to society;

its total impact is far from what one might call "sound." Its implications of frustration, worry, and self-doubt reveal the other extreme of Kenji's poetry.

In talking about the nature of poetry, however, Kenji completely ignored this darker side. He preferred to look at what poetry could do, rather than what it was doing for him. Part of the reason for this may be that when he discussed the nature of poetry he was usually addressing someone, whereas when he wrote poetry he wrote it for himself. But his attitude must also be related to his basic mental outlook. He was an idealist, and when he talked about the beauty of poetry he did so in terms of ideals rather than reality.

Variations on 7–5

"Poetry is a rhythmical language that spontaneously flows out from the innermost part of the soul. . . . The sound, the melody, the tone, the wording, all come out automatically." According to a student's note, Kenji said something to this effect in one of his lectures. In keeping with his conception of poems as imagery sketches and his idea that the creative process begins with the submersion of self in natural surroundings on a preconscious level, his idea of poetic form seems to have centered on spontaneity: a poet, in touch with the cosmic mind, instinctively and automatically sketches his inner vision. The touchstone of this half-conscious singing out is the rhythmical language in which it occurs: the course of Kenji's poetic development shows that he came to consider a flow of strongly rhythmical language to be the essence of poetic form. Unlike Hagiwara Sakutarō, he seems to have been less concerned with an individualized rhythm and shape for specific poems than with rhythmical language per se. From his initial involvement with experimental tanka through his move to free verse, his prosody remained quite regular, and it grew more so in the course of his career. Thus the form of his poems comes to echo their content: as imagery sketches they portray slices of the infinite continuum of time and space; as variations on 7–5, they are slices of the rhythm echoing throughout all previous Japanese poetry—above all, through popular marches and songs.

Kenji stated explicitly his emphasis on the basically musical nature of poetic language in an apologetic letter written home to his father in 1926 during a three-week stay in Tokyo, where he was indulging his enthusiasm for classical European music by taking daily organ lessons. "You may wonder," he wrote, "why I have to pain myself unnecessarily to learn music. But I need it badly, as it is a foundation for the language of literature, especially of poetry and children's drama." The link between poetry and children's drama may indicate that he was thinking primarily of rhythm, since in the East as in the West, children's literature tends to be marked by a strongly rhythmical quality.

There was room for individual variation in the poetic rhythm, however, as his story "The Dragon and the Poet" makes clear. The young poet Surdatta, now knowing how he composed his contest-winning song, is tormented by the suspicion that he may have unconsciously stolen it from a wise old dragon. He remembers that when the song came to him in his sleep he was on a headland where the dragon lived. But the dragon, when hearing Surdatta's misgivings, reassures the young poet:

Surdatta, that song is yours as well as mine. . . . At that time I was the cloud and the wind. And you were the cloud and the wind, too. The poet Alta would probably have sung the same song if he had meditated then. But, Surdatta, Alta's language would have been different from yours, and yours from mine. The same thing can probably be said about rhythm, too. For this reason that song is yours, and it is also ours to the extent that it belongs to our spirit that controls the clouds and the wind.

Here Kenji implies that the spirit moving all poets is the same, but that it takes different forms when different poets verbalize it. Each poet has his own individuality, which colors sound, melody, tone, and wording, resulting in a mode of expression uniquely his own.

Kenji began his career as a poet by writing tanka, and he used that form almost exclusively until he was 24 years old. He was a prolific tanka poet: a collection of tanka he himself compiled contains more than eight hundred poems. In choosing the 31-syllable form, he may have been influenced by the examples of Yosano Akiko and Ishikawa Takuboku. Many middle-school students who aspired to literary fame in those days wrote tanka; even Hagiwara Sakutarō wrote in that form as a secondary school student. For the young Kenji, Takuboku's influence must have been particularly great. Takuboku had been born near Kenji's hometown, had attended the same secondary school, and had published poems and essays in local newspapers. It must be more than coincidence that Kenji began writing tanka seriously in January 1911, several weeks after the publication of *A Handful of Sand*. "Various Kinds of Poetry," Takuboku's essay eloquently advocating the merits of tanka—his kind of tanka—had been published at about the same time. No explicit proof of Kenji's indebtedness to Takuboku has been preserved, but in theme, imagery, diction, and style his tanka have a good deal in common with those in *A Handful of Sand*. The most convincing evidence of direct influence is that he consciously manipulated the length of lines and their appearance on the page, as did Takuboku. In practice Takuboku wrote only three-line tanka, but Kenji used two-, three-, four-, and five-line forms, following closer in fact to what the older poet preached in theory.

A couple of Kenji's tanka will illustrate Takuboku's influence. The first was written in 1914, the year Kenji graduated from middle school and began to help in his father's pawnshop on a full-time basis. His nose was operated on for ozena in the spring, and the resulting complications kept him in the hospital for more than a month.

> My friends'
> matriculation tests must be soon.
> Having been ill, I dig up
> a small lily.

Compare this with a poem from *A Handful of Sand*:

> The day when all my friends seem superior to me,
> I bring home a flower
> and cherish my wife.

Both tanka portray a young man comparing himself with his friends and suffering from an inferiority complex; in an effort to overcome his feelings, he pays attention to a flower, something outside of competitive human society. The two poems use similar themes, materials, and images, except that the bachelor Kenji could not refer to a wife. Also, both verses look like fragments of a diary, recording the poet's emotion of the moment. Of course, Kenji also utilized the multi-line form characteristic of Takuboku's tanka.

As another example, here is a tanka Kenji composed in 1915:

> Dokugamori Woods,
> Mount Nanshō, and the rest of the range
> suddenly leap up and hang over my forehead.

This can be traced back to another poem in *A Handful of Sand*:

> I think of an October morning
> when Mount Iwate's
> first snow closed in over my eyebrows.

Although Takuboku's tanka records a recollection rather than an immediate experience, the center of interest in both poems is a colossal mountain towering above the poet, who for an instant feels both awe and a sense of purification. Again, both poems use the multi-line form.

Other tanka by Kenji also suggest his indebtedness to Takuboku. Indeed, many resemble the older poet's not only in form but also in that they record the emotions the poet experienced from day to day, in sharp contrast to most contemporary tanka, which copied nature in the way advocated by Shiki. Kenji even grouped poems by date of composition when he compiled his tanka anthology, so that the collection looks almost like a diary. Thus Takuboku's theory that poetry should be a diary, that it should record the poet's thoughts of the moment in the fragmentary way they come to mind, may have laid the foundation for Kenji's own later theory of imagery sketches.

In 1921, at the age of 24, Kenji almost completely stopped writing tanka and then slowly began to write free verse. The fact that his later tanka include many rensaku, or sequential compositions, may evince an increasingly urgent need for a verse form longer than 31 syllables. A rensaku collectively entitled "Andersen's Swan," for instance, is a sequence of ten tanka, but because each tanka has a varying number of lines—from two to five—it looks more like a free-verse poem consisting of ten stanzas. Its first tanka especially, which contains five lines of three, two, seven, five, and fourteen syllables, does not look like a tanka at all. From this type of tanka to free verse, the distance is very short. In a sense, Kenji's shift from tanka to free verse had already been determined when he began to emulate Takuboku by allowing the needs of each poem to dictate its line divisions.

On the other hand, Kenji seems to have carried the rhythm of traditional poetry into his free verse, and the 7–5 pattern is basic to a considerable number of his "imagery sketches." For instance, the line-by-line syllabic scheme of "Clearing the Wild Land," a nine-line poem cited earlier, is:

$$7$$
$$7-7$$
$$7-5$$
$$7-5$$
$$7-5$$
$$7-5$$
$$8-7$$
$$7-5-9$$
$$7-7$$

The basic rhythm of seven and five syllables is so distinct that one is tempted to view the poem as several tanka glued together or as a variation on rensaku. Likewise, the 52 lines that constitute "Spring and Asura" include sixteen 7–5 lines (and variations), eighteen 5–7 lines (and variations), and seven 7–7 lines. "Green Blades of Spears," another poem in *Spring and Asura*, presents an extreme case: it is neatly divided into seven parts by a one-line refrain, each part consisting of four lines with the syllabic scheme:

```
7-7
7-5
7-7
7-5
```

The rhythmic pattern is so regular that one feels hesitant to call it free verse. Most of Kenji's imagery sketches show the 7–5 scheme less markedly than do these examples, but many of them have one or two 7–5 lines or variations at a crucial spot in the poem, thereby providing a rhythmic undercurrent for the entire piece.

Kenji's predilection for the 7–5 syllabic pattern links his work to the rhythm of the traditional Japanese song, utilized in popular Buddhist hymns as well as in folk songs and songs for children. One of the strongest popular uses of this rhythm is in marching songs. When Kenji himself wrote a marching song in a story called "Hydro Poles on a Moonlit Night," he used the 7–5 pattern for its basic rhythm; he did the same when he wrote a school song for Hanamaki School of Agriculture, clearly keeping in mind that the song would be used to accompany students' marches. Being the basic rhythm of a march, the 7–5 pattern conveys a sense of progress, comradeship, and exaltation; Kenji, who wanted his poetry to produce a "sound" impression, may have exploited this effect in his free-verse poems. Perhaps he hoped that the march rhythm would help a poem move forward in time and space, as it were. The rhythm can be used for laborers' processions, too, and its popular valence can make it seem a "workers' rhythm."

Kenji would have denied consciously using a syllabic scheme, however, for he believed that the language of poetry was spontaneous. He would have insisted that the language of his free verse automatically had the basic 7–5 rhythm. For him, that was probably true: the rhythm sometimes flowed out even when he wrote prose, as in some sections of such stories as "Tales of Zashiki Bokko" and "General Son Ba-yu and Three Physicians."

Kenji was sensitive not only to the rhythm of a poem but also to the aural effect of the individual words used in it, and he

made some interesting remarks on the subject. According to a
student of his, for instance, he once said in a lecture that a poem
loaded with consonants sounds rough. In the same lecture he arranged the five vowels of the Japanese language according to degree of tonal brightness: the order was, from the brightest to the
darkest, "a," "i," "o," "e," and "u." On another occasion, when he
offered critical comments on a children's story written by a
friend, he observed that Rirura, a name given to one of its characters, sounded too smooth to fit the ill-natured character of the
child. His suggestion was to change one of the three "r"s to either "m," "s," or "h." In his own story "Windflowers," the narrator observes that *okinagusa*, the usual Japanese word for a windflower, does not have aural qualities that suggest the gentle,
youthful beauty of the flower; he prefers its alternate name,
uzunoshuge, whose tonal qualities suggest to him the black petals,
pale green leaves, and gleaming pappi of a windflower. In yet
another revealing example, an idyllic poem called "A Picture of
Flowers and Birds: July," Kenji presents a young man and his
sister standing on the edge of a river and enjoying the scenery
on a summer day. The sister notices a bird that has alighted on a
power line and points it out to her brother, who responds:

> "Oh, that's a kingfisher.
> A kingfisher, you know—the one with crimson eyes.
> Say, Michia, this is another hot day, isn't it?"
> "What is Michia, brother?"
> "That's his name.
> 'Mi' refers to the smoothness of his back;
> 'chi,' to the way his bill is pointed;
> and 'a' makes it a pet name."

Here Kenji has coined a name for the kingfisher purely on the
basis of the aural effects produced by three syllables. This example, together with the others cited, shows that Kenji's imagery
sketches included not only visual images but auditory ones as
well.

Kenji's preference shifted from imagery sketches in the colloquial language to shi in classical Japanese as he grew older. Especially in the last five years of his life, largely a period of illness, he

liked writing poems in the classical language. There is no doubt
that he thought quite seriously about those verses, for he called
them shi, and not the modest-sounding imagery sketches. Even
as he lay dying, he continued to revise, copy, and compile them
into two anthologies entitled *Fifty Poems in Classical Japanese* and
One Hundred Poems in Classical Japanese. He died before he had
time to finish compiling a third. All in all, the poems he wrote in
this form total more than three hundred.

Many of those poems are adaptations of imagery sketches or
tanka he had written earlier. It appears that the ailing Kenji,
lying in bed, took out old manuscripts and reworked them. One
example is a free-verse poem he wrote in July 1926:

> *Opus 728*
> As the rainshower pours down
> a smoke of dust rises.
> 　In the billowing steam
> 　I, all alone, am angered at my work.
> 　　Dead leaves of fern,
> 　　wild roses' roots,
> 　　and busily scurrying ants
> 　　around their collapsed castle.
> The cedar trees hang streams of rain
> and send faint, white splashes.

Kenji crossed out this poem, presumably when he made the first
draft of a shi some time later on the margin of the manuscript.
He then copied the final draft on a new sheet of paper:

> *Rainshower*
> As the rainshower pours down, the tilled ground
> sends up a smoke of dust.
>
> In the lukewarm steam a person stands,
> his figure dark with groundless anger.
>
> When wild roses' roots have been washed
> and ants scurry around their nest
>
> the cedar trees hang banners of water
> and splashes faintly extend.

The most obvious difference between the two poems is in form.
"Rainshower" is more deliberate and formal, a quality that is

even more evident in the original because it is written in classical
Japanese. The sense of immediacy present in the language of
the earlier poem is all but gone, for better or for worse. It has
been replaced by the strong rhythm of a well-regulated prosody:
the second poem consists of four stanzas, each with two lines
of an identical 7–5 syllable pattern. No wonder Kenji had to
change "I" to "a person" in the latter poem, placing greater distance between the poet and the experience depicted. In it, the
poet's anger is neatly framed.

"Rainshower" typifies the prosody of Kenji's poetry in classical
Japanese. The form he considered standard had four stanzas,
each consisting of a couplet, with each line consisting of seven
and five syllables. Many pieces in *Fifty Poems in Classical Japanese*
and *One Hundred Poems in Classical Japanese* are written in this
form, and the others can be seen as variations on it. Kenji's predilection for this form can also be surmised from a note entitled
"A Study of Four-Couplet Poetry in Classical Japanese," apparently an outline for a projected essay with that title:

1. Introduction. The Fixed Verse Form in Classical Japanese. A Poem in Four Couplets. Its History. Imayō. Tōson, Yau, Hakushū.[8]
2. Beginning, Development, Change, and Conclusion in a Four-Couplet Poem.
3. Prosody. Composition of a Line.
4. Rhyme.

Sketchy though it is, the note suggests Kenji's idea of his favored
verse form in classical Japanese. The sequence of four couplets
had precedents in the Japanese poetic tradition, its origin going
back to the imayō of the late Heian period. Several modern
poets before him had experimented with the form, too. He conceived the poem's structure in terms of the time-honored method
of development used in classical Chinese verse, the first couplet
constituting a "beginning," the second a "development," the
third a "change," and the fourth a "conclusion." He gave no further explanation of prosody or rhyme, but he clearly regarded

[8] As mentioned in the Introduction, imayō were popular songs of the middle
and late Heian period. The modern poets Shimazaki Tōson, Yokose Yau (1878–
1934), and Kitahara Hakushū experimented with the form.

these as important elements of shi. The reference to rhyme is odd, for Japanese poetry had never utilized that device in its long history. No extant shi by him has a distinct rhyme scheme, either.

Kenji's poems in classical Japanese have usually been ranked lower than his free verse. They have been described as less fresh, less vigorous, and less original, and this has been attributed to the fact that the poet, confined to bed, had no new experience to stimulate his mind, no new images to sketch. However, Kenji's poems in classical Japanese sound more melodious than his imagery sketches. The 7–5 rhythm, which was submerged in his free verse, appears openly and resounds throughout his shi. Perhaps Kenji thought of these works more as songs than as poems. He wanted them to be read less by literary critics than by the general public, for whom free verse was still an import, whereas the 7–5 pattern was easy and familiar. In allowing that strong, popular rhythm, anchored by the four-couplet form, to prevail in his last poems, Kenji was true to his desire to be both a Buddhist poet and an agrarian artist—he was attempting to write poems that would sing out of the minds of ordinary people, as well as out of the cosmic mind of wind and clouds and trees.

Art in a Turnip Field

Roughly speaking, Kenji's view of the use of poetry evolved in three stages. At first he expected a good deal out of literature, linking it with religion and envisioning much usefulness for it at both personal and social levels. Then he came to admire a farmer's life so highly that art began to seem a luxury. In later years he tried hard to resolve the dichotomy between art and manual labor, as is evident in "Agrarian Art." One cannot, however, clearly demarcate the three periods; it is more accurate to say that elements of the three co-existed to varying degrees, on the whole moving in the general direction of a dialectical synthesis of labor and art.

At the personal level, verse writing early functioned as a means of relieving loneliness for Kenji. His early tanka are full of insecurity, uneasiness about the future, self-accusation, unfulfilled desire, causeless anger, gloom, and even despair. Writing poetry seems to have been one of the few, if not the only, means he had to vent those emotions. A tanka he wrote in 1916 is typical:

> Steel pen, steel pen,
> steel pen: all alone, you
> move on the barren moor
> of my doubts.

The picture is brighter in "A Biography of Guskobudori," his pseudoautobiography, in which the hero is described as feeling so lonely in childhood that he sings songs and scribbles words on tree trunks in the woods. Yet the idea that poetry relieves loneliness remains. Kenji's most direct statement of it appears in a letter he wrote to a friend in 1932. Referring to his motive for writing poetry, he said, "I have not been writing imagery sketches to please the public. It is all because I could not bear loneliness, because I could not resist my desire to own something beautiful. If a handful of readers were to completely share my feelings and say a few words to me to that effect, that would be about all I hope for."

Although it may sound as though Kenji were writing verse only for himself, significantly he mentions his hope for "a handful of readers" to share his feelings completely. He was not blind to the social functions of poetry, and the preceding quote shows his awareness that poetry can serve as a means of uniting people. In general, he stressed the social functions of poetry more than its personal uses, and we have seen him presenting a particular kind of social function in an early story, "The Dragon and the Poet," in which Surdatta is praised for his ability to envision a model of truth and beauty for tomorrow's world. This story shows the main drift of Kenji's early views on the function of poetry: he saw the poet as a prophet, an architect, a seer—as a moral leader like a man of religion.

From early youth Kenji seems to have seen literature as allied to religion. It is widely assumed that he began writing free verse and juvenile literature seriously in 1921, after a high-ranking

Buddhist priest named Takachio Chiyō advised him against entering the priesthood, explaining that in the Hokke sect a believer was expected to try to reach a higher level of faith while following his line of business. The priest further suggested that if Kenji felt gifted as a poet, he should pursue that art until his faith in Buddhism manifested itself in his poems without conscious effort. Kenji seems to have taken the advice to heart. The words "Through Reverend Takachio's advice, creation of literature for the Flower of the Law" are recorded in one of his notebooks, and a letter from the same year declares: "The religion of the future is art. The art of the future is religion."

In what sense can poetry serve as a religion? Kenji's answer would have stressed poetry's ability to widen our perspective. The kind of poetry collected in *Spring and Asura* helps a person to transcend the human and merge with the true mind, the single, shared consciousness that is reality. It helps a person know his true self and experience his true place in the scheme of things.

Unfortunately, Kenji could not unwaveringly keep his belief in such a lofty view of poetry. Especially in his later years, he doubted poetry's capabilities more and more. A devaluation of poetry is already evident in a preface he wrote for his unpublished second collection of imagery sketches, entitled *Spring and Asura II*. Toward its end he entreated magazine editors not to press him for more poetry after they read the collection. Explaining why he disliked such solicitations, he said, "Incompetent man though I am, I have a farm to till, and in winter I have to set up an 'office' with jute sacks at various places and advise rice farmers on fertilizing. My head is filled with thoughts about those works, which are somewhat more humble than such declarations as 'Let us march on full stride' or 'Let us make a pledge,' and so on." Although he did not deny the value of poetry, Kenji implied that he personally attached equal or even higher importance to other things that were generally considered lower than poetry in the hierarchy of human activities. Foremost among those other things were farming and helping people to farm. To Kenji, poetry began to look less meaningful because a poet merely promised without making the physical effort to fulfill his promise.

Kenji's misgivings about the capabilities of poetry came to take more direct expression in later years. An extreme case is his poem "Love and Hate for Poetry," an imagery sketch that he published in a magazine in 1933. The poem is about an electrical engineer on a night shift at a hydroelectric plant. As he sleepily watches over the gauges on the master panel, there appears before him a sweet-voiced woman whose body is made of ice and through whose chest show three radiant hearts. The engineer, who apparently has a complex about art, recognizes her as Poetry and strikes up a conversation:

"Just as I suspected,
you have three hearts, don't you?"
As the engineer sadly mutters,
the beautiful lady, heaving her chest in pride, says
"How could anyone write a play
without three or four hearts?"
That angers the engineer.
"What is a play anyway?" he asks.
"Because of your petty education
and silly vanity
those children in the field out there
cannot buy
little red pants or even a pair of socks.
At the year's end, the heads of their families
must go to the market for fish and medicine
and roam the streets, sighing,
until the night falls.
Who is the master artist
deserving that kind of sacrifice?
Where is the work of art
rivaling that kind of sacrifice?
If what is known as art
remains an imitation, a fake
or a place of refuge for incompetents and cowards
for ever and ever,
we should smash it to pieces!"

When the engineer realizes that his words have been a bit too violent, it is too late. The shocked lady collapses to the floor and disintegrates, whereupon the engineer's vision vanishes, too.

In "Love and Hate for Poetry," Kenji criticized poetry for ig-

noring current social conditions, and thus helping to create
them. Yet Kenji must have felt a certain affection for his Lady
Poetry, since the engineer belatedly regrets having blasted her,
and the poem's title includes the word "love" as well as "hate."
The later Kenji loved poetry so long as it presented a vision of
beauty and truth mankind could seek, but he had to reject it
when it did little or nothing to actualize that vision.

Kenji tried hard to resolve the dichotomy between art and life,
between vision and reality, in his later years. His endeavor was
twofold: on the one hand he attempted to transform real life
into art, and on the other he tried to bring art close to the life of
workers. In other words, he attempted to bring art and life together by reorienting each toward the other. His attempt to see
art in a worker's life has already been glimpsed in "Opus 1063"
and "To My Students." It took even more direct expression in
the following poem:

Third Art

As I ploughed the field for turnips,
a stocky, gray-haired man
sneaked up behind me
and asked what I planned to sow.
Red turnip seeds, I answered.
The man, saying a turnip field
should be ploughed like this,
quietly stretched out his hand
for my hoe
and drew a curved furrow with it.
Stillness ringing in my head,
I stood there vacantly
as if entranced by a magic potion.
There were the sunshine, the wind,
our two shadows cast on the sand,
and a stream gleaming in the distance.
Yet I was in a trance, wondering
what brushstroke in black ink
or what fragrance of a sculptor's chisel
could ever surpass that furrow.

Here the old farmer is identified as a master artist who uses a
hoe for his paintbrush and the earth for his canvas. His art is
that of the Third Estate, or "third art." By extending the mean-

ing of art to include the consummate skill of an experienced laborer, Kenji was attempting to unify life and art.

On the other hand, Kenji tried to bring art into laborers' lives, for he felt that too many workers never knew the enjoyment afforded by beautiful things. That feeling is expressed in such poems as this:

Opus 739
In the dense fog the hands are freezing.
  The horse's thighs tremble, too.
Toss me the rope. The rope!
  The plumes of pampas grass are loaded with frosty dew.
  Would that sunrise be soon!
A pheasant is crowing. A pheasant
appears to be in your house.
   Striding through the vacant house,
   looking for food
   and crying. Isn't that a pheasant?

The poem, written in 1926, depicts farmers working in the field on a chilly autumn morning. On the dusky farm before sunrise, their minds are occupied with work and with their wish for the sun to bring some warmth. Kenji, however, wants them to think of a pheasant, a beautiful bird that symbolizes art. He believed the farmers would get a bit of relief from their hard work if they could divert their minds to things of beauty from time to time.

Kenji's twofold approach to a synthesis of art and life found its definitive expression in "Agrarian Art." The title of the essay suggests its purport, a unification of art and farm life; that unification is attained when all artists become farmers who physically till the land and all farmers become artists who are sensitive to the beauty of nature and of their own work. As has been noted, Kenji criticized contemporary artists for monopolizing beauty, an old, unproductive kind of beauty. In the same essay he had this message for artists:

Look at those long-haired ones sipping coffee, their faces vainly waiting for something.

Burn up all your worries and merge with the soul of all that exists.

Communicate with the wind, obtain energy from the clouds.

And he had this message for farmers:

Set your gray labor aflame by means of art.
Here is our ceaseless, pure, and happy creation.

He explained, "Labor is something instinctive. It is not always pain. It is always creation. Creation is always a pleasure. When a person sacrifices his humanity and enslaves himself for productivity, it turns into pain." Ultimately, Kenji was trying to restore humanity to art as well as to workers' lives, making it the basis of both. Of course, in his vocabulary "humanity" had unusually large connotations, including the cosmic mind that man shares with all other beings. Agrarian art as conceived by Kenji was based on this kind of humanity; it should enable all men to join together in a common spirituality and a shared work.

Such a view of the use of art is open to criticism when seen against the backdrop of contemporary society. In the first place, Kenji's identification of a higher type of art with agrarian life is too limited in scope, for labor is not limited to farm labor. Life on a farm provides more opportunities for the artist to merge with nature and to receive creative energy from it than does life in a factory. But Japan had already begun transforming herself from an agrarian into an industrial nation, and Kenji appears to have regarded that fact too lightly. Second, he was too optimistic in his expectations for the role of art in agrarian life. He thought art would relieve the hardships of peasant life, but he seems to have overlooked the fact that the main cause of those hardships was the existing social order, which heavily favored landlords. Poetry might bring emotional relief, but it could not cure social inequities. Takuboku eventually found that out, but to the last Kenji does not seem to have felt it of paramount importance.

Be that as it may, Kenji's vision of the use of art remains an attractive ideal. Long after his death Japan has not yet solved the problems that concerned him. Many artists still suffer from a dichotomy between art and life, as evidenced by the life and death of the novelist Mishima Yukio (1925–70). Like Kenji, Mishima in later life came to recognize that art was powerless to improve existing conditions. Earlier he had tried to create the kind of art that would positively contribute to the spiritual well-being of his countrymen, but in the last phase of his career, he seems to have given up hope that art could make an active contribution to social welfare.[9] Other novelists, like Abe Kōbō (b. 1924), have written extensively about alienation, a prevalent problem in contemporary, urbanized Japan, and have tried to find some way to facilitate meaningful communication between individuals.[10] Kenji's poetry, and his idea of poetry, address these and other problems that are still vital today. His solution requires an idealistic and spiritualistic belief beyond the grasp of many, but his proposal of uniting through art with both the world and one's fellow humans is appealing. And the honesty, sincerity, and intensity with which he made that proposal are exceptional, moving all who read his biography and his writings. He not only conceived a unique view of poetry; he lived it.

[9] The dichotomy between art and life, and his lifelong endeavor to resolve it, are outlined by Mishima himself in the autobiographical essay *Sun and Steel*.

[10] The best treatment of this theme is Abe's celebrated novel *The Woman in the Dunes*.

CHAPTER SIX

Takamura Kōtarō

To MANY Japanese readers, Takamura Kōtarō (1883–1956) represents "the conscience of Japan." Some poets have called him the "father of contemporary Japanese verse" and have paired him with Hagiwara Sakutarō, whom they consider its "mother." The high respect accorded him in Japan has not been echoed, however, in other parts of the world. Kōtarō's poetry seems uninspiring to many Western readers. In the context of world literature, his imagination appears limited, his ideas simplistic, and his style prosaic. Even his Chieko poems, so lavishly praised in Japan, lose much of their lustre when placed beside the best European love poetry. The discrepancy between his national renown and international apathy is remarkable.

Kōtarō himself seemed to anticipate such a discrepancy. Toward the end of his career, in a poem entitled "My Verse," he declared:

> Despite the fervent love I have for Western poetry
> my verse stands on a different base.
> The Athenian sky and the Christian fountain
> gave birth to the language and thought of Western poetry.
> Full of beauty and strength, it comes flowing into me
> and yet its physique, built on flour, butter, and beef,
> would not translate into my Japanese.

Presumably, the different base he spoke of has an irresistible charm for many Japanese readers but is an enigma to Westerners.

There is also the problem of Kōtarō's anti-British and anti-American poems. Until the late 1930's, he was known as a humanist poet and a member of the idealistic White Birch group, composed of writers and artists who had a profound faith in the basic goodness of human nature and advocated respect for individuality, love for all mankind, and freedom from all forms of hatred and violence. Like other members of the group, he ardently admired idealistic humanists of the West such as Tolstoy and Romain Rolland; indeed, he was the first person ever to undertake a Japanese translation of Rolland's masterpiece, *Jean Christophe*. Yet when the war broke out he became one of the most outspoken poets supporting the militarist government. Before then he had published only two books of poetry, *The Journey* (1914) and *Chieko Poems* (1941). Suddenly he began producing many poems in praise of the war, filling three anthologies: *These Great Days* (1942), *Uncle's Poems* (1943), and *The Records* (1944). After the war he regretted having written these works and tried to explain:

> The Emperor is in danger!
> That one cry
> decided everything for me.

This, however, does not completely explain how he reconciled humanism and militarism.

Finally, throughout his life Kōtarō insisted that he be considered a sculptor rather than a poet. He even refused to be inducted into the Japanese Academy of Art as a poet, fearing that his acceptance of the honor would jeopardize his chances of being elected as a sculptor. We might assume, then, that his poetry would be a sculptor's verse, that it would be influenced by his concern for another medium. An examination of his poetic should shed light on his relation to the two art forms and on the other enigmas and contradictions of his career.

I Talk of Natural Life

An observation that appears toward the end of a short but perceptive essay called "Human Heads," published in 1927, suggests Kōtarō's idea of representation:

A man's head shows two types of beauty, innate and acquired, their close intermixture creating an overall harmony. Of course I like innate beauty, but I find myself attracted even more to acquired beauty. The latter is human beauty derived from a person's life experience. I like aged people partly for this reason. A photograph merely reproduces innate beauty, failing to capture the other type. Accordingly, all babies look beautiful in photographs. It is only through living eyes that acquired beauty can be recognized; it cannot be captured by mechanical means. People who look more attractive in photographs are endowed with innate beauty, whereas those who do not look good in photographs but who are charming when seen in person have plenty of acquired beauty, the beauty derived from their respective careers, life-styles, personalities, and education.

Kōtarō did not explicitly say how acquired beauty could be recorded, but he undoubtedly implied that an artist, with his living eyes, can catch and record the kind of beauty that a camera cannot.

Elsewhere in his writings Kōtarō repeatedly emphasized the superiority of art to photography, his favorite example being the statues by Michelangelo known as "Day" and "Night" in the New Sacristy of San Lorenzo in Florence. He once saw a photograph showing living people in the same pose as Michelangelo's statues and was deeply impressed by the much greater force of the artist's creation.[1] He concluded that there were two ways of copying nature. Photography is a low-level copying, and so are illustrations of news reports and drawings of specimens in school textbooks; Kōtarō felt that many bronze statues standing throughout Tokyo belonged in this category, too. True art, in contrast, should attempt to imitate nature at a higher level.

If Kōtarō's view of photography seems unfair, we should remember that he made his observations at a time when photographic art was still in its infancy in Japan. Furthermore, his criticism was directed less at photography than at factual reality. According to him, the real subject of a work of art can look less beautiful than the work that draws on it. For instance, a nō mask, which imitates a human face, at times looks more alive than a

[1] The photograph was published in G. H. Stratz, *Die Darstellung des menschlichen Körpers in der Kunst* (Berlin, 1914).

living actor's face on the stage. Auguste Rodin's statue of Balzac is, in Kōtarō's judgment, the Balzac among Balzacs; it is more like Balzac than was the real person. "When it is a true work of sculpture," said Kōtarō, "a portrait of a person will be more like the person than he is himself. An image of a cicada will be more like a cicada than the actual insect, and that of a rock will be more like a rock than the actual stone. The image may not be a complete replica of the original, yet it will look more like the original than the original does itself." This is because the original as we see it is confused by its connections with what is not its own essential life. "A living person has residues," Kōtarō explained. "He possesses things that are not his molecules, things that are nonessential, ambivalent, and wasteful."

Kōtarō's concept of artistic representation, then, implies copying the essential, inner core of the subject. He seems to have arrived at this idea through personal experience as a sculptor. As he remembered, one day in his youth he was trying to carve a wooden replica of a wreath shell.[2] He made five carvings, but none of them satisfied him because although they resembled the model closely enough, they somehow looked weak. After many painful hours he finally discovered that a wreath shell has an "axis." He was able to rotate the shell when he held the two ends of its axis. Apparently the shellfish had grown around this axis, adding spines one by one. The discovery made his work much easier. He carved a new replica with the axis in mind, and was able to complete a work that looked firm and well settled. From then on he made a habit of not beginning to carve anything until he had discovered the "axis" in his model.

Kōtarō's idea of mimesis is simple to apply as long as the subject is a relatively uncomplicated object like a wreath shell. But one runs into difficulties when the subject is more complex. What, for instance, is the axis of a fish, a bird, or an animal? And what happens when the subject is a person? From Kōtarō's essay

[2] A wreath shell (*Turbo cornutus*) is a kind of shellfish living in the waters near Japan. Its shell, shaped like a small wreath made of tree branches, is used ornamentally.

on people's heads, we can infer that an artist carving a human portrait tries to represent the inner forces that shaped the model's past history and thereby present the "acquired beauty" that photography cannot capture. But perceiving those inner forces is not easy; a person is harder to examine than a shell. In his youth, Kōtarō experienced that difficulty when he was studying art in Paris. Being Japanese, he felt he simply could not understand his French model. Her white body seemed, he said, as inscrutable as a tiger in the zoo. At last he decided to go back to Japan and use a Japanese model.

Back in Japan, however, Kōtarō often experienced a related difficulty: that all people may not see the essential inner forces in the same way. On one such occasion, he was carving the head of a wealthy industrialist. The old man, full of self-confidence, said while posing for him:

> "An artist who copies nature is no good.
> A portrait need not resemble the model
> if only it shows him to be a great man.
> Yes—yes (his mouth stretching six inches wide),
> I can be excused now, can't I?
> You say you can't carve an image of Buddha?
> That's because your art is not good enough.
> Don't copy nature.
> Do you know the phrase 'the spirit's circulation, life's
>   motion'?[3]
> I came up with this satirical poem this morning."
> Examining this lump of avarice from top to bottom
> I copy every bit of its contours
> and record the whole development of capitalism in the
>   Japanese Empire, shown in the grotesque face.

Here both the industrialist and the artist share the view that art should not copy nature's surface but represent its essence. Yet in determining what that essence is, the two differ vastly.

Kōtarō tried to resolve the conflict between subjective judgment and objective representation by recognizing distinct roles for different forms of art, in particular for poetry and sculpture.

---

[3] The phrase is one of the most famous—and controversial—terms in Chinese and Japanese painting. Its basic meaning seems to be that a painting is vibrant with life only when the painter's spirit circulates through it.

This is suggested in his poem "Portrait," from which the quotation above is taken. The poem voices the sculptor's disgust with his model, yet we might wonder whether the sculptor should not have expressed that disgust by means of sculpture rather than poetry. Kōtarō, however, felt that poetry was far more capable of expressing emotion than was sculpture. Both arts demand that the artist represent the essence of his subject, but sculpture's demand is more rigorous: since it translates forms into other similarly three-dimensional shapes, it is a more directly mimetic art. Because Kōtarō felt his repugnance as a subjective feeling, he expressed it in a poem; in his portrait head he presented, or thought he presented, the more objective forces that shaped both the life of his model and the recent history of the country.

Kōtarō elaborated on this distinction in a short essay called "My Relationship with Poetry," which gives an account of his student days, when his sculpture became too poetic. At one time he witnessed some young children employed by a circus company going through their ruthlessly rigorous training. Stricken by humanitarian wrath, he created a sculpture showing circus girls in tears, with their young male partners gesturing as if to defend them. At another time he became interested in portraying a Buddhist priest forsaking his holy mission, and carved a statue of a priest tearing up sutras in a dramatic gesture. However, soon Kōtarō came to realize the foolishness of forcing sculpture to perform what poetry does better. Thus, in order to protect his objectivity in sculpture, he began writing poetry more seriously. "For this reason," he explained, "in both my tanka and my shi there are few nature poems or poems of objective description. Many of them present my personal thoughts directly. My desire for objective description is fulfilled in sculpture. In this sense, poetry is my safety valve."

On another occasion he put the issue from an opposite angle, treating sculpture as the "safety valve" of his poetry. In a panel discussion entitled "Beauty and Life," he observed that contemporary free verse had been dominated by imagism, a trend he personally disliked. "I've never been an imagist; I can't be one,"

238 Takamura Kōtarō

he said. "That is because I am a sculptor. Sculpture is all imagery. When I want to present images, I don't have to write poetry. At a time like that I produce sculpture." Kōtarō drew a neat distinction between the two arts, a distinction no doubt related to the fact that abstract sculpture had not yet been introduced to Japan.

In Kōtarō's opinion, then, poetry expresses essential life forces as they are experienced within the artist's own life; sculpture captures the same forces observed from without, in the life of another. Yet what are those inner forces, the subject of poetry as Kōtarō saw it?

A traditional Japanese answer would be that the subject of poetry is intense, genuinely felt emotions, something like Akiko's jikkan. Some of Kōtarō's statements and many of his poems appear to substantiate this answer. Nevertheless, there is evidence that his stand was more unusual. For instance, in an essay called "Characteristics of Japanese Verse," he defined poetry as energy and considered emotion nothing more than one of the media that help convey that energy. "The true being of poetry lies in an emanation issuing forth from the whole of the poem," he said. "Things written down in the poem, such as subject matter, emotion, and intellect, are no more than media for that emanation." Kōtarō's favorite metaphor for the energy conveyed by a poem was electricity. In an essay entitled "I Would Not Speak on Poetry," he said he wrote poetry from a strong inner impulse and compared it to accumulated electric energy seeking release. The metaphor also appears in the poem "Stormy Mountains":

No poetry lies in meaning.
Meaning is no more than a medium that carries electricity.

In Kōtarō's view, a poem may embody the poet's intense emotion—or, for that matter, penetrating intellect or engaging subject matter—but its ultimate purpose is to convey a kind of psychophysical energy from the poet to the reader.

Kōtarō may have felt that this all-important energy could not be explained in analytical terms, since he preferred to talk of it in a more impressionistic manner, often in poems or aphorisms. Here are two examples:

My View of Poetry

Poetry is no more than an emanation from the core of the way in which a man lives his life.

It has neither a fixed form, nor a theorem, nor a house. It cannot be captured, and yet it abounds in man. Hence, poetry transforms itself in an infinite number of ways.

Poetry Itself

Vitamins can be extracted. Life cannot be. Life is always incarnate in matter. Poetry cannot be extracted, either. Poetry is always incarnate in subject matter. A true poet is never afraid of any subject or thought, because he knows poetry is invisible and universal like life. Only a second-rate poet who is frightened about the choice of subject matter for his poetry and who thinks his poem should extract poetry is concerned about the art of composition. Such a poet is like a man who mistakes vitamins for life.

From these aphorisms we can infer that Kōtarō believed poetic energy to be identical with the very source of life, the energy that keeps a thing alive.

A look at another of his poems, "The Starting Point," will further clarify the concept:

I talk only of fundamentals,
I sing only of the fountainhead
in a simple language even a child can speak
or rather, only a child can speak.
When people say they have a headache
I don't talk of medicine,
I talk of natural life.
Holding their heads in their hands, they complain:
What a silly answer!
Probably it is silly.
But I know only one thing—
to follow Nature's laws.
In a bag, seeds of cedar from Katori Shrine[4]
look like tiny particles of dust,
yet once in the soil they are awakened,
regain life, and sprout up through the ground.

[4] The Shinto shrine, located in Chiba Prefecture, is dedicated to a war god. Many cedar trees grow in its precincts.

This is the only sort of thing
I know and am truly impressed with.
I always make it a starting point.

Clearly the theme of the poem is an awareness of a fundamental
life-force deep within a living being, a force that makes a seed
germinate and a poet sing out. Kōtarō called it "Nature." I will
capitalize the word in his usage, to distinguish it from "nature"
in the ordinary sense. This concept is central to Kōtarō as man
and poet.

Kōtarō's attitude toward the basic life-force, or Nature, was
strongly affirmative, almost reverent. It stood out distinctly in
contemporary Japanese literature, which was dominated by naturalism. Influenced by Darwinism, naturalist writers conceived
of the life-force as amoral and instinctive, functioning for the
prime purpose of maintaining life and the species. Because of
this force, they imagined, plants vie for sunlight, animals devour
one another, and human beings struggle for survival. Kōtarō,
along with other members of the White Birch group, revolted
against that prevailing notion. He thought of the force as mor-
ally positive. To him, anything that followed its natural life
seemed good. Nature's laws should take precedence over man's
laws, he felt; indeed, they were *the* laws. His concept of Nature
also showed a more optimistic outlook than the traditional idea
of nature, which presumed a set of neutral, superhuman forces
controlling the universe. Since olden times the Japanese had
associated aspects of nature with anthropomorphic gods, who
could be violent and ruthless when angered. Kōtarō believed
that humankind has nature-given strength to withstand such violence. In his view, even the destructive forces of nature are
good because they nurture human strength and courage.

Kōtarō's optimistic idea of Nature and its presence in man is
succinctly expressed in a two-line poem called "The Poet":

> No matter how tightly I am blindfolded, I turn in the di-
> rection I am expected to.
> No matter how many times it is rotated, the needle points
> toward the celestial pole.

This poem speaks a strong confidence in the workings of Nature within man. His senses may temporarily be blinded, yet perceptions rooted deeper in his body are never blinded; they are like a compass needle always pointing north. All a poet need do is follow the basic impulse deep within him.

At this point we can see a connection between the "axis" of a sculptor's subject and the poet's vital energy, which is the core of his topic. They spring from the same source and point toward the same pole because both follow Nature's laws. To rephrase the difference between poetry and sculpture, then, a poet tries to express the basic force of Nature through an energy within himself, whereas a sculptor expresses the same force by dissolving his personal identity into the energy within his subject. In both instances the energy is essentially good, according to Kōtarō.

To sum up, then, in Kōtarō's view art imitates nature through Nature. The artist copies reality, concentrating on the basic life-force that resides deep within him, as well as within his subject. Art is mimetic because the life-force is within every object in the universe, but art is also expressive because the life-force can be found within the artist himself. A poet tends to try to capture that vital energy by looking inside himself, whereas a sculptor does so by observing an outer object; yet the main purpose of both artists is the same.

Although Nature always occupied a central place in Kōtarō's view of art, his treatment of it varied considerably in the several distinct phases of his poetic career. To trace its vicissitudes, one can examine representative poems in chronological order to see how his approach to Nature developed. As befits a poet whose ideal poetry depended on the expression of inner impulses and an inner energy, the changes in his attitude toward Nature, and by extension to the relation between poetry and the world, are bound up with stages in his biography.

Kōtarō's first book of poetry, *The Journey*, includes 107 poems written between 1910 and 1914. It represents the work of his Sturm und Drang period, a time of emotional turmoil and rapid fluctuations in his personal life while he groped for spiritual direction and a vocation. In 1909, after he returned from three years in the West, Kōtarō joined a group of young artists who called themselves decadents, and with them he spent many nights in drinking and sensual indulgence. Soon growing dissatisfied with that life, he planned to be a dairy farmer and traveled northward to Hokkaido. However, his farming plans ended in failure, too. In rapid succession, he then had a love affair with a geisha, opened and closed an art gallery, turned down an offer of a college post, and declared that he had no intention of heading the Takamura family in the future. *The Journey* contains a number of poems that reflect these painful experiences and Kōtarō's effort to rise above them. Its title poem, written toward the end of this period, gives a sense of the direction he eventually found:

> There is no road ahead of me.
> The road follows behind me.
> O Nature,
> father,
> magnificent father, you gave me independence.
> Watch over and protect me forever.
> Always fill me with your vitality
> for this long journey of mine,
> for this long journey of mine.

Here the poet is a seeker of the Way, a person groping for moral guidance. And he begins to find it; it is Nature within him, a life-force given by a magnificent father. The identification of Nature with a father rather than a mother is characteristic of Kōtarō, who wanted to see strength, rather than gentleness, at the core of man's existence. In the poem the speaker has not yet found the road to follow in the journey of his life, but he has found a way to build that road—namely, the strength and energy given him by Nature.

Most other poems in *The Journey* are variations on the same theme. Early pieces, such as "Night in a Studio," "The Land of Netsuke," and "Father's Face," reveal Kōtarō's frustration with present reality, whether that of art, that of other Japanese people, or that of the Japanese within himself, and they suggest his ardent desire to overcome and surpass that reality. The winter poems, such as "Winter Comes," "Winter Has Come," and "Winter Poem," all reiterate his determination to arrive at his goal despite his harsh surroundings. "Lonely Road" and "Night" closely resemble "The Journey" in portraying a wanderer seeking for the right way to live, whereas later poems in the collection, such as "Mountain," "I Dance with Millions of Things," and "The Soil in May," depict such a wanderer in touch with Nature and thereby gaining courage and strength to venture further in the same direction. The poems in *The Journey* do indeed trace the poet's journey from darkness to light.

After publishing *The Journey*, Kōtarō planned a second book of poetry entitled *Wild Beasts*. It was never published during his lifetime. As the proposed title indicates, the poems to be collected in the anthology all centered around animals. Here is one of them, "The Ragged Ostrich," one of the best-known poems by Kōtarō:

> What is so amusing about keeping an ostrich?
> In the muddy four-yard square of the zoo
> aren't his legs too large to stride?
> Isn't his neck too long?
> Aren't the wings too tattered for life in a land with
>   snowfall?
> He will eat biscuits when he gets hungry,
> but aren't his eyes always gazing into the distance?
> Aren't they blazing with insufferable anguish?
> Aren't they waiting, ever so eagerly, for an emerald wind?
> Isn't that small, homely head whirling with boundless
>   dreams?
> He is no longer an ostrich—don't you agree?
> Men,
> stop doing this sort of thing.

The anger in this poem is directed to all who suppress the Nature in living creatures. Wild animals and birds provided a model for Kōtarō because their actions are faithful to the source of life within themselves. Unlike them, many modern people have not only lost sight of this source but unwittingly impose on others a life directly counter to it. The poem has been called humanistic and humane; it is so, but that humanism is derived from the poet's positive faith in Nature, or the "wild beast," within a living being.

A similar affirmation of Nature constitutes the main theme of many other poems by Kōtarō that feature animals and birds. Like the poem just cited, "Polar Bears" and "Elephant's Bank" portray wild beasts caged in a zoo, the former focusing on the poet's attraction to the stern nonconformity of the bears, and the latter on his sympathy for the tame elephant. Based on Kōtarō's personal observations in the United States, the poems also reflect his unfavorable impressions of contemporary American culture. In poems like "Lion Licking His Wound," "Elephant," and "Gorilla in the Woods," wild beasts either have been captured or have almost been trapped by the cunning schemes of humankind but succeed in breaking out of their imprisonment and returning joyfully to their native habitats. "Fastidiousness," "Thunder Beast," and "Dragon" all depict imaginary creatures that are Nature incarnate and that in their innate fastidiousness show how filthy the world of men really is. "Catfish" describes a sculptor carving a catfish, in touch with Nature within the fish he is modeling. It may seem strange that Kōtarō should have chosen an awkwardly shaped fish as an embodiment of Nature, but to his sensibility a catfish was a "wild beast" precisely because of its unrefined form. A goldfish would never have served the purpose.

Thematically there is only a short distance between these poems and the pieces collected in *Chieko Poems*, Kōtarō's next book of poetry, for through his love of his wife Chieko he returned to the Nature within himself. In a more literal sense, Chieko herself reverted to a "wild beast" when she became insane. It is difficult to select just one poem from this popular anthology, as it covers Kōtarō's work from 1912 to 1941;[5] nevertheless, the following poem will illustrate his views on Nature, love, and their interrelationship:

[5] This refers to the first edition. An expanded edition of *Chieko Poems* was published in 1956, shortly after Kōtarō's death.

Cattle at a Frenzied Run

Oh, are you frightened
by what you just saw?
Like demons thundering
through a deep forest, shaking the yew pines
and causing an avalanche into the silence,
they bolted away to a place unknown,
a herd of cattle at a frenzied run.

Let us stop working for today.
Off triangular Mount Hotaka's ridge, which we were
 sketching,
clouds of terre-verte have appeared.
Over the cerulean Azusa River
carrying the icy water from Yari Peak,
mountains have begun to lean.
Far in the valley, white aspens blow in the wind.
Let us stop sketching for today
and build the fire we like,
not so large as to pollute this sanctuary.
Be seated on the moss there
Nature has swept clean.

Are you frightened
because you saw that young bull, bloody and distraught,
breathlessly chase
a herd of stampeding cows?
Some day you will recall with sympathy
the animal nature bared on this holy mountain.
Some day, after you have experienced many more things,
you will recall it, and smile in quiet love.

This could be called a "wild beast" poem because of its affirmation of the animal energy revealed in stampeding cattle. But
here that energy is related to the romantic love between the poet
and a young woman, presumably Chieko. The maiden, inexperienced in love, does not notice that relationship, but the poet
is sure she will come to learn about it as she matures. He feels
she will in time understand, and even admire, the frenziedly
running animals.

Chieko must have found Kōtarō's idea of natural love attractive, since eventually she married him. For a time their life together, as described by many who visited them, seemed to represent a model of such love. But such a life-style inevitably has

latent dangers. First, it presupposes the complete isolation of the two lovers from the rest of the world, for their pursuit of love confines them to a private world all their own. The two need extraordinary motivation and willpower to fight off the intrusion of elements alien to their life together, and there is always tension between them and the external world. Second, if love is based on a complete affirmation of natural impulses, as Kōtarō said it should be, disharmony as well as harmony will arise: both amorous pursuit and antagonism are implied in "Cattle at a Frenzied Run." Kōtarō seems to have underestimated or ignored these aspects of love, and the ensuing pressures must have contributed to Chieko's insanity. Finally something had to give. What gave was Chieko's sanity, the link between Kōtarō's studio and the outside world. Through her madness she returned to Nature, to a truly private world where not even her husband's love could follow her.

The book *Chieko Poems* traces the evolution of their love. Its early poems, such as "Fountain of Mankind" and two poems both called "To a Person," embody Kōtarō's fervent longing for Chieko the maiden, identifying that longing with an instinctive desire for the archetypal fountain that gives life to all living things. The next group of poems, such as "Dinner" and "Two under the Tree," by and large praise sensual love as the source of human vitality. The mundane world outside creeps into the lovers' minds at times, as described in "Two at Night" or "Person Who Delivers Beauty to Imprisonment," but they—especially Kōtarō —stubbornly stick to their principles and will not easily compromise their idealism for material comfort. Chieko, however, has moments of weakness: "Child's Talk" describes her longing for her native countryside, like a caged ostrich longing for his native wilderness. Then comes the third group of poems, in which Chieko has lost her sanity. Kōtarō keeps believing that his wife is still on her journey back to the wilderness, and so he portrays her in such poems as "Chieko Riding the Wind" and "Chieko Playing with Plovers." But he cannot bear the sadness of being left alone, and that feeling finds an outlet in such poems as

"Invaluable Chieko" and "Two at the Foot of the Mountain."
The last group of poems in the collection is made up of elegies
written after Chieko's death. The poems are pervaded by deep
grief, but consolation comes to Kōtarō in two ways. He believes
that in the last moments of her life Chieko regained sanity and
rejoined him as his loving wife. He also believes that after death
she has been reunited with Nature and therefore has become
part of himself. The first belief is given beautiful form in "Lemon
Elegy"; the second, in "To a Dead Person." Even after the catas-
trophe of Chieko's madness and death, Kōtarō's faith in Nature
was unwavering.

The Chieko poems reveal not only the strength and persistence with which Kōtarō believed in Nature but also his increased
isolation from the rest of the world because of that belief. Since
Chieko was the "fountain of mankind" for him, he had no need
of other people: his longing for openness with Nature was satisfied as long as his wife was with him. When Chieko died, he lost
that invaluable partner. To fill the void in his heart, he had to
reestablish his ties with the rest of humanity and to find a new
source of Nature. What he found in the outside world was a war-
bound country whose citizens were increasingly ultranationalistic. There, following the tenets of the nationalistic Shintoists, the
grief-stricken Kōtarō replaced love of Chieko with love of Japan
by discovering a new fountain of mankind in his Japanese ances-
try. He was captivated by the idea that war was divine as long as
the Emperor, the ultimate Shinto authority on earth, sanctioned
it. Thus he came to write poems promoting the war.

Kōtarō published three books of war poems in rapid succession. The following example, from *Uncle's Poems*, shows the sort
of message many of these poems sought to convey:

Those Who Return to the Source
Throughout the millennium the Great Deity has reigned.
Those who know the source of life gain a strength
that enables them to do deeds out of proportion to their
    stature.
Those oppressed with self-doubt
are in utter darkness, with no knowledge of the great cause.

Those who simply return to the source
see the bright sun and moon;
without questioning living or dying
they respond to His will with all they have.
Winter, spring, summer, and autumn have passed,
and December 8 is here again.
Soldiers killed in the war are not dead;
their life shining brightly, they guide us.
Now is the time to serve the country with dedication and
    courage.
Let all of us, each in his way,
return to the source of life.
Powerful are those who return to the source!

The poem bears the stamp of the former Kōtarō, for the poet is anxious to return to Nature, the source of all life. But that concept of Nature is now tied up with Shinto doctrines and through them with patriotism, Emperor worship, and justification of the holy war that began on December 8, 1940. Especially noteworthy is Kōtarō's categorical rejection of people who are "obsessed with self-doubt." He feels self-examination is characteristic of a person who is not yet initiated; a critical mind is a sign of ignorance and lack of faith in Nature. When the poet says those who "simply return to the source / see the bright sun and moon," he sanctions those who follow their inner impulses without intellectual scrutiny. For Kōtarō the path leading to Nature was emotional, not critical. There lay a pitfall. Although his prowar poetry had other roots as well, such as his complex feelings about being Japanese and his unhappy experiences in the United States, and although he did write a number of nonwar poems during the war years,[6] there is no doubt that his concept of Nature merged readily with ultranationalistic Shintoism, even at the sacrifice of humanism.

After the war, Kōtarō was intensely repentant. Although his name was not blacklisted by the occupation forces, he voluntarily banished himself to a humble hut in the wilds of northeastern

[6] Kōtarō apparently planned to publish these poems under the collective title *Songs of Little Stones*, but the manuscript burned when his house was demolished by an air raid in 1945.

Japan so that he could spend a life of penitence alone. Looking back, he came to feel he had been a model of folly; that feeling was so overwhelming that he gave the title *The Model* to the last book of free verse he published during his lifetime. In his view, he and all the other wartime leaders who misled the nation were models of folly, providing a lesson for the younger generations of Japanese. His concept of Nature in this last phase is revealed nowhere better than in its title poem, "The Model":

> The simple-minded snow continues to fall,
> and the hut is silent as a deaf-mute.
> The hut shelters a model,
> a model of folly,
> who was so steeped in the peculiar ethics
> prevalent for three generations in this peculiar country[7]
> that, to his rebellious eagle-wings,
> he applied his own pitifully sharp, coercive nails
> and broke his flight feathers by his own will,
> bringing on himself sixty years of life in a steel cage,
> a life of sitting, obeying,
> and living by those ethics to the dictates of his conscience:
> this creature as simple-minded as the continuing snow.
> Freed at last, he stretches his wings
> and discovers a sad truth:
> three rows of his flight feathers are gone,
> and his blinking eyes have dark-green blind spots.
> Yet, amid the ruins of crumbled walls,
> he bates his breath
> and prepares to dare the boundless expanse ahead—
> this model of folly.
> The mountain hut shelters the model,
> the simple-minded snow buries the hut.
> Irresistibly the snow continues to fall,
> covering everything.

The poem resembles "The Ragged Ostrich"; indeed, it could be retitled "The Ragged Eagle," since it centers on the "wild beast" in man and its conflict with the outside world. Nevertheless, there is a significant difference between the two poems. In

[7]"Three generations" refers to the reigns of Emperor Meiji (1852–1912), his son Emperor Taishō (1879–1926), and his grandson Emperor Shōwa (*b.* 1901). Kōtarō felt contemporary Japanese ethics emphasizing loyalty to the Emperor had begun during the Meiji period.

"The Model," the main culprit restricting the free manifestation of the poet's inner energy is not the materialism and inhumanity of modern life but the feudalistic ethics of early modern Japan, which formed his conscience. Instead of being trapped by forces in the outer world, the poet-eagle has been shaped from within by a particular national ethics, and because of that distortion of his nature he has been induced to cripple himself. He feels a fool, yet he berates himself, not for trusting Nature, but for allowing himself to be bound by traditional patterns of thinking.

Thus, in the last phase of his poetic career Kōtarō began to sense complexities and even contradictions inherent in his concept of Nature. He had optimistically thought that to achieve a better life all he need do was let his inner Nature freely follow its course. As it turned out, however, his inner impulses betrayed him and proved to be, not the spontaneous promptings of an inner life-force, but habits of thought conditioned by the prevailing ethics. Nature was too "simple-minded" not to allow itself to be led astray. Yet Kōtarō would not forsake Nature. On the contrary, he preferred to steep himself deeper in Nature, despite his realization of its limitations. He was determined that if Nature was simple-minded, he would be simple-minded too, and would live his life as a simpleton. He did not have anything else to believe in.

In his lifelong faith in Nature, Kōtarō was heir to some of the most prominent premodern Japanese men of letters, despite his declared adherence to Tolstoy, Rodin, and Romain Rolland. Like many medieval Japanese poets and their followers, such as Priest Saigyō, Kamo Chōmei (1153–1216), and Bashō, he chose to conceive Nature as transcendental, and in doing so he did not place much emphasis on the role of man. In his insistence on the importance of an inner life-force, he tended to be more pantheistic and cosmological than humanistic, especially as he grew older. For him, "return to Nature" implied turning his back on human society. As a younger man he had no need for other people's company if he could be with Chieko or if he felt he shared

life with a wild beast. His solitary life in the mountains as an old
man seems a natural outcome of his earlier life and beliefs, even
though a historical factor, the war, was the ostensible cause. It
is not difficult to see in Kōtarō the image of a medieval poet-
hermit who is disillusioned with strife-ridden society and re-
treats to the life of a sage in the wilds, although Kōtarō himself
may not have been aware of the connection between his stance
and Japan's long tradition of hermit poets.

The Merits and Faults of Spontaneous Writing

On May 21, 1943, the national radio broadcast a special news
bulletin that stunned everyone in wartime Japan. Admiral Yamamoto Isoroku, the highest-ranking field commander of the
Imperial Navy, had been killed when his plane was shot down at
the front. Hearing the news, Kōtarō immediately took up his
pen and began writing an elegy:

> Admiral Yamamoto was killed in action.
> The news struck me like a sudden flash of lightning.
> All the blood rushed into my head,
> and my pen could make only an illegible scrawl.

The poem goes on for seventeen more lines, extolling the late
admiral's virtues, grieving over his loss, and expressing the poet's belief that his brave death will greatly inspire all servicemen.
That belief, the poem concludes, finally steadied the poet's pen
and calmed his mind. Kōtarō entitled the poem "Death of an
Admiral" and published it in the newspaper *Asahi* the following
morning.

The episode exemplifies Kōtarō's view of the verse-writing
process. A poem, he believed, is spontaneously produced when a
poet is galvanized by a forceful energy that affects him like electricity. The view is consistent with his theory of mimesis, which
emphasizes the role of Nature and by extension implies that poetic composition is instantaneous. The news of the admiral's
death struck a chord in the inmost part of the patriotic poet's
heart, activating Nature within him. Kōtarō, a passive agent,

moved his pen according to Nature's dictates, and the poem was completed in no time. The manuscript of the poem, which survives today, substantiates its spontaneous composition, for the handwriting shows hardly any hesitation of the pen or revision through afterthought. The poet himself scrawled, in the margin of the manuscript, "3 P.M. on May 21, 1943. Written for the *Asahi* on the very day and time of the event."

Kōtarō's belief in the spontaneity of verse writing is frequently voiced in his essays and letters. "Poetry comes out of the poet," he once wrote, "in the same way frost crystallizes on the great earth." On another occasion he wrote, "A poem emerges spontaneously; it is inevitable. It is like a rooster announcing the time of dawn." "Being a poet is not a privilege," he wrote more than once. "It is an inevitability." Kōtarō held the same idea of the creative process in other arts. "Whether in painting or in sculpture, a work of art must be something absolute on the artist's part," he said. "Something written according to predetermined plan does not satisfy me. To my way of thinking, an artist must grab a palette or clay the moment Nature strikes his heart, so that he may transmit that instantaneous inspiration in his product." By "an inevitability" and "something absolute" Kōtarō referred to the vitality and autonomy of the prime force that motivates the artist. In his view, a work of art should be a spontaneous manifestation of Nature and free from all artificial rules. Only a second-rate poet, he thought, is concerned with the art of composition.

However, among Kōtarō's own poems those that show little or no evidence of revision, and hence can be called the most spontaneous, are generally inferior to those whose manuscripts or publication history show signs of reworking. No one would count "Death of an Admiral" among Kōtarō's best poems, even disregarding its ultranationalistic overtones, for the words sound stereotyped and the emotion is grandiose. In contrast, the manuscripts of his better poems show many traces of revision. A well-documented example is "Rice-Planting Song," an imitation folk song that humorously describes rice farmers planting their

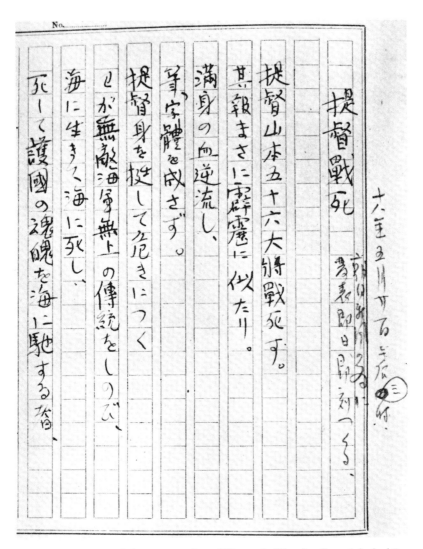

提督戦死

提督山本五十六大将戦死す。

其の報まさに霹靂に似たり。

満身の血逆流し、

筆、字體を成さず。

提督身を挺して危きにつく

己が無敵海軍無上の傳統をしのび、

海に生きく海に死し、

死して護國の魂魄を海上に馳する哉。

The first page of the manuscript of Kōtarō's "Death of an Admiral."
The note in the margin at right says that the poet wrote the verse imme-
diately after he heard the news. Reproduced from Kitagawa Taichi, ed.,
Takamura Kōtarō zen shikō, by permission of Mr. Takamura Tadashi and
Nigensha.

fields. Its first draft is so full of revisions that in many places it is difficult to make out what the original wording was. According to his diary, Kōtarō went to see a performance of rice-planting dances on March 7, 1947. He began writing the poem on March 13 but did not finish it until April 30, making at least three different drafts in the meantime. He worked on the poem on March 13, 15, 16, 20, 21, 22, 24, 25, and 29. He then asked a local schoolteacher to look over his use of dialect in the poem, and after getting her comments on April 27, he revised for another couple of days. Thus the poem cannot by any stretch of the imagination be said to have formed itself naturally like frost condensing on the earth or a rooster crowing at dawn. The same can be said of the way in which "New Order in the Orient" was written. Kōtarō first thought of writing a poem about Oriental poetry on or before July 22, 1948, but he had difficulty getting started. His diary reveals that he tried to write the poem unsuccessfully on July 22 and 25, was able to produce a little on July 29, August 1, and August 4, and then wrote a good deal on August 5 and 6. He polished the poem on August 8, made a clean copy on August 21, and finally mailed it out to a magazine on August 23. Again, it is evident that this poem did not come into being simply by instantaneous inspiration.

As a matter of fact, Kōtarō once wrote a poem expressing the agony of prolonged composition. Dated 1949, it is called "Wicked Woman":

> The poem I began on those snowy days
> is still not finished after cherry blossoms are gone.
> In the grip of this wicked woman
> I cannot take even a single forward step.
> In a wrinkle of my brain
> an idea is stuck, and that alien object
> has clogged the path of my creative impulse.
> The impulse, independent as it always is,
> takes no notice of the situation
> and tries to pull me into a world of exquisite beauty.
> Yet the wicked woman, breathing hard,
> holds me lustfully all day and all night.
> I am late for sowing,

my potatoes are rotting,
brackens are becoming overgrown,[8]
the charcoal fire went out some time ago.
Already grapnel flowers[9] are in bloom everywhere,
and occasionally hailstones hit my shoulders.
What shall I do with that wretched idea?

According to his own theory, Nature should have activated Kōtarō's creative impulse and produced a poem in no time, but
the reality was far different. Cherry trees, grapnel flowers, and
everything else seemed to follow their natural courses, but the
poet's mind did not, even though he could recognize Nature's
impulse deep in himself. He was painfully aware of something
within him trying to express itself, but he could not find a
proper means to release it. Whether he eventually succeeded in
doing so is not known, for he gave no clue as to the identity of
the poem he was working on. Be that as it may, he is confessing
that the creative impulse, activated by Nature, is sometimes not
enough for successful composition of a poem. He must have realized that intense energy alone cannot produce a good poem,
and he did produce some fine poems. How did he do it?

Kōtarō did not explicitly answer that question, since he had a
profound disdain for all poetics and refused to recognize that
there was such a thing as an art of verse writing. However, many
surviving manuscripts show that in actual practice he often
thought about ways to improve his draft poems. By analyzing
some examples of his creative process, one can infer his un-
expressed views on the subject.

Kōtarō composed our first example, "Life with a Distant Aim,"
on January 22, 1935, after more than two years without writing a
poem. He had been too busy tending his ailing wife. Chieko's illness was especially serious in late 1934 and early 1935; she refused to eat, smashed things, screamed at everyone, and ran
about hysterically. But on the night of January 21, Kōtarō managed to scrawl a short poem:

[8] Young shoots of brackens are eaten in Japan.
[9] They are so called because the flower is shaped like a grapnel. The Latin
name is *Epimedium grandiflorum*.

Life with a Distant Aim

A bird flies out from under my feet.
My wife takes poison.
My wife loses her mind.
The sight is set at 3,000 meters.
This gun has too distant an aim!

He made a clean copy of the poem the following day. He then remembered that a friend, Nakahara Ayako (*b.* 1898), had asked him to write a preface to her new book of poetry. He did not know if he would have time to oblige, so he added the words "For a Preface" in parentheses after the title and sent it to her, explaining the situation in an accompanying letter. Madame Nakahara, however, decided not to use the poem in her book, fearing that it might embarrass Chieko. Eventually Kōtarō published the poem in a magazine in August of that year—after, of course, erasing the parentheses. Then, in December 1939, the poem was republished in an anthology of contemporary poetry. Sometime between the two publications, Kōtarō reworked the manuscript. The anthology version reads:

Life with a Distant Aim

A bird flies out from under my feet.
My wife goes insane.
My clothes become ragged.
The sight is set at 3,000 meters.
This gun has too distant an aim!

The version that appeared in *Chieko Poems* two years later was the same, as were all other subsequent ones.

The second version is definitely better. In the original draft, the second and third lines are repetitive in both wording and implication: the repetition of "my wife" is bothersome, and the third line merely reiterates what is implicit in the second. The reference to the poet's clothes in the revised version indicates that he too is suffering, that their life together is suffering. It points to the fact that the sight of the gun had been set by the two of them, for both the poet and his wife were idealists who set their aim at a great distance, and that was the cause of their downfall. In the poem's original draft the poet discovers his fatal mistake through his wife's insanity; in the second draft he does so through his own suffering, as well as through hers. He has become more objective, for he observes not only his wife but also himself. Consequently, the second version portrays the situation more fully than the first, indicating deeper insight.

Kōtarō took less time to arrive at the final version of our second example, "Odd Poverty," but the revision was more drastic. Its initial draft was made on December 12, 1936:

Life in a Cave

My poverty is an odd one.
When I'm loaded, I eat the best there is;
when strapped, lettuce and yam gruel days on end.
My craft can, but doesn't, bring money in;
the harder I work, the more behind I run;
for a commission, I can't even get back the cost.
I give away whatever there is,
and when there's nothing, I skip cooking.
Having no child, and my wife in a hospital,
I live alone in a cave.
The best and the worst—these two
alternate in my life.

For whatever reason, Kōtarō did not publish the poem. Then, on December 3, 1939, he gave a new title to the poem and revised it extensively:

Odd Poverty

His poverty is an odd one.
When he's loaded, he eats the best there is;
when strapped, lettuce and yam gruel days on end.
His craft can, but doesn't, bring money in;
the harder he works, the longer it takes to do the job;
bewildered, people stay away from him.
That easy solution, "the middle way,"
does not suit his inborn character.
Wifeless and childless, his empty house
accumulates only dust, dirt, and chipped wood.
His sleeves ragged, his clogs broken,
he drinks water, then stands alone in the chilly wind.
Yet he does not consider himself poor;
he takes the best and the worst in alternation as they come,

and clutches them like a rosary.
Something rich and blessed
is waiting for him wherever he goes—
so believing, he gazes into the depth and beauty of this world
with hungry eyes and a thankful heart.
Neither happiness nor misery exists in this world;
one must simply march on.
There are the sky, the earth,
the wind, the water,
and the sun rising each morning.
His odd poverty
seems strange to him, too.

The poem was published in a magazine the following month. Later it was collected in *These Great Days* with no change in wording.

The most obvious change in the revised version is in the treatment of the man portrayed, who is described in the third person rather than the first and who is now depicted as an artist. The poet, now outside the poem, describes the poor artist more objectively. He can explain why the man has to suffer poverty in spite of his professional skill and can delineate his outward appearance in more detail, producing a clearer portrait. There is also a change in the poem's philosophical outlook. "Life in a Cave" merely portrays a man who reflects on his strangely destitute life. "Odd Poverty" goes beyond that: it presents a man who has found positive value in such a life. He is an enlightened sage living in a hermitage, who discovers happiness in accepting whatever Nature bestows on him. The second poem is technically more skilled and philosophically more substantial.

Kōtarō revised many other poems, although in most cases the interval between first and final drafts was not as lengthy as in the two examples given above. His revisions are similar to those of other poets. He polished words and expressions, making them more precise. Although he made considerable additions in "Odd Poverty," normally he cut words and lines as revision progressed. An extreme case is "The Journey," which originally had 102 lines; he reduced it to just nine lines in the final draft. The revisions also indicate a process of objectification. As is evident in the two examples cited, Kōtarō was able to look at himself and his thoughts from a greater distance as time went on, and that distance gave him an opportunity to develop his thoughts more fully. In this respect, he was similar to Hagiwara Sakutarō.

In other respects, however, there is a great difference between the creative processes of Kōtarō and Sakutarō, resulting in two very different types of poetry. The most noticeable difference is at the beginning of the verse-writing process. In drafting a poem, Sakutarō began with fragmentary thoughts, feelings, or images, which were often so vague and incoherent that he himself did not understand what they meant. In contrast, Kōtarō started with clear, well-defined thoughts or feelings. He had a good idea of what he was going to write, and he had it well under control in his conscious mind. In the manuscript of "Death of an Admiral," his handwriting is hurried and scrawly, leading one to conclude that he wrote the elegy spontaneously "on the very day and time of the event," as he said he did. Yet the poem's structure is orderly, its thought clear, its grammar correct, and its orthography (with one minor error) impeccable. The same can be said of "Life with a Distant Aim" and "Life in a Cave." To be sure, Kōtarō revised those poems; yet the original version of each, although handwritten in a tentative manner, suggests the poet's complete control over his material. The first drafts of the two poems have a more finished appearance than the final drafts of many poems collected in *Howling at the Moon*. To use Sakutarō's term, Kōtarō's poems have not been "liquefied."

There seems to have been a considerable discrepancy, then, between theory and practice in Kōtarō's view of the creative process. He insisted on spontaneity in verse writing, subscribing to an inspirational theory and maximizing the role of Nature. But when he followed that principle in practice, by and large he produced inferior poems. In most cases, abstract ethical thinking seems to have intervened between his initial inspiration and the first draft, resulting in a carefully worded, neatly structured poem. Nevertheless, he generally produced a finer poem when he deliberately went about revising a first draft. This discrep-

ancy between theory and practice may have been rooted in his
basic temperament, as well as linked to his main profession. He
was an intensely ethical person, who turned in the "right" direction even when blindfolded. He did not want—or was afraid—
to express the dark impulses of his subconscious until he could
get a grip on them and turn them in an ethically right direction.
Being a sculptor, he was more form-conscious than are most
other people; as a poet, he would not take up his pen until the
material within him took definite shape. He would not allow
himself to jot down incoherent, ungrammatical words on paper,
even for his own use. As we have noted, he wrote, "No matter
how many times it is rotated, the needle points toward the celestial pole." Most other poets would have wanted to catch the
waverings of the compass needle before it settled, but Kōtarō
wrote a poem only after it had stopped.

In Praise of Wintry Beauty

As a sculptor, Kōtarō was bothered by the fact that the general
public found sculpture less easy to appreciate than the other
arts. He believed this was because other arts, such as painting
and music, appeal more immediately to the senses. The fact an-
noyed him, however, and therefore he never begrudged the
time to give talks or write essays explaining the charms of sculpture to laymen. A crucial passage of one such essay, entitled
"The Charms of Sculpture," contains the following remark on
nude statues:

Human figures made of stone or bronze or wood are often too far removed from nature. Nevertheless we look at them with interest, not because they reproduce nature but because they enable our eyes to see a
vision of nature's soul—because they enable our ears to listen directly to
nature's breathing, enable our fingers to touch nature's pulse. By this, I
do not mean the reproduction of shape. The phrase "abstract beauty
made concrete" may sound almost senseless, but sculpture is an art that
makes this strange idea come true. Some people say they have been em-
braced by ghosts. According to their accounts, something shapeless and
invisible, like smoke, came to them and covered their bodies, whereupon they felt their hearts suddenly begin to beat fast. Works of sculpture affect a spectator in this way: the spectator feels his heartbeat
quicken all of a sudden.

The passage reveals what Kōtarō thought about the effect of a work of art on the spectator. Although he was talking about sculpture, his comments also apply to the other arts, including poetry.

The basic thrust of the passage is that the main charm of art lies in its ability to make the spectator see "nature's soul." The idea is a corollary of Kōtarō's concept of artistic verisimilitude because he believed art should represent a life-force, which he called Nature. (His own term for it in this passage is "nature's soul.") By looking at a work of art, he is saying, the spectator comes close to Nature. Although nature may have impure residues, Nature is purer and more beautiful; a work of art that represents Nature therefore moves the spectator.

Kōtarō's other writings indicate that at least four main types of aesthetic effects would emerge from a work of art that embodied Nature. For convenience, these might be labeled soundness, lack of sentimentality, wintry beauty (a baring of essentials), and sincerity. They are interrelated, and sometimes their implications overlap.

Soundness for Kōtarō seems to have implied either a primitive directness or the free manifestations of natural forces. Once, when a photographer for a women's magazine asked him to cite what he thought was the most beautiful thing in Japan, he pointed to vegetables lying in the kitchen. In the passage accompanying the photograph of those vegetables, he exclaimed, "How dazzling are those white, green, and pinkish things born out of the great earth! How beautiful are those magnificent roots that grew in the soil!" Clearly he was stating his reaction to the Nature that nurtured those vegetables. In the same vein he sang of the beauty of vegetation in the month of May:

> Two acres of wheat sway in whitish green,
> an acre of turnips is lined up in a solemn ceremony,
> and innumerable little things sprouting everywhere
> with the eyes of a baby look toward the blue sky.

The animals and birds Kōtarō described in his "wild beast" poems emanate the same soundness, the same sense of a healthy and unrestrained exercise of natural impulses—or at least they did when they were in the wild.

Kōtarō liked works of art created by ancient peoples because he thought they reflected Nature in a sound and healthy way. He was fond of ancient Egyptian sculpture, for example. "Its techniques are primitive and rough, paying little attention to tiny details," he observed, "but in its abandonment there is a vitality that moves the spectators." Although he was not a Christian, he liked reading the Psalms for what he perceived to be a similar primitive artlessness. "I think they are ridiculously naive," he said. "So thinking, I still read them." Another Christian work of art that impressed him deeply was Notre Dame Cathedral in Paris. "Cathedral in the Rain," a long poem recording his impressions of it, is one of his better-known works; the poem can be read as a hymn in praise of soundness eternalized in a work of art. Gazing at the cathedral in a rainstorm, the poet came to feel as if the stately structure were an eagle or a lion, and the wild energy with which it fought the storm moved him deeply.

Kōtarō approved of the works of later artists to the extent that they showed the same quality of soundness found in older art. Among sculptors, he liked Donatello, Michelangelo, and Rodin because he felt their works had sprung out of the "true life-force." Among Western composers his special favorite was Bach, who he imagined "ate everything and was healthy and big." He believed that Bach composed the Brandenburg Concertos by "responding to the laws of nature's force." Among modern Western poets he especially liked Whitman. According to him, Whitman "had nourished unusually sharp animallike senses as well as an honest plantlike heart, had been healthy and pious, and had gained true freedom within himself." In Kōtarō's opinion, the soundness of Whitman's verse is derived from the fact that the poet was in touch with Nature. "Nature is extremely heterogeneous, complex, and full of conflicts and discriminations," he wrote, "and yet it is one and all and a flow and a penetration. Whitman's poetry is not a special product created by a certain man's special personality but only the voice of Nature uttered through a personality."

In Japanese art, Kōtarō saw the best expression of soundness in *haniwa*, clay images made in prehistoric times. "The haniwa dolls made by our ancestors are all sprightly and simple, and they indicate the joy of having absorbed beauty directly from Nature," he said. "They show no signs of indulging in the grotesque or the unhealthy. What they do show is exceedingly innocent, unvarnished beauty expressed through the soundness of daily life." Kōtarō liked the beauty of haniwa so much that he not only considered it the source of Japanese aesthetics but made it one of the prototypes of beauty in the history of world art. According to him, there are four such prototypes: Greek, Egyptian, Chinese, and Japanese. Egyptian beauty is dark and melancholy, since it originated in *The Book of the Dead*; Greek beauty is complex and somber; and Chinese beauty is extremely intricate. In contrast, Japanese beauty is sprightly, simple, and free from gloomy doubts. Kōtarō's classification shows a partiality to his own country, perhaps because he formulated it during the war years. Nevertheless, his predilection for soundness is consistent with his Nature-based aesthetic, which predated the war.

However, health and soundness have not always been considered the hallmarks of beauty. In an essay called "Soundness in Beauty," Kōtarō complained of the ease with which people are diverted from these qualities to appreciation of less vigorous types of aesthetic effect:

Beauty is sound by its own nature. True, there are such things as decadent beauty and fragile beauty, and since these penetrate the human heart more easily, people have come to hold a special appreciation for the beauty of something that seems ready to perish at any minute. Consequently there has emerged an aesthetic that prizes fragile, perishable beauty. However, this must be considered a degradation of beauty.

Aware and yūgen, the ideals traditionally most prized in Japanese literature, epitomized for Kōtarō the "aesthetic that prizes fragile, perishable beauty."

To Kōtarō's chagrin, in the course of history the primitive simplicity and directness that characterized haniwa had gradually faded from Japanese art. Buddhism, which he felt was more concerned with death than with life, had cultivated a darker, gloomier ambience, *aware* or "pathos." In medieval Japan it developed into the combination of elegance, mystery, and quiet resignation known as yūgen. Although Kōtarō admitted the importance of *aware* and yūgen in Japanese culture, to him those ideals seemed too passive, too sentimental, and devoid of health and vigor. His feelings are most clearly expressed in a poem written for New Year's Day, 1950:

> *Greeting*
>
> Stop playing Nippon's music in the minor mode.
> Things gloomy, doleful,
> shady, forlorn, destitute,
> and yet with humble
> and quiet grace,
> making one see Mount Sumeru [10] in a sesame seed—
> those "beautiful" things:
> discard them all and raise your eyes higher.
> Fling your baton in a big curve
> and play music in a strong, positive, major mode,
> reforming those "beautiful" things in Nippon.
> To change the minor mode and create magnificent music
> with Destiny knocking on the door,
> first discard the chilly yūgen.
> That is my New Year's greeting.

He could understand, and even liked, medieval poets like Priest Saigyō and their latter-day followers like Bashō, but he felt the Japanese of the twentieth century should go beyond them. "I think it is a waste of effort to try to reenter their world," he said. His poem on Bashō, called "Ailing on a Journey," characteristically ends with the line "I will walk one step beyond," hinting at his determination to pick up where Bashō left off.

Kōtarō's distaste for *aware* and yūgen is reflected in two articles entitled "The Charms of Sentimentalism" and "Autumn and Literature in Japan." In the former, he stated that everyone has a tendency to indulge in excessive emotion, and cited the example of Verlaine, whose poetry he thought was generally free of

[10] A towering mountain located in the center of the Buddhist universe. Its top is some six million miles above sea level; its bottom, another six million miles below sea level.

sentimentalism but whose diaries written in prison and while
sick clearly showed it. Kōtarō's real target, however, was contemporary Japanese literature, which he believed contained even
more sentimentalism than Verlaine's diaries. That criticism is
echoed in the latter essay, in which he emphasized Japanese
poets' stereotyped response to autumn. It seemed to him that
traditionally the Japanese were fonder of autumn than of any
other season. He could accept this fondness, but he found objec-
tionable the fact that the Japanese considered autumn a rueful
season and had developed a sentimental aesthetic based on it. To
him, autumn was a beautiful and pleasant season with lower humidity, cleaner air, and bluer sky, a season when people regained
their appetites and felt more energetic than in summer. He
urged Japanese writers to reconsider their autumnal aesthetics
and restore "richness" and "unadorned health" to their work.

Kōtarō's own favorite season, however, was winter. He explained his feelings in a short article entitled "Two Notes on
Winter":

When I walk across a moor alongside foothills on a windy winter day,
I am struck at once by the warm density of the perfectly still earth, by
the infinite cleanliness of the landscape, which looks as if thoroughly
washed, and by the beauty of something thick and invisible that fills the
air. The earth entrusts everything to the elements, and yet it follows
the laws of necessity without fail, working indefatigably from within.
Whenever I witness the infinite energy of the great earth, I find my
heart stirring, gaining the kind of courage that I could never get elsewhere, even after listening to one hundred sermons. Leafless bushes
and trees, dead grass and seeds—the things of nature have been arranged with true tact and delicacy. All things that are to fall have fallen,
all things that are to be prepared have been prepared, revealing everything clearly and with no complications. That austere beauty is the most
beautiful of all.

Kōtarō went on to declare his conviction that "the ultimate in art
lies in such wintry beauty."

In his attraction to winter, Kōtarō was drawn to nature stripped
of all surface adornment. He felt he could come closer to the
heart of nature—that is, Nature—more easily at such a season,
so he preferred tree trunks to verdant foliage, the bare skeleton

to the beautifully dressed figure. Indeed, he once wrote in a poem that "winter's beauty is the skeleton's beauty." Perhaps his partiality to wintry beauty was related to his being a sculptor who worked with wood most of the time. As a carver, he created artistic form by shaving off all the unneeded parts from his material; the season of winter seemed to him like a gigantic chisel cutting away all that was unnecessary from everything on earth. "Like a blade, winter has come," he wrote in one of his poems. He actually felt his chisels become sharper in winter. "A chisel dislikes summer humidity," he said. "A sharp chisel abhors even the slightest sign of people getting sweaty."

Kōtarō's poetic chisel became sharper in winter, too, and he produced a disproportionately large number of poems on that season. "Winter Comes," "Waking on a Winter Morning," "Winter Poem," "Winter Has Come," "Winter's Departure," "Children in Winter," "Winter's Words"—one could go on listing such titles. Here is one of Kōtarō's winter poems, entitled "A Fellow Named Winter":

> When that fellow Winter sneezes
> the sonorous sound startles all—
> even the ocean tide turns transparent at once.
> With a sulky face, that fellow
> winds the light-brown spring
> tightly in the center of the hollow sky.
> With a white, mathematical logic, that fellow
> persistently follows a weak soul
> and chases it into a tight corner.
> Even when I read a morning newspaper
> my cold fingertips sense
> that fellow's determination.
> All the mental landscape of last night and before
> was just a wrinkled mirage.
> That fellow Winter beats me, and beats me again.
> He skins my face.
> He makes me forsake my body.
> He breaks me to pieces and buries me in the snow.
> He then orders me to stand up.
> I say to myself, "I will!"

This poem differs from Kōtarō's other winter poems in that the season is conceived as more physical than metaphysical. Yet its theme is the same: winter skins all things on earth, laying bare their essential being. When wintry beauty is translated into human conduct, the beauty of sincerity emerges, for sincerity means a bared conscience, a response not from the "skin" but from the bottom of the heart. Kōtarō highly prized the unadorned expressions of an honest heart. "An honest expression of emotion is always truthful and beautiful," he once wrote in a newspaper article, entitled "Beauty Equals Truth." He applied, or claimed to apply, that concept in screening amateur poets' works when he was the poetry editor of a women's magazine. "It goes without saying that a certain amount of skill is needed in writing poetry, but I value an abundance of truthfulness more highly than a small amount of skill," he said in explaining his policy of selection. "I seek poems that contain true outpourings from the heart." In his opinion, a poet preoccupied with technique is less than totally sincere in venting true emotion. "No artist," Kōtarō advised, "needs to think of his end product in advance."

Kōtarō's dislike of excessive technical skill may have led him to take a particular interest in amateur artists' works. During his lifetime he was well known for his readiness to contribute to "little magazines." His attraction to what seemed rough and spontaneous no doubt motivated him to serve as poetry editor of a women's magazine, and he honored an unusually large number of obscure poets by contributing forewords to their poetry collections. Conversely, he was hard on well-established artists whose works showed, in his opinion, too much skill and too little sincerity. His early essays reviewing major art exhibitions in Tokyo were notorious for the sharpness with which he attacked the works of professionals. The professionals, in turn, charged that Kōtarō never entered his works of sculpture in reputable competitions because he was afraid of reprisals.[11] In literature, he was harshest on a great novelist of his time, Tanizaki Jun'ichirō (1886–1965). He charged that Tanizaki's stories were written ac-

[11] Kōtarō's own explanation was that he refrained from entering large competitions because his father, a famous sculptor, was usually on the panel of judges.

268   Takamura Kōtarō

cording to plans carefully designed in advance, not as the novelist's heart was moved by specific themes. "His works are lacking
in sincerity," Kōtarō charged. "An ability to describe things is of
no special value." His dislike of Tanizaki was lifelong; almost
forty years after making this remark, he spoke unfavorably of a
later masterpiece by Tanizaki. "*The Makioka Sisters* is a mere
story," he said. "It offers nothing that appeals to the soul." His
point was the same as before: Tanizaki was a skillful storyteller
but not a man who honestly bared his feelings.

Kōtarō's taste for sincerity was shared by many contemporary
readers. Since olden times Japanese prose literature has prized
the direct expression of honest feelings, and it has produced
more diarists and essayists than have many other national litera-
tures. Throughout history prose fiction was dominated by a confessional type of novel. Although *aware* and *yūgen* were prized
in traditional poetry, the primitive simplicity of *The Collection of
Ten Thousand Leaves* was often revived as a poetic model: Shiki's
ideal of makoto and Akiko's principle of jikkan can be considered its modern variations. Traditionally Japanese readers have
had a distaste for artifice and have appreciated nature and the
natural. Seen in this context, Kōtarō's predilection for sincerity
was rooted in the Japanese literary tradition, and readers were
well prepared to accept it. They readily forgave him, too, when
they knew he sincerely regretted his wartime activities.

Disorder in Theory, Order in Practice

One day in March 1947, Kōtarō received a parcel post pack-
age from Miyazaki Minoru, a relative of his and a longtime admirer of his poetry. When he opened it, he was surprised to find
the handwritten manuscript of a collection of his tanka, compiled by Miyazaki without his knowledge. Miyazaki wanted to see
the collection published and had already secured a publisher.
Kōtarō, however, did not like the idea. He was ashamed of the
early tanka that had appeared in *The Morning Star*, and his later
tanka were written for personal pleasure, not for publication. In
reply, he wrote to Miyazaki, "The fact is that I do not expend my

full efforts in writing tanka nowadays. I may scrawl one in the margin of a letter to express my feelings of the moment, but my tanka are no more than such scribbles. Should that sort of thing get published? I am sure I would feel guilty if I were to permit that to happen."

Miyazaki did not heed his words, and published the tanka collection in November.[12] Kōtarō was upset. When a copy reached him, he took a glance at it, immediately wrapped it up, and put it away on a shelf. He protested to Miyazaki and the publisher, and eventually reached a compromise solution: the sale was to be limited, and each copy was to carry an explanation of the situation. To one of the readers who had already bought the book, Kōtarō sent a note of apology, saying, "That tanka collection was printed by the publisher and the editor without my permission. It was done completely against my will. I had never checked its contents. I think it is a senseless, absurd publication, and I feel sorry for those who bought it."

The episode reveals with what strong conviction Kōtarō thought of himself as a writer of free verse and nothing else. The vehemence with which he defended his position seems extraordinary, especially since he had written some two thousand tanka by his own count and had even acquired a pen name, Saiu, for writing in the 31-syllable form. Many of his tanka had already been published in magazines and had been well received; certainly they had not met with the harsh criticism suffered by some of his postwar shi, which he published first in magazines and later in *The Model*. Kōtarō said his tanka were scribbles venting his feelings of the moment, but did he not regard all poetry as such?

An interest in Japan's other traditional verse form, haiku, had preceded Kōtarō's involvement with tanka. He began writing haiku in his late teens, and at times was quite successful: once his haiku won first prize in a nationwide contest, and others were published in a prestigious haiku magazine, *The Cuckoo*. But, as he recalled, "a desire for lyricism" gradually intensified within

---

[12] Called *The White Hatchet*, it included 268 tanka by Kōtarō.

him, leading him away from haiku and toward tanka. When he
came across the masculine, heroic tanka of Yosano Hiroshi in
newspapers, he was greatly moved by them. He began writing
tanka in the same style himself and soon became a member of
the New Poetry Society. As for free verse, he had no interest in it
whatsoever. Free-style poetry in Japan was dominated at the
time by the followers of French Symbolism, and their esoteric,
high-flown vocabulary led him to believe that free verse was
quite alien to his temperament.

Although Kōtarō's early poetry was often quite traditional, at
times it foreshadowed his later themes. On the conventional side
is a haiku he wrote at the Basilica of St. Anthony in Padua during his trip to Italy in 1909:

> As I enter the church
> how cold are the stones!
> Spring rain . . .

In spite of its European setting, this is very much a traditional
haiku, suggesting a harmony between the spring rain and the
feel of the stones. However, a tanka written a little later the same
year, shortly after Kōtarō returned to Japan from his three-year
sojourn in the West, is less conventional:

> My homeland
> smells like the site
> of a fire:
> people walk along
> smoking cigarettes.

The poet's critical mind impinges on the lyricism of this tanka.
One feels Kōtarō wanted to criticize the Japanese at greater
length but could not do so because of the brevity of the form. In
fact, he treated the same theme in free verse a year later, producing "The Land of Netsuke," a more successful poem.

Kōtarō's transition from tanka to free verse took place in the
years following his return from abroad. While in Paris, he had
discovered that French Symbolist poetry was not as esoteric as
its Japanese admirers made it seem to be. Then, returning to
Japan, he found that a new generation of poets had begun writ-

ing shi that were closer to social reality. Awakened to the potential of the form, he too began writing free verse. Although he continued to write tanka off and on, he did not approach it with the same seriousness as he did free verse.

At least three factors may explain why Kōtarō came to prefer free verse in his mature years. The first is the brevity of tanka and haiku. "The contents to be embodied were too much for the tanka form," he said, recalling his first impulses to write free verse. On another occasion he remembered, "I came to conceive a desire for writing free verse when I became dissatisfied with an art like tanka, which is based on momentary feelings." In other words, he wanted a longer verse form capable of articulating sustained thoughts and emotions. He may have felt a subconscious need for a longer form even when he was writing in traditional forms, for many of his early tanka and haiku, including the two examples cited earlier, are rensaku; a sequence of tanka or haiku on a common theme moves in the direction of the more sustained development of a long shi.

Another factor prompting his move toward free verse was his strong dislike of such traditional Japanese ideals as *aware* and yūgen, to which tanka and haiku were closely tied. Although Akiko, Takuboku, and other modern poets had tried to create a new aesthetic for those forms, they had not totally succeeded in their efforts, at least not in Kōtarō's eyes. To him, any poet writing in a traditional verse form seemed haunted by what he called "ghosts of the past." In "New Order in the Orient," he wrote:

> Japanese poetry pursued ethereal beauty to such an extreme
> it reduced itself to incantational phrases.
> So many tanka and haiku poets having forsaken the world,
> poetry barely survived in monasteries and hermitages.
> As life's realities always contain the unbearable,
> only those who deserted the world were able to speak up.

Kōtarō did not actually say that those who wrote tanka and haiku were cowards who chose to avoid the real issues of life, but there is no doubt he thought he would have taken a different, more daring alternative if he had been in their position. He would have squarely faced "the unbearable" in life's realities, speaking up loudly from a battlefield. Perhaps it was easier to speak up loudly in free verse, a new form liberated from the ghosts of traditional Japan.

Freedom, not only from traditional aesthetics but also from any conventional syllable count, must have been Kōtarō's third and probably most immediate reason for selecting free verse. The language of free verse is less arbitrary, more colloquial, and more variable than the 5–7–5 or the 5–7–5–7–7 form. As has been mentioned, he believed that poetry is "no more than an emanation from the core of the way in which a man lives his life" and therefore that it has "neither a fixed form, nor a theorem, nor a house." Free verse seems closer to raw emotion and thus, for Kōtarō, to reality. In a two-line poem entitled "Reality," he suggested to would-be poets:

> Cut the branches and leaves of emotion.
> Grab the roots of feeling.

Such branches, leaves, and roots have myriad shapes and colors, and Kōtarō did not wish to cast them in some predetermined mold.

Yet free verse does have its own form and structure. Since Kōtarō was almost completely silent about the art of composition, one can only glimpse his view of poetic form through a poem he wrote to suggest the kind of poetry he held to be ideal:

The Poem

The poem incites the reader to write poetry.
The poem gives a roaring start to his dynamo.
The poem is ultimately what it is.
The poem is the highest of numerous phases assumed by
    the source of life.
The poem looks disorderly.
The poem looks contradictory and incoherent, too.
The poem is controlled by a movement in its deepest
    interior.
The poem is a display before the settlement of an account.
The poem is an inevitability allowing no random thought.
The poem has a physiological structure.
The poem flows torrentially through space.
The poem falls, ascends, perishes, comes to life again.

The poem destroys a form and gives birth to a form.
The poem is repulsion and affinity between electrons.
The poem lives right before one's eyes.
The poem is strict and yet somehow personable.
The poem looks, strangely enough, as if it could be grabbed
    in the hand.
The poem is written on the paved sidewalk, too, as those
    who look will find.

The fifth, sixth, tenth, and thirteenth lines of this didactic poem, which specifically concern poetic form and structure, are worthy of our attention.

Of these, the thirteenth line is the easiest to interpret. By saying that the poem "destroys a form," Kōtarō implies that a poet should break through the ordinary diction designed to express routine thoughts. He may even be suggesting that traditional verse forms like tanka and haiku should be destroyed, since they are inextricably entwined with the stereotyped sentiments of the Japanese people. Kōtarō wanted each poet, or rather each poem, to create a new form.

That new form should appear "disorderly," "contradictory," and "incoherent," according to the fifth and sixth lines. These descriptions are relative, for in the very next line Kōtarō says the poem is "controlled by a movement." He is referring to the freedom, independence, and tension inherent in poetic form: a poem follows its own emotional logic so faithfully that it may seem contradictory or even incoherent to those who are used to the syllogistic structure of a treatise or to the orderly syllabic patterns of haiku and tanka. In Kōtarō's view, free verse seems disorderly in outward form because it verbalizes the poet's response to Nature before that response is hardened by discursive logic. In its "deepest interior," it is controlled by that response and therefore is given an inner unity. Another name for this unity is the "physiological structure" mentioned in the tenth line. Kōtarō implies that a poem has a structure like that of a living organism, that its parts are united by an organic, not an abstract, logic. "Disorderly" really means "illogically arranged" or, more precisely, "physiologically arranged."

One might legitimately ask, however, whether a poem that a poet feels is physiological in structure might seem that way to a reader with a different sensibility. Kōtarō anticipated this question, and wrote that a work of art can be understood only by those who have the same "octave"—that is, the same range of feeling—as the artist. Elsewhere he confided that he thought no work of art could be completely understood except by its maker.

Kōtarō himself need not have worried about art's ability to communicate, since his own poetry has been read and admired by a large number of people in Japan. The main reason, however, seems less that his tuning fork caused answering reverberations in the hearts of a great many people than that his poems are not as abstruse as those of most contemporary shi poets. For ordinary readers, his works are much easier to understand than the poems of, say, Hagiwara Sakutarō. Despite his insistence on physiological structure, Kōtarō's poems tend to progress logically, by means of lucid, grammatical statements, neatly punctuated. In most instances they do not look "disorderly," "contradictory," or "incoherent," even in their first drafts. The piece called "The Poem" is itself a good example: each of its eighteen lines is a prose sentence that makes a clear statement. More than the verses of any other major contemporary poet, Kōtarō's poems create the impression of having been written after the feelings that prompted them had cooled. They do not have the spontaneity of Takuboku's poetry, the fresh sensuality of Sakutarō's poetry, or the murky all-inclusiveness of Kenji's poetry. Even Kōtarō's poems on sex, such as "Lust," are healthy, moral, and a bit sermonizing.

It seems appropriate to conclude, then, that the poetic ideal Kōtarō expressed in "The Poem" was merely that—an ideal. He longed for a poem so vibrant with life that its form would appear incoherent. Yet he was too much a man of reason, morality, and self-discipline to write such a poem himself. He was a sculptor, who worked with tangible, carefully shaped forms, and he wrote his "physiological structure" into similarly neat, presentable forms. Consequently his poetry gained respectability, the kind of respectability that has made him one of the most popular poets among compilers of school textbooks. But it lost something along the way.

Why, then, after he became a confirmed free-verse poet, did Kōtarō keep writing tanka, even though he knew the form was too brief for his purpose, too traditional in its aesthetics, and too rigid in syllabic pattern? He once hinted at an explanation in the pages of *The Morning Star*, where he wrote that the tanka he composed nowadays were "idle-talk poems" (*itazuragoto uta*), the kind of poems Yosano Hiroshi would not approve of. Yet, he added, he had to write them because he "wanted to proceed from the reality hidden behind what my free verse expressed." Here he seems to have admitted that his free verse indeed lost something in the process of expression, and that his tanka retained part of what the free verse had lost.

Kōtarō did not elaborate on this point, but one can learn more about it from the fifty samples of "idle-talk" tanka he published at about the same time. Of the fifty tanka, twenty are on the subject of cicadas, apparently because Kōtarō was then carving a wooden cicada. Here are the eighth, ninth, tenth, and eleventh poems from that group:

> All of a sudden
> a shrill cry or two, and then
> silence again.
> How forlorn you must be,
> cicada in the cage!

> Nowhere in its body
> does it have the filthiness
> of a living being:
> this dry, almost weightless
> *abura* cicada.[13]

> In my hand
> the cicada does not try
> to fly away . . .
> It crawls slowly, leaving
> an itchy feel on the palm.

[13] *Graptopsaltria calorata*. A black, medium-sized cicada, it is known for its vigorous chirping.

Is there anything
I can give to this cicada
whose mouth
I cannot locate? No,
I have nothing to give.

Compare these tanka with the following free-verse poem, "I Carve a Cicada." Although the poem was written sixteen years after the tanka, the resemblance is evident:

Facing the winter sun on the south window, I carve a
    cicada.
Dry, inanimate, and weightless on the palm, the *minmin*
    cicada[14]
has nothing of the baseness of a living being.
I cannot even locate the mouth it eats from.
The cicada crawls on a corner of the Tempyō desk.[15]
I gaze at its wings.
Fragile, thin, transparent fragments of heaven—
the ethereal wings of this insect
have gentle, slow-curving contours,
softly covering its black and green armor.
From the cypress wood I am carving
a fragrance ascends and fills the room.
I forget the hour, the place, and the time;
I forget people, or even to breathe.
This tiny studio of four mats and a half
seems hanging somewhere in heaven.

Clearly the second and third lines of this poem are based on the ninth tanka on cicadas; the fourth line, on the eleventh tanka.

Despite the apparent connection, the tanka and "I Carve a Cicada" are markedly different in both theme and style. The free-verse poem is a portrait of the artist at work. It has an orderly, logical structure, beginning with a description of the setting and ending with an expression of the artist's feelings. The main theme is the artist's feelings—his devotion to and enjoyment of the creation of beauty—and the poet goes about describing them step by step, using vocabulary anyone could un-

[14] *Oncotympana maculaticollis.* A large cicada, black with green dots, it has a pair of transparent wings with green nervures.
[15] A small, low desk in the style of the Tempyō period (A.D. 729–49), originally used for reading Buddhist scriptures. Kōtarō had one in his studio.

derstand. In its strict adherence to normal syntax, "I Carve a Cicada" is almost a prose poem. In contrast, the four tanka present raw, fragmentary impressions. A little surprise at a cicada's sudden cry or at its weightlessness, the itchy sensation of a cicada crawling on the palm, a helpless feeling of the difference between a man and a cicada—these are the ingredients of the tanka. On the surface their form is a rigid syllabic pattern, yet the language sounds more fresh and pliant because it is less controlled by the dictates of the grammar of Japanese prose.

It is also significant that the eighth and tenth tanka of the rensaku were not incorporated into "I Carve a Cicada." The reason must be that they did not fit the theme of the poem. The eighth tanka, about a caged cicada, produces an impression close to *aware*. Because Kōtarō would have been ashamed of creating such an impression, there is no way he could have integrated the poem into his later shi. The tenth tanka is about a cicada that refuses to fly away. The image certainly does not fit well with the cicada in the artist's studio, which he imagines came from heaven. Those two tanka are the "leftovers" of Kōtarō's shi, raw materials that were not incorporated into the free-verse poem. They must be what he meant by "the reality hidden behind what my free verse expressed." To a lesser extent the same can be said of the ninth and eleventh tanka, as well as of the others not cited here. These examples make clear why Kōtarō thought of tanka as "idle-talk poems"; they were raw, private, fragmentary, and therefore not public. For this reason he did not want Miyazaki to publish his tanka collection.

There is, then, a basic contradiction between Kōtarō's theory of form and his practice, just as there was a discrepancy between his view of the creative process and his actual method of writing verse. In theory, he aspired to poems with a physiological structure, poems so close to the source of life that they would look disorderly and incoherent to a man of reason. He therefore moved away from fixed verse forms and toward the unfettered shi, a verse form that he thought would allow more disorderliness and incoherence. In practice, however, his free verse looks just as orderly and well-regulated as his tanka and haiku. Indeed, sometimes his shi seem less alive because they allow a greater invasion of reason and logic. Traditional Japanese verse forms, by their extreme brevity, often defy the rules of grammar and prevent a logical statement from entering a poem. Shi has no such restrictions, and Kōtarō was free to present his comments and observations at a distance from sensory impressions. The result was a structure more logical than physiological, and a language more reasoned than impassioned. In contrast to his wife, he had too much sanity.

A Giver of Spiritual Vitality

Kōtarō wrote only one play. Called *The Young Artist*, it was published in the April 1905 issue of *The Morning Star* and was staged by his friends shortly afterwards. The hero is a young, happily married painter named Sayama, who as the play opens is jolted by the news of his sister's suicide. From her last letter to him, he learns that she had leprosy and that he too must have inherited the disease. He suffers alone, unable to reveal the truth to his pregnant wife for fear of upsetting her. Subsequently he seeks solace in a life of debauchery, not returning home for days on end. His strange behavior is too much for his gentle wife to bear; she goes insane and dies after giving birth to a son. After that, Sayama falls into even deeper despair and contemplates suicide. Just then a friend intervenes and succeeds in awakening him to his pride as an artist. The reformed Sayama produces a masterful oil painting, which wins him a high honor at the World's Fair in St. Louis. On the day of the celebration party given by his friends, however, he kills his infant son and shoots himself.

The play, melodramatic though it is, reveals young Kōtarō's view of the use of art. Unlike most of the other romantics associated with the New Poetry Society, he seems to have realized the limitations of art. There is no way to interpret Sayama's death as a glorious one; it is pathetic. The play's message must be that art cannot be a final savior, even though it may somewhat diminish the pain of living: to an ailing man the highest honors awarded an artist do not mean much. That seems to be what Kōtarō believed at age 22.

Interestingly enough, Kōtarō came to recognize the value of art more and more as he grew older. When he was in his sixties, he even thought art could overcome the fear of death, serving as a substitute for religion. He changed his stance as dramatically as did Takuboku, who followed the reverse path of holding excessive expectations of poetry in his youth but abandoning them in later years.

The older Kōtarō recognized art's usefulness for both the artist and the spectator. For the artist, the use of art lies in the joy of creating. Even the leper Sayama was able to forget his illness, albeit temporarily, while he was painting. In a later essay Kōtarō made the same point more emphatically: "The spirit of art enables a person suffering from the miseries of life or the pain of an ailment to step aside a little and contemplate the miseries or pain from a nonrealistic standpoint." The joy of creation is the main theme of some of his poems, such as "I Carve a Cicada" and the following example, called "Sitting Alone":

> Late at night, a violent rainstorm besieges my house.
> Sitting in a lonely room, not even a mouse for company,
> I hold a half-finished wooden carp.
> My palm is strangely cold as it touches the scales
> and I feel things dense but invisible
> approach from the four corners of the room.
> The carp's eyes stare at me.
> Without moving my hand, I hold my breath
> and listen to the rainstorm of a late summer night.
> I feel as though I were in a far-off land,
> as though I were out of this world.[16]

The rainstorm is figurative as well as literal, symbolizing his stormy life with the insane Chieko. Art, however, had the magical power to transport him to a blissful, far-off land.

Kōtarō made a small but significant distinction between the uses of poetry and sculpture: he seems to have thought working

---

[16] Kōtarō began carving a wooden carp in 1935, but he was never able to complete it, despite several years of intermittent work. This poem was written in 1938.

with wood created a more positive pleasure than did working
with words. "When I am sculpting," he wrote, "my heart is filled
with a feeling that this life is worth living. Writing poetry gives
me no such pleasure; rather, it gives me pain. Or I should say I
write poetry because I feel pain. The pain vanishes when I vent it
in words." His poems about the pleasure of artistic creation are all
about carving. Why sculpture should give him great satisfaction
and verse writing produce only a passive sort of pleasure, Kōtarō
did not explain. The difference can perhaps be attributed to his
distinction between representation in the two arts. As we have
noted, he considered sculpture a more directly mimetic art than
poetry and tried to exclude all subjective thoughts from his work
in it. That attempt may have rid him of painful emotions, enabling him to feel as if he were far from his grief-laden world. In
contrast, writing poetry put him in the midst of those painful
emotions, forcing him to work with them in order to put them
into words.

On the other hand, a joyful creative process did not always
lead to a happy result. Kōtarō may have felt unearthly bliss while
carving a wooden carp, but the carp was never completed. His
poems far outnumber his sculptures. Such comparisons may be
irrelevant, since numbers are not related to quality; nonetheless,
one cannot but feel that the totality of his work as a poet outweighs the totality of his work as a sculptor, in spite of the fact
that he always considered himself more a sculptor than a poet.
After all, the Japanese Academy of Art wanted to induct him for
his poetic, not his sculptural, achievement.

Unlike Shiki or Akiko, however, Kōtarō seldom tried to per-
suade others to become artists on account of the pleasure creative activities impart. He was more eager to make them readers
of poetry or viewers of painting and sculpture. When he spoke
or wrote about the use of art for nonartists, he stressed its didactic function more than its pleasurable effects:

Art is not to entertain people; it is to strengthen them. It is not to make
people laugh; it is to make them think. It is to lift them up, to make
them advance and settle down. It is not to soothe their daily suffering by

patchwork; it is to give them basic strength to withstand the suffering. It is not refreshment that consoles people tired of living in this world; it is nourishment that prevents them from being tired. It teaches people a mysterious magic by which to keep their souls vigorous even when their bodies are exhausted. Those who open their eyes to art will see a world of light before them.

Here Kōtarō implies that art can provide spiritual and moral strength for those who appreciate it. We have already seen where in his view that strength comes from: it is derived from Nature, embodied at the core of a work of art. According to Kōtarō, by looking at a true work of art people recover a basic life-force that is often buried under the unhealthy routine of modern life.

Kōtarō's faith in the didactic function of art strengthened as he grew older. During the war, he submitted an "Artist Mobilization Proposal" to the government, which had appointed him to one of its advisory councils. In it, he proposed sending artists to factories all over the country to decorate dormitories, dining halls, and recreation rooms. Explaining the proposal, he said: "To elevate our national morale, the mental hygiene of factory workers throughout the country is extremely important. . . . We cannot overlook the fact that a mentally healthy life is nourished by sound beauty seen everywhere in one's environment." Kōtarō was not worried about farmers and fishermen, who worked in the midst of nature, but he was afraid factory workers would lose their spiritual vitality if they looked at nothing but dreary machines day after day. He also suggested that the Ministry of Welfare require each factory to set aside a certain percentage of its construction budget for art, or make it obligatory for each large factory to hire an advisor on art, although he did not include this in the proposal. Characteristically, he was strangely blind to the fact that the factory workers whom he wanted to be surrounded by beauty were manufacturing brutal weapons for modern warfare.

The government, which had its hands full with other matters, did not act on Kōtarō's proposal for mobilizing artists. But he mobilized himself, at least, becoming an outspoken prowar poet and producing a number of militant poems that he thought would contribute to a mentally healthy life for his countrymen in wartime. In believing in the social function of poetry and expressing that belief through action, he went further than any other major Japanese poet writing in the shi form. Neither Takuboku nor Sakutarō, both of whom in theory recognized the "journalistic" function of poetry, wrote so many didactic poems.

When the war ended, Kōtarō's belief in poetry did not waver. In time he repented his wartime activities, but he remained convinced that his poetry had served at least one important purpose: it kept national morale high. In "Short Biography of a Fool" he says he wrote prowar poems to "prevent the moral degradation of my countrymen." He was more specific in an unpublished poem written at about the same time:

> *People Went to Die after Reading My Poetry*
> Bombs were falling all around my house.
> From a power line, a woman's thigh hung.
> Death was always nearby.
> To ease my fear of death
> I put all my heart into writing "The Time for Sure Death."
> My countrymen read the poem on the battlefield.
> After reading it, some went to face their deaths.
> Others reread it every day and wrote back to their homes.
> The submarine captain soon sank with his boat.

"The Time for Sure Death" must symbolize Kōtarō's wartime poems in general, since he never wrote a poem by that title. Here he expresses his hope that his war poems helped his countrymen to keep up their courage and overcome their fear of death.

This position on the use of art is opposite to the stance Kōtarō adopted in his youth. In *The Young Artist* he implied that art could not ultimately cure an ailing man: Sayama, despite his great achievements as an artist, destroys himself in the end. The play's conclusion would have been drastically different if Kōtarō had written it forty years later: by the saving power of art, Sayama would have overcome the fear not only of leprosy but of death itself. To the Kōtarō of later years, art was tantamount to religion, a provider of spiritual and moral strength. It is a wonder that an artist who lived through the turbulent years of two world wars, the Great Depression, and the Allied occupation could believe in the saving power of art so purely for so long. Kōtarō's optimistic view of human nature, his genuine, idealistic temperament, and his habit of looking at the sunny side of things remained intact to the end of his life; any adversities he encountered merely increased his faith in art as a savior. He lived and died with a strong belief that art can make a great contribution to human life.

CHAPTER SEVEN

Ogiwara Seisensui

ONE OF THE most intriguing developments in modern Japanese poetry was the emergence of free-style haiku (*jiyūritsu haiku*), a movement to liberate haiku from its two traditional requirements: the 17-syllable pattern and seasonal reference. The movement, which began around 1909,[1] shocked contemporaries. To many of them, free-style haiku seemed a flat contradiction in terms. How could haiku, a fixed verse form, be free in style? If a poem is written with no predetermined prosody, wouldn't it be more appropriate to call it free verse? Some radical-minded poets like Shiki's disciple Hekigodō were willing to participate in the experiment, but most established haiku writers were skeptical of its future success, and conservatives vehemently attacked the movement as deviating from the time-honored tradition. Nevertheless, free-style haiku has survived, although it has not gained as many followers as its initial promoters hoped it would. Their chief magazine, *Layered Clouds* (which was founded in 1911), continues to publish the works of old and new poets who write haiku in the free style. Moreover, Ozaki Hōsai (1885–1926) and Taneda Santōka (1882–1940),[2] two outstanding prac-

---

[1] In this year two pioneering magazines of free-style haiku, *Verdant Heat* and *Smoke*, were founded. They lasted for only a couple of years, but other magazines that followed, such as *Layered Clouds* and *Quince*, picked up the movement.

[2] Both Hōsai and Santōka came from affluent families, but midway through their careers they abruptly abandoned their homes to become Buddhist monks. Each spent a large part of the rest of his life wandering and begging for alms. Many of their poetical works became known to the general public only after their deaths, mainly through the efforts of their mentor Seisensui.

titioners of free-style haiku, have attained prominent positions in the history of modern Japanese poetry.

The free-style haiku movement would not have enjoyed its degree of success had it not been for the sustained, dynamic leadership of Ogiwara Seisensui (1884–1976). He was more a reformer, critic, and teacher than a poet, although his poetic achievement was considerable and his literary criticism gained a measure of strength from the fact that he was a practicing poet. The role he played in the formative years of free-style haiku is comparable to Shiki's for traditional haiku in early modern Japan. But Seisensui was more fortunate than Shiki in that he was endowed with both health and wealth. Born into an affluent merchant family, he was able to found *Layered Clouds* and to give it financial stability for many years. And his life was long and vigorous: he was still actively writing poetry and prose in his late eighties. Altogether, he published some four hundred books. He also gave many lectures promoting free-style haiku, both in person and over the national radio. If he seemed more a teacher than a poet, this was not because his poetry was deficient but because it was overshadowed by his other activities.

Haiku in Spirit, Free Verse in Form

As a teacher Seisensui was headstrong and fearless. If the occasion required, he did not hesitate to "correct" poems that had been considered masterpieces of haiku. Even the following poem by Bashō, probably the most famous of all haiku, did not escape his criticism:

> The old pond:
> a frog leaps in—
> the water's sound.

Seisensui felt the first line was superfluous. He proposed changing the poem to:

> a frog leaps in—
> the water's sound

Here is his explanation:

What motivated Bashō to write this haiku was the sound of a frog jumping in, and nothing else. That instant he was awakened to the fact that
the common phenomenon of a frog jumping into the water was in truth
not a common phenomenon at all. Therefore, if one were to give expression to that awakening, the words

> a frog leaps in—
> the water's sound

would be sufficient. In point of fact, those were precisely the words that
came out of Bashō's mouth at the time. But the words did not have the
needed seventeen syllables, so he felt there was something lacking.
Therefore he tried to put an additional line before them. Reportedly
Kikaku[3] proposed "mountain roses" for the line, but Bashō settled on
"the old pond" instead. With "mountain roses," the poem's scene would
have become too artificial. No such artificiality exists when it is replaced
by "the old pond." In other words, the addition of "the old pond" is so
unobtrusive that the new three-line poem does not differ very much
from the original two-line verse. For this reason I like Bashō's version
better than the one Kikaku proposed. Yet, if I may speak from my current standpoint, I would say the two-line version omitting "the old
pond" expresses the poet's feeling better. Obviously Bashō held a conventional idea of form and felt that

> a frog leaps in—
> the water's sound

did not constitute a haiku. I contend that these two lines definitely form
a haiku.

In explaining Bashō's composition of the famous haiku, Seisensui drew on his own basic idea of verse writing: that poetry is
a spontaneous expression of the poet's feeling in a given instant,
nothing more or less. A fixed verse form, like 5−7−5, is a hindrance to the process of expression. Seisensui speculated that
even a master poet like Bashō fell victim to his own conventional
idea of form and conceived a weak first line when he wrote the
frog haiku. In Seisensui's view, the poem shows the need for
breaking down the 5−7−5 pattern; a free-style haiku can be
truer to what the poet feels at the creative moment, for it does
not restrict the expression of emotion by imposing a predetermined form.

Seisensui offered various metaphors to elucidate the func-

[3]Takarai Kikaku (1661−1707) was one of Bashō's leading disciples. The episode mentioned here appears in a book by Kagami Shikō (1665−1731), another
of Bashō's disciples.

tional difference between conventional and free-style haiku. On one occasion he compared the 17-syllable poem to a suitcase and the free-style haiku to a *furoshiki*, a square piece of cloth used for wrapping things to carry. A suitcase is convenient to have, he said, because one can toss anything into it, but a problem arises if the object is too large and will not go into the suitcase or if it is too small and rattles around. A furoshiki, on the other hand, can wrap a large object or a small one, freely fitting its size and shape. On another occasion Seisensui compared the traditional haiku poet to a person trying to use a bamboo basket to scoop up little things floating on the water. The basket can catch big things, but more tiny and delicate things slip through its meshes. Seisensui wanted a poet to use his bare hands and to resist the temptation to get a basket. An article manufactured for a pre-determined purpose, such as a suitcase or a basket, serves that purpose very well, but its limitations become evident when it is indiscriminately applied to the myriad sizes and shapes found in nature. Ideally, one should invent a new tool to exactly suit each of them. Likewise, Seisensui advocated "one rhythm per haiku." Each haiku, he insisted, should have its own unique rhythm because each subject is different. He charged that those who impose the 5–7–5 form on all subjects ignore the fact that everything in the universe is alive and changes from moment to moment.

Seisensui tried to show the superiority of free-style haiku by specific examples, too. One was his poem:

> dandelions
> dandelions
> on the sandy beach
> spring
> opens its eyes

According to his explanation, he composed the poem one winter day when he suddenly came upon dandelions blooming on the beach. In them he felt the intensity of nature's life; he thought he actually saw nature opening its eyes. In his opinion, that vivid, immediate sensation could never be conveyed in a 17-syllable haiku, such as:

Dandelions
without waiting for spring
open their eyes.

He concluded that "my haiku expresses something before it settles down into the 17-syllable form."

On another occasion, Seisensui compared two haiku on fireflies. One was a well-known 5–7–5 poem by Bashō:

The instant it seemed
to fall from a blade of grass,
it flew up: a firefly.

The other was a free-style haiku by one of Seisensui's students, Ōhashi Raboku (1890–1933):[4]

fireflies
begin to glow
two of them
crawling

Seisensui thought Bashō's poem was good, but not as good as Raboku's. In his opinion, Bashō's haiku was a descriptive poem that skillfully depicted a firefly's movement as observed by the poet, whereas the poem by Raboku contained "the breath issuing forth from the fireflies' life, which the poet felt to be his own." The latter haiku embodied the rhythm of life; the former merely presented a picture. Seisensui concluded that this difference occurred not because Bashō was inferior to Raboku as a poet but because 17-syllable haiku was inferior to free-style haiku as a poetic form.

Seisensui's comments are not likely to convince everyone, but they do make clear his view of the relationship between poetry and the world. In his opinion, a poet is to capture the delicate life of nature, make it his own, and articulate it in all its freshness and liveliness. The traditional 17-syllable pattern seemed a hindrance in this process.

The same urge to make the poem faithful to its subject moti-

---

[4]Raboku was a latecomer to the *Layered Clouds* group but became one of its most active members. Impressed by his devotion, Seisensui once called him a "haiku incarnate."

vated Seisensui to criticize the use of season words, required in traditional haiku. He believed that this age-old practice had some virtue for beginning students because it forced them to be aware of nature, but too frequently it tempted them to come up with a stereotyped response or to falsify their true observations or feelings. Many haiku teachers still asked their students to write haiku on fulling blocks and cuckoos, which were favorite themes in classical haiku but had little to do with modern urban life; the students consequently had to concoct haiku using bookish learning. Even when the seasonal theme was something they could personally observe, such as the moon or young leaves, students were prone to be restricted by the associations of the traditional season words. Poets living far away from the Kyoto-Osaka area, where season words originated, had an especially hard time reconciling the gap between their actual observations and the images evoked by season words. The north wind, for example, was traditionally a season word for winter because the wind usually blows from the north in the Kyoto-Osaka area during the winter months. The same phrase implies summer for people who live in northern Honshu, but northerners who followed the traditional rule had to use "the north wind" in their winter haiku nonetheless.

Seisensui thought that even the innovative Shiki was at times a victim of this unreasonable convention. Although Shiki was aware of the evils of stock response and advocated shasei, he adhered to the convention of seasonal reference. As a result, Seisensui felt, he did not pursue shasei to its ultimate conclusion. Seisensui believed Shiki himself became vaguely aware of the contradiction of insisting on shasei while observing the requirement of season words, and that for this reason Shiki seemed more eager to write tanka than haiku in his later years. Seisensui felt that Shiki's later haiku were markedly inferior to his later tanka, and he warned that any haiku poet who followed Shiki's path would encounter the same difficulties.

Seisensui's stand against arbitrary formal requirements resembles that of Ezra Pound, who helped promote an Anglo-

American free-verse movement early in this century, as well as the views of modern free-verse poets in Japan. Yet unlike those other formal innovators, Seisensui wanted to claim for his own work a traditional name. Since to attack the requirements of 17-syllable length and seasonal reference is to attack the formal definition of haiku, Seisensui had to substitute an analysis not based on formal elements per se. His attempts to do so and to defend his work as haiku against the criticisms of the major free-verse poet Kitahara Hakushū are at the core of one of the livelier literary controversies in modern Japan.

In refuting Hakushū, as well as in his other extensive writings on the topic, Seisensui distinguished free-style haiku from free verse on two main counts. The first was subject matter: free verse treats all kinds of subjects, but the matter of haiku is limited to nature; in particular, haiku expresses a special relationship with nature that developed in the course of the verse form's history. The second was treatment: free verse is linear and discursive in structure, tracing the course of a poet's mental experiences; on the other hand, haiku is centripetal, focusing an instantaneous, intuitive perception. Seisensui touched on these points in "On Free Verse and Haiku," a long article he wrote in response to Hakushū:

Poetry treats all kinds of subjects—lyrical matters, epic matters, natural scenes, human passions, social thoughts. But, in my opinion, haiku is to treat just one thing, "a flavor of nature" captured through contemplation of nature. The realm of haiku is very small indeed, as it picks up just flavors of nature from the wide world of poetry. Of course, a flavor of nature can be treated in other types of poetry, too, but in haiku it does not take the form of "expression" in the ordinary sense of the word; it seeks "submersion," which is the opposite of expression. This makes the realm of haiku even smaller.

"A flavor of nature" was, in Seisensui's view, the essence of the premodern haiku tradition. He repeatedly cited Bashō's dictum "Follow nature and return to nature"; another of Bashō's sayings he liked was "When you are composing a verse, let there be not a hair's breadth separating your mind from what you write." To Seisensui, "return to nature" meant becoming one with na-

ture and feeling its pulse within his body. He expressed this idea
in his own dictum "Listen to nature." Old haiku masters did not
"see" nature but "listened" to it, he believed. Quoting Bashō's famous haiku

> The wild sea:
> extending over Sado Isle,
> the River of Heaven,

he said that here the poet was "listening" to the scene, not
"watching" it, that the poet's soul expanded to the size of the sky
and that he listened to the words of the stars. In Seisensui's opinion, this close relationship with nature is unique to the haiku
tradition.

Although Seisensui sometimes attacked the wording of Bashō's poems, then, he revered the spiritual attitude those poems
expressed. He believed that in his own work he sought a similar
relationship with nature, and since his poetic project was the
same as that of the earlier master, he felt justified in calling his
free-style poems haiku and placing himself in a tradition with
Bashō at its head. At times he even sought a precedent in Bashō
for his own formal innovations. He could not claim that the sev-
enteenth-century master actually wrote free-style haiku, but he
pointed out that Bashō frequently relied on an inner rhythm
more than on an outer one, so that many of his finer haiku have
a more complex rhythm than 5–7–5. "If Bashō had not been
restricted by the idea that haiku must be 5–7–5, I am sure he
would have written more good poems," Seisensui daringly—and
self-servingly—observed.

For instance, Seisensui thought it more natural to break down

> Gathering the rains
> of early summer, how swift
> the Mogami River!

as

> Gathering the rains
> of early summer
> how swift
> the Mogami River!

He believed that in some cases Bashō found his desire to follow
an inner rhythm so strong that he had to break down the outer
rhythm of 5–7–5. For example, in

> A banana plant
> in the autumn gale:
> I listen to the dripping of rain
> into a basin at night.

the syllabic pattern is 3–5–7–5 or 8–7–5, no matter how carefully a conservative reader may analyze it. Seisensui thought
Bashō was inadvertently using the principle of free-style haiku
when he paid close attention to the inner rhythm, the rhythm
unique to his subject.

The second major difference between free verse and free-
style haiku, a difference in treatment and structure, is the gist of
an exchange between Seisensui and Hakushū concerning Hakushū's three-line shi entitled "View on a Beautiful Day":

> How beautiful!
> As I look afar, sailboats
> and magnificent Mount Fuji's peak.

Criticizing the poem in one of his essays, Seisensui observed that
this subject matter had been treated by generations of haiku
poets and that, seen from the viewpoint of haiku, the words "As
I look afar" were superfluous. A haiku poet would have said:

> How beautiful!
> Magnificent Mount Fuji's peak
> and a sailboat.

Changed in this way, he said, the poem's focus is sharpened, and
it presents the poet's feeling in a flash of light. He concluded by
observing that Hakushū's poem was like liquid jello in a con-
tainer waiting to set.

In a counterattack, Hakushū said that his poem was a lyric,
which allowed greater play in time and space than did a haiku.
His poetic sentiment at the time, he said, was not instantaneous
but progressive; therefore the words "As I look afar" had to be
included to indicate the lapse of time. His range of sight was
wider than Seisensui's revision implied, for it encompassed more

than one sailboat and the peak of Mount Fuji far in the distance. He concluded that Seisensui was like an overeager photography buff whose sole concern was to focus the camera, and likened Seisensui's haiku "How beautiful . . ." to a seafood dish dried out from overcooking.

Who was right? Hakushū's poem appears the more attractive of the two because his verse form is fresher, whereas Seisensui's haiku suffers because it uses the conventional 5−7−5 form to express a conventional and extremely hackneyed theme, the beauty of Mount Fuji. Seisensui himself was aware of the poem's triteness and said it was the kind of haiku that could be found in anyone's haiku collection. On the other hand, Hakushū's poem is not much better, for although his form is new his theme is not. Seisensui was right when he pointed out, in his rebuttal to Hakushū's charge, that the theme was an old one in the haiku tradition and gave no sense of fresh life. However, Seisensui was not entirely fair when he transformed a free verse on a conventional theme into a conventional haiku, in effect doubling the conventionality.

Be that as it may, Hakushū's poem and Seisensui's revision provide a fine example of the structural difference between free verse and free-style haiku. According to his own analysis, Hakushū's poem progresses in three stages: first the poet feels the beauty of the scene as a whole, then he discovers sailboats, and finally he looks up toward Mount Fuji. In Seisensui's haiku, the poet has an instantaneous flash of inspiration in which the beauty of the scene, a sailboat, and Mount Fuji are brought together. "The rhythm of shi, like that of tanka, progresses temporally," he observed, "but the rhythm of haiku is more spatial."

Elsewhere Seisensui explicitly described haiku's structure as a focusing. "The sentiment is condensed into one glow," he said. "Then that glow is verbally recorded, all the words serving to bring together the nearby rays of light into a single point. That is the basic structure of haiku." He used several other images to compare shi and haiku. Once he likened all poetry to a pyramid and said that long poems were located at the bottom of the pyramid, whereas haiku was like its pointed top. On another occasion

the comparison was to flowing water. "When one's poetic sentiment is flowing with a riverlike rhythm, it should take the form
of a long poem with many lines," he said. "But when the flow
increases in speed and finally falls over a cliff, the expression becomes shorter and leaps like a waterfall. That, I believe, is the
structure of haiku." The last set of similes brings out an important point: the structural difference between haiku and free
verse is derived from a difference in the nature of the poet's sentiment. Haiku expresses an instantaneous perception, a brief
submersion of self in nature, whereas the longer shi traces a
train of thoughts or feelings.

On one occasion Seisensui wrote his own free verse to contrast
with this free-style haiku:

> toward the sky
> wheat ears
> must be growing
> I hold a child

To his free-verse rendering he gave the appropriate—perhaps
too appropriate—title "Paraphrase":

> The child rollicks in my arms,
> clothed in white, feathery wool
> and enjoying the warmth like a little bird.
> She must be rejoicing at the rare sight of this clear, bright
>   sky.
> Should I loosen my hold for a moment,
> she would soar to the sky the next.
>
> In the field, a skylark must have begun to sing
> and wheat ears must be growing, too.
> Yes, under that pale purple of the sky
> there should be the transparent green of wheat ears.
>
> In the sky, a large paper balloon:
> a fluffy cloud floating on the early summer wind.
> In the sky, a large loaf of bread:
> a cloud looking as if deliciously baked.
>
> The child rollicks, gazing skyward.
> She waves her hands toward the sky.
> All she can say is "Papa" and "Mama,"
> but she chirps the tune all day long.
> My skylark!
> Grow tall and healthy, like full-eared wheat.

The "paraphrase," although a bit overdone, does illustrate the structural difference between haiku and shi: the latter traces the poet's mental experience, whereas the former concentrates on the focal point of that experience.

The two distinguishing features of haiku, a submersion in nature and instantaneous insight, are related to each other. Seisensui commented on that relationship in one of his earliest writings, an essay called "Poetry of Enlightenment":

> We want to see nature within ourselves or, to put it differently, we want to contemplate nature from within. Instead of interpreting it by knowledge or appreciating it by aesthetic taste, we want to feel it instinctively with our entire being. We want to base our spiritual life on such an enlightenment. . . .
> If we take a wrong approach we will not be able to gain this kind of enlightenment, no matter how desperately we may try. We must live intensely with a humble heart, whereupon, like a divine revelation, it will show itself mysteriously but clearly in our mental mirror. It will be a valuable symbol.
> Such an enlightenment will bring a joy comparable to religious exaltation. A similar experience has been described by Goethe:
> > At that joyous moment
> > I felt myself so small and so great.[5]
> A person feels so small because he is woven into nature; he feels so great because he encompasses all of nature.
> We must not miss this flash of lightning. We must capture the sensation of this valuable instant. We must constantly strive to deepen our perception and gain a greater enlightenment by recording and expressing our feelings of these moments.
> The haiku form is short, sharp, and intense because it aims to record the rare glowing moment at which our life radiates rays of light. It is very small and very large, mirroring what we are.

Here Seisensui unites pantheism and poetics. The poet's aim is to arrest nature, which is at once inside and outside of him. He is to record the precious moment of enlightenment wherein the self and all others, man and nature, the subjective and the objective, merge. Such an experience lasts only for an instant because of the constant pressure of the conscious mind; hence a verse form that aims to record it must be short.

[5] The lines are from *Faust*, Part I, scene 1. They are translated into English here in a manner that approximates Seisensui's Japanese translation.

Seisensui believed in the eternal life of all-pervading nature, which manifests itself in myriad forms. As a young student he had admired European literature, especially Goethe, but unlike many contemporary intellectuals he never experienced a vague longing for Christianity, a mysterious religion of faraway countries. Rather, his study of Western literature increased his interest in the Japanese cultural tradition. He became more and more attracted to Buddhism, especially after he lost his wife and mother in the aftermath of the Great Tokyo Earthquake of 1923. He even thought of becoming a monk. Although he did not, he attained enlightenment during Zen meditation on Mount Kōya in central Japan. Accordingly his pantheism was Buddhistic, and quite unlike that of Takamura Kōtarō, who saw physical energy as the link between man and nature. When Seisensui talked about nature, his models were the vegetable and mineral worlds.

Ultimately, Seisensui's idea of mimesis comes close to that of Bashō, who also endeavored to catch the inner life of a natural object by submerging his own ego within it. Seisensui pushed that principle a little further, placing even greater emphasis on spontaneity and instantaneous perception. He felt such perception could be recorded with a higher degree of immediacy if the mode of expression was unrestricted. In effect, he proposed writing free verse using Bashō's idea of mimesis, and if he had called the resulting poems free verse, few people would have objected. But he wanted to call them haiku because he believed he was working within a poetic tradition initiated by Bashō and was changing it to fit a new age. His belief turned out to be a minority opinion. Persistent debater though he was, Seisensui seemed to have conceded defeat in his last years. The last book he published during his lifetime was entitled, not *An Introduction to Haiku*, but *An Introduction to Short Verse*.

Light, Water, and Fertilizer

Seisensui wrote extensively about the process by which a poet produces free-style haiku. His best exposition of the subject is contained in *A New Introduction to Haiku*, a book intended for those with little or no verse-writing experience. In it, he remarked that a would-be haiku poet needs three things: "light," "water," and "fertilizer." The remark is central not only to the book but to his entire pedagogy.

Seisensui explained the meaning of "light" in the following passage:

"Light" is the essence of all that is beautiful. Where there is light, there is beauty. Of course you can see light inside your room or under an electric lamp at night, but I suggest you go out into the sunlight. Because Japan is blessed with a mild climate, you neither feel the summer sun unbearable nor become a prisoner of winter storms, except in certain small areas of the country. Go out into the sun and write haiku as much as you can. Seek out haiku directly from the light. . . . Long ago, among the Ten Disciples of Bashō, there was a man from Kaga Province named Hokushi. He loved to play with children. One day, when he took out an oak staff and prepared to go on his usual stroll, a child called out to him and asked where he was heading. Hokushi answered, "I'm going haiku-picking." Haiku can be found in the balmy light of spring, in the pleasant light of autumn, or (it does not have to be in a favorable climate) in the glaring light of summer. Each season offers a kind of haiku that cannot be picked at any other time.

Like Shiki, Seisensui warned against visiting famous places, saying that a haiku about a weed on the roadside can be more interesting than one about a renowned Buddhist temple.

By "light" Seisensui meant nature, especially the vegetable and mineral worlds celebrated in traditional Japanese poetry. Like Shiki he advocated shasei; unlike Shiki, however, he rejected ordinary seasonal themes. Such themes, he contended, are convenient for an inexperienced poet who does not yet know how to focus his camera, but haiku on traditional themes are often hackneyed, even when they are based on actual experience. Accordingly he recommended that a beginning poet try to invent his own themes, such as "A Family Scene," "Sunday," or "At an Aquarium." He also recommended composing several haiku on a single theme.

Even if a poet goes out into the light and discovers a fitting theme, he will not be able to write a single haiku unless he enters a mood appropriate for composition. To describe this state of mind, Seisensui used the metaphor of water:

Water does not directly fertilize trees and grass, and yet it is indispensable for their biological needs. Likewise, for your training in haiku you should get a constant supply of "water," a haiku-mind that remains active day in and day out. . . . If you have this haiku-mind, you will always find yourself surrounded by things that can be made into haiku. Don't neglect making these things into haiku. They will fade away unless you actually transform them into poems.

Seisensui suggested that an amateur poet always carry a notebook with him, so that he could jot down whatever came to mind; another suggestion was to use the margins of a diary.

"Water," then, is what Seisensui called the "haiku-mind" (*kugokoro*), without which material fitting for haiku would disappear unrecorded, just as a seed that has begun to sprout will die unless water is supplied. In essence, haiku-mind strives to attain an instantaneous perception of the life in natural things. To explain the idea, Seisensui once quoted Bashō's famous saying "Learn about a pine from a pine and about a bamboo from a bamboo," and said that by "learn" Bashō meant "learn the heart of nature." A mind that is ever ready to blend with nature and find its innermost secrets—that is haiku-mind.

How does one go about attaining haiku-mind? Seisensui gave an answer in another of his primers, *How to Write and Appreciate Haiku*:

"Merge your mind with nature" may sound like a very difficult teaching to follow, but actually it is nothing other than returning to childhood. How excited we used to feel when snow fell and rapidly piled up! We jumped into it and played. We befriended nature. We merged with it. But we lost this kind of excitement as we grew older. If as adults we feel anything at all on a snowy day, it is likely to be concern about having muddy streets for the next few days. This is so because the world of adults has hardened our minds, filling them with thoughts of personal gain and loss. But in truth we have never completely lost a longing for nature; we have only forgotten it is there. Therefore, when we see a magnificent scene on a trip or some similar occasion, we are deeply impressed and feel as though we had returned to the homeland of our hearts.

Here again Seisensui was following the teachings of Bashō, who reportedly said "Heed what children do" and "If you want a haiku, let it be composed by a child three feet tall." Seisensui

even ascribed the famous frog poem to Bashō's childlike mind,
comparing him to a little child who might have sung out:

> Into an old pond
> Mr. Frog
> Jumped in.
> Plop!

Although part of Seisensui's purpose may have been to criticize
those who give an overintellectualized reading to the poem, it
cannot be denied that Bashō did write some haiku that are
clearly childlike, as did some other major haiku poets, notably
Issa.

Suppose that a poet, with this childlike haiku mind, has come
upon an interesting subject in nature. What happens next? Does
the mind go out and become one with the subject? Or vice versa?
How does haiku emerge out of the merging? Seisensui believed
that usually the mind takes the initiative. He admitted that there
were cases in which the subject takes the first step, but he thought
that even in such instances the poet's subconscious mind seeks the
subject to externalize itself. At all events, the poet instantaneously
feels that there has been a union and at the same time feels an
urge to verbalize it. The process of verbalization takes only a short
time with some poets, much longer with others.

Seisensui offered a number of examples to clarify the process
of the merging of mind and nature and the subsequent verbalization. To begin with a simple one, here is a free-style haiku by
Hōsai:

> I meditate
> a mud snail walks

According to Seisensui's explication, the poet was pondering
some serious topic, perhaps what human life was all about or the
course he should take in the years to come, as he sat by a country
lane. Suddenly he noticed a mud snail crawling in front of him,
whereupon his mind went out and became one with it. In that
instant he was the snail, and the snail he. "Yes, this is nature,"
Seisensui thought the poet said to himself. "This is the peace of
mind belonging to one who enjoys nature-given life." The poet

immediately verbalized the situation in the simplest words possible, telling about himself in the first line and about nature in the second. He put the two lines side by side, and had a free-style haiku.

Needless to say, the mind-nature division that exists in the initial stage of the creative process is less clear in many finished haiku because objects in nature are often used literally, or metaphorically, or both. The following haiku by Santōka consists of images only:

> into my begging bowl also
> hailstones

A hailstorm had come up as the beggar-poet hurried along an open road one winter day. Small pellets of hail fell into the begging bowl he was carrying; they looked like the white grains of rice given by the benefactors he had visited. Instantaneously he was struck by inspiration: the hailstones were a gift from the greatest of all benefactors, heaven. Seisensui surmised, "With a childlike mind, the poet held out the metal bowl and received what was coming down from heaven." The poet's mind had merged with the begging bowl.

A more secular example is a poem by Seisensui himself:

> straw-thatched houses:
> falling
> snow
> piling up

Explaining how he wrote the poem, Seisensui said that he was gazing at the falling snow with a vacant mind. Fragmentary thoughts flashed through him: "Oh, it's falling, the snow—falling on straw-thatched houses—oh, piling up—oh, piling up." When the trance had passed, he realized that his breathing had been perfectly at one with the rhythm of the falling snow. He tried to record the ecstasy as it had been, and this poem came into being.

What Seisensui called "fertilizer" in *A New Introduction to Haiku* can be interpreted as a means of aiding amateur poets to attain haiku-mind. By "fertilizer" he meant books, especially collections of haiku by master poets of the past. The advice to read books is surprising, coming from such a fiercely independent poet, but his chief intent was to help would-be poets discover how generations of haiku poets had submerged themselves in nature. For him, the essence of haiku—indeed, of Japanese culture—lay in a close relationship with nature. In *A New Introduction to Haiku* he made a bold generalization about the identity of Japanese culture:

Generally speaking, people in the West believe that "nature" is opposed to "man," that the force of nature is to be resisted by human will. Look at their architecture. A Western house is built sturdily so as to withstand the onslaught of the elements. Its walls are thick, its windows small. In contrast, a Japanese house is supported by slender pillars and enclosed with storm doors.[6] When the doors open, the wind blows freely in and out. What separates indoors from outdoors is nothing more than paper screens, which we call *shōji*. We are never afraid of nature; we feel nature is our friend. To take another example, look at Western clothes, which cover bodies like suits of armor; it is as if they were afraid to take a chance of exposing their skin. Japanese kimonos have wide-open sleeves and are quite loose at the bottom. Western clothes are intended to protect man from nature; ours are designed to make us relax in nature. In eating habits it is the same. Western food is placed on the table only after it is dead and absolutely safe. In Japan many more things are eaten alive, like raw fish; the fresher the food is, the more we enjoy it. These facts again prove that in the West raw nature is considered dangerous, whereas in Japan people are not afraid of nature and befriend it.

Haiku exemplified this Japanese cultural trait, Seisensui continued. His contrast between Japanese and Western cultures, with its convenient examples and sweeping generalizations, is all too familiar, but the passage helps explain why for many years he so adamantly maintained that his poetry was haiku and not free verse. He considered free verse a product of Western culture and did not want his poetry to be associated with it. For the same reason, he wanted beginning students to read the classics

---

[6] A traditional Japanese house has fewer outer walls than its Western counterpart. In place of a wall there is a set of sliding wooden doors called *amado*, or "storm doors," which is closed at night as well as on stormy days.

of haiku and to use them as "fertilizer" to help cultivate their
haiku-mind.

Seisensui warned against reading famous books of haiku indiscriminately, however, for he thought that some well-known
classical poems did not capture the vital haiku moment. He frequently criticized Buson and Shiki for this fault. Although he
was well aware of their poetic talents and often paid them high
respect, he felt they too frequently wrote as bystanders, seldom
letting their minds merge with nature. For instance, he did not
like this well-known poem by Buson:

> The peony falls—
> lying upon each other,
> two or three petals.

He admitted that it was masterfully written, but he felt it lacked
vitality. Explaining the reason for his criticism, he said, "The
poet worked so hard at depicting the peony that he became a
slave to his own contrivance. As a result, he succeeded in creating an interesting picture of the peony, but failed to absorb its
life into his own mind." Elsewhere Seisensui cited eight other
peony poems by Buson that showed no trace of Buson the man.
"In my opinion," he continued, "these are paintings and not poetry. Haiku, being poetry, should reveal the poet's self. It should
contain the sense of a union between the subject and the poet's
self."

Seisensui more harshly criticized Shiki, who was largely re-
sponsible for popularizing Buson among modern haiku poets.
His reason was, again, that Shiki's poetry resembled painting
and did not show enough of the blending of mind and nature.
In theory Shiki preached shasei, yet what he practiced was, in
Seisensui's words, "photography-ism" instead of shasei-ism—he
merely recorded what he saw. The following comparison with
Bashō demonstrates the point.

> Red as usual—
> on the morning after a gale,
> pepper pods.

According to Seisensui, this haiku, attributed to Bashō, is not a mere photograph but suggests "the poet's heart going out to the life of a tiny, lovable thing amid all that is desolate." In contrast, Shiki's poem

> Wintry rain:
> cockscombs are black,
> chrysanthemums white

has "no warmth of subjectivity." Whereas Bashō's red is poetic, Shiki's black and white are only colors used in painting. Seisensui insisted that colors in haiku must suggest the life of the subject matter felt in the poet's heart. Shiki's colors do not do so and therefore have reduced the poem to "a tiny fragment of glass."

Of course, excessive objectivism is not limited to the poetry of Buson and Shiki. Seisensui saw many worse instances in the haiku of his own time, as well as in those of the past. He thought even Bashō was not always immune to the disease. One example is a Bashō poem cited earlier:

> Gathering the rains
> of early summer, how swift
> the Mogami River!

Apparently the original draft of the poem differed from this by one word:

> Gathering the rains
> of early summer, how cool
> the Mogami River!

Seisensui did not like this version, and he speculated that Bashō did not like it either. In the earlier draft the poet is merely standing on the riverbank gazing at the water; his heart and the water have not attained union. Seisensui imagined that Bashō later went aboard a boat and let himself drift on the river, whereupon he felt as though he and the water were one. That experience inspired him to revise the poem. In Seisensui's judgment, the substitution of "swift" for "cool" improved the poem greatly, for the new poem conveys a sense of the poet's heart "flowing with

the stream of nature's life." In this instance Bashō himself cured
the disease of excessive objectivism.

The example points to the importance of stylistic revision and
polishing, which Seisensui considered the last significant stage of
the creative process. He himself did a good deal of revising,
sometimes changing a poem written many years earlier. Moreover, he actively sought other people's opinions of his draft poems. At times, he sounded as though he considered group discussion a necessary phase of verse writing. For this reason he
recognized the value of verse-writing sessions. He participated
in many such gatherings and sometimes published records of
the discussions that took place.

For instance, he once wrote a series of poems on leaves and
presented it to a group of haiku poets for discussion. One of the
poems was:

> in the field
> night stalls are set up
> a lantern
> a lantern
> leaves

One poet said he could not clearly see where the leaves were; he
did not know whether they were lying on the ground, still on the
branches, or in the process of falling. Another imagined they
were dark, dry leaves sparsely remaining on a tree. None of
those present was able to visualize the scene as Seisensui had
hoped they would. The scene he wanted to depict was a rustic
fair on a winter night, with one tiny stall here and another there
along a lane. A lantern spotlighted each booth, dimly showing
cheap, miscellaneous items for sale; they looked unreal and
could hardly be distinguished from the fallen leaves mixed with
them. Although leaves must be lying everywhere, they were visible only where a lantern was. A lantern, fallen leaves; another
lantern, fallen leaves—Seisensui wanted to create this impression. Hearing what other poets had to say, he realized the poem
did not do what he had wanted it to. Afterwards he changed the
haiku to:

```
in the field
lanterns are placed
night stalls
leaves
```

He felt that the line "night stalls are set up" in the original draft sounded too explanatory and that the lantern should appear before the stall because this was the order in which one would see them. He was not entirely satisfied with the revised poem, but believed that it was more faithful to his initial impression of the scene.

In another instance, Seisensui could not decide between an initial draft and a revised one, and so he presented the problem to his colleagues. The haiku was about a "floating island," a grass plot in a muddy lake, gradually disappearing into the evening dusk. The original draft was:

```
floating island's
undarkening
green also
darkens
```

Later he revised it to read:

```
floating island's
green also
drowns
in my night
```

This time there was a consensus among the poets participating in the discussion; they all favored the revised version. One felt that the first draft was too artificial and did not articulate the poet's feeling faithfully. Another liked the words "my night," which he thought expressed a sense of becoming one with the night. A third also preferred the second draft because he felt it did away with the idea of the passage of time, which dominated the first version. Hearing all this, Seisensui no longer had any doubt which to choose; he adopted the second.

Seisensui and his followers held many such sessions to scrutinize each other's haiku. The discussion sometimes resulted in revision, at other times not; in either case it contributed to a poet's

awareness of his own creative process. The debate became quite
heated on some occasions. One involved the following haiku by
Aoki Shikunrō (1887–1968):[7]

> a pot of
> yellow chrysanthemums

Most of those at the session disliked the poem; some, indeed,
wondered whether it could even be called a poem. They admitted that yellow chrysanthemums were more poetic than white or
red ones because their color created the impression of collecting
the rays of autumn sunlight, but they criticized the poem for not
expressing the poet's feeling. One of them even said it was merely
the title of a painting, and a trite one at that. At last they turned to
Seisensui, who had considered the poem highly enough to publish it in *Layered Clouds*.

Seisensui, now playing a defense attorney's role, first proposed that they compare the following three compositions:

> A: the pot
>   is of yellow chrysanthemums
>
> B: there is a pot of
>   yellow chrysanthemums
>
> C: it is a pot of
>   yellow chrysanthemums

Seisensui contended that A was not poetry, B was close to but not
quite poetry, and C was in the realm of poetry. According to his
contention, A stated a recognition that was intellectual and
hence not poetry; B portrayed an existing object that lay outside
the poet. In contrast, C presented a perception that had been
internalized, the poet's heart having touched the essence of his
subject. Seisensui argued that Shiki and his followers tended to
write "there-is" haiku, haiku like B, because they tried to sketch
an object from the outside. "In opposition to them," he said, "I

---

[7] Shikunrō was a leading member of the *Layered Clouds* group from 1915 to
1940. Seisensui often praised his sensitivity to rhythm. He published seven volumes of haiku.

would like to advocate an 'it-is' haiku, a haiku emphasizing perception." He proposed revising Shikunrō's poem to read

yellow chrysanthemums'
one pot

because that would approach closer to C. He felt the poem thus
revised would articulate the poet's satisfied feeling of owning the
whole beauty of autumn.

Seisensui's argument did not convince all the people present.[8]
One of them remarked that if Shikunrō's lines deserved the
name of haiku, such lines as

a pile of
tangerines

would have to be called haiku also, and that one could easily
compose any number of haiku using the same format. Another
participant questioned whether any and all perceptions could
become poetry, or whether a true work of art would not demand
more than a simple expression of perception. Seisensui's replies
to both these questions were long and vigorous, but not very
convincing. In the end he had to concede that he regarded Shikunrō's haiku as poetry but that he did not count it among his
great favorites.

This episode suggests a weakness in Seisensui's concept of the
creative process. He wrote a great deal, quite eloquently, about
the art of writing free-style haiku, urging beginning poets to go
out into the sunshine and observe nature freshly, to submerge
their hearts in nature and feel its pulse within themselves. That
feeling, he taught, should be expressed with brevity, precision,
and a natural rhythm. He also taught the importance of showing
poems to other people for criticism. But by and large his advice
stopped there. Most of his books on the art of verse writing were
for beginners; their titles often included words like "introduc-
tory" and "how to." Although they are lucid and stimulating,

<hr>

[8]Shikunrō, who was not present but heard about the discussion, was not convinced either. The difference of opinion eventually led him to leave Seisensui
and the *Layered Clouds* group.

those books are not deeply philosophical. Seisensui was a missionary, not a theologian.

Toward Naturalness and Simplicity

In April 1938, Seisensui gave a talk in English, which was broadcast overseas. Its title was "Naturality [*sic*] and Simplicity." Although the text of the talk has not been preserved,[9] one can reconstruct its substance, for naturalness and simplicity were the twin principles of Seisensui's haiku aesthetics, and he frequently wrote about them.

Seisensui's emphasis on naturalness was a direct outgrowth of his belief that haiku should capture the life of nature through a merging of the poet's mind with his subject matter. He used the term to refer to an alignment with, or expression of, nature and natural forces:

The word "naturalness" can be interpreted in many ways, but I believe its true meaning has to do with one's perception of the force of life. Naturalness does not imply a retreat from society into nature. It does not refer just to viewing the moon or the clouds. Rather, it asks one to absorb the great power and light possessed by nature and to hold the happiness of nature in one's heart during the course of one's life.

"Power" and "light" were two words Seisensui was fond of using whenever he tried to explain the beauty of nature. Of the many types of natural beauty, he favored vigor, strength, directness, clarity, and related qualities, which he thought were attributes of the basic life-force. One of his oft-repeated dictums is: "New haiku is poetry of light. It is poetry of strength."

Seisensui used many classical haiku to illustrate naturalness. In addition to Bashō, he especially favored, somewhat surprisingly, Takebe Ryōtai (1719–74).[10] In such haiku as

The young grass:
soaking through its green
the spring rain falls

[9] An article Seisensui wrote in English and published in the July 1938 issue of *Cultural Nippon* is apparently based on this talk, but how closely it follows the talk is not known. The article is entitled "The Haiku, or the Japanese Poetry in Seventeen Syllables."

[10] Ryōtai is the haiku name of Takebe Ayatari, a painter, classical scholar, and

Seisensui recognized Ryōtai's successful attempt to capture the vigorous life of nature. He thought the use of two verbs, "to soak" and "to fall," especially effective in conveying a sense of nature's force.

Seisensui believed free-style haiku could convey this type of beauty as well as, or better than, the traditional 5–7–5 form. He speculated that Ryōtai, who was especially eager to capture naturalness in his poetry, inwardly felt an impulse to break through the 17-syllable form. The pattern of his haiku on spring rain is 5–7–7 (or 5–7–5–2). Seisensui believed that if Ryōtai had been more conventionally minded, he would have followed the usual 5–7–5 pattern and written a haiku like:

> The young grass:
> how dazzling its green is
> in the spring rain!

Seisensui rightly noted that this 17-syllable poem focuses on the beauty of the fresh green grass, not on its vigorous growth. In his opinion, as soon as a poet utilizes the conventional 5–7–5 form he feels the pressure of conventional haiku aesthetics and is inclined to write haiku embodying stereotyped sentiments. Using a bold metaphor, Seisensui asserted, "The beauty of a 17-syllable haiku is similar to that of a crystal. It is inorganic and belongs to the mineral world. What we seek is more organic and biological. A poem that looks like a crystal can never convey the sense of life." The word "never" in the last sentence is undoubtedly too strong, because by his own admission Bashō, Ryōtai, and other premodern poets had been able to write "biological" haiku.

Seisensui inadvertently used the strong word "never" because many contemporary 17-syllable haiku did seem to be trapped in a stereotyped haiku aesthetic. One particularly shocking example was:

> After lighting
> incense, he killed himself:
> the spring rain.

---

writer of prose fiction. He is best known for his adaptation of the Chinese novel *Water Margin*.

The poem treats an actual incident. The suicide had been well planned; the man had even seen to it that his body would be discovered in a beautifully scented room. In his presentation, the poet chose to create a harmony between the incense and the spring rain, pushing the suicide into the background, as he had been taught in traditional haiku lessons. Consequently his poem failed to convey "a life burning within the incident" or "a great power of nature lying in contradictions," in Seisensui's words. The conventional requirements of the 5–7–5 pattern and seasonal reference had induced him to avert his eyes from the heart of the event.

This example suggests that under Seisensui's aversion to the 17-syllable form lay a distaste for traditional Japanese aesthetic concepts. Classical poets like Bashō also aimed at naturalness in their poetry, yet to Seisensui their type of naturalness seemed lacking in dynamic energy. Explaining the beauty of Bashō's poetry to young would-be poets, he wrote:

The impression created by Bashō's works can be described as the transparent serenity of a moonlit night. Bashō called it *sabi*. It is the kind of beauty many old folks have a taste for. I would not deny the value of sabi in haiku, but it is not something I can recommend to young haiku poets. We have to break out of the mood of a moonlit night and advance into the mood of dawn.

Aware did not fare any better in Seisensui's aesthetic:

Bashō conceived nature to be a harmonious world. He recognized *aware* in the departure of a season. From that standpoint he injected a new meaning into the 5–7–5 form and the season word. Indeed, the 17-syllable form was perfect for embodying his harmonious world. . . . But I do not see nature as something quiet or in terms of the four seasons alone. I see active movement in it. I see a force in it.

These statements distinguish between the traditional kind of naturalness and the kind favored by Seisensui, who wanted to see a positive, dynamic force in haiku. As we have seen, his naturalness did not mean "a retreat from society." Instead, he wanted his fellow poets to be in the midst of modern society, which was anything but quiet and harmonious, and he wanted them to convey a sense of that vigor in their poetry.

In Seisensui's definition, then, "naturalness" covers a wider range of meaning than it did in premodern poetics. A modern haiku can depict the beauty of contemporary urban life and still produce naturalness. Seisensui illustrated this point with some apt examples, including:

> a truck
> loaded with steel:
> trees along the street
> about to bud

This free-style haiku portrays the dynamic force of nature through the image of winter trees, which are outwardly as frigid as steel but inwardly brim with strength. They will shoot forth myriad buds at the first sign of spring. The steel bars on the truck are also full of life as they hurry to a construction site; soon they will become part of the lives of the people who occupy the building. "We recognize a force of life not only in the trees but in the truck also," observed Seisensui. "The truck loaded with steel is linked to the trees through this life-force." The haiku, then, shows naturalness, the kind of naturalness Seisensui wanted to see in twentieth-century poetry.

The other of Seisensui's twin aesthetic principles, simplicity, also had its origin in premodern haiku. He thought it was related closely to the Japanese love of nature. "I have said that the Japanese are great lovers of nature, and now I say that they are also lovers of simplicity," Seisensui said. "Indeed, one cannot fully appreciate the beauty of nature without loving its simplicity, for beauty and simplicity are inseparable in nature." Like Shiki, he believed that nature was simple. He was fond of illustrating this point by referring to two things the Japanese thought represented the ultimate in natural beauty: Mount Fuji and a pine tree. The shape of Mount Fuji, he said, is so simple that one could outline it with three matchsticks. And a pine tree, especially the kind frequently sketched by Japanese painters, has a simple form with very few branches. Seisensui speculated that Mount Fuji and pine trees had attained such simple beauty because they had been in place for many years, while the elements stripped them of anything superfluous. In their simplicity they showed the ultimate form of nature and its force. According to Seisensui, the art and poetry of Japan, especially haiku, had cultivated such simple beauty.

Like naturalness, then, simplicity is a manifestation of the essential force of nature. Again, like natural beauty it is dynamic. Seisensui observed:

"Simplicity" does not mean something passive, something done on a reduced scale. It works on complex, multifarious, disorderly things until it finds a core and unifies them into a single entity. Only something that has strength can do this. It is the same with man's mind: when the mind is unified by a single, powerful purpose—for instance, admiration of the great power of nature—it becomes extremely simple.

The passage explains not only the meaning of simplicity but also the way in which a haiku poet works on his material. Composing haiku is a process of simplification, of centering complex material around a single core, and this can be done when the poet's mind attains the simplicity of a natural force.

Seisensui cited many haiku showing the beauty of simplicity— an easy task for anyone. Here is an example, a haiku by Bashō that Seisensui translated as:

Day by day ripens the wheat;
The skylarks—how gaily they sing!

In a long explication in English, Seisensui pointed out that a skylark, called "a messenger to the sun," is often seen singing over wheat fields, which change their color subtly day by day, from lemon yellow to apricot yellow, to orange yellow, to burnt orange, and so on. He then asked his readers, "Do you not picture the skylark facing towards the sun and singing to tell of the Good Earth, so full of peace and happiness? Does it not seem that the wheat, which is shining so brilliantly, expresses the infinite 'life-power' of Mother Earth? In other words nature is a harmonious simplicity." Seisensui's point is that by condensing the vast scene of the summer countryside Bashō succeeded in capturing nature's simplicity. He contended that the haiku, in fewer than twenty syllables, was able to create an impression of the bright and sunny atmosphere of wheat fields that Words-worth took more than thirty lines to portray in "To a Sky-Lark."

Seisensui undoubtedly considered free-style haiku a more fit-ting vehicle to present the simplicity of nature than the 5–7–5 form. We have already seen him change Bashō's famous frog poem into a free-style haiku by dropping its first line. Whether the change makes this a better poem is open to question, but in some cases the 17-syllable requirement has undeniably forced a poet to insert a word or two that is not absolutely necessary. A free-style haiku eliminates such a need, enabling a poet to sim-plify to the bare minimum as, for instance, Shikunrō did when he wrote:

> grasses
> moonlit night

In Japanese only six syllables make up this poem, which portrays a vast, grassy plain, a nocturnal world of nothing but grass and moonlight that extends into an infinite distance. Seisensui cor-rectly observed that not a single syllable could be added to this haiku. Of course, the 17-syllable rule would not have allowed such simplification.

The simplicity of the haiku form inevitably demands the ac-tive participation of the reader. Because there is so much blank space in the picture, the reader must use his own imagination to fill it in. To explain such a poet-reader relationship, Seisensui often used the metaphor of a circle. In his opinion, each haiku is a circle of which only one half is completed by the poet. The other half must be supplied by the reader. "In short," he said, "a haiku can be properly appreciated only when there is teamwork by the poet and the reader. Only those who are capable of writ-ing haiku can truly understand haiku written by other people." Because of its extreme brevity, haiku asks every reader to be a poet to a greater degree than do other forms of poetry. "One can enjoy a novel, a play, a painting, or music while being a mere reader, spectator, or listener," Seisensui said. "In haiku, however,

only practitioners can appreciate the product." He once estimated that 99 percent of the people who read haiku in contemporary Japan had written haiku themselves.

In Seisensui's view, then, there is no clear-cut distinction between the poet and the reader, for reading a haiku is in many
ways similar to writing one. Strictly speaking, no haiku is a
finished work of art; every poem is waiting for a reader to come
and finish it. "I think," Seisensui remarked, "haiku can be said to
be an art presenting not something that is expressed but something that expresses. It focuses less on a completed work than on
a heart that is creating a work." He implies that a haiku is a catalyst that initiates or promotes the process that is verse writing.
Although the idea can be applied to all poetry, because of its
brevity haiku demands greater participation from the reader.
This close poet-reader relationship goes back to the very origin
of haiku, to the time when it was the first verse of a linked poem.
In haikai, every reader had to be a poet; he was required to add
his own verse to the poem being composed in his presence.

The extreme brevity of haiku and the resulting demand it
makes for the reader's participation bring up the questions of
ambiguity and plurality of meaning. Seisensui implied that a
haiku was 50 percent finished by the poet and that the other 50
percent must await completion by individual readers, but some
of his followers wrote haiku that seem only 20 or 30 percent
finished. He once criticized several haiku by his students, saying
that they were more like stanzas of a linked poem, which expected other stanzas to follow. On another occasion he remarked
that an overly ambiguous haiku was usually just a witty quip or at
best a Zen riddle, in either case not deserving the name of a
work of art.

That Seisensui's concern with excessive ambiguity was justified is dramatically revealed by an examination he gave at a
Tokyo women's college where he taught for a time. The test
listed five free-style haiku the students had never seen before
and asked them to explicate each. As it turned out, one of the

five haiku was so ambiguous that of the 120 examinees only one gave a "correct" answer. The poem in question was:

> calling back
> with only one word

Some of the answers Seisensui received were:

A: The poem reminds me of the day when I left home for Tokyo. Doesn't it express the affection of a parent who, seeing off a child, inadvertently calls out aloud? Calling back the child with one word—that is the situation.

B: The occasion is a lovers' parting. At the last minute the man says a word to call the woman back. He still recalls the day from time to time.

C: Just one word would have been enough to call back the person, but he could not say it. He has regretted that ever since. The poem expresses the empty, sad sentiment of parting.

D: At a crowded place in town the poet thought he saw an acquaintance, but because he was not sure he could not decide whether he should call out. The poem embodies that hesitant feeling.

E: When the poet spoke to a person lying sick, the answer that came back was just one word. The poem indicates the lonely, helpless feeling of that voice.

In Seisensui's judgment, A was the correct answer. He labeled all the other answers wrong because they did not sufficiently focus on "affection," which he thought was at the core of the poem. However, he did not explain why a reading that focuses on affection should be considered correct. Apparently, the right type of reader grasps the right meaning by instinct. "In haiku, the meaning is understood instantaneously, as soon as the reader reads the poem," he said. "There is nothing we can do about those who do not understand or catch the meaning instantly." This makes reading haiku an esoteric practice reserved only for the initiated. When 119 out of 120 college students do not understand the meaning of a poem correctly, isn't there something wrong with the poem, or shouldn't a teacher at least ponder that question? Seisensui did reflect on whether the haiku was defective in expression. But he could find no fault with the poem and so laid the blame on the students' lack of experience in reading poetry.

Seisensui's comments on another of the five haiku and its varying interpretations reveal his general scheme of ranking different readings of a poem. The free-style haiku presented to the students for explication was:

> a beret
> is hanging on the pillar—
> a funeral urn

On reading the students' answers, Seisensui was pleased to find that more than half of them had interpreted the poem in the way he wanted. The answers of about one-third of the remaining students were not wrong but in his opinion could not be said to be correct, either. Here are some typical answers:

A: The beret is hanging on the pillar just as it was before. But why has its owner turned into an urn? The poem suggests the poet's grief as well as his memories of the dead person.

B: I wonder if the dead person was an obscure painter. The room looks bare. The only conspicuous thing is the beret he was fond of wearing. The scene is reminiscent of the lonely life he lived.

C: The child is dead and lies inside the urn, but its beret is still hanging on the pillar. This is a grief-laden poem.

D: The kindergartner was killed in an accident. The red color of the little girl's beret, which still hangs on the pillar, increases the poet's grief.

E: The poet has been sick, and his beret has been hanging on the pillar all these days. It looks like an urn. The poem expresses the aging poet's sadness.

Seisensui considered A and B correct answers. He liked B better, because he thought it probed deeper into the meaning of the poem. He said that C and D were possible but not very good: their writers had identified the owner of the beret as a little girl, and that seemed inappropriate. He pointed out that if the dead person were a little girl the bereaved family would never have left her beret hanging in the room, since it would be a painful reminder of the days when she was alive. The students who read the poem along the lines of C and D had never been mothers themselves, he speculated, so they had come up with such possible but unlikely interpretations. As for E, the student who wrote it had an insufficient knowledge of haiku structure. "A beret" and "a funeral urn" are juxtaposed in the poem, for after the second line there is a caesura characteristic of haiku. The student was ignorant of that practice and equated the two images, mistaking the urn for a metaphor.

The principles of haiku interpretation that emerge from Seisensui's comments are a strange combination of the familiar and the esoteric. In explicating the beret poem he showed that a correct reading of haiku is possible for anyone who pays close attention to the wording, structure, and imagery of a poem as well as to the workings of the human mind. But in discussing the haiku on parting he placed undue emphasis on instantaneous, instinctive understanding. When all but one student gave inadequate interpretations, he blamed the students for not possessing that mysterious capacity. Here lies the dilemma of the free-style haiku theorist. On the one hand he must advocate free interpretation of the poem, as must any haiku critic. But on the other he must emphasize the identity of free-style haiku and ask the reader to try to reach for the poem's core, which is a mystical union of man and nature. Drawn toward these opposite poles, Seisensui did not know how to reconcile them. Because of the subjective nature of literary interpretation, that reconciliation is not easy in the literary criticism of any period or culture; the problem is multiplied in dealing with haiku, a verse form especially susceptible to multiple interpretations. Seisensui extolled the simple beauty of haiku, but simplicity also means ambiguity, and he could not quite resolve that difficulty.

The Boundaries of Freedom

No one discussing free-style haiku can avoid the question of the appropriate length of an individual poem. How long, or how short, can a poem be in free-style haiku? Can it be written in just three syllables? Or in as many as 30? For someone to write a poem of 100 syllables and call it a free-style haiku would defy common sense. Although to draw precise rules to stipulate a poem's length would go against the very principle of free-style haiku, there must be some agreement about a poem's length, as long as it is to be called a haiku and not free verse.

Seisensui's answer to this question in *A New Introduction to Haiku* was that a free-style haiku should have "a length that can be read out in one breath." He said this had to be so because haiku was primarily an exclamation indicating admiration for the beauty of nature. He did not elaborate, except to point out that a tanka was difficult to read out in one breath. Thus presumably he thought a free-style haiku should be shorter than 31 syllables. In another book, *Critical Comments on Free-Style Haiku*, he said a free-style haiku could sometimes become rather long but not "ridiculously long" and added that an ordinary haiku consisted of four parts and that each part could contain as many as seven syllables. It follows, then, that the longest haiku would have a total of 28 syllables. "A haiku longer than that is rare," he said. As for the shortest, he cited Shikunrō's haiku about the grassy plain on a moonlit night, which, as we have seen, consists of just six syllables. "Such extremely short poems are few," he said. "Ones that are too short tend to look crippled." From these comments one can gather that Seisensui thought the length of an ordinary free-style haiku should fall between six and 28 syllables.

To test this premise, I counted the syllables of all 283 poems published in *Critical Comments on Free-Style Haiku*, a book intended to bring together poems representative of the genre at the time. The greatest number of free-style haiku in the anthology are written in 19 syllables; there are 40 such poems. The second largest number (25) are written in 21 syllables. After that the order is 21 syllables, 22 syllables, 18 syllables, 16 syllables, and 17 syllables. Only one poem has more than 28 syllables; no poem has fewer than nine. Sixty-five percent of the poems have between 17 and 22 syllables. It can be said, then, that our premise is correct: over 99 percent of the haiku in the anthology contain more than five and fewer than 29 syllables.

Critical Comments on Free-Style Haiku was published in 1935. In subsequent years poets seem to have become more liberal about the length of free-style haiku. One extreme case is Shikunrō, who wrote some of the shortest poems in Japanese, including this one:

> face

This haiku—if it can be called a haiku—consists of only two syllables in the original Japanese. At the other extreme, some extraordinarily long "haiku" have been published. Some of the longest, such as the following, were written by Matsumoto Kazuya (*b.* 1928):[11]

> sky-piercing
> blue
> second weeding
> third weeding
> and yet
> from inside rice plants
> they grow
> it doesn't straighten any more
> my back

This poem has 55 syllables! The two examples cited fall outside of the general guidelines set up by Seisensui, but both authors contend they are haiku. Are they really? Would Seisensui have approved of them as exceptions?

I believe Seisensui would not have approved of them, although he was generous about the length of free-style haiku. These two poems are not consistent with his poetic. Seisensui defined a haiku as a poem capturing the momentary perceptions of a man who had attained a mystical union with nature. He distinguished it from free verse by the presence of an instantaneous

---

[11] Kazuya was a member of a group promoting haiku in colloquial Japanese. The example cited here is from a book of his haiku published in 1959.

insight and the absence of a temporal progression of thought. An extremely short poem, like Shikunrō's, is hard put to portray or to suggest with any depth the poet's union with nature. If a poet is limited to two or three syllables, he has just one Japanese word to work with, and the best he can do is to present a lone image, as Shikunrō did. The resulting poem is too cryptic; at best it is a Zen riddle, which Seisensui thought did not deserve the name of a work of art. On the other hand, an extremely long "haiku" like Kazuya's inevitably approaches what is generally known as free verse because its very length creates the impression of passing time. A poem with 55 syllables cannot be read out in one breath, and a sense of time inevitably enters the reader's mind as he reads the poem from beginning to end. Kazuya's poem definitely suggests the passage of time, since it mentions the second and third weedings, between which there is an interval of several weeks. The poem conveys a sense of the farmer-poet looking back in time and pondering; it is not an instantaneous flash of insight.

Seisensui found it easier to characterize free-style haiku by its structure than by its length. According to him, the basic factor in the structure of free-style haiku is the caesura, a major break that occurs once in a poem. The caesura has been a conspicuous structural feature of traditional haiku for centuries: the 17-syllable poem usually has a "cutting word," a word indicating a major break in the flow of meaning. Seisensui valued this feature in traditional haiku and observed that a haiku without a caesura was not really haiku but *hiraku*, a "flat verse" in the main body of a linked poem.[12] Such a verse, he said, was "like a stick" and "without any sign of haiku rhythm." He prized the caesura in haiku because he thought it helped to express "a cubic sense of nature." In his opinion, a caesura-less poem is too flat.

Seisensui cited a number of examples to illustrate the value of the caesura, among them this free-style haiku by Raboku:

[12] Strictly speaking, *hiraku* refers to any of the stanzas constituting a linked poem except the first three and the last, but here Seisensui meant any haikai verse except the first stanza.

emaciated
a crescent moon rises
yam leaves

He pointed out the presence of a caesura after the second line,
which, he said, caused the reader to hesitate and ponder for a
moment. That pause creates a sense of how the yam leaves,
which have been in the dark, suddenly receive the white rays of
the moon and loom dimly on the surface of the earth. He invited
the reader to compare the poem to a conventional 5–7–5 haiku
on the same theme:

Emaciated
a crescent moon rises
over yam leaves.

The second haiku does away with the caesura by adding the
word "over." The result is a flatter, more descriptive poem without the sense of the poet suddenly discovering yam leaves in the
dark. Seisensui described the effect of this haiku as "lukewarm,"
"commonplace," and "explanatory."

His high regard for the caesura led Seisensui to insist that a
haiku is structurally a two-line poem. For this reason, when he
romanized classical haiku he wrote each poem in two lines; likewise, whenever he translated a haiku into English he rendered it
in an unrhymed couplet. (An example has been cited—Bashō's
haiku on skylarks.) Seisensui was very unhappy when the translation committee of the Japan Society for the Promotion of Scientific Research,[13] in one of its projects, decided to translate all
haiku in three lines. As a member of the committee, Seisensui
argued vehemently for two-line translation, but others did not
listen to him, because, according to him, many of them were spe-
cialists in English literature and had no understanding of the
rhythm of haiku.

Seisensui published some of his own haiku in couplet form.
Here are two examples, both written in 1914:

[13] Nippon Gakujutsu Shinkōkai. The project referred to here resulted in
Haikai and Haiku (Tokyo, 1958), one of the standard haiku collections available
in English today.

a sail in the distance
the wind blows hard at the steersman's eyes

not a single grave unlighted
this place alive with villagers

He wrote many similar two-line poems around this time, but he gradually came to have doubts about the propriety of calling them haiku. In haiku, he felt, one of the lines is semantically more weighty because a haiku has a single focus. "I became aware," he confessed, "that a haiku should have a focus collecting all the rays of light." Rereading the first haiku cited above, he admitted that there were two focuses—the sail and the wind. In order for the poem to be a haiku, he felt it should concentrate on one of them, and he rewrote it to focus on the wind before including it in his haiku collection.

Seisensui did not, however, give up two-line poetry. Instead, he attempted to develop it into an independent verse form. The attempt climaxed in 1918, when he published a number of such couplets as well as a long essay laying a theoretical foundation for the experimental form. In sum, that foundation was the poet's desire to write a short poem that permits the passage of time, in contrast to haiku, which crystallizes a momentary insight devoid of temporal elements. "The life of haiku lies in its focused moment," Seisensui explained. "It cannot truly represent the rhythm of time. But a two-line poem seems able to suggest a temporal rhythm." In other words, he tried to use the new form to express experiences that seemed too long for haiku. Here are two examples:

Hot Spring
From the bathtub's edge
Time quietly overflows.

Winter
The sky deepens day by day.
Every tree in sight becomes bare.

Like these—and unlike haiku—many of his couplets have titles. They also show a more logical structure than ordinary haiku.

Both these facts may be due to the presence of temporal elements. Whereas a haiku poet expresses an insight before it has time to harden, a writer of couplets chooses to meditate on his insight, allowing time for his intellect to come into play. A poem thus written is likely to have a more concrete theme and a better-ordered structure; it cries out for a title, too.

Seisensui's call for two-line poetry fell on deaf ears. Hardly anyone responded, except a small group of his own students. It is easy to see why. Two-line poems have a fixed verse form, with less freedom of expression than free verse and without the centuries of tradition that polished tanka and haiku. If a closed form contributes little or nothing to poetic expression, one might as well write free verse. Seisensui's own two-line poems did not promote the cause, either, for in general they were less than inspiring. The two-line form was an interesting experiment, but little more.

In addition to stressing the importance of the caesura in haiku and developing that break into an experimental couplet form, Seisensui recognized other, shorter pauses that he thought gave complexity and variation to a haiku's total rhythm. "Pauses" may not be the right word, since the reader does not necessarily stop reading at these points; they are more semantic than elocutionary. In essence, one occurs when a phrase or some grammatical unit ends and a new one starts. According to Seisensui, in most instances a haiku will have three, four, or five such phrases; the combination of their number and length gives the haiku its unique rhythm.

That a haiku can be a three-phrase poem is easy to see. A traditional haiku, with its 5−7−5 pattern, readily breaks into three parts separated by two pauses. For instance, in Buson's famous haiku

> Mustard flowers:
> the moon in the east,
> the sun in the west

there are three distinct phrases corresponding to the divisions of the 5−7−5 pattern. Seisensui proposed to illustrate this structural feature using a triangle. (See Figure 1.) The figure has the advantage of showing that the phrases "the moon in the east" and "the sun in the west" not only correspond to each other but respond to "mustard flowers" from their respective positions. Seisensui observed, "The scenery extends far to the east and far

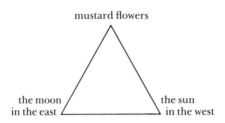

mustard flowers

the moon
in the east

the sun
in the west

FIG. 1. Analysis of Buson's haiku, I

to the west, with the vast expanse of mustard flowers connecting the two. Indeed, this is a huge triangle. It is as if the immense triangle covered everything between heaven and earth."

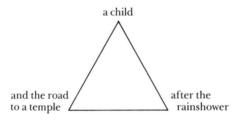

a child

and the road
to a temple

after the
rainshower

FIG. 2. Analysis of Sensuirō's haiku, I

Seisensui also found a triangular form in this free-style haiku by Sakai Sensuirō (d. 1964): [14]

> a child
> and the road to a temple
> after the rain shower

[14] Sensuirō was a founding member of an early free-style haiku magazine, *Experiment*, but became a regular contributor to *Layered Clouds* after meeting Seisensui in 1914. He also edited his own haiku magazine, *Window*.

(See Figure 2.) He likened the haiku to a painting entitled "Landscape with Child." The poem made him visualize a child in the foreground, some lingering rainclouds in the background, and a temple and its road midway between the two. The three features of the landscape made up the three points of the triangle.

Seisensui believed, however, that Sensuirō's haiku could also be made into a square; indeed, he liked that better. The poem's shape would then resemble Figure 3. The square allows the

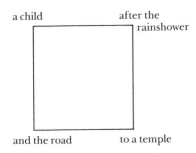

a child   after the
                               rainshower

and the road   to a temple

FIG. 3. Analysis of Sensuirō's haiku, II

child and the temple to face each other, and it separates the road from the temple and brings it closer to the child. Seisensui thought these changes helped the reader to visualize the child on the road. The square also suggests that the child and the temple are related—Japanese children often play in temple yards—and thus brightens the image of the temple, making it fit the refreshing feeling of the air after a rain shower.

In general, Seisensui seems to have preferred to dissect a haiku into four parts, whether the haiku had a 5–7–5 pattern or not. "A traditional haiku has 5, 7, and 5 syllables," he wrote. "Each 5-syllable part normally represents one semantic unit, whereas the 7-syllable part contains two units. Consequently many haiku comprise four units of meaning." In his view, free-style haiku is more faithful to the idea of a four-part poem since it is not restricted by the 5–7–5 pattern. "You may feel haiku to be a restrictive verse form if you consider it a 17-syllable poem," he said. "But try to think of it as a four-unit poem. Then the poem's length—namely, the number of syllables—will be determined by the length of the words contained in each unit. The poem may include 18 or 19 syllables, or just 15 or 16 syllables in all. If you regard haiku as a four-unit poem . . . you will find haiku to be something exceedingly free and natural." The argument in this passage is basically the same as the one presented when Seisensui urged haiku poets to follow the inner rhythm rather than the outer 5−7−5 pattern, save that he conceived that inner rhythm as consisting of four parts.

Seisensui offered a number of examples to support his theory that a haiku consists of four parts. As we have seen, he broke down Bashō's 5−7−5 pattern into four divisions:

> gathering the rains
> of early summer
> how swift
> the Mogami River!

Another example he cited was Bashō's haiku on banana plants, which even more clearly showed its four parts. Yet another example was a free-style haiku by Seisensui himself:

> the wheat grows
> a *temari* ball bounces

Temari, or "handball," is a simple game played by little girls in Japan. It entails bouncing a small ball continuously, and the winner is the player who can bounce the ball the greatest number of times without a break. A girl often practices it by herself, as seems to be the case in this poem. Seisensui broke the poem down into four parts and placed each part at the corner of a square, as shown in Figure 4. He then observed that the figure made clear two parallels: one between the wheat and the ball, the other between growing and bouncing. According to his explanation, the verb "to grow" suggests the poet's affection for the wheat, because an indifferent person would never notice its imperceptible daily growth. That affection has something in common with his love of the child who is bouncing the ball. The parallel between the wheat and the ball allows them to define each other: the wheat must be growing near a house because a

little girl is playing nearby, and she must be enjoying her play in
the same carefree way as the wheat grows on the farm. The
haiku portrays a quiet countryside on a balmy spring day, with
all its four semantic units echoing each other to define the
scene.[15]

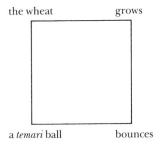

the wheat   grows

a *temari* ball   bounces

FIG. 4. Analysis of Seisensui's haiku

Although Seisensui believed most haiku have a square form,
he also said that some haiku are pentagonal. He believed, for example, that Buson's haiku on mustard flowers could also be seen
as five-cornered, as shown in Figure 5. A pentagon reveals the

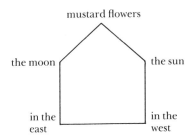

mustard flowers

the moon   the sun

in the   in the
east   west

FIG. 5. Analysis of Buson's haiku, II

poem's symmetry better than the triangle does, for it sets up a
separate parallel between the sun and the moon and between
the east and the west.

[15] In view of Seisensui's analysis, one might argue that this haiku should be
translated in four lines. However, the pause after "grows" seems more pronounced than the other two; hence my two-line translation.

According to Seisensui, longer free-style haiku are often shaped like Buson's poem, although the figure may be turned upside down. The following poem by Raboku is an example of a five-cornered haiku written in free style:

> downy hair
> of the baby in my arms
> softness
> of the evening wind
> I love.

(See Figure 6.) The pentagonal diagram shows that the words "I love" refer not only to the wind but to the baby as well, even though grammatically they modify the former alone. It also suggests that the softness of the wind is like the baby's hair, that young leaves are budding on the surrounding trees, and that both the hair and the leaves are blown gently in the wind.

FIG. 6. Analysis of Raboku's haiku

Seisensui's analysis of haiku structure in terms of geometrical forms is interesting and helpful, especially for those who are not used to reading haiku. However, it is all too easy to find in haiku any number of pauses one may choose. Not only are there thousands of examples to pick among, but any Japanese sentence of ten to thirty syllables has two, three, four, or five pauses, whether it is a haiku or not. Therefore Seisensui would have needed to argue for a particular number, patterning, or treatment of pauses to characterize adequately the structure of haiku.

Nevertheless, Seisensui's haiku geometry did make a contribution to Japanese literary scholarship. For one thing, it was virtually the first attempt to analyze the structure of haiku. Poets and critics before Seisensui had theorized about the cutting word, but they were averse to dissecting haiku, or any form of poetry, because they felt a poem was a living organism. Seisensui, one of the first Japanese to major in linguistics in college, had no such aversion. His discovery of pauses smaller than the caesura led him to break up a haiku, but that did not bother him, since it had a precedent in linguistic analysis. His comparison of haiku to geometric figures also had the virtue of showing—although he may not have noticed it—that a haiku was not a linear poem, reinforcing a point he stressed in his controversy with Hakushū. He argued, in effect, that the word ending a haiku did not create a sense of finality in the way the ending of a free-verse poem might, that it always linked with the beginning or with another earlier word, thereby completing a geometric shape. A pioneer in free-style haiku, he was also one of the first to venture into an analytical study of the haiku form.

Everything We See Becomes a Flower

In the preface to *How to Write and Appreciate Haiku*, Seisensui listed three pleasures haiku can afford. He called them the pleasure of creating, the pleasure of appreciating, and the pleasure of seeing. His ideas on the enjoyment of poetry center on these three concepts.

The observation that haiku brings the pleasure of creating is based on the premise that most people involved in haiku are not merely readers but writers as well. As we have seen, Seisensui estimated that 99 percent of all haiku readers were also poets; he believed haiku made an artist out of everyone. "The pleasure of creating comes close to gratifying a human instinct," he said. "When a man in primitive times molded a bottlelike object out of clay, he must have felt a very human joy in having created something with his own hands, even though he made it for a practical purpose." Composing a haiku, he insisted, was easier than making a bottle or almost any other art object, since it required hardly any time, material, or equipment. "Even an elementary school child can write a haiku that looks genuine," he remarked. "Practically anyone can be a haiku poet. Almost no time is needed; one hour after supper will suffice. With a notebook and a pencil, a commuter can compose haiku during his morning or evening ride on the train." Seisensui himself was introduced to this pleasure during his student days. He recalled:

One spring vacation I went on a haiku journey from Kasumigaura to Tsukuba and then to Haruna, carrying with me a notebook and a pencil, which I held dearer than my life. I was determined to compose 100 haiku each day. It was a reckless attempt, but I was able to write that many. Those were the happiest days of my life, because I could write as many haiku as I wanted. A haiku poet's pleasure lies not in becoming an expert but in creating—in being able to create.

Shiki had spoken of the same kind of pleasure. In his student days, he too had the habit of going for a stroll with a notebook and a pencil in hand.

In addition to the joy of creation, Seisensui recognized a cathartic pleasure in writing haiku. He believed one was able to relieve grief by transforming it into haiku because the grief was objectified in the process. "When a person concentrates on writing haiku," he explained, "his observation of himself becomes clearer, and his vision of himself grows more distinct. Since grief and pain are subjective, it is inevitable that they depart when he objectifies himself thoroughly." He compared haiku to weeping, to a confession, and to the healing of a skin rash. He was aware that other types of poetry also had a therapeutic effect, but he seemed to feel that for many people in Japan haiku was the most readily available cure because it was brief and familiar and required no special training. It was available even to elementary school children.

To catharsis is added the pleasure of feeling that a painful emotion will be shared by other people who read the poem. To view it from the other side, the reader can be said to experience a cathartic pleasure, too, since he identifies with the poet's emotion and feels relief when the poet vents the emotion through the poem. This is what Seisensui termed the pleasure of appreciating. "When a person reads a haiku," he explained, "he enjoys imagining the scene or emotion the poet experienced. The act is enjoyable because the poem touches the reader's heart and causes a psychic phenomenon that can be called resonance." In other words, reading haiku gives one the pleasure of communicating with others and sharing an experience with them. Such pleasure can be obtained by reading other types of poetry, too, but Seisensui seems to have believed that a haiku reader can taste a greater enjoyment than other readers because he is a more active reader. In haiku the pleasure of appreciating and the pleasure of creating meet; to use Seisensui's metaphor, the haiku reader has to complete a circle that is only half finished. To a greater degree than other forms of poetry, haiku induces the reader to become a poet and to taste the pleasure of creation, and its accompanying purgation, himself.

Seisensui felt haiku's role in creating "resonance" was increasingly important in modern society, where a lack of heart-to-heart communication was more and more apparent. Seisensui saw in poetry a potential for filling this gap. "It is only through poetry," he asserted, "that we can truly talk to each other as fellow human beings, transcending the differences of age, occupation, and social class." Haiku was especially fit for this purpose, because since olden times it had had a social function. It had also been the most democratic and the most popularly appealing of all Japanese verse forms. Hence the resonance between heart and heart caused by reading haiku not only brings pleasure but also assumes social and moral significance.

The third pleasure of haiku as conceived by Seisensui was more personal but just as significant nonetheless. By "the pleasure of seeing," he meant enjoyment of the beauty of nature. He wrote:

Everyone can see and enjoy the beauty of flowers and blossoms. But between those who know haiku and those who do not there is a difference. When people are awakened to haiku, they begin noticing the beauty of nature in such unlikely things as a weed or fallen leaves, the kind of things they would have wanted to throw away before their awakening. Although some classical poets sang of excrement, I am not advocating a beautification of sordid things; what I am promoting is a realization that there is nothing filthy in nature. Buddhism teaches: "Grass, trees, the land—everything is a Buddha." Buddhahood is manifest in every tree and weed. Bashō said, "Everything we see is a flower." A stone by the roadside or a cobweb under the eaves is just as beautiful as a flower. Living in this world will become very enjoyable if one acquires such a viewpoint. One could be awakened to this viewpoint by way of Buddhism, but that route requires an exceedingly hard training. There is an easier, more enjoyable route: haiku.

The multiple implications of the pleasure of seeing stated here range from the elemental to the sublime. In the end, the pleasure becomes a kind of moral enlightenment, and haiku becomes a kind of religion.

At a basic level, Seisensui believed that haiku cultivates a person's aesthetic sense. Not only does it deepen his appreciation of nature by sharpening his sensibility, but it broadens his aesthetic experience by helping him to discover beauty in ordinary things. In this respect Seisensui's belief is similar to that of medieval Japanese tea masters who cultivated *wabi*, the beauty of paucity and plainness, although he probably would not have liked his idea to be associated with a premodern aesthetic concept. As with the tea masters, in Seisensui's poetic such an aesthetic sensibility is tied to a moral attitude. In his view, a haiku poet must not merely recognize beauty in nature; in order to capture that beauty, he must immerse himself in nature and share it himself. The poet must gain haiku-mind, through which he transcends his small ego and becomes part of something much larger, something cosmic. Seisensui observed that an artist has two aims in life, one aesthetic and the other moral. An artist must strive to create a great masterpiece of art, but he is also a human being and should want to live a spiritually rich life. "It would be a most satisfying experience for the artist," Seisensui said, "if he could submerge his small ego in great nature and attain a realm of perfect liberation in everyday life." In this statement, the phrase "the pleasure of seeing" becomes equivalent to the joy of attaining spiritual enlightenment, an ecstasy gained when one sees nature so intensely as to lose oneself in the act. One is reminded that Seisensui used the phrase "religious exaltation" in a similar context, citing lines from Goethe. The title of the article in which he did so, "Poetry of Enlightenment," indicates his view of the ultimate use of haiku.

For Seisensui, writing haiku was a way of life, a moral discipline. It served many of the same functions as a religion. Composing haiku helped to allay grief in the face of tragedy. It enabled one to live a spiritually satisfying life even when materially impoverished. It helped to restrain passions, which, if left free, could expand to monstrous size. It brought peace and calm amid the bustling modern age. In short, writing haiku helped one attain a supremely happy state of mind.

To support his contention, Seisensui cited examples of people for whom haiku functioned as a kind of religion. One was Kaitō Hōko (1902–40),[16] a young tubercular patient who was first attracted to Christianity but later sought solace in haiku.

> a red dragonfly too
> has come for a visit
> all alone
> satisfied

This free-style haiku by Hōko suggests that not only the dragonfly but also the sick poet was satisfied. He knew he was dying, for tuberculosis was incurable in those days, yet he was calm both physically (otherwise the dragonfly would have been too frightened to come near him) and spiritually (otherwise he would not have been able to write a haiku). He had been able to attain that peace of mind by identifying with a dragonfly, a part of nature.

Seisensui's favorite examples of the supreme, religious function of haiku also included poems by the monks Hōsai and Santōka. The following haiku of his own, written during an illness, could serve as well:

> now in bed
> now out of bed . . .
> plumes of wisteria
> are visible
> from the bed too

---

[16] Hōko joined the *Layered Clouds* group in 1925. Many of his haiku, collected in *Three Cranes*, reflect his prolonged, losing battle with tuberculosis.

Clearly Seisensui's illness was not as serious as Hōko's, since he was able to get out of bed once in a while. But he was not strong enough to stay up for many hours, and the slow process of recovery irritated him at times. What pacified his mind was composing haiku, and through haiku approaching close to nature and appreciating its beauty.

These examples are free-style haiku, and they well illustrate Seisensui's ideas concerning the use of poetry. Yet one wonders whether those ideas might not apply to the entire haiku tradition just as well. Almost everything Seisensui said about the pleasure and usefulness of free-style haiku can be traced back to Bashō. Seisensui did not disguise that fact; indeed, he often cited Bashō to support his arguments. With respect to the use of haiku, he was not at all an innovator. But that fact is proof that the new form of poetry to which he dedicated his life was haiku and not free verse. There was no doubt in his mind that he was faithfully following the path of traditional haiku. The question of form aside, Seisensui conceived of haiku in quite a traditional way, even though many of his contemporaries did not recognize that he did.

CHAPTER EIGHT

Takahashi Shinkichi

TAKAHASHI SHINKICHI (*b.* 1901) is a Zen poet, the only poet of major stature in modern Japan who can be so designated. A few other poets have shown an interest in Zen Buddhism, but none has followed its rigorous discipline with such dedication and persistence. Shinkichi's connection with Buddhism began in childhood, for his father's family religion was Zen and his mother had a profound faith in the teachings of the Shingon sect. When he was twenty, he spent eight months as an acolyte in a nearby Shingon temple. Six years later, after meeting with Master Ashikaga Shizan (1859–1959), he embarked on a serious training program in Zen. Although he did not become a Zen monk as he had initially hoped he would, he continued to attend Zen lectures, participate in Zen meditation, and study under various Zen masters. By age 51 he had received from Shizan "The Moon-on-the-Water Hall," a testimonial certifying completion of the entire course of Zen training under the master. He himself has recorded the experience of attaining satori, or enlightenment, more than once. He has read extensively in Buddhist literature and has himself written four books on Zen. In terms of activities and attainments in Zen, no other poet in contemporary Japan comes even close to him.

And yet Shinkichi is a modern poet baptized by Western civilization. He specializes in free verse, a form imported from the West; he writes neither haiku nor kanshi, the two poetic forms traditionally associated with Zen. In fact, he was considered one of the most daringly experimental poets in the Western style when he made his poetic debut in 1923 with *Dadaist Shinkichi's*

Poems, whose title indicates its indebtedness to Tristan Tzara and others associated with dadaist movements in Europe and America. Although notices about dada had appeared in some newspapers, Shinkichi's book was the first work to attract much attention to the movement in Japan. If modern Japanese poetry is an amalgam of East and West, Shinkichi epitomizes that blend in a highly individual manner.

From Dada to Zen

Shinkichi first learned of dada through two articles published in a newspaper on August 15, 1920. Under the headlines "The Latest Art of Hedonism" and "A Glance at Dada," the articles reported on the current state of literature and the arts in Europe and America, with a focus on recent dadaist activities. Although the articles were largely descriptive and showed no special enthusiasm for dada, they made a profound impression on nineteen-year-old Shinkichi. To borrow his expression, he was hit over the head and knocked out cold. He was particularly attracted to three comments made in the articles. The first was a citation from Tzara's "Dada Manifesto of 1918": "I proclaim opposition to all cosmic faculties that squirm in the putrid sun. . . . Dada is an abolition of the future."[1] The second was Walter Serner's assertion "The world view is a confusion of words." And the third was the report that dadaists often printed words horizontally, vertically, and diagonally on the same page. Shinkichi was not to see the articles again for the next forty years, but he was to recall these comments over and over.

For young Shinkichi, then, the appeal of dada lay in the aggressively assertive attitude with which it pointed out and ridiculed the meaninglessness of things. He had been leading a wretched life for several years before his encounter with dada. His first love affair had ended in frustration and sadness when the woman he loved married another man, and in his ensuing depression, he had dropped out of secondary school just before

[1] Retranslated from the Japanese so as to approximate what Shinkichi read in the newspaper.

graduation, much to the chagrin of his parents. Leaving his home in Shikoku, he had roamed restlessly from one job to another; then, penniless and undernourished, he contracted typhoid and came close to death. Afterwards, he spent two months in a rehabilitation center in Tokyo as a charity patient, waiting to become well enough to return to Shikoku. The articles on dada, read at this juncture in his life, gave him hope that he might be able to rebound from despair by asserting it to the world. Recalling the significance dada had for him at this time, he wrote, "The word 'Dada' refers to a wooden horse in French; in Rumanian it is equivalent to the French word *oui*. Inherent in Dada, therefore, is a positivism that affirms all after denying and destroying all."

It took some two years—he called it an "incubation period"—for Shinkichi to begin writing dadaist poems. In August 1922, he made his first serious attempt to write free verse. The result was a poem entitled "Dagabaji's Assertion." Since Dagabaji is a corruption of Shinkichi's family name, the poem's title implies an assertion by the poet in thin disguise. "Assertion" here must mean an existentialist assertion by which to turn all negatives to positives or, more precisely, by which to eliminate all distinction between positives and negatives. The poem's two stanzas are:

DADA asserts and denies all.
Infinity or nothingness or whatever, it sounds just like
    a cigarette or petticoat or word.
All that oozes up in imagination exists in actuality.
All the past is included in the future of fermented
    soybeans.
Things beyond human imagination can be imagined
    through a stone or a sardine's head—so imagine a
    ladle, a cat, and everyone else.
DADA recognizes ego in all.
It recognizes ego in vibrations of the air, in a germ's
    hatred, and in the smell of the word "ego."
All is one and the same. From Buddha's recognition
    there appears the remark "All is all."
All is seen in all.
Assertion is all.

The universe is soap. Soap is trousers.
Anything is possible.

To a Christ pasted on a fan, jelly wrote a love letter.
All this is true.
How could it be possible for nonsmoking MR. GOD to
imagine something that cannot be asserted?

Tzara's all-negating manifesto is echoed in such lines as "DADA
. . . denies all" and "All the past is included in the future of fermented soybeans." Serner's assertion about words resounds in
many nonsensical comparisons, such as those between infinity
and a cigarette, between the ego and vibrations of the air, and
between the universe and soap. Although Shinkichi did not have
the poem's words printed in a drastically unconventional way,
the orthography does include some unorthodox deviations. The
words "petticoat" and "true" are written in *katakana* syllabary instead of ordinary *hiragana*, for no apparent reason.[2] Roman
letters are used for "DADA" and "MR. GOD," the former printed
vertically and the latter horizontally. The traits of dada, as understood by Shinkichi, are unmistakably present.

The tone of the poem, however, is surprisingly affirmative.
Whereas Tzara proclaimed opposition to all cosmic faculties,
Dadaist Shinkichi asserts and denies all in the very first line of
the poem and goes on to make more assertions than negations.
He accepts infinity, imagination, the past, religion, the ego, the
whole universe. His negations, on the other hand, are all elim-
inations of distinctions. He denies the distinctions between the
finite and the infinite, between reality and fiction, between past
and future, between self and others, between part and whole.
Indeed, he is able to accept all because he denies all distinctions.
The remark "All is one and the same" in the eighth line sums up
the meaning not only of the first stanza but of the whole poem.

Undoubtedly the positive tone of the poem led Shinkichi to
entitle it "Dagabaji's Assertion." The word "assertion" was retained when the title was changed to "Assertion Is Dadaist" upon
its re-publication in *Dadaist Shinkichi's Poems* a few months later.
The same assertive tone pervades other poems included in the

[2] There are two sets of syllabaries in the Japanese writing system. *Katakana* is
used only in special cases, such as in transcribing foreign words. *Hiragana* is employed in all other cases.

anthology, although in degree it differs from poem to poem. It is less pronounced, for example, in such short pseudolyrics as "Three Dada Poems" and 66 verses collectively called "Poems of 1921," which make use of broken syntax, chance association, and arbitrary lineation. Still, behind the audacious pose and carefree style we sense a poet who believes in the interrelatedness of all things, no matter how disparate they may appear on the surface. The image of this poet becomes clearer in the longer pseudonarratives included in the anthology. "ShinDA Renkichi,"[3] for instance, introduces a poet who comes to feel, while watching another poet die, that the past has merged with the future. "Voice-copying Gramophone" portrays a sexologist who has ostensibly destroyed all the old myths about sex but who nevertheless follows a routine, everyday life with his wife and child. "Nosebleed" depicts a destitute Bohemian poet who finds no meaning in life and dreams of draining himself of all his blood, but whose suicide attempt turns out to be a mere dream. In these and other pseudonarrative poems the plot is muddled and the characterization sketchy, yet there always emerges a main character who perseveres in living on, even in a world that he knows is chaotic and hostile.

Shinkichi's concept of poetry during the dadaist phase of his career can be summed up in one statement: poetry is assertion. He had discovered that denouncing can also mean accepting, for through exposure to dada he had learned that a word meaning "a wooden horse" in French can mean "yes" in Rumanian, that things seeming meaningless on the surface can be meaningful in another sphere. Poetry gave him a means of presenting an all-inclusive, all-assertive world in which disparate things coexist, in which disorder becomes order simply by being what it is. To rephrase Serner's dictum, poetry for Shinkichi is a confusion of words that presents a world view.

Dadaist Shinkichi's Poems appeared in February 1923. In July 1924, Shinkichi published a long pseudonarrative entitled *Dada*.

---

[3] "ShinDA" is a whimsical joining of DADA and *shinda*, a Japanese word meaning "dead." Shinkichi probably had in mind the futurist poet Hirato Renkichi, who died in 1922.

は梯子
と
J

　　　の上に居る
鋸を金槌で掻き鳴らした
　　　彼女は寝巻く擲ねよ゛
エレベーターの廻轉が止った
　　金庫の娃娠
Lが梯子を上る　Jが鯖鈴がくのをする

KKKKAZUKO MUSK

聴診器を持った PRICKLE

MELONMELONMELON

幻は焼かれた
フキルムは切れた。

VENTILATION

49

䷀䷁䷂䷃䷄䷅䷆䷇䷈䷉䷊䷋䷌䷍䷎䷏䷐䷑䷒

俺
忠

Portions of two poems from the first edition of *Dadaist Shinkichi's Poems*, showing some of the striking visual effects characteristic of Shinkichi's early poetry. The opening line of Poem 49 (second line from left) creates the impression of piled dishes by stacking up the character *sara* ("dish"). The poem was later entitled "Dishes." Reproduced from a facsimile published by Meicho Kankōkai.

But the very next month, from aboard a boat bound for Korea, he threw the book into the sea as a symbolic act indicating his determination to part with dada. Three years later he did just that.

Shinkichi has repeatedly explained why he decided to forsake dada. According to his explanation, it was because he discovered dada to be merely "an imitation of Zen." Even while he was an eager follower of Tzara, he had noticed some similarity between dada and Buddhism. "Dagabaji's Assertion" includes more than one reference to Buddhism; in fact, its thematic statement "All is one and the same" uses a Buddhist idiom. Shinkichi's interest in Buddhism intensified as his fervor for dada cooled, until in 1927 he decided to become an acolyte at a Zen temple. Later he was to recall, "Because I did not know French, my dada was philosophically a Buddhist dada." The comment implies that Shinkichi, unable to read about dada firsthand, tried to interpret it in his own way; inevitably he did so in a Buddhist way.

What were the elements common to both dada and Zen, as seen by Shinkichi? He pointed out several in "Dada and Zen," an essay written more than fifty years after his dadaist phase. They can be summed up as antirationalism, indivisiveness or "oneness," dissolution of the self, absolute spontaneity, and mistrust of language. In Shinkichi's view, Tzara's staunch opposition to abstraction and conceptualization is like Zen, which does not teach a single "law" to its followers. Tzara's realization that "he existed nowhere" seems an echo of what is known as nonself in Zen; his effort to abolish all logical distinctions shares a common goal with the Zen ideal of oneness; his faith in spontaneity has its counterpart in Zen's "now-ness"; and his insistence on "the dislocation of language" appears to echo nonverbalism in Zen, which teaches that five thousand volumes of sutras amount to nothing more than the noisy cries of crows and magpies. The similarities between dada and Zen were not immediately apparent to young Shinkichi; hence his initial enthusiasm for dada. But as they gradually dawned on him, he chose to return to the Buddhist tradition. In Europe dada paved the way for surrealism; for Shinkichi, it cleared the way for Zen.

In October 1928, Shinkichi embarked on his first serious Zen training at a temple in central Japan. At first the rigorous program proved too much even for this young man with a strong physique, and he had to return to his home in Shikoku for several years to recover from physical and mental exhaustion. He had to give up his plan of becoming a Zen priest, too. But he never wavered in his determination to pursue Zen, and that determination has continued. His deep faith in Zen is reflected in most of the books of poetry he has written since his departure from dada—*Gion Festival* (1926), *Words in Jest* (1934), *Solar Eclipse* (1934), *Rain Clouds* (1938), *Kirishima* (1942), *Father and Mother* (1943), *The Body* (1956), *The Bream* (1962), *The Sparrow* (1966), *Afterimages* (1976), and *The Hollow* (1981)—as well as in several editions of *Takahashi Shinkichi's Collected Poems*. Since 1924 he has been a Zen poet, with the exception of a short period during World War II when he wavered between Buddhism and Shintoism.[4] "I don't care how other people may criticize me for this," he once said, "but I know of no way to live except by articulating my cosmic view in poetry. My life would lose its meaning if I were to stop trying to preserve the tradition of Zen."

The cosmos that Shinkichi has endeavored to depict in his later poetry is a world of Zen and all that is held to be meaningful and true in Zen. With him, poetry presents—or represents—less nature than Zen-nature. This assertion, however, contains a basic paradox, for Zen disparages language and favors nonverbal communication, whereas poetry uses words as its medium. Recognizing this contradiction, Shinkichi once asserted, "My poems deny language; they deny poetry." How has Shinkichi resolved the dichotomy?

Shinkichi has addressed this question in several of his essays. In "Modern Japanese Literature and Zen," for instance, he stressed the uselessness of words in capturing the inexpressible essence of Zen and described existing literary works as "rubbish piled on the surface of our society." He did add, however, that at

---

[1]During this period Shinkichi produced two books of poems, *Visits to Shinto Shrines* (1942) and *Islands of Yamato* (1943).

times pure gold was buried under the rubbish, and he concluded, "One might be able to enter Zen by way of literature, although inevitably it is a roundabout way." In an essay entitled "The Unsung Poet," he again disparaged the function of language and criticized poets and philosophers who believe that reality can be expressed in words. He then observed, "Poetry comes closest to truth, but it is not truth." The most direct expression of his view of the relationship between poetry and truth in Zen is found in an essay called "Under the Tower of Babel." Once again he begins his argument by minimizing the value of language, saying, "Words, whatever kind they may be, are forever incapable of expressing truth. We, the human species, who created words arbitrarily in our brains, have put up with expressions that do not exactly correspond to truth. Just as we are content with television, which merely shows images of people and things, we let our brains take care of daily life by using language because it is simpler to do so." He goes on to disparage literature because it is built on words, then reflects on the fact that he is himself a man of letters. The essay almost becomes a soliloquy at this point:

> What, then, do I want to say when I write? I want to transmit truth. I know I have just said truth cannot be expressed in words. Truth is inexpressible. And yet I write because I want to convey that very fact to readers.
> One might tell me that it is also impossible to convey the inexpressibleness of truth. To that remark, I would respond as follows.
> It is impossible to transmit truth to readers, but it is possible to make them verbally understand it. To those readers content with verbal understanding, one is able to present in writing something similar to truth. Because what lies in the presentation is not truth itself, those who try to understand it are wasting their time. The experience, however, may help them some day in some way. It may help them to grasp truth when they have a chance to do so.

From these comments one can gather that Shinkichi considers verse writing a waste of effort from a purely Zen point of view but recognizes in it some pedagogical value.

In brief, Shinkichi believes poetry is a verbal substitute for truth. In his view, truth itself can be grasped only by intuition, after a long period of meditation and other Zen exercises. As he has been fond of pointing out, all Bodhidharma did to attain satori was to sit and meditate facing the wall for nine years. Yet a beginning student of Zen needs advice and direction; consequently a number of books on Zen have been written in China and Japan over the centuries. The Rinzai school, in particular, has long utilized kōan, questions to which there are no rational answers, as an important means of inducing trainees to break away from logical patterns of thinking. Shinkichi, whose Zen training was in the Rinzai school, is aware of the merits of kōan and once observed that they contain something delicate and indescribable that helps students. Possibly he considers his poetry a kind of kōan or a popularized version of kōan. Most Japanese seldom have a chance to come in contact with kōan today; even when they do, they do not gain much out of the kōan because it is written in classical Chinese and intended for the use only of serious Zen trainees. In comparison, poetry has a better chance of being read by the general public. An attempt to approach Zen by way of poetry is, in Shinkichi's words, "a roundabout way," but few people in modern times have the time, motivation, or physical and mental toughness to undergo the rigors of Zen training. Shinkichi thought poetry might fill the gap.

The bulk of Shinkichi's later poetry seems consistent with such a view of verse writing. He does not write poetry with this view in mind; more often, the view comes to permeate his poetry as a natural outcome of his being a Zen Buddhist. Still, by way of poetry he has tried to give a verbal semblance of truth in Zen. His poems deal with such themes as nonself, timelessness, the Zen eye, nonattachment, nondivisiveness, enlightenment, and mistrust of language. They no longer show the explosive energy or the rebellious spirit that dominated his dadaist poems; rather, in a reflective tone and restrained style they try to activate the reader's mind by way of surprise or irony.

One can cite any number of Shinkichi's poems to illustrate those characteristics; a composition entitled "Death," which first appeared in the 1952 edition of *Takahashi Shinkichi's Collected Poems*, will serve the purpose. It consists of just one line:

Nobody has ever died.

In terms of vocabulary and grammar, few Japanese sentences are simpler than this. But semantically the poem resembles a kōan because it defies logical understanding. If there is one sure thing in this unpredictable life, it is death, so how can one say nobody has ever died? Shinkichi puts that question to his reader just as a Zen master would pose a kōan to his student. No rational answer is possible, so to respond the reader has to try to go beyond the bounds of intellect. Few readers, if any, will be led to satori by pondering the question, but the experience may help them open their minds some day by some chance.

The implications of the poem "Death" become clearer when it is juxtaposed with the climactic scene of an autobiographical story by Shinkichi called "The Eel." The protagonist of the story is a middle-aged man by the name of Takeha Yasuzō, who all through his life has desperately sought peace with the world and with himself. He has tried Buddhism, Shintoism, and other possible means of salvation, but all in vain; people call him a madman, and indeed he has had more than one mental breakdown. Finally one autumn he visits a Zen temple for week-long *sesshin* —a program of meditation and study under a master. Unexpectedly, he is rewarded with satori. The enlightenment comes one afternoon, just before he faces his teacher in a personal study session. His mind has been especially serene that day, as he sits waiting for his turn outside the teacher's room. When his turn comes he strikes a bell with a mallet twice, following the rule. He cannot believe his ears, for the bell rings out with unearthly beauty, the like of which he has never heard before. In that instant a thought flashes through his mind:

This is what it means to live. Like a sound, like a cloud.
There is nobody who is living. We human beings are allowed to live. Like a sound, like a cloud.
I had read volumes of scriptures and seen the word "nonself" a countless number of times, but I had never understood the true meaning of the word.
We human beings are like that sound. There is no such thing as the self. Only "nonself" exists.

The next moment Yasuzō enters the room and sits down facing the teacher. Later he cannot remember what he said to the teacher, but he does remember what the teacher said to him. "I am no match for you," the master said with a smile. "Go out and have a rest." The strict teacher had never said anything approaching this before, and as he left the room, Yasuzō was filled with incomparable happiness.

The poem "Death" tries to lead the reader to the state of mind attained by Yasuzō in this episode. As Yasuzō came to realize, nobody is living, and therefore nobody has died. To put it this way is nothing more than verbalization, and the reader who understands the truth at this level has understood it merely as a concept. Yet that is all poetry can do.

Shinkichi's longer poems are generally less cryptic and less like kōans, but many of them similarly try to awaken the reader to some aspect of Zen truth. They frequently feature an animal: a cat, a mouse, a cow, a groundhog, a rooster, a duck, a pigeon— all are visualized as living in a Zen world. Shinkichi was particularly fond of writing about a sparrow. The poem below, simply called "The Sparrow," is an example:

> when the sparrow
>   took a hop
> flowers
>   withered away
> the sparrow's
>   head feathers are ruffled
>   and its chest feathers tremble
>   as it crouches there
> the sparrow
>   blinks its eyes
>   and in that instant
> ten billion years of history pass

It is consistent with Zen that the poem should center on such a plain little bird, for in Zen there is no such thing as profound, esoteric truth; if there is something that comes close to it, it lies in everyday things seen by everyone. The third stanza of the poem, by painting an ordinary image of a sparrow, brings home

that point and links other stanzas, which defy our usual ways of
conceiving the bird.

Shinkichi's fondness for sparrows seems to have had its roots
in a childhood experience:

> It happened when my older sister died and I went to the funeral,
> which was held at her husband's home deep in the mountains. She was
> buried in a graveyard in a pine forest located at the edge of a pond.
>   As I was trudging toward home, I came upon a dead sparrow lying in
> the road. I was struck by the thought that the sparrow was my sister.
>   I came to believe that my sister had been a sparrow.
>   Since then, whenever I see a sparrow, I recall my sister who died
> young.

Note that the young Shinkichi saw a dead sparrow—not a new-
born one—on the day of his sister's funeral. This was not a case
of transmigration and rebirth, which is rejected by Zen. Rather,
the sight awakened him to the oneness of a sparrow and a human being, and of the past, the present, and the future. His sister died with a physical sparrow but is living in a Zen sparrow
that exists outside of time. The bird that appears in "The Sparrow" and many other poems by Shinkichi is such a sparrow, a
creature that transcends all divisions and distinctions recognized
by the intellect.

In technique "The Sparrow," with its clear imagery and indented layout, looks like an imagist poem. A good many of
Shinkichi's Zen poems similarly try to suggest the essence of Zen
through images. Others, however, do not. A poem on the nature
of the human mind, entitled "The Beginning and the End," is
representative of this second type. It also signifies a landmark in
Shinkichi's Zen training, for it deeply impressed his teacher,
Shizan. Shinkichi has not explained the specific circumstances
under which it was written, but he did say something about the
kind of problem he was having during his Zen training under
Shizan at that time. In a short essay entitled "Blend Your Mind
with Your Breathing" he recalled, "Once my teacher said, 'Leave
your doubting mind as it is.' I did not understand what he meant.
I was naive enough to think that he was referring to the idea that
both beautiful and ugly thoughts lay in one and the same mind,

that there was no distinction between them. Only recently have I come to learn that man's mind has no right or left because the mind itself does not exist."

No doubt it was after a similar awakening that Shinkichi wrote the poem "The Beginning and the End":

> One cannot say where the mind exists.
> It exists everywhere. The universe is filled with it.
> The mind is beyond being large or small.
> It never vanishes.
> It continues to exist after the body dies. From its view-
> point, there is no such thing as dying.
> This mind was present before we were born.
> It is never born.
> Nothing exists outside it.
> All that exists is the mind.
> One cannot say it exists.
> But, clearly, the mind is moving.
> That is the beginning of all.
> The mind always lies in the beginning.
> And it is forever ending.
> Everything is nothing but the mind.
> Between the beginning and the end there is not a hair's
> breadth.

When he sent the poem to Shizan, in return the old Zen master gave him a signed piece of calligraphy that read "I have set your mind at peace." As Shinkichi immediately recognized, the words were those of Bodhidharma's reply to Hui-k'o, a Zen trainee, who had asked, "I have been seeking the mind but cannot get it." The moment Hui-k'o heard his teacher's words he attained sa-tori, and he later became the second patriarch of Zen. Shizan's reply to Shinkichi, then, was intended to do what Bodhidharma's reply did for Hui-k'o; it positively verified Shinkichi's attainment and thereby brought his mind to rest. It also indicated that he had correctly understood the teaching "Leave your doubting mind as it is."

Shinkichi has also written poems that are not ostensibly Zen. Generally these seem to be more popular with the reading public, since they are more lyrical and less abstruse. Yet in them one can still see the pose of a Zen poet, unobtrusive though it may be. Here, for instance, is a short lyric called "Flowering Rose Mallow":

> What is the rose mallow's whiteness?
> Its petals are whiter than snow
> as it opens in the warmth of a summer day.
> White as a distant cloud
> and translucent as tissue paper
> the scentless flower blooms with its head drooping.
> What can it be? White and faintly echoing in the eye,
> the dreamlike flower will vanish at a touch.

The poem has been praised for its lyrical beauty and is among the most popular of Shinkichi's works. Critics have said that it catches the pure, fragile beauty of the rose mallow, a beauty approaching yūgen. One can appreciate the poem at that level, and many readers have done so. But another layer of meaning emerges when one remembers Shinkichi's remark "Buddhism is a theory that places nothingness behind matter." By "nothingness" he meant the void that contains all. If one interprets the poem from this angle, one discovers in its poet a Buddhist reaching for that nothingness. When the poet asks about the rose mallow's whiteness, he has started his quest for what lies behind the visible flower. He then notes a series of seeming contradictions: a summer flower whiter than winter snow, a distant cloud right in front of him, a flower that has no scent, and a whiteness that echoes in his eyes. Finally, by transcending these dichotomies he reaches the invisible reality behind visible matter, as physical reality becomes dreamlike and vanishes at a touch.

To conclude, then, Shinkichi's concept of artistic representation is a paradoxical one. In his view, art imitates nature, which is ultimately nothingness. In his younger days he often depended on dadaist means to reduce being to nothingness; in dogmatic assertions he denounced all systems by which people ordered the world. In his mature years he has concentrated on verbalizing various aspects of Zen reality, which transcends and yet includes the physical world. However, the essence of Zen cannot be expressed in words, and this creates a dilemma for the poet. Nevertheless Shinkichi has continued to write poems, believing that they may by chance give a clue to those striving for enlightenment. In a poem entitled "Footnotes" he wrote:

> Is that white thing a rooster?
> All words are imperfect; they are footnotes.

In his view, poetry is a footnote trying, in its imperfect way, to comment on a Zen text that is invisible to common eyes.

Like a Cloud in the Sky

The titles of Shinkichi's essays are sometimes deceptive. In a piece called "My Method of Writing Poetry," he merely recalled his early days as a dadaist poet and mourned the alienation of contemporary poets from the general public. In an essay entitled "How to Write and Appreciate Poetry," he did describe how he appreciated three specific modern poems, but he said nothing about methods of writing poetry. His essay "My Poetry and Zen" is largely about the life of a Zen priest who risked his life to save a valuable copy of a Zen classic when his temple burned in a fire. The discrepancy between the titles and the contents of these essays seems due not so much to the author's irresponsibility as to a lack of self-awareness about the creative process. When he wrote down those titles on page one, Shinkichi was quite sincere, yet he simply did not know his own method of writing poetry and therefore could not write about it in the pages that followed. He probably has seldom thought about the art of poetry per se, for abstract speculation is rejected by Zen.

In his voluminous writings, however, there are some passages that touch on the subject in a casual manner and thus shed light on his idea of the verse-writing process. For example, in an essay called "A Talk on Poetry and Zen" he stated:

In the *Analects* Confucius is reported to have said, "If I am to sum up in one sentence all the 300 poems [in *The Book of Poetry*], I would say they are free of devious thoughts." A composition written with devious thoughts can never be called a poem. In Confucius' view, a piece of writing that contains devious thoughts is nothing more than rubbish, no matter what strenuous effort may have been expended in its making.

One must prize words that come to mind by chance and without premeditation. When my writing is a faithful record of what floated into my mind like a cloud in the sky, I do not have the self-loathing I usually feel whenever I read my own work later.

Some might say that such a natural, spontaneous method of verse writing may be possible for short lyrics but not for epic poems like Homer's. But there are few long pieces in ancient Chinese poetry or in *The Collection of Ten Thousand Leaves* and *The Collection of Ancient and Modern Poems*. Confucius' remark on poetry is valid.

The passages point toward three elements of the creative process that Shinkichi held to be important. The first is the need for a specific state of mind, a state free of "devious thoughts." The second is the casual, incidental manner in which inspiration visits the poet. The third is the spontaneous nature of the creative process, which dictates the brevity of the poem produced. All three elements follow along the lines of traditional Japanese poetics, with some noteworthy modifications.

Shinkichi implied that a poet must attain a serene frame of mind, devoid of all impure thoughts, before the verse writing process begins. This, however, is not a Confucian idea, for consciously or unconsciously he misinterpreted the words "devious thoughts." By these words Confucius meant ethically unacceptable thoughts, but Shinkichi used them to designate thoughts that are not natural and spontaneous. Thus Shinkichi's stand is consistent with Zen, which discourages deliberate, willful speculation. As a Zen Buddhist, he wanted to purge all calculated thoughts from the mind of the poet waiting for inspiration. To extend his metaphor, a poet's mind must be as clear as a cloudless sky; when the mind is ready, poetic inspiration will come as naturally as a cloud appears in the sky. Shinkichi once said, "I have written poems as they naturally emerged; there is no other way to make seeds of poetry germinate. One will never be able to produce moving poetry if one uses a method in the same way as one would cultivate flowers in a greenhouse or other man-made environment." Although the metaphor is different, the implications are the same: the beginning of a poem cannot be forced.

In Shinkichi's view, then, a poet is a passive agent who has to wait for the visit of poetic inspiration. He can take no deliberate action to make it come; instead, he must patiently persevere, always ready for the crucial moment. "He must always strive for it, until he finds himself doing so even in his subconscious mind," Shinkichi advised. "When he keeps trying for it, something accumulates within his body without his knowledge, until finally it seeks an outlet and comes pouring forth. Thereupon a seed of poetry germinates." Such poetic inspiration has various ways of manifesting itself, and the poet does not know when or how it will do so. Sometimes it emerges purely by chance in an unexpected place. For instance, one day Shinkichi was waiting for a bus at a bus stop, when suddenly the line "A railway station appeared before my eyes" came to his mind. Inspired by the line, he began composing a poem, which was eventually entitled "The Railway Station." But there are other occasions, too, on which some external stimulus helps trigger an inspiration. As examples of such stimuli, Shinkichi mentioned reading a poem or a book, seeing a movie, and listening to music. He might have added looking at a work of art, for he wrote the poem "Peach Blossoms and a Pigeon Painted by Hui-tsung" after seeing the Chinese painting of that title and "Yakshi" after seeing a statue of an ancient Indian spirit; there are many similar examples. An actual experience can be a stimulus, too. One of his better-known poems, "Dishes," was written while in his youth he worked as a dishwasher in the dining hall of a Tokyo newspaper press. He has also written many travel poems, such as "Mount Fuji," "From Pusan," and "Ruins of Pompeii," all based on actual experiences during his trips in and outside of Japan. In this respect, Shinkichi's theory and practice have been no different from those of most other poets.

Shinkichi's third point about the creative process is more unusual: he feels that a poem should be completed by the force of the initial inspiration and therefore that it has to be short. He believes that not only should the inception of verse writing be natural but the entire process should be spontaneous, too. Referring to the seed of poetry, he said, "Once a seed germinates, the rest is just a matter of waiting for its natural growth." He also explained, "It resembles what a baby goes through in the womb until the time of delivery." Both metaphors stress the naturalness of the creative process and reject a premeditated scheme or correction by afterthought. Shinkichi was more explicit in another comment: "Another method would be to jot down anything and everything as a novelist does and then go about cutting out the unneeded. But I seldom use this 'draft' method." Probably he fears that revision would destroy the spontaneity of the initial inspiration. There are exceptions, but generally he seems to have been faithful to his words in actual practice. Referring to the 1949 edition of *Takahashi Shinkichi's Collected Poems*, he wrote, "I scribbled those poems in the margin of paper scraps or notebook pages whenever they happened to come to mind. I expended no great pains in writing any of them; in no case did I follow a plan or make revisions by afterthought. To draw a comparison with painting, this is like a collection of rough sketches. But that very roughness may have resulted in a kind of artless beauty." He went on to note that most of the poems were necessarily short.

Shinkichi's liking for short, inspirational poetry does not necessarily imply that the verse-writing process, too, is short. Of course some poems may be completed relatively quickly, but in many instances Shinkichi seems to have worked on a poem over a period of time. His metaphors for the creative process, already cited, indicate this: it takes nine months for a baby to be born after its conception, and it takes weeks or months for a plant to flower after its germination. We have noted that *Dadaist Shinkichi's Poems* needed an "incubation period" of some two years after their original inspiration. In Shinkichi's opinion, inspiration can be retained intact in the mind for a long time, especially if it is strong. Of the poem "The Railway Station," he recalled that he wrote nothing for several months after conceiving its first line, but that the initial image was so vivid and powerful that it never disappeared from his mind. Finally he was able to write the second line; after that the words came smoothly, and he was able to complete the poem in several hours.

A couple of examples will clarify Shinkichi's idea of the verse-writing process. The first is a poem called "The Fly":

> I wanted to live for an infinity of time.
> Infinity was in a fly.
>
> At a flick of my hand
> the fly lazily glided away.
> Its leisurely manner
> awakened a friendly feeling in me.
>
> Late at night
> under a bright lamp
> and with the sound of rain outdoors
> I was reading a book.
>
> On the pages of the open book
> a fly
> happened to cast a lonely shadow.
>
> Like the fly's leg, infinity
> is slender and bent.

Shinkichi explicated the poem in an essay also called "The Fly." As he explained, he was reading a book at home one rainy autumn night when suddenly a fly came out of nowhere and flew over the pages of the open book. He stopped reading and watched the fly for a while. Presently, without being driven away, it flew off with a slow, feeble movement, looking as if its strength were almost gone. The poet never saw the fly again.

This incident inspired Shinkichi to write the poem. He did not say with which line he began to write, but he did mention that the first line expresses something that had been bothering him, perhaps unconsciously preparing his mind for poetic inspiration. "Every human being harbors a desire to live a long life," he said. "Although there are some who kill themselves, most people have occasion to wish that they could live for a thousand or ten thousand years if at all possible. I was no exception; hence I wrote that I had wished for eternal life." But then he had an awakening, after which he no longer wished to live forever. To make that clear, he wrote the second line. This line, he said, is extremely important but difficult to explain. "The more seriously you ponder the line, the more difficult it will become," he speculated. "Even if you spend your whole life studying it, you may not be able to solve the problem. This line demands that much contemplation." In effect, then, the second line is a kōan. Shinkichi did not try to interpret it; he just gave some hints, one of which is a line from "Dagabaji's Assertion" that reads "Infinity or nothingness or whatever, it sounds just like a cigarette or . . . word." What he implied is the Zen concept of oneness: there is no difference between the infinite and the finite, whether in a fly, a cigarette, or whatever. To understand the true meaning of infinity one needs to attain satori; hence the difficulty of comprehending the line.

Shinkichi felt that the first two lines of the poem contained everything he wanted to say. But he did not stop writing at this point because he thought some people might want him to show why infinity is in a fly. In the lines that follow, therefore, he tried to describe the relationship between the fly and himself.

The second stanza defines that relationship as "a friendly feeling." No doubt the feeling was awakened in him because he saw an image of himself in the feeble flight of the late autumn fly. He said he considered calling the poem "The Winter Fly," since he was attracted to the lone fly barely surviving the cold autumn days. The words "lazily" and "leisurely" are significant; he saw the fly accepting its destiny with composure, neither fighting against nor hurrying toward death. There is a bit of fiction: in the poem he flicks his hand to drive away the fly, which he did not do in actuality. That change dramatizes his shift of mood from hostility to friendliness.

The third and fourth stanzas mainly describe the physical setting. The lateness of the hour, the sound of the rain, a man reading a book by himself—all enhance the atmosphere of loneliness and prepare for a climax in the last line of the fourth stanza. Explaining that line, Shinkichi said, "It depicts the lonely figure of a fly hovering, but because I myself cut a lonely figure one might say that the fly is my shadow, or perhaps that I am the fly's shadow." In other words, there is no distinction between the poet and the fly, between his life and its life, or between his solitude and its solitude.

Now that the relationship between the poet and the fly has been established and explained to the reader, Shinkichi comes back to recapitulate the poem's main theme in the two concluding lines. These lines echo the previous line "Infinity was in a fly" and elucidate its meaning through a more specific image—a fly's leg. Shinkichi explained, "Here I may sound as though I had a firm grip on infinity, as though no one else understood it better than I did. But I wrote those lines in view of such things as Einstein's theory of relativity, which says that the universe is mathematically finite." By his reference to Einstein, Shinkichi probably means to imply that infinity is itself a relative term. A fly's leg is tiny, fragile, finite—more poignantly so when the season is late autumn. Yet all that seems so because the fly is viewed from the standpoint of the human species, much bigger in size and longer in life span. From the point of view of the universe, man too would seem tiny, fragile, and finite. And the universe itself might seem tiny and finite in relation to some other cosmic system. One can go on and on in this way, infinitely. Shinkichi has demonstrated, then, that infinity is, and is not, in a fly.

At the end of the essay "The Fly," Shinkichi states that he made almost no additions or deletions in wording once he had written the poem. That is consistent with his idea of verse writing. Yet he made some changes later on. The poem was originally published in a newspaper in January 1951. When it was included in the 1952 edition of *Takahashi Shinkichi's Collected Poems*, the following version was printed:

> I wanted to live for an infinity of time.
> Infinity was in a fly.
>
> At a flick of my hand
> the fly lazily glided away.
>
> Its leisurely manner awakened a friendly feeling in me.
>
> Late at night under a bright lamp
> and with the sound of rain outdoors, I was reading a book.
>
> On the open book, a fly
> cast a lonely shadow.
>
> Like the fly's leg, infinity
> is slender and bent.

A comparison with the original poem shows that the words "the pages of" and "happened to" have been omitted in this version. The change is a definite improvement, for it tightens the poem. The number of stanzas has been increased from five to six, whereas the number of lines has been reduced from fifteen to eleven. The result is a more proselike poem, creating a greater sense of calm and contemplation. The change, however, has reduced what Shinkichi has called "a kind of artless beauty."

The making of the poem "The Fly" reveals how a trivial incident may strike a chord in the poet's mind and set off the creative process. In the next example, the cause-and-effect relationship is more pronounced. The incident that sparked the creative process occurred shortly after the end of World War II, when Shinkichi was near physical and mental exhaustion in the chaos of war-ravaged Japan. Without wife or child and with hardly any money or other belongings (his apartment had been destroyed in an air raid), he barely managed to keep himself alive. Trying to gather the courage to live on, he began reading the Lotus Sutra, even though he had read it several times before without understanding its meaning. This time, however, he was deeply moved. He felt he understood something of the sutra's profound meaning, and he wanted to record the experience in words. "I was anxious," he recalled, "to sum up my feelings within myself and make a note of them for my later use. So I wrote the poem." The poem, called "Not Home," consisted of just three lines:

> Tell them I am not home.
> Tell them nobody is here.
> I'll be back in five hundred million years.

Shinkichi did not say how long it took him to write this poem or whether he made any changes after its first draft. He probably wrote it in a spontaneous manner because it is short, colloquial, and, to use his word, like a note. It also belongs to the group of poems he said he expended no great pains in writing. Perhaps its "artless beauty" appealed to Japanese readers, since it gained popularity with the passage of time. The people in his hometown even erected a stone monument with the poem carved on it. Shinkichi is quite fond of the poem himself and once boasted that a poem of this calibre has been rare in modern Japanese poetry since Hagiwara Sakutarō.

Again, the making of "Not Home" is consistent with Shinkichi's idea of the creative process, perhaps more so than the making of "The Fly." He held that poetic inspiration can result from reading a book, and the Lotus Sutra sparked it for him. From the sutra he learned that "our life is not so simple or shallow as to fade away in five hundred million years or one billion years." To most readers, something like this is bookish knowledge. It had been so to Shinkichi, too, each time he read the Lotus Sutra before. But this time the book hit him hard, penetrating through the intellect and reaching the deepest part of his being. What he found in those depths, he did not spell out in the poem. One can surmise, however, that it was similar to a childhood experience he described in an essay called "Nothingness." One day when he was a young boy, he was walking along a path that paralleled a stream when suddenly a thought flashed into his mind:

I am currently strolling alongside a brook lined by wax trees. Imagine a long string stretching from my present location to a spot in the past several hundred millions of years ago. Then imagine another string that similarly extends into an infinitely remote future. The two strings would be the same length.

I am always at midpoint between the past and the future. If I walk a little over thirty minutes along this embankment, I shall leave the countryside and arrive in a city. But if I try the same experiment again in that city, the lengths of the two strings will remain the same. This is because both the past and the future have the same infinite length. The situation will be unchanged in fifty or sixty years, although I shall be an old man by then.

I am, then, always at the same spot. Minute by minute the time I experience vanishes and is reduced to nothing. Both the time that has passed and the time to come crumble minute by minute, and there always exists nothing but my own self, located at midpoint.

This mystical childhood experience points toward the Zen concepts of timelessness, the void, and nonself. It echoes the words of Master Rinzai (*d.* 867),[5] which Shinkichi was fond of quoting: "There is neither Buddha nor the human race. There is neither the past nor the present."

In the end, however, Shinkichi seems to have remained unwavering in his belief that verse writing is a waste of effort from the point of view of Zen, even when it is done in a natural and spontaneous way or provides a record of inspired moments. He was not completely sure until one day he asked his Zen teacher Shizan to write Confucius' words "free of devious thoughts" for him. Apparently he thought to keep the calligraphy by his side as a constant reminder of the proper manner in which to write poetry. Shizan obliged, but on handing over the finished calligraphy he whispered to Shinkichi, "You don't need 'thoughts,' either." Shinkichi did not quite understand the meaning of the teacher's words at the time, but as he reflected on them afterwards he came to know what they meant. As a Zen poet he had believed he should get rid of all deliberate, willful ideas until his mind was filled with nothing but spontaneous thoughts. Yet Zen demanded that he eliminate even those spontaneous thoughts. The mind had to become completely vacant. Could a person with a completely vacant mind ever write a poem? There, again, is the paradox of the Zen poet.

Zen Buddhist as Literary Critic

Largely self-educated, Shinkichi has been an avid reader since childhood. As he recalled, he was captivated by Dostoevsky's *Crime and Punishment* at age twelve, and after that he read any Western book available in Japanese translation—Tolstoy, Plutarch, Plato, Chekhov, Strindberg, Flaubert, Max Stirner, Romain Rolland. He was so hungry for new books that when he was seventeen he ran away from home and went to Tokyo, where the largest library in Japan was located. Once in Tokyo he visited the library every day, sleeping at a nearby public lavatory at night. When he became a Buddhist acolyte three years later,

[5] Rinzai, or Lin-ch'i in Chinese, was a Zen priest who lived during the T'ang dynasty. He founded the Rinzai school of Zen, to which Shinkichi belongs.

he often hid in a closet and read religious classics rather than doing assigned chores. His passion for books did not abate after he became an adult. "I neither got steady employment nor settled into a married life," he recalled later. "Reading books was my job." Soon he began to publish book reviews and essays on literary and art criticism. As the years have passed, his critical writings, those on modern Japanese literature in particular, have accumulated. If these were sorted and arranged in proper order, they would form a book that could be called *A Short History of Modern Japanese Literature*.

As a critic, Shinkichi has adopted an uncompromisingly moral stance. He has sought truth, as he came to understand it through Zen, in all the works he reads. Thus in his evaluations he often measures a work against Zen beliefs, then passes judgment on its strengths and shortcomings in relation to that standard. Typical is his comment on a short poem by Hagiwara Sakutarō entitled "Is Thought Only a Pattern?":

> Letting a thought stroll
> under the trees in a dense forest
> Buddha felt nature glowing in the dark.
> The moonlight was so very beautiful
> it breathed life into any kind of meditation
> and merged it with any kind of nirvana.
>
> "Is thought only a pattern?"
> Treading on the moon's rays, Buddha
> asked his gentle heart.

Shinkichi gave the following reading:

This poem has no syllabic pattern; instead, it has a deliberate inner rhythm. It is given a natural unity by its calm, smoothly flowing mood.

Allowing himself no lazy redundancy, the poet has presented a symbolic portrayal of a human being. Sakutarō's poetry often suggests the decadence of an ailing mind, but no such penchant for the bizarre can be recognized in this poem.

"Pattern" [*ishō*] is a new Japanese word. Sakutarō wondered whether a thought was nothing more than an arrangement of colors and designs. His faith in Buddhism was passive. Probably he learned about Buddhism in an indirect way—by reading Nietzsche and Schopenhauer. . . . I do not think the words "any kind of" are necessary in the sixth line, for there is only one nirvana. Such words as "glowing in the dark" [*sōmei*] and "meditation" [*meisō*] seem obsolete in today's usage, but perhaps Sakutarō liked the way they sounded when pronounced. If the thought walking in the moonlit forest belongs to the Buddha who existed in history, the setting must be during his training days and before he perceived the Law. Not having attained satori yet, he could not have been called Buddha. The poet wrote "Buddha felt nature," but he did not elaborate on it. Sakutarō seems to have approached Buddhism by way of emotion.

Clearly Shinkichi set out to find Buddhist values in the poem; he was pleased to the extent that he uncovered them, and displeased to the extent that he did not. Overall, he tried to interpret the poem too literally and as too faithful to his own beliefs. Sakutarō probably used the expression "any kind of nirvana" because different sects of Buddhism seem to picture different kinds of nirvana; he also visualized a metaphysical Buddha rather than a historical one. This freedom bothered Shinkichi, devout Buddhist that he was. He felt Sakutarō had approached Buddhism "by way of emotion" when he should have done so through rigorous training.

As can be seen from this example, Shinkichi did not have a high regard for Sakutarō, probably the most prestigious of living Japanese poets in his time. In his estimation, Sakutarō was overly eager to absorb Western culture and neglected the traditions of the East, especially Buddhism. Sakutarō was too "passive" a Buddhist; whatever knowledge he had of Buddhism had been retranslated from Nietzsche and Schopenhauer. In Shinkichi's opinion, Sakutarō in his last years came to realize his mistake: late in his career he lamented, "All the literary education I received in the past was basically wrong." But Shinkichi thought Sakutarō was better than most of his followers, for they paid even less attention to Buddhism, thereby causing a hopeless degradation of contemporary poetry. In an essay called "The True Nature of the Poet," Shinkichi declared, "A species called poetry once lived on this earth, but those creatures are now presumed extinct. We discover fragments of their bones once in a while. Finding poetry is more difficult than discovering a snowman in the Himalayas." He has been equally harsh toward some novelists of modern Japan. The two major figures who have taken the brunt of his attack are Tsubouchi Shōyō (1859–1935) and Tanizaki Jun'ichirō, both of whom he felt went too far in importing the ideals of Western literature to Japan. He thought Shōyō was so busy translating Shakespeare and introducing Western literature that he became blind to the values of Zen and Japanese culture and therefore made the outrageous comment "Our traditional verse must be said to be the product of a primitive country." Tanizaki, an ardent admirer of Western aesthetics in his youth, did realize the value of his country's cultural heritage later on and wrote a number of novels utilizing the native tradition, but Shinkichi felt the novelist was still too partial to just one aspect of the Japanese literary heritage, popular Edo fiction;[6] as a result his novels were more entertaining than philosophical or religious. Shinkichi was especially incensed by Tanizaki's seeming inability to sniff out Zen elements in Japanese culture and said that the novelist must have been suffering from a chronic inflammation of the nose.

Predictably, Shinkichi has been more generous toward authors whose admiration for the West did not prevent them from valuing Buddhism and Japanese culture. He was delighted, for instance, when he learned that Futabatei Shimei (1864–1909), a novelist and translator of Russian literature, had practiced Zen meditation for a time in his later years. He also approved of the novels of another one-time practitioner of Zen, Natsume Sōseki (1867–1916), but he thought Sōseki's understanding of Zen was too intellectual. "No matter how many times you read all of Sōseki's works," he said, "you will never be able to learn the essence of Zen. But you may get a distant view of its outer landscape." As for Mori Ōgai, Shinkichi considered him basically a Confucian; yet, having been educated in nineteenth-century Japan, Ōgai had in him "the traditional Oriental sentiment breathing," which led him to write several stories with distinct references to Buddhism.

[6] Many entertaining stories intended for popular consumption were published during the Edo period (1600–1868). Tanizaki was an avid reader of these in his youth. In later life, however, he became much more interested in Heian literature.

Shinkichi liked Mishima Yukio for his interest in traditional Japanese culture and for his effort to study Buddhism in his later years, but could not approve of Mishima's fascination with Wang Yang-ming's philosophy because he thought Wang's teachings incorporated the degraded Zen Buddhism of the Ming dynasty rather than the more orthodox beliefs of T'ang and Sung times.[7] Shinkichi also commended Kawabata Yasunari (1899–1972) for lecturing on Zen in his Nobel Prize acceptance speech, but was disappointed when he killed himself. "Kawabata had not learned true Zen after all," Shinkichi reflected. "A person should keep on living as long as he can, no matter how old and ugly he may become. Whatever the circumstances may be, suicide is not right. That is my opinion."

Shinkichi has had similarly mixed feelings about major modern poets. He liked Takuboku's poetry because it had something of the flavor of Buddhism; he attributed that flavor to Takuboku's having been born in a Zen temple. At age seventeen or eighteen, Shinkichi was an enthusiastic admirer of Takuboku's poetry, but later he thought his admiration had been like coming down with the measles: after a while the fever was completely gone. "I agree with many critics who consider Takuboku's tanka shallow and unartistic," he said. His appraisal of Miyazawa Kenji's poetry was more favorable, but not by much. Although Kenji was a dedicated Buddhist, he belonged to the Hokke sect, which highly valued the Lotus Sutra, and that fact apparently antagonized Shinkichi. When Shinkichi received a copy of the sutra from Kenji's family, he sold it to one of his acquaintances. His respect for Kenji rose when he was awakened to the value of the Lotus Sutra and came to realize the ultimate oneness of the Zen and Hokke sects. Still, he considered Kenji's poems too unpolished, too prosaic, and too dogmatic to be called mature works of art. "I understand that Kenji valued the Lotus Sutra

[7] The Neo-Confucian thinker Wang Yang-ming (1472–1529) taught the unity of knowledge and action, advocating moral effort as the correct road to spiritual enlightenment. Mishima was attracted to this emphasis on action, but to Shinkichi the idea that enlightenment could be attained through practical morality perhaps seemed too facile.

more than anything else in the world," he said. "Yet that fact is not manifest in his verse. One will be disappointed if one expects to find the flavor of the sutra in his poetry." His criticism of Kenji's poetry may have been unfairly harsh because he saw a rival in that Buddhist poet.

Shinkichi was more generous toward Takamura Kōtarō, whom he knew personally; they were members of the same poets' group for a time. Also, Kōtarō had studied Zen as a young man, and Shinkichi was pleased to discover in his *The White Hatchet* a couple of tanka based on that experience. Yet he was disappointed that Kōtarō had not continued with Zen and believed that this manifested a certain "fragility" of mind. In his view, the poet-sculptor should have squarely confronted reality when Chieko went insane or when Tokyo lay devastated by air raids; instead Kōtarō beautified his wife in his imagination and escaped to the remote northeast. For that reason Shinkichi did not like *Chieko Poems* and "Short Biography of a Fool."

It is not easy to find poets who have been given unconditional approval in Shinkichi's critical essays, but the two who probably come closest are Bashō and Shiki. The main reason, of course, is their connection to Zen. Shinkichi greatly admired Bashō's haiku, saying that they embody "the purest soul of the Japanese." In his opinion, Bashō was able to become a great poet by practicing Zen under Priest Butcho (1642–1715) in his younger days. "Bashō mastered Zen with Butchō's help," Shinkichi observed. "Without considering that fact, no discussion of Bashō's haiku can be of any value." Shinkichi cited Bashō's poem

> The moon fleeting fast,
> foliage atop the trees
> holds the rain

as suggesting the kind of Zen he learned from Butchō. This was a new interpretation, since no scholar had mentioned a connection between this haiku and Zen. Unfortunately, Shinkichi did not spell out the nature of the connection. Possibly the moon that swiftly appears from and disappears into the clouds symbolizes the Buddhist Law as seen by men, and the foliage washed by rain is suggestive of the fresh, serene state of mind the poet was in at the time. Describing the scenery, Bashō wrote, "There was the moonlight, there was the sound of rain—the beauty of the scene so overwhelmed my mind that I was left without a word to say." Probably Shinkichi saw something of Zen in Bashō's experience.

Shinkichi's attempt to tie Shiki to Zen was more striking, for no other scholar had done so. Shiki himself wrote poems that seem to point toward atheism. But according to Shinkichi, Shiki learned Zen from Amada Guan (1854–1904), a priest and the author of the popular *Diary of a Pilgrim*. "Because he suffered from chronic ill health, he does not seem to have practiced Zen meditation," Shinkichi wrote of Shiki. "But it is impossible to think that such a sensitive mind as his was not inspired when it was introduced to Zen. I believe that the basis of Shiki's thought was ultimately nothing other than Zen, the kind of Zen that goes back through Guan to Tekisui, Gizan, and Hakuin."[8] Shinkichi combed Shiki's works to find proof of the older poet's serious commitment to Zen. One example he cited was this haiku:

> Have they come here
> to peck at my living eyes?
> Those hovering flies!

Again Shinkichi did not explain specifically why this haiku had Zen implications; he only observed that it suggested "Shiki's eyes gazing at his own death." But he wrote, in concluding his comments on Shiki:

> Where could such a thing as life exist?
> We are dead as we are.

Possibly Shinkichi thought the haiku represented a Zen state of mind, the kind of state that made the ailing poet feel "we are dead as we are."

Not being proficient in European languages, Shinkichi wrote

---

[8]Tekisui (1822–99), Gizan (1802–78), and Hakuin (1685–1768) were all well-known Japanese Zen priests of the Rinzai school. Tekisui, who studied Zen under Gizan, later became Guan's teacher.

little about Western literature. The little he did write often concerned men of letters whose thoughts he felt appeared to be Zen. He mentioned, for instance, that when he read *Nausea* in translation he felt that Sartre's epistemology was close to a Buddhist's. In an essay entitled "Rimbaud and Zen," he set some lines from the French poet side by side with Zen sayings and asserted: "I am certain that if Rimbaud had been born in Japan he would have practiced Zen of the Rinzai school and attained enlightenment—even though that would not have prevented him from contracting syphilis." Likewise, in "Dada and Zen" and other essays he compared a number of passages from Tzara's works with Zen phrases and found a good deal of common ground. "By reading 'A haute flamme' and other poems by Tzara," he wrote, "I can tell he had entered the realm of Zen." In "Stray Notes on T. S. Eliot" and other writings, he said he discovered in Eliot's poetry something similar to Zen, citing lines from *Four Quartets* that he thought were reminiscent of a Zen point of view. He was a little perturbed by Eliot's great popularity in Japan and remonstrated, "If you are a Japanese and write poetry in Japanese, you need not study Eliot's writings. A surer way to learn from Eliot is to read Buddhist scriptures and Zen books."

All in all, Shinkichi's critical writings make stimulating reading. He is a far from impartial critic: he is not a scholarly, well-informed reader, either. Yet his biased, impressionistic method sometimes uncovers hitherto unnoticed meanings in a poem. He has been virtually the only critic to approach modern Japanese free verse from a Zen point of view. The approach, although sometimes unfair, is effective to the extent that Buddhism has become an integral part of Japanese language and culture, however hidden it may seem under the veneer of modernization. Thus his stand counterbalances those of critics who tend to underestimate the role of Buddhism in contemporary Japanese life and poetry. His critical voice has been a lone one, yet it is the kind of voice that must exist for the health and welfare of Japanese poetry.

Poetic Form for a Modern Intellectual

As we have noted, the literary expression of Zen took two major forms in Japan, kanshi and haiku. The connection between Zen and kanshi goes back to China, where Zen originated. Following the example of Chinese monks, Zen adherents in Japan wrote verse in classical Chinese; this type of poetry reached its peak in the fourteenth and fifteenth centuries with the Zen-inspired poems known as *gozan bungaku* or "literature of the Five Mountains." Then in the seventeenth century haiku became associated with Zen. The most admired master of haiku, Bashō, practiced Zen in his youth and incorporated it into his poetry and poetics. For many poets who followed him, writing haiku was a spiritual discipline not unlike Zen. Haiku, in turn, came to be considered a literary form capable of suggesting the essence of Zen.

Why, then, did Shinkichi not write kanshi or haiku? Why did he choose to write in a poetic form that was imported from the West and that, according to Seisensui, embodied a clearly anti-Japanese attitude toward nature?

Shinkichi was born a little too late to obtain the kind of education that would have enabled him to write Chinese with ease. If he had received a good education in nineteenth-century Japan, he might have gained enough proficiency in classical Chinese to compose poems in it. Natsume Sōseki, born one generation earlier, could and did write kanshi. Shinkichi was able to read classical Chinese, and by all indications he read a large number of Chinese poems. His admiration for ancient Chinese verse, such as the poems in *The Book of Poetry*, has been mentioned earlier. He also read many Chinese Zen poems, as any Zen trainee is expected to do. But apparently he did not like *gozan bungaku*; to him, the Japanese Zen monks who wrote it seemed too concerned with the art of poetry. "Their works seem worthless in comparison with the verses of Chinese Zen monks," he observed. By reading *gozan bungaku* he undoubtedly learned the futility of trying to write a good poem in a foreign language.

Shinkichi has said why he did not become a haiku poet. He wrote haiku as a young boy, and he even had a haiku name, Makuwauri ("Melon"). Yet in a couple of years he stopped writing in seventeen syllables, for two reasons. First, his interest in writing haiku was vitally connected with a local haiku group of which he and his father were members. When the leader of the group, an employee of a large organization, was transferred to another locale, the group became inactive and Shinkichi lost his motivation for writing haiku. Second, in one of the haiku gatherings he heard an older poet predict the invention of a haiku-producing machine. The prediction shocked young Shinkichi. "I felt," he recalled, "that if a machine could compose every conceivable haiku, there was no sense in racking my brains to write one." Years later he realized that his argument was invalid, but he still could not completely drive misgivings from his mind.

Interestingly enough, Shinkichi has written more tanka, a verse form traditionally less close to Zen, than haiku. He does not know how many tanka he has produced, but he estimates the total to be fewer than three hundred. Below is an example, written one day in 1945 after an air raid had devastated a famous mausoleum in Tokyo:

> Trampling the hot
> roof tiles, I push my way
> through a bombed area.
> lying dead in my path,
> a blue sparrow.

As this example shows, the imagery and diction of many of the tanka have Shinkichi's stamp, yet his tanka are generally more incidental in theme and more lyrical in overtone than his shi. They give the impression of having been written in a more spontaneous manner and with a less serious intent. Except for a few that are tacked onto shi, Shinkichi has not included any of them in his collection of poetry. Apparently, like Takamura Kōtarō, he does not regard his tanka as serious poetry.

The main reason Shinkichi has not tried seriously to write tanka or haiku in his mature years appears to lie in their brevity.

He is not lacking in respect for these forms; as we have noted, the two poets he admires most are Bashō and Shiki. He is also quite appreciative of *The Collection of Ten Thousand Leaves* and has said he recognizes "unparalleled beauty" in those poems. Yet he continued, "I look at them in the same way as I look at antique paintings; I do not feel like composing my own poetry in imitation of them." To his sensibility, tanka and haiku are archaic or are rapidly becoming archaic. "To be competitive with the poetry of the rest of the world, tanka and haiku are too short," he said, and then added, "I suspect tanka and haiku will be absorbed into free verse in the future." On another occasion he was more impatient and declared, "Tanka and haiku are already things of the past."

Shinkichi does not favor short verse forms for modern use, basically because he feels the psychology of a modern man demands a poetic form that is longer, more flexible, and more inclusive—a form that allows more than lyricism. In his view, human life has become considerably more complex than it was in Bashō's time or even in Shiki's time, and many problems have emerged that cannot be solved by taking refuge in nature. Shiki's followers tried to modernize tanka and haiku, but they were not entirely successful. As an example, Shinkichi cited the following modern tanka written by a resident of Okinawa. The poem was inspired by an unfortunate incident in which an American soldier stationed in Okinawa shot and killed a local woman:

> A mother
> of three little children
> was shot to death.
> Perish, America!
> Perish, America!

About this tanka, Shinkichi observed:

In this instance, the mother in the poem may stand for all Okinawans, who share the same ideology, or she may represent the whole Japanese race. But what kind of response did the author expect from the readers by screaming "Perish! Perish!"? I can understand how the author, on hearing about the callous slaying of a mother, was angered by the lawless situation and had to cry out in protest. Yet if that cry amounted to nothing more than this single tanka, it might be taken for the mumbles of a sick man in delirium.

Shinkichi was referring to the complex political and social reality that existed in Okinawa before its reversion to Japan in 1972. There was a great deal of tension between the American occupation forces and local residents; incidents like the one mentioned in the tanka made the issue more emotional. Shinkichi understood the situation and the feelings of people involved, but he was critical when those feelings took a form like this tanka. In his view, a tanka can powerfully express a simple, straightforward emotion but is too short to do justice to the totality of a complex psyche responding to a complex reality. He feels that because of this fact modern tanka poets tend to write rensaku. "But," he has said, "a verse form that requires thirty poems to make a point clear is not a suitable vehicle of expression for a busy poet. Doesn't it save our energy if we write free verse? I may seem to be promoting my own cause, but that is what I think." He said nothing about haiku in this connection, but the same statement can be applied to it as well, or even better, since it is shorter than tanka.

Shinkichi once made the same point from another angle, presenting a free-verse poem of his own that he thought could never be written in tanka or haiku form. It is called "The Turtle":

The turtle has no basic doubts.
He is on the side of the status quo.
When confronted by a principle, he breaks down and shows
    his belly.
Look at the turtle paddling slowly in the waters of morality.
His muddy webs push aside the waves of culture.

His head looks masochistic, yet it is too short for self-
    sacrifice.
His shell resembles a feudal castle.
That amphibian fellow, always ready to compromise and
    wait for a chance!

The turtle sneaked into a yard overgrown with weeds.
He plucked bashful white flowers, only to throw them away.
He trampled dark shadows the wilting grass had craved.

When a flower opens, the turtle spits on its redness.
He hates the depth of earnest love among the verdant trees.
He has a savage mouth.
When he exhales, he does not think of the air he will
    inhale—
not in the way the earth thinks of evaporating water when
    it lets the rain fall.
With what peace of mind he spends his days, not
knowing there is no such animal as a turtle!

One morning the turtle forgot his coat
at the Dog Star's.

He must lead an indomitable life.
Turtle, forsake those petty, loachlike pleasures!

Would that happen if he denied life by death?
Death is built on the foundation of life.
All that is distant from the earth supports the earth.
If his shell is broken, the turtle will lose his life.

War is a speed.
A great speed is needed.
Where there is no speed, there is death.
Slowness is not the turtle's virtue.

Will the turtle fight with the sun?
Won't he be slain by sunset?

Referring to this poem, Shinkichi said, "In order to go beyond
the realm of haiku and tanka (which specialize in nature poetry)
and create a new form, I felt a need to write this kind of poem,
which is intellectual in expression." One does not need his statement to see the point. "The Turtle" could never be made into a
tanka or haiku, for its main theme, an attack on Philistinism, is
too complex a subject to be effectively articulated in 17 or 31 syllables. If a haiku (or its comic counterpart, a senryū) were to
treat the subject, it would merely smile at people content with
the routines of daily life. If a tanka were to do so, it would cry
out in protest at their follies as emotionally as did the Okinawan
poet. In either case there would not have emerged a reflective,
metaphysical poem like "The Turtle." Haiku and tanka are too
short to develop a set of images as fully as Shinkichi did in this
poem or to probe into a theme as deeply. The poem is longer
and more intellectual than the average Shinkichi poem; the
theme demanded that. It is a satirical poem, looking at people

and society from a transcendental point of view not unlike a Zen Buddhist's. Free verse is a poetic form flexible enough to include all those elements.

Basically, then, Shinkichi has wanted maximum freedom of poetic expression. He rejected fixed verse forms because they seemed too restrictive and favored a verse form that could be long or short, lyrical or intellectual, traditional or radical. His general stand on the question of poetic form is revealed in a short poem entitled "Words":

> Words can be of any kind,
> form can be of any kind, for
> what must be captured is only one;
> it has nothing to do with words or form.

If the poem captures truth, Shinkichi couldn't care less about words or form. Because truth is difficult—ultimately impossible—to capture, he has wanted maximum freedom of choice in his attempts to set it down.

Shinkichi has had very little to say about the form and structure of free verse itself. He chose to write shi precisely because of the freedom of expression it afforded him; he would not want to restrict that freedom by favoring a certain form or structure within free verse. Nevertheless, when one reads his poems and essays one is tempted to make a couple of tentative generalizations. First, he seems to prefer relatively short poems. Second, his lines tend to be more assertive than suggestive, more philosophical than mystical.

In spite of his declared dislike for the brevity of tanka and haiku, his poems, excluding prose poems, are relatively short. In fact, he once observed that "the length of a poem would do best to remain within fifteen or sixteen lines, or twenty lines at most." He mentioned two reasons. First, he had read poems in the *New York Times* and noticed that they were all short. Second, he was too poor to produce a long literary work; he would starve to death if he were to write a long one! Clearly Shinkichi was not completely serious when he made these comments. The main reason his poems are short probably has to do with his high regard for an inspirational creative process. As we have seen, he believes that a poem must be composed by the force of inspiration; he considers a poem to be primarily the spontaneous record of "what floated into my mind like a cloud in the sky." Presumably inspiration, an intuitive insight into truth, is of short duration. Referring to the poems in the 1949 edition of his collected works, Shinkichi himself stated that "the diction is lucid and most of the poems are short." He was right on the last point, at least: of the 134 poems included in the collection, only one has more than twenty lines. Although the ratio of long poems to short is larger in other of his anthologies, most of his poems are shorter than twenty lines, and he has written a sizable number of poems that consist of only one or two lines. A one-line poem called "Death" has been cited; here are two more examples:

The Sun
The sun is shrinking every day.

Potato
In a potato
there are mountains and rivers.

That these are inspirational poetry is evident. The first poem records an inspired moment in which the poet transcended the limits of the ordinary human senses and acquired a cosmic point of view: measured on the astronomical clock, the sun is shrinking visibly every day. In the second poem, he went to the other extreme, viewing things with a microscopic eye. At one inspired moment, he thought he saw the world in a potato.

The poem "The Sun" consists of seventeen syllables; "Death," of twelve syllables; and "Potato," of twenty syllables. As far as syllable count is concerned, they may seem less like free verse than like haiku; certainly they are well within the standard syllable count of free-style haiku as proposed by Seisensui. Yet these short poems by Shinkichi differ from free-style haiku in grammar and syntax. The language of haiku deliberately destroys ordinary relationships between words, so that it can transmit truth that cannot be expressed in logical statements. Shinkichi's short poems do not; by and large they retain the normal grammar and syntax of Japanese prose. Each of the three short poems mentioned above comprises a complete sentence, with all its normal linguistic relationships intact. There is no way to mistake them for free-style haiku. The same applies to Shinkichi's longer poems: his lines usually make grammatically complete sentences. The only major features differentiating the language of his poetry from ordinary prose are frequent line changes and the omission of punctuation. Nevertheless, his lines strike the reader as being poetic because the statements he makes are striking. He shocks his readers by stating, in a grammatically perfect sentence, that the sun is rapidly shrinking or that nobody has ever died. He tosses out an enigmatic idea and hopes it will awaken in readers thoughts to which they have never been exposed before. This is fundamentally different from the method of haiku, which stimulates a reader's imagination by presenting a grammatically incomplete sentence. Shinkichi's method is more intellectual. It appeals to modern Japanese readers, who have been exposed to too much Western literature and philosophy to have complete faith in an anti-intellectual approach to truth. Ultimately, Shinkichi is anti-intellectual; more precisely, he wants to go beyond intellect. But he goes through the intellect to reach for the realm beyond it, and he knows many contemporary readers cannot bypass intellect as some haiku poets seem to do. A lifelong concern with the dichotomy between science and religion also stems from his refusal to underestimate the achievements of intellect in modern times. He wants to write poetry from the perspective of a modern man, a man well aware of the potential of human intellect. The language of his poetry reflects this fact.

The structure of Shinkichi's poems often follows the line of his philosophical speculation, and as a result the poem looks like a philosopher's monologue. The poem's unity is attained through a progression of thoughts expressed in a sequence of complete sentences. Unlike Hagiwara Sakutarō, who tried to verbalize feelings before they became ideas, Shinkichi waits until feelings harden into ideas and then speculates about them. In this respect he is more a philosopher than a poet, and some of his poems indeed look like aphorisms. On the other hand, he is distinctly a poet in relying on images, metaphors, and symbols in giving form to his thoughts. He could be said to be a metaphysical poet, although he has never called himself such.

On the whole, however, no generalizations about Shinkichi's structural method hold true, for it is too diverse. He rejected tanka and haiku because of their formal restrictiveness, and he would not like to be confined to any specific method of unifying a poem. With him, a poem is the outcome of meditation, and its structure and wording must be free to follow the way in which his meditation progresses. The structure can be logical, associational, or narrative, depending on the way his cogitations evolve at the time. He conceives shi to be an all-inclusive verse form freely allowing him to do all these things; that must be part of the reason he thinks free verse will in time absorb both tanka and haiku. The language of his poetry is as flexible as free verse can be.

For Those Who Do Not Hear the Rooster

A good deal has already been said about Shinkichi's view of the use of poetry. In general, it is not very favorable. At times, when provoked, he has even conceded that poetry is not only useless but harmful. As we have seen, poetry seemed to him nothing more than "rubbish" at one time, "footnotes" at another. Similar derogatory words abound in his writings. The most disparaging of all appear in the essay "The True Nature of the Poet," in which he called poets liars, thieves, and father-killers. Although much of this abuse is rhetorical, there is no doubt that he assigns a secondary importance to poetry in his scheme of things. Of prime importance to him is religion. For a brief period of his life that religion was dada; then it was replaced by Zen Buddhism.

During Shinkichi's dadaist phase, poetry functioned as a vehicle for making assertions and thereby transforming negatives into positives. Believing with Serner that "the world view is a confusion of words," he found poetry useful because it provided explosive power with which to destroy existing systems of thought and reduce them to more primordial, preintellectual matter. Presumably he could have done the same in prose, yet poetry is more pliant in form, more capable of being loaded with intense mental energy. It can express the spirit of rebellion in a freer, more immediate, and therefore more forceful form. As Shinkichi portrayed himself in "ShinDA Renkichi":

> I write with a finger.
> I write with snot.
> I write on a piece of soiled toilet paper.
> For those who drink seminal discharge with a tobacco pipe
> my poetry has no use.

His poetry was useless for the genteel middle-class, but served a function for a youthful rebel.

In this concept, poetry is ultimately a means to an end. Young Shinkichi was trying to find a way to come to terms with himself and the world; he thought dada showed him one such way. To him, dada was more a mode of thinking and living than a literary and artistic movement, and unlike many European dadaists, he made almost no effort to propagate dada among his fellow poets and artists. He was content that it help him in his own spiritual quest. Writing poetry provided him with an effective means of making dadaist assertions and thereby striving for the end he sought. Thus it was relatively easy for him to give up being a poet and become a Zen trainee in 1928, because he was first and foremost a seeker for a better spiritual life. He had been a poet only secondarily.

The role of poetry became even less significant in Shinkichi's thought after his serious commitment to Zen. Indeed, his earlier exposure to poetry came to seem a drawback when he began his Zen training. He recalled:

I continued to write poetry and prose fiction only to make a living; my heart was not with literature but with Buddhism. I read a great deal of Buddhist literature indiscriminately, trying to search out the essence of Zen by way of literature. All that was a waste of time and energy; many times I stumbled, hurt myself, and had to beat a retreat.

He was implying that his orientation as a poet was a disadvantage in his quest for satori. When he was a dadaist, poetry was at least of help in pursuing his goal, but as a Zen student he found literature harmful.

Poetry can be harmful in Zen training because the poet uses words; thus he may be deluded into thinking that he can express truth in words. From a Zen point of view, seeking truth by means of language is as hopeless as trying to complete the Tower of Babel. After all, words are a product of the mind, and the thinking mind represents only one—and a nonessential—part of human life. "I do not believe," Shinkichi said, "that the functions of my mind are related to the whole of my being. I believe my mind is performing its functions on its own within just one part of my being." In his view, there is another, more essential part. That part can be reached, he thinks, only through Zen exercises.

Zen and Buddhism have lost much of their popular appeal in modern times. Since Japan under the Meiji government decided on wholesale Westernization, people have become believers in science instead of religion. "It would not be an exaggeration to say," Shinkichi once observed, "that due to the Meiji government's anti-Buddhist policy, as well as to the invasion of Marxism and Leninism, virtually no Japanese has continued to believe in Buddha or to study Buddhism." His assessment of the situation is basically correct, although he has indeed exaggerated, despite his protestation to the contrary. Buddhism has become only a nominal religion for many Japanese, no longer providing them with a way of coming to grips with their existence.

Here Shinkichi saw a potential use for literature in general and for poetry in particular. Many Japanese have stopped going to temples in search of salvation, but they read novels, short stories, and poems. Shinkichi sees much contemporary literature as nothing more than "rubbish piled on the surface of our society," yet sometimes, he thinks, pure gold may be buried beneath the rubbish. To quote his words again: "One might be able to enter Zen by way of literature, although inevitably it is a roundabout way." It is a roundabout way because literature is dependent on words. But literature has a universal appeal. For the general public, it is more approachable than Zen.

For Shinkichi, then, literature is most useful when it helps readers in their quest for religious truth, even though it can do so only in an indirect way. Literature can be no more than a verbal substitute for truth, but it may serve as a catalyst in their quest some day. Poetry, in particular, is capable of functioning as a Zen kōan because of its capacity to be more illogical, more provocative, and more removed from everyday reality than prose. To Shinkichi's way of thinking, poetry is most useful when it acts as a kōan—when it plunges the reader's mind into a Zen type of meditation. Shinkichi has written many poems of this kind in his later years. His poem "Death," for instance, tries to open readers' eyes to the eternity of cosmic life. "Flowering Rose Mallow" leads them to see the nothingness hidden behind physical being. "The Fly" makes them begin to contemplate the questions of infinity and relativity. "The Turtle" shocks them by letting them see how meaningless are their daily lives. One can go on and on citing such examples.

It is no wonder that almost all of Shinkichi's later poems feature a Zen Buddhist either as the poem's speaker or as its main character, with or without disguise. Only on rare occasions can one sense the voice of a poet per se. "The Eastern Sky" is one of those few poems. Based on an experience during Shinkichi's Zen training, it will serve as a fitting conclusion to this discussion of his view of poetry:

> Early in the morning a rooster is crowing.
> I want to get a chisel
> and carve that living rooster.
> With the sharp, stainless blade
> I want to gouge its throat.
> The distant crow of a rooster
> is what I want to carve.

The rooster's crow is like the elusive moment of satori. A poet's task is to capture that moment and present it to the uninitiated reader, who is unable to hear the crow by himself. There is a problem in doing so, because the moment dies as soon as it is verbalized; it is like the image of a rooster instead of a live one. Yet the poet keeps trying to capture that precious moment. Even if he fails, he will still present a semblance of the moment or at least a record of his efforts, and his attempt may help the reader in his own spiritual quest. In Shinkichi's view, therein lies the only usefulness poetry can claim.

Conclusion

F ROM SHIKI TO Shinkichi, Japanese poetry has undergone
many changes and diversified in many directions. Shiki was a
radical poet in his day, but even he could never have imagined
that something so Oriental as Zen would find expression in free
verse, an import from the West; a haiku consisting of two syllables or a tanka written in romanization would have been beyond
his wildest dreams. Given such diversity, it is difficult to general-
ize about modern Japanese poetry. Yet after examining the theory and practice of eight major poets, we can discern certain general trends that typify the modern age. In the following pages
we shall focus on these trends and thereby try to identify the
contributions our eight poets have made to the evolution of Japanese poetry.

The belief that art imitates nature is inherent in all of our
poets' theories. Yet the definition of "nature" has expanded considerably. In premodern tanka, to write about nature meant to
write about plum blossoms, cuckoos, or pampas grass—objects
that emanated elegant, courtly beauty. Haiku poets widened this
realm by including crows, weed flowers, and such, yet by and
large they were hesitant to venture outside topics that were traditionally considered poetic. The introduction of European poetry to early modern Japan changed that convention. The idea
that the more sordid aspects of reality could be used to a pleasing artistic end had been alien to traditional Japanese aesthetics,
but exposure to Western realism began to erode that attitude.
An early sign of the trend was Shiki's essay "Haiku on Excre-

ment," which pointed out that a poetic effect could be created using scatological materials. A couple of decades later Takuboku defended a tanka that portrayed a man urinating. By the time Shinkichi began to publish, the realm of poetic subjects had so widened that hardly anyone objected when he used such images as snot and seminal discharge in his verse.

An even more important change was that Japanese poetry began to address intellectual topics. Having been dominated by a lyric tradition for centuries, premodern verse had never presented philosophical or moral themes in sustained arguments; it could not do so because of its brevity. The intellectualism of European poetry provided a fresh stimulus to poets in early modern Japan, inducing, as we have noted, a Tokyo University professor to write a poem on the principles of sociology. The longer, more flexible shi form enabled poets to expound concepts in a reasoned manner. Sakutarō, Kenji, and Kōtarō all wrote tanka in their youth but became free-verse poets as they matured: Sakutarō's Schopenhauerian nihilism, Kenji's agrarian populism, and Kōtarō's Shintoistic pantheism contained too much intellectual substance to be adequately expressed in 31 syllables. Even the Zen poet Shinkichi, who could have turned to haiku, chose to write in free verse because he did not want to bypass intellect in his search for truth. Although many haiku and tanka are still being written, on the whole Japanese poetry has come to tolerate discursive reason to an extent never known before.

On the other hand, many Japanese poets have remained skeptical about the usefulness of the intellect as a means of grasping ultimate reality. Sakutarō, probably the most intellectual of our eight poets, had a high regard for human reason but saw its power as manifested largely outside of poetry. In his opinion, poetry is preintellectual: what a poet senses by intuition is verified by reason later on. "Poetry deals with images floating in a dream at night," he said. Many other poets, notably Akiko, Kenji, and the young Takuboku, also associated poetry with a world of dreams and visions.

Given these poets' reservations about the function of discursive reason, their concepts of mimesis had to stop short of naturalistic realism. They did not want to represent experience as it is rigidly marked out by the commonsense mind—into this and that, internal self and external world, or dream and reality. To use Sakutarō's metaphors, they expected poetry to deal not with solid matter but with liquids and to be more like painting than photography. Likewise Shiki, who advocated "sketches from life" for beginning poets, advised advanced students to portray a vision of nature more beautiful than everyday life—that is, to represent the truth of their personal vision as well as external objects truly observed. Takuboku, who was so attracted to naturalistic realism that he decided to write prose fiction, did not succeed as a novelist partly because he was not able to keep at a distance from his own fictional characters and so represent the world as separate from his own feelings; Kōtarō wrote verse because in poetry, unlike sculpture, he could be as subjective as he liked. Mimetic theories in Japan have always shown an aversion to objective, photographic representation of nature, and they have retained this orientation in the modern period.

One reason Japanese poets prefer not to distinguish rigidly between the self and the external world is their pantheistic concept of nature. We might recall Seisensui's words, "In the West raw nature is considered dangerous, whereas in Japan people are not afraid of nature and befriend it." None of the traditional religions in Japan has conceived of human identity as distinct from other existences in nature; man has always been considered part of nature and therefore able to return to it. The result is that instead of objectively observing his subject and delineating its outlines, a poet is expected to submerge himself in nature and capture its life from within. Seisensui concentrated on the vegetable kingdom, Kōtarō on the world of wild beasts, yet both recognized a basic life-force flowing through man and the universe, and both considered that force the prime source of energy for creative activities. To Sakutarō the comparable vital impulse was a nostalgic yearning for the forms that define experience, which lie beyond the grasp of the conscious mind; for

Kenji it was the craving of all creatures to ascend to Buddhahood. An extreme case is that of Shinkichi, who as a Zen Buddhist refused to distinguish between any objects in nature. Seisensui's dictum "Merge your mind with nature" characterizes
the typically Japanese idea of mimesis.

However, none of our eight poets has been very specific about
the initial stage of the creative process, in which the mind merges
with nature. This is because they believed that stage lies in the
subconscious and is not known to the poet himself. They were
not convinced, as were some people in premodern Japan, that a
poet at work is divinely possessed, but they agreed that he is a
passive agent who does not have complete control over himself.
Sakutarō offered a modern metaphor: a poet is an automated
machine. There is therefore no agreement about methods for
inducing poetic inspiration, but poets have given various bits of
advice. Shiki, Akiko, and Seisensui stressed the importance of
traveling, especially in the wilds. Although neither Kenji nor
Shinkichi mentioned this method, both often wrote poems during a trip, and apparently a change of scene provided the needed
stimulation. Sakutarō, not a nature poet, preferred to stay indoors, but he emphasized derailing the mind from its daily routine. Takuboku and Kōtarō, who led stormy lives, did not seem
to worry about inspiration because they had plenty of external
stimuli. Agonized by the illness of loved ones, they sought emotional relief by venting their pain. To use Akiko's distinction,
they relied more on passive jikkan than on positive ones.

One uniquely Japanese method of verse writing continued to
be practiced in the modern period. It is a verse-writing party, a
gathering of poets for the purpose of producing poems. The
practice runs contrary to the idea of inspiration, yet Shiki,
Akiko, Takuboku, and Seisensui all seem to have enjoyed it
enormously. Primarily a game played in a lighthearted mood, a
verse-writing party provides participants with a chance to improve their craft in a painless way. Such parties are part of a centuries-old tradition and were therefore limited to the two tradi-

tional verse forms, haiku and tanka. Free-verse poets were left to struggle for inspiration on their own.

When visited by an inspiration, most poets would hasten to note it down. Since olden times an inspiration had been thought to be a fleeting thing that faded away in a short period of time. In medieval Japan, for instance, it was popularly believed that Lady Murasaki conceived the rough outline of *The Tale of Genji* while praying at a Buddhist temple one night and immediately scrawled it down on sutra paper that happened to be lying near at hand. Bashō advised that an inspiration be committed to writing instantaneously, like "felling a massive tree" or "cutting a watermelon." Many modern poets had similar ideas and attempted to jot down, as soon as possible, what came to their minds in inspired moments. Shinkichi used the margins of his diary or a convenient scrap of paper; others made a habit of carrying a notebook for this purpose. Such notebooks have been published in the collected works of Sakutarō and Kenji, and they give valuable hints about the creative process. By and large the poet's notes are fragmentary and sometimes even incoherent, showing that he himself did not at first completely grasp the meaning of an inspiration. In time, however, he came to understand its meaning, and as he did so he gave it a more comprehensible verbal form. The poet, who is a passive agent at the time of inspiration, slowly assumes a more active role as composition progresses.

All of our poets emphasized the importance of completing composition before the inspiration cooled. Akiko had an apt metaphor: poetic emotion is a molten ball, which must be cast while it is hot. At the extreme, Kōtarō insisted that a poem has to be completed spontaneously, that only a second-rate poet is concerned with the art of composition. Evidence shows, however, that all of our poets revised to some degree. Shiki's moon poem, for example, went through six different versions. Sakutarō's "Howling Dog" has at least three known drafts; Kenji's "Mother," at least two. Kōtarō himself reworked many of his poems, and in general the ones he revised are superior to those completed on the spur of the moment. This fact points to the truism that inspiration and composition are not antithetical, that the result is most satisfying when the art of composition helps to give inspiration the best verbal form it can possibly take.

Many of our poets believed that no revisions should be attempted long after the initial composition. Sakutarō, for instance, criticized Akiko on this count, feeling that she had revised her earlier tanka after her shiseishin had qualitatively changed. On the other hand, Kenji held an interesting minority view: he thought a poem could be revised at any time because in his opinion there was no such thing as a final form in poetry or anything else; all things, he believed, are eternally in flux. Shinkichi also seems to have tacitly subscribed to this view, since many of his poems appear in different forms in different editions of his collected works.

Modern Japanese poets have formulated few new concepts about the creative process; in practice, too, by and large they have followed premodern methods of verse writing. They have, however, significantly expanded the range of aesthetic effects created by poetry. Many traditional ambiences still persist: Shiki's makoto and plainness, Akiko's truth, Takuboku's kokoro, Kōtarō's sincerity, and Seisensui's naturalness and simplicity are all variations on aesthetic ideals cherished by Japanese poets for centuries. Yet modern poets have also created some ambiences that were largely unknown in premodern poetry. These seem to cluster in four main areas: the sublime, the vigorous, the hortatory, and the intellectual.

The sublime was proposed by Shiki as an antidote for elegance, the courtly beauty admired by earlier Japanese poets. It gives the impression of strength, courage, magnificence, or violence. Shiki himself did not write many poems that produced this sort of effect, perhaps because he was ill for much of his adult life and had few chances to sketch a magnificent natural scene or a heroic deed from personal experience. Later poets succeeded better, however, and Kōtarō's "Cathedral in the Rain" and Kenji's poem about peasant women entitled "Opus 1063" exemplify the sublime. They have nothing of the delicate, exquisite quality that dominated premodern Japanese poetry.

Vigor is the antithesis of *aware*, another traditional ambience that had been admired by generations of poets since the Heian period. It overlaps the sublime in its implications of strength, but it emphasizes vitality more than magnificence or grandeur. It is the beauty of a healthy wild animal in opposition to the beauty of *aware*, which focuses on the evanescence of life. Its implications are more humanistic and less otherworldly. Kōtarō, who wrote many "wild beast" poems, was a champion of this aesthetic. Interestingly enough, the Buddhist Kenji, who might have been expected to be partial to *aware*, also promoted a healthy, robust poetry, since he belonged to the Hokke sect, which advocated making a positive contribution to contemporary society. His agrarian poetry represents one of the farthest departures from the aesthetic ideals of Heian tanka.

Kenji mentioned contribution to society as an ingredient of a sound, vigorous poetry. Sakutarō spoke of shiseishin as pedagogic and of poetry as "journalistic." What I have arbitrarily labeled "the hortatory" refers to such attempts to edify the reader and move him to action. Some of the later poems of Takuboku, who also equated poetry and "journalism," affect the reader this way; Kōtarō's war poems provide another set of examples, seeking to move readers in a completely different direction. So insistent an inclusion of political, social, and moral messages was unknown in premodern Japanese poetry, although a small number of political poems had been written in Chinese.

Modern poetry has emphasized intellectual content to a degree unknown to premodern readers. Traditionally haiku and tanka poets abhorred intellectual speculation, preferring to work with raw feelings before reason had interfered. Modern poets allow intellection more room in their works. Even Shinkichi, who as a Zen Buddhist has a basic mistrust of the intellect, has written "The Turtle," which relies on conceptual argument. Takuboku included "thoughts" among the four souvenirs he believed a poet could give the reader, and many of the ideological poems he wrote in his last years make an intellectual appeal. Sakutarō felt the intellect was the domain of prose, yet his poetry seems to have grown increasingly intellectual in his later years, until he wrote only prose poems, aphorisms, and essays. By and large free verse is more capable of accommodating discursive reason, and therefore it has come to produce a kind of philosophical poem entirely new to the Japanese poetic tradition.

If modern Japanese poetry has become more diverse in the types of effect it produces, it has become even more varied in form and style. The adoption of the shi form was the greatest single modern innovation, but haiku and tanka have undergone many formal and stylistic changes as well. At first poets were pessimistic: Shiki, for instance, predicted the early deaths of haiku and tanka. Yet these forms have survived the challenges of modernization and free verse, in part because they were able to change.

Modern poets have, for instance, begun to make greater use of the rensaku technique, writing a series of haiku or tanka on a common topic and publishing them together under a single title. This device responds, at least partially, to the oft-emphasized complaint that 17 or 31 syllables is too short to do justice to the complex mind of a modern man or the intricacy of modern life. In rensaku, a haiku or tanka becomes like a stanza of a free-verse poem, and the poet can go on writing any number until he feels his theme is exhausted. He can even give the entire series a coherent structure in the manner of a shi; a good example is Shiki's "Forcing Myself to Take Up the Pen." Akiko and Takuboku wrote rensaku, too, although no examples have been quoted.

Modern poets have also taken greater liberty with syllabic patterns. Haiku written in more than 17 syllables and tanka containing more than 31 syllables have become more common. The purpose is partly to add freshness and individuality, partly to answer the charge that these fixed verse forms are too inflexible. Some radical haiku poets, led by Seisensui, went further and invented free-style haiku. Takuboku kept the 31-syllable form, but had his tanka printed in three lines. Kenji wrote tanka in schemes varying from two to five lines, and Toki Aika experimented with romanized tanka. With such flexibility of form, haiku and tanka have come closer to free verse; indeed, free-style haiku might be considered a variety of free verse. In the process, they have been severed from premodern aesthetic and moral values. No critic would think of evaluating a romanized tanka by the standard of *The Collection of Ancient and Modern Poems*; no one would call it feudalistic and old-fashioned, as conventional tanka were sometimes called in early modern Japan.

But free verse has also highlighted the strong points of haiku and tanka. Because in some respects these forms cannot compete with free verse, they have been forced to cultivate what they can do best. As modern poets have discovered, their main strength is their open, inconclusive form and their resulting ability to present fragmentary thoughts in fragmentary language. Akiko liked the tanka form because it embodied random fragments ripped from life; Takuboku favored it because it could record momentary thoughts fleeting through his mind; and Seisensui felt haiku could express a spontaneous feeling with all its spontaneity intact. Kōtarō's practice also indicated where the domain of tanka lies: in his later years he wrote shi to show to the public but used the 31-syllable form when his feelings were too personal for formal presentation. We see, then, haiku and tanka complementing free verse and finding thereby their raison d'être.

Japanese free verse has in turn been affected by traditional forms. One conspicuous result is its brevity. Although Kenji and Kōtarō wrote several long shi, most free-verse poems produced in modern Japan are relatively short. Akiko advised that a beginning poet write free verse in ten lines at most; Shinkichi was a little more generous and extended the desirable maximum length to twenty lines. Some of Hakushū's shi were so short that Seisensui was tempted to turn them into haiku—to the wrath of the free-verse poet. There is no simple way to explain the Japanese predilection for shortness. One explanation may have to do, as Akiko has pointed out, with the tradition of lyricism in

Japanese poetry: heightened lyrical moments cannot last very long. Another explanation may be related, as Shinkichi has suggested, to elements of Zen in Japanese culture that promoted a distrust of the expository function of language. No doubt one could cite many more reasons, but none is likely to be satisfactory in itself. Critics have long tried, with little success, to explain why the short story has been the dominant form of prose fiction in Japan for many centuries; a similar situation exists in poetry.

The language of Japanese free verse has been influenced by the traditional rhythm of alternating five- and seven-syllable lines. In fact, in the formative years of shi most poems were written in this syllabic pattern, and even in later years poets like Kenji utilized it in free verse. Eventually Kenji abandoned free verse altogether in favor of the five- and seven-syllable pattern. At the other extreme were poets like Sakutarō, who consciously avoided anything resembling traditional prosody. Sakutarō felt that the repetition of five- and seven-syllable lines was too monotonous, that such a rhythm created a sense of routine daily life and was therefore unfit for modern poetry, which in his opinion should soar high above everyday reality. Seisensui seemed to agree, but in his mind the 5–7–5 syllabic pattern represented conformity to and dependence on traditional values. In both these poets' works the absence of the 5–7 pattern is conspicuous—so conspicuous that when on rare occasions they use it the lines stand out clearly. The poets, of course, calculated this effect.

Japanese poets writing in free verse have tended to depend on the visual effect of the written poem more than on the auditory qualities that emerge when it is read aloud. Again this tendency is related to the practice of haiku and tanka poets, who since olden times have exploited the visual elements of the language. One may or may not agree with Sakutarō's contention that Japanese is an unmusical language, but the fact remains that premodern poets never seriously attempted to explore its prosodic potential beyond the 5–7 syllabic pattern. On the other hand, they made profuse use of visual imagery in their works, so much so that there emerged an idiomatic phrase defining poetry as verbal painting. Haiku and tanka have also incorporated the art of calligraphy. Indeed, one of the qualifications of a poet was once that he be a good calligrapher. Free-verse poets do not pay much attention to their handwriting, yet they carefully consider the visual effects of hiragana, katakana, and Chinese characters so that lines in their poetry will look artistically satisfying when written or printed. If they want to create a rugged effect, for example, they make more use of Chinese characters, which have many angular shapes. If a graceful effect is desired, they depend more on hiragana, which have many curved lines. Of course, this aspect of their craftsmanship would go unnoticed if their poetry were read aloud to an audience. Perhaps because of this, Japanese poets seldom give poetry readings. Far more widespread is the practice of writing poems on decorative cards to give to admirers. The card, called *shikishi*, is framed and hung in one's living room.

The language of shi, except in its early years, has been modern spoken Japanese. The use of the vernacular in verse writing is another contribution made by poets in our time, for during the preceding centuries poetry had always been written in classical Japanese, the language of the Heian period. Some early modern poets experimented with using the vernacular, but it took Sakutarō's genius to transform colloquial Japanese into a respectable poetic language. Sakutarō himself had to retreat to classical vocabulary in his last years, as did Kenji, yet today modern spoken Japanese is firmly established as the language of shi. Haiku and tanka, being classical verse forms, still usually employ the classical language; however, Seisensui and his group have consistently advocated writing haiku in the vernacular. During the early years of this century, Takuboku was already using colloquial phrases in his tanka, and colloquialisms and recent borrowings have continued steadily to invade haiku and tanka, so that nowadays it is not unusual to find loan words from English or French in these centuries-old verse forms. *Kurisumasu* ("Christmas"), for example, has now been widely accepted as a season word in haiku. The language of Japanese poetry has been modernized as life in Japan has been modernized.

No such dramatic change has occurred in Japanese views on the use of poetry. As in the West, traditional views ranged between the two poles of hedonism and didacticism, conceiving poetry as giving pleasure or edification or both to the reader as well as the poet. Modern views also fall within this range. Most of our eight poets readily recognized the pleasure of reading or writing poetry. To Shiki, verse writing was play as opposed to work; to Takuboku, it was a puff of tobacco after a hard day; to Seisensui, it was a means of relaxation after supper. In other words, poetry has been conceived as a relief from the pain of life. Illness, poverty, domestic discord, loneliness, unfulfilled desire—all are vented in poetry and thus mitigated. Poets and readers share their personal problems with each other, and the sharing lessens their suffering. When Akiko was desperately in love with a married man, when Sakutarō had a running feud with his wife, or when Takuboku heard that his daughter was in a coma, poetry was there to help. It even helped to raise Shiki's spirits as he lay dying. The view that poetry is a release for painful emotions has remained strong in modern Japan.

Several of our eight poets conceived of a more positive pleasure to be derived from writing poetry. Both Akiko and Seisensui stressed the joy of creation, of owning and loving something that one has brought into the world. In their view, verse writing provides one of the readiest opportunities to fulfill the creative instinct, for a pencil and paper are all that is needed. Most of our poets seem to have felt this kind of pleasure in their student days, although for Kōtarō sculpture seems to have given it more than did poetry.

Modern poets often believed that poetry was not only pleasurable but didactic. As poets, they considered themselves seers, prophets, bearers of messages from a future world. But they differed about what that world would look like. To Akiko, it was a humanistic society in which all people, including women, would be able to realize their full potential as free human beings. To

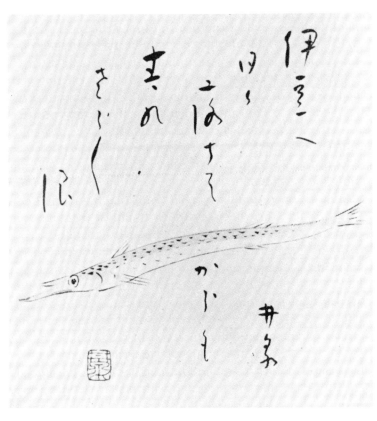

A shikishi by Seisensui. The haiku reads:

Izu e	in Izu Peninsula
hi ga	the sun
ochite kara mo	has gone down, yet
haru no	spring
sara sara	continues to murmur
nami	with the waves

Reproduced from Ogiwara Seisensui, *Haiku no te* (Jitsugyō no Nihon Sha).

Sakutarō, it was a new, Westernized Japan, a modern nation completely liberated from feudalistic morality and culture. To Kenji, it was an agrarian society in which all poets would farm and all farmers would write poetry. Most of the poets seem to agree in principle about why a poet can be a seer. In their opinion, a poet is an idealist whose aspiration for a better existence is so intense that he is able to sense what others do not. To borrow Sakutarō's words, a poet is endowed with shiseishin, which enables him to soar high above mundane reality. On his return to the earth, he presents his vision in terms comprehensible to the ordinary senses.

When that world of higher reality is conceived in religious terms, poetry is identified with religion. Many of our poets did indeed turn poetry into a religion. Kenji and Shinkichi identified poetry with the teachings of their Buddhist sects. Shiki and Seisensui saw haiku as part of a pantheism like that nurtured in the premodern haikai tradition. Kōtarō shared a similar belief, except that he emphasized the dynamic energy of living creatures. These poets did not necessarily consider poetry more effective than traditional religion in its saving power; in fact, Kenji and Shinkichi seem to have believed it to be less effective. Yet they all knew the diminishing role of religion in twentieth-century Japan. With the influx of Western rationalism, Buddhism and Confucianism had lost much of their appeal to the general public; Shinto, associated with militarism, fared even worse after Japan lost the Second World War. In contrast, poetry retained more popular appeal; it could spread religious messages without the rituals and formalities of an established religion and could even sweeten those messages with entertainment.

It cannot be denied, however, that poetry too has been losing its popularity in the last few decades. People are more inclined to watch television or look at comic books than to appreciate poetry. Or they read popular fiction, seeking to be entertained by stories. Although poetry has continued to function at a personal level, its social function has diminished considerably. It has lost the power to move people—a great many people—to action. Already Takuboku and Kenji recognized that sad fate, and they became, or wanted to become, workers rather than observers, men of action rather than men of letters. Sakutarō also foresaw poetry's fate and predicted that public libraries would shelve books of poetry in an unobtrusive corner because few readers would be interested. Will Japanese poetry survive? A century ago Shiki asked the same question and gave a pessimistic answer. Yet poetry survived, even proliferated, and he himself helped it to. We can only hope that history will repeat itself.

Rōmaji Renderings of Haiku and Tanka Cited

The numerals at the left indicate page numbers in this book. In the original editions, some of Takuboku's tanka have indented lines, as shown in the English translations in Chapter 3.

CHAPTER ONE. MASAOKA SHIKI

26 Sanbashi ni wakare o oshimu tsukiyo kana
27 Sanbashi ni wakare o oshimu fūfu kana
27 Miokuru ya yoi no sametaru fune no tsuki
28 Haru no yo ya byōbu no kage ni mono no iki
28 Chamise ari shirouma tsunagu momo no hana
28 Nagaki yo ya omoidasu toki kaze ga fuku
29 Kōbai no rakka moyuran uma no fun
29 Meigetsu ya usagi no fun no akarasama
30 Ōkami wa fun bakari de mo samusa kana
30 Samidare ya taiga o mae ni ie niken
31 Mononofu no yanami tsukurou kote no ue ni kasumi tabashiru
    Nasu no shinohara
32 Yama no yu ya hadaka no ue no amanogawa
32 Neshizumaru sato no tomoshibi mina kiete amanogawa shiroshi
    takeyabu no ue ni
32 Kogarashi ya kane hikisuteshi michi no hata
32 Waga niwa no ogusa mo moenu kagiri naki ametsuchi ima ya mi-
    dori sururashi
33 Mugimaki ya tabane agetaru kuwa no eda
33 Yukihatenu natsuno no michi no michi haruka hiru suguredomo
    hito ni awanu kamo
34 Yamazato wa u no hanagaki no hima o arami shinobine morasu
    hototogisu kana
34 Yamazato no u no hanagaki no yūzukuyo shinobine morasu hoto-
    togisu kana
35 Fuyugomoru yamai no toko no garasudo no kumori nugueba tabi
    hoseru miyu
35 Kangofu ya utatane samete hae o utsu
35 Garasudo no toi wa tsuki akashi mori no ue ni shirakumo nagaku
    tanabikeru miyu
35 Hana chitte mizu wa minami e nagarekeri
36 Hechima saite tan no tsumarishi hotoke kana
36 Tan itto hechima no mizu mo ma ni awazu
36 Ototoi no hechima no mizu mo torazariki
42 Aizō wa hae utte ari ni ataekeri
42 Daiichi ni sen no haibun sono tsugi mo mata sono tsugi mo shasei
    shasei nari
42 Kōbai no rakka moyuran uma no fun
43 Hachiue no kikyō utsurou kosame kana
43 Yamazato no momiji ni asobu hitotoki wa aki no hikage mo
    nodokekarikeri
44 Hito mo kozu haru yuku niwa no mizu no ue ni koborete tamaru
    yamabuki no hana
44 Tomoshibi no hikari ni terasu mado no soto no botan ni sosogu
    haru no yo no ame
44 Ichihatsu no hana sakiidete waga me ni wa kotoshi bakari no haru
    yukan to su

101 Aki no sora kakuryō to shite kage mo nashi / amari ni sabishi / ka-
rasu nado tobe
101 Tōkai no kojima no iso no shirasuna ni / ware nakinurete / kani
to tawamuru
101 Hatarakedo / hatarakedo nao waga kurashi raku ni narazari /
jitto te o miru
106 Nani ga nashi ni / hai no chiisaku nareru gotoku omoite okinu /
aki chikaki asa
109 Borōjin to iu Roshia-na ga, / naze to mo naku, / ikudo mo omoi-
dasaruru hi nari.
109 Tomo mo, tsuma mo, kanashi to omou rashi— / Yamite mo
nao, / kakumei no koto kuchi ni tataneba.
109 Yaya tōki mono ni omoishi / terorisuto no kanashiki kokoro
mo— / chikazuku hi no ari.
111 Iki sureba / mune no naka ni te naru ne ari. / Kogarashi yori mo
sabishiki sono ne!
111 Aru hi, futo, yamai o wasure / ushi no naku mane o shite minu— /
saishi no rusu ni.
111 Niwa no soto o shiroki inu yukeri. / Furimukite / inu o kawamu
to tsuma ni hakareru.
114 Jibun yori mo toshi wakaki hito ni, / hannichi mo kien o ha-
kite, / tsukareshi kokoro!
115 Tawamure ni haha o seoite sono amari karoki ni nakite sanpo
arukazu
115 Hyōzen to ie o idete wa hyōzen to kaeritaru koto sudeni itsutabi
115 Furusato no chichi no sekisuru tabi ni ware kaku sekisuru to
yamite aru
116 Mizutamari kure yuku sora to kurenai no himo o ukabenu aki-
same no nochi
117 Aki no sora kakuryō to shite kage mo nashi sametaru hito no kokoro ni mo nite
118 Mizutamari / kure yuku sora to kurenai no himo o ukabenu / aki-
same no nochi
118 Aki no sora kakuryō to shite kage mo nashi / amari ni sabishi / ka-
rasu nado tobe
118 Hyōzen to ie o idete wa hyōzen to kaeritaru koto sudeni itsutabi
118 Hyōzen to kuni o idete wa hyōzen to kaeritaru koto sudeni
itsutabi
119 Hyōzen to ie o idete wa / hyōzen to kaerishi kuse yo / tomo wa
waraedo
119 Kagiri naki kokorobososa yo! / me o tojite / mune no itami o ko-
raetearu hi!
119 Kaishin no isha no ososa yo! / me o tojite / mune no itami o jitto
koraearu hi
119 Kaishin no isha no ososa yo! / itami aru mune ni te o okite / ka-
taku me o tozu.

CHAPTER SIX. TAKAMURA KŌTARŌ

270 Tera ni ireba ishi no samusa yo haru no ame
270 Furusato wa kajiba ni nitaru nioi suru tabako o nomite hito no
     ayumeri
275 Dashinuke ni jiji to koe tate mata damaru kanashiki semi yo kago
     no naka no semi
275 Iki no mi no kitanaki tokoro doko ni mo naku kawakite karoki
     kono aburazemi
275 Te ni toreba tobō to mo sezu noro noro to tenohira kayuku aruki
     mawaru semi
276 Doko ni kuchi ga aru ka wakaranu kono semi ni nani o ataen
     atauru mono nashi

CHAPTER SEVEN. OGIWARA SEISENSUI

285 Furuike ya kawazu tobikomu mizu no oto
285 Kawazu tobikomu mizu no oto
286 Kawazu tobikomu mizu no oto
286 Kawazu tobikomu mizu no oto
287 Tanpopo tanpopo sunahama ni haru ga me o hiraku
288 Tanpopo ya haru o matazu ni me o hiraku
288 Kusa no ha o otsuru yori tobu hotaru kana
288 Hotaru hikarisometaru nihiki ni te ayumi
291 Araumi ya Sado ni yokotau amanogawa
291 Samidare o atsumete hayashi Mogami-gawa
291 Samidare o / atsumete / hayashi / Mogami-gawa
292 Bashō nowaki shite tarai ni ame o kiku yo kana
292 Uraraka ya / miwataseba hokake-bune / reirō to Fuji no mine
292 Uraraka ya Fuji reirō to hokake-bune
294 Mugi no ho no detarashii sora e ko o daku
299 Kangaegoto o shiteiru tanishi ga aruiteiru
300 Teppatsu no naka e mo arare
300 Waraya furu yuki tsumoru
302 Botan chitte uchikasanarinu nisanben
302 Ōkaze no ashita mo akashi tōgarashi
303 Shigururu ya keitō kuroku kiku shiroshi
303 Samidare o atsumete hayashi Mogami-gawa
303 Samidare o atsumete suzushi Mogami-gawa
304 No ni dekita mise no hi ga hi ga ko no ha
305 No ni hi o oite mise wa ko no ha
305 Ukisu no kuretaru aosa mo kuretaru
305 Ukisu no aosa mo waga yo ni oboreru
306 Hitohachi no kigiku
306 Hitohachi wa kigiku de aru
306 Hitohachi no kigiku ga aru
306 Hitohachi no kigiku de aru

Source Notes

This section is primarily for those who read Japanese and wish to consult the original sources. In the notes below, the numbers at the left refer to page and line in this book. The two following italicized words are the end of the quotation or the final words of the sentence or phrase that is being annotated. Translations of all quotations from Japanese sources are the author's.

INTRODUCTION

1.14. *any branch.*" Basil Hall Chamberlain, *The Classical Poetry of the Japanese* (London, 1880), p. 14.

6.27 *Latin verses.*" *Ibid.*, p. 15.

CHAPTER ONE. MASAOKA SHIKI

Volume and page references are to *Shiki zenshū*, 25 vols. (Tokyo: Kōdansha, 1975–78).

10.26. *great genius.* 11: 289.
10.30. *complete failure.*" 11: 290.
11.15. *at nightfall.* 4: 578–79.
11.24. *sinking sun.* 7: 45.
12.34. *briefest words.* 14: 248.
13.34. *beautiful clothes.*" 4: 577.
14.12. *or space.*" 4: 395.
14.18. *without fins.*" 4: 640.
14.21. *autumn gale.* 4: 524.
14.30. *the blizzard.* 1: 142.
15.15. *tengu mask.* 3: 458.
15.20. *them all.* 6: 428.
16.7. *mountain roses.* 6: 410.
16.10. *an ant.* 3: 365.
16.15. *to life.* 6: 409.
16.18. *my death.* 3: 243.

17.27. *he did.* 7: 144–45.
18.16. *the poem.*" 4: 577.
18.20. *humanity objectively.*" 4: 482.
19.26. *or two.* 7: 245.
20.10. *no more.* 14: 190.
20.19. *reader's emotion?*" 14: 190–91.
20.33. *more convincing.* 4: 458–59.
21.21. *the same.* 4: 449–50.
22.7. *poetry is.*" 7: 30.
22.15. *therefore uninspiring.* 7: 30.
22.26. *exhaust yourself.* 4: 392.
22.37 *less hackneyed.*" 4: 392.
23.15. *full bloom.* 5: 262.
23.20. *green wheat.*" 5: 262.

23.26. *more interesting.*" 5: 263.
24.4. *be hackneyed.*" 4: 405.
24.7. *all good.* 4: 351.
24.17. *American literature.*" 4: 406.
25.2. *entirely imaginative.*" 4: 405.
27.17. *glaring faults.* 12: 247–51.
28.14. *the light.*" 7: 65.
28.19. *and "humorous.*" 4: 345.
28.20. *of each.* 4: 415–38.
28.25. *something breathes.* 4: 428.
28. 29. *white horse.* 4: 430.
28.33. *to rise.* 4: 436.
29.14. *by little.* 5: 442.
29.19. *of grass?*" 12: 125.
29.25. *on loincloth.* 5: 392–406.
30.27. *close range.* 4: 373.
30.31. *withered fields.* 4: 378.
30.36. *of houses.* 4: 375.
31.5. *at Nasu.* 7: 28.
31.27. *one exception.)*" 4: 243.
32.7. *of Heaven.* 1: 346.
32.12. *bamboo grove.* 6: 139.
32.15. *the roadside.* 2: 368.
32.20. *spring green.* 6: 125.
33.33. *into bundles.* 5: 463.
34.3. *a soul.* 7: 160.
34.18. *summer day.* 7: 161.
34.27. *low cry.* 7: 56.
35.3. *low cry.* 7: 59.
35.19. *the clothesline.* 6: 266.
35.22. *a fly.* 3: 56.
35.27. *of trees.* 6: 326.
35.30. *flowing southwards.* 2: 206.
36.31. *gourd vines.* 3: 473.
39.1. *new form.* 14: 199–201.

39.5. *to come.* 14: 30.
39.8. *writers last.* 11: 18.
39.18. *premodern times.* 4: 165–66.
39.23. *haiku alone.* 4: 541.
40.7. *in 1892.*" 11: 215.
40.29. *inspire them.* 14: 12–14.
41.4. *matches feeling.*" 14: 134.
41.20. *something irregular.* 4: 441–
42, 539–41; 7: 14.
41.27. *cannot predict.*" 4: 441.
42.23. *over again.* 6: 221.
43.3. *beautify dung.*" 5: 392.
43.14. *autumn leaves.* 12: 122–23.
43.19. *of Haiku.*" 4: 383.
44.3. *the world.*" 7: 105.
44.11. *mountain rose.* 6: 119.
44.16. *ceaselessly falls.* 6: 280.
44.21. *my life.* 6: 411.
44.35. *the water.* 3: 148.
44.38. *a peony.* 2: 506.
45.3. *its close.* 2: 406.
46.5. *same theme.*" 11: 147.
47.28. *autumn flowers.* 11: 180.
49.11. *each day.* 12: 563–65.
49.17. *blossom viewing.*" 5: 461.
49.34. *a masterpiece.* 11: 213.
50.18. *and earth.*" 7: 68.
50.24. *are penniless.*" 12: 283.
50.29. *or impiety.*" 14: 92.
51.1. *is harmful.*" 4: 576.
51.9. *of haiku.*" 12: 379.
51.21. *his spirit.*" 14: 9.
51.28. *in life.*" 14: 76.
52.10. *instant death.* 12: 316.

CHAPTER TWO. YOSANO AKIKO

References are to *Teihon Yosano Akiko zenshū*, 20 vols. (Tokyo: Kōdansha, 1979–81), if no title is cited.

53.5. *poetic reform.*" 12: 476.
55.10. *a lyric.* 13: 39.
56.2. *termed lyrics.*" "Yosa Buson," in Yamamoto Sansei, ed., *Haiku kōza* (Tokyo, 1932), 5: 151.
56.15. *totally mistaken.*" Ibid., p. 152.
56.21. *be painted.* 17: 385.

56.22. *the artist.* 17: 387.
56.24. *the self.* 17: 386.
56.31. *an image.* 19: 147.
57.22. *of nature.* 13: 275–76.
57.27. *kabuki play.* 19: 147.
57.35. *my jikkan.*" 13: 7.
58.1. *younger days.* 13: 256–57.
58.8. *each poem.*" 13: 122.

58.14. *actually possess.*" 13: 21.
58.22. *specific occasion.*" 13: 398.
58.29. *extraordinary excitement.*"
    20: 300.
59.27. *7–7 pattern.*" 13: 82.
60.10. *and beautiful.*" 13: 10.
60.23. *of love.*" 13: 17.
61.3 *in Europe.*" 16: 146–47.
61.34. *human life.* 20: 37.
62.15. *specific occasion.*" 18: 245.
62.30. *experience love.* 19: 17–18.
63.8. *of love.*" 13: 258.
63.15. *it is!* 1: 12.
63.20. *magnolia blossom.* 1: 10.
63.25. *am I.* 1: 38.
64.20. *inner wishes.* 13: 9.
64.24. *of vision.* 13: 273–74.
64.29. *new life.*" 13: 273.
64.32. *a "romantic.*" 13: 275.
66.5. *hopelessly entangled.* 1: 152.
66.10. *him more?* 1: 18.
66.15. *black butterfly.* 1: 21.
66.28. *younger days),* 13: 37.
67.27. *emerged spontaneously.* 13:
    39; 20: 300.
67.32. *in town.* "Yosa Buson," p.
    152.
68.6. *be stimulated.*" 20: 300.
68.19. *a tanka.* 13: 42.
69.5. *key word.* 13: 40–41.
69.10. *my consciousness.*" 13: 24.
69.21. *for money.* 13: 45.
69.27. *an operation.* 13: 24.
70.10. *write poetry.* 13: 50.
70.19. *bud swell.*" 13. 253.
70.23. *the need.*" 13: 254.
71.7. *poet's powerlessness.* 18:
    249–52.
71.13. *an emotion.*" 18: 244.
71.33. *tanka form.* 13: 28.
72.10. *was black.* 20: 301.
72.14. *morning sun.*" 20: 302.
72.18. *verse writing.* 20: 311.
72.29. *of contrast.* 11: 405–6.
73.15. *7–5 rhythm.* 16: 148–49.
74.7. *good books.* 13. 102–18.
74.16. *the daylight.* 13: 102.
74.31. *or modern.*" 13: 109.

75.8. *it fresh.*" 13: 111.
75.17. *emotional capacity.* 13: 117.
76.10. *my breast.*" 14: 363.
76.18. *writing poetry.* 12: 473.
76.25. *to say.* 12: 472.
77.3. *be invented.*" 18: 247.
77.6. *this regard.* 12: 473.
77.8. *Modern Poems.* 4: 87.
77.17. *in admiration.* 18: 56.
77.27. *and dislikes.*" 18: 58.
77.34. *"beauty"* (bi). 13: 46–47.
78.3. *largely immature,* 13: 37–38.
78.13. *not lonely?* 1: 6.
78.18. *spring night.* 1: 7.
78.23. *spring evening.* 1: 38.
79.20. *in verse.*" 13: 83.
80.14. *each poet.*" 13: 75.
80.21. *modern men.*" 13: 420.
80.33. *my reveries.* 13: 402.
80.38. *sun subside.* 13: 405.
81.5. *crimson butterfly.* 13: 411.
81.32. *beautiful woman.* "Yosa
    Buson," pp. 175–76.
82.9 *first love.*" 13: 317.
82.27. *great statue.*" 17: 389.
83.4. *popular song.*" 13: 57.
83.15. *17-syllable form;* 18: 221.
83.29. *tanka rhythm.*" 13: 30.
84.3. *a spool.*" 13: 30.
84.6. *poet's emotion.* 18: 221.
84.15. *the wind.* 18: 221.
84.22. *the sky.* 13: 260.
84.35. *one breath.* 9: 294.
85.9. *come by.* 16: 151.
85.24. *human life.* 14: 362.
86.3. *tea bowl.* 13: 266.
86.8. *as shi.* 13: 266–67, 391–92.
86.16. *31 syllables.*" 20: 308.
86.21. *he used.* 20: 307.
86.22. *free-style haiku.* 13: 44.
86.25. *the originals.* 13: 64.
86.35. *outdated diction.* 13:
    267–68.
87.2. *contemporary age.* 13:
    268–69.
87.28. *symbolic art.*" 17: 484.
88.2. *author's emotion.* 13: 276–77.
88.26. *of age.* 13: 277.

89.7. *my heart.* 13: 278.
89.13. *symbolic poetry.* 13: 279.
89.20. *the universal."* 13: 279.
90.7. *slide away.* 13: 280.
90.17. *a bat.* 13: 281.
90.22. *to time."* 13: 281.
90.35. *symbolist poem.* 13: 283–84.
91.17. *is valuable."* 13: 282.
91.34. *the arts.* 13: 49.
92.6. *writing poetry.* 18: 452.
92.11. *and loneliness.* 18: 453.

92.15. *in art."* 14: 438.
92.32. *sell flowers."* 17: 379.
93.11. *humanistic education.* 17: 375–84.
93.23. *of creation.* 17: 367–68.
93.26. *highest floor."* 20: 302.
93.32. *of gold.* 4: 171.
94.2. *someone else.* 13: 52–53.
94.9. *small self."* 17: 386.
94.20. *the future.* 17: 420.
94.33. *and develops."* 17: 391.

CHAPTER THREE. ISHIKAWA TAKUBOKU

The collection of Takuboku's works referred to below is *Ishikawa Takuboku zenshū,* 8 vols. (Tokyo: Chikuma Shobō, 1978–80).

97.8. *fleeting vision.* 2: 12–13.
97.28. *the universe."* 6: 358.
98.5. *heart's desire.* 1: 142.
98.10. *not where.* 1: 142.
98.15. *sleeping child!* 1: 311.
100.26. *a story.* 5: 143.
101.3. *his own.* 4: 130.
101.21. *something fly!* 1: 42.
101.24. *a crab.* 1: 7.
101.27. *my hands.* 1: 19.
102.19. *starving friends!* 2: 461.
104.21. *his life."* 4: 296.
105.8. *or falsehood.* 4: 217.
105.20. *preconceived purpose.* 4: 218.
105.24. *the ground?"* 4: 218.
106.16. *getting better.* 6: 218.
107.3. *its author."* 7: 323.
107.11. *to masturbation.* 4: 253.
107.24. *transfixed objects.* 4: 219–20.
108.9. *conscious life).* 7: 293.
109.2. *V Narod!"* 2: 416.
109.23. *mind today.* 1: 96.
109.26. *of revolution.* 1: 97.
109.29. *of late.* 1: 97.
110.28. *write tanka."* 7: 323.
110.34. *tanka form."* 4: 214.
110.36. *sad toys."* 4: 300.
111.10. *autumn gust!* 1: 79.
111.13. *come home.* 1: 101.
111.16. *a dog.* 1: 103.

113.5. *prose fiction."* 5: 272.
113.7. *ripped open."* 5: 273.
113.31. *red ink."* 2: 171.
114.13. *a tanka:* 6: 189.
114.16. *mind is!* 1: 87.
114.29. *other shi."* 5: 324.
114.37. *120 tanka.* 5: 287.
115.8. *wrote them."* 5: 287.
115.15. *three steps.* 1: 234.
115.20. *times already.* 1: 234.
115.25. *in bed.* 1: 233.
116.27. *good, however.* 5: 323.
116.34. *autumn rainfall.* 1: 246.
117.5. *awakened man.* 1: 246.
118.12. *autumn rainfall.* 1: 39.
118.36. *times already.* 1: 152.
119.3. *of mine!* 1: 8.
119.23. *my chest.* 1: 205–6.
119.26. *my chest.* 1: 295.
119.29. *my eyes.* 1: 93.
121.8. *and true.* 6: 358.
121.31. *the heart,"* 7: 247.
121.33. *truly thought."* 7: 219.
122.6. *been falsified."* 5: 300.
122.12. *to fall.* 1: 229.
122.17. *completely gone.* 1: 151.
122.31. *in vigor."* 5: 299.
122.37. *I love. Myōjō,* July 1908, p. 53.
123.5. *of mine. Ibid.,* p. 52.
123.17. *penetrating jikkan."* 4: 298.
123.36. *of struggle."* 5: 16.

124.11. *nation's women.* 2: 418.
124.27. *heart aches.* 1: 24.
124.30. *autumn rain.* 1: 24.
125.25. *his own."* 5: 195.
126.7. *deep sorrow.* 2: 416–17.
127.3. *a poet."* 4: 113.
127.17. *human life?* 4: 231.
128.16. *modern man."* 7: 224.
128.22. *the mind?* 4: 287.
128.34. *31 syllables."* 4: 288.
129.7. *rhythmical complexity."* 4: 288.

130.23. *my hometown.* 1: 97.
130.26. *and yet—* 1: 94.
133.1. *of cowardice."* 4: 215.
134.5. *morning, too.* 1: 87.
134.28. *to God,"* 6: 358.
134.29. *of mankind."* 5: 68, 99; 6: 358.
135.12. *a game.* 7: 232.
135.32. *tiny bit?* 4: 294–95.
136.5. *a cigarette,"* 7: 234.
136.10. *I think."* 7: 297.
136.31. *than crying."* 2: 171.

CHAPTER FOUR. HAGIWARA SAKUTARŌ

The latest edition of Sakutarō's collected works, *Hagiwara Sakutarō zen shū,* 15 vols. (Tokyo: Chikuma Shobō, 1975–78), is the text referred to below.

139.12. *aristocratic (antidemocratic).* 14: 127–28.
139.33. *the outset."* 14: 76.
140.1. *the future.* 9: 208.
140.24. *exasperating place.* 1: 43–44.
142.34. *their longing."* 6: 36.
143.13. *beside it.* 6: 36.
143.22. *certain being."* 5: 162.
143.32. *of moths!* 1: 144.
144.14. *all creatures."* 11: 198.
144.21. *or reptiles."* 5: 164.
145.20. *my reach.* 1: 191–92.
146.8. *creaking wagon.* 1: 37.
146.21. *elegant appetite.* 1: 189–90.
147.10. *Western civilization.* 5: 288–91.
147.27. *not photography."* 5: 177.
148.2. *in Germany.* 10: 26–28.
148.37. *my rage.* 2: 113–14.
150.5. *conscious life.* 5: 137.
150.25. *of solitude.* 2: 126.
151.3. *creative mind.* 12: 412–14.
151.15. *an instant,"* 12: 412.
151.17. *the mind."* 11: 248.
151.18. *divine inspiration";* 11: 248.
151.19. *physiological anomaly."* 12: 58.

151.32. *too much!* 12: 5.
152.15. *artificial means."* 9: 191.
152.18. *subjective Ideas."* 14: 73.
152.24. *her associates.* 6: 380.
153.2. *called poetry."* 5: 143.
153.14. *artistic expression.* 6: 112–14.
153.29. *prosaic description."* 9: 363.
153.35. *aesthetic instinct."* 1: 230.
154.7. *your ear."* 14: 67.
154.9. *connotative function."* 14: 68.
154.23. *Shimazaki Tōson.* 11: 155–60.
154.30. *my life."* 9: 220.
155.26. *muddy cat.* 2: 78–79.
155.35. *instinctive fear.* 9: 225.
156.29. *the poem."* 14: 88.
156.30. *desolate graveyard."* 14: 88.
157.25. *fluorescent light.* 12: 11.
158.9. *moonlit night.* 12: 12.
158.42. *moonlit night.* 1: 341–42.
159.32. *moonlit night.* 1: 341–42.
160.23. *my part.* 13: 168.
161.6. *has written."* 10: 280.
161.13. *of gunshots.* 10: 413.
161.15. *"profound" ones.* 10: 280.
162.19. *a stream.* 10: 279.
162.36. *was lacking.* 10: 279.
163.17. *and time."* 7: 66.

164.9. *never seen.* 7: 41.
164.36. *photographic skill."* 7: 422.
165.14. *never seen."* 7: 186.
165.24. *Gessō's interpretation.* 10: 282.
166.26. *not own."* 5: 110.
167.30. *verbal nuances.* 6: 328–43.
168.8. *the term."* 6: 332.
168.14. *from rhythm."* 6: 370.
168.34. *aural quality.* 6: 377–78.
169.12. *same function."* 6: 336.
170.4. *so on)."* 10: 59.
170.33. *realism differ."* 6: 146.
171.31. *the haiku.* 6: 377.
172.7. *and dull."* 6: 164.
172.12. *approaches verse."* 6: 165.
172.27. *contemporary Japan."* 7: 287.
172.36. *express them."* 6: 248.
173.15. *today's Japan."* 6: 475.
173.37. *bore readers.* 9: 85.
174.20. *modern Japanese.* 6: 431–32.
174.33. *it aloud."* 6: 240–41.

175.1. *impressionistic prose":* 6: 265.
175.14. *rhythmical beauty,"* 6: 266.
175.23. *with words."* 1: 242.
176.8. *dark-skinned girl.* 2: 73–74.
176.13. *automatically unwinding."* 14: 91.
177.17. *wild roses.* 8: 19–20.
178.40. *Too-Ru-Mour Too-Ru-Mour.* 1: 164–66.
179.9. *Too-Te-Cūr Too-Ru-Mour.* 15: 278.
179.19. *shameful retreat."* 10: 38.
180.2. *my time!* 10: 38.
180.10. *consoling hand,* 1: 13.
180.25. *are synonymous."* 10: 52.
180.34. *new one.* 7: 250.
181.4. *by businessmen."* 10: 53.
181.10. *vice versa."* 10: 66.
181.16. *is science."* 10: 128.
181.19. *precedes thinking."* 10: 101.
181.29. *-novelist, too."* 10: 213.
182.19. *the public."* 10: 228.
183.2. *select readers."* 5: 123.

CHAPTER FIVE. MIYAZAWA KENJI

Kōhon Miyazawa Kenji zenshū, 14 vols. (Tokyo: Chikuma Shobō, 1973–77), is the edition used here. Volume 12 is divided into two parts; all the page numbers mentioned below refer to Part 1.

185.32. *lamp vanishes).* 2: 5.
186.20. *as before.* 9: 142.
187.23. *imagery sketches.* 2: 5–6.
187.34. *full-scale study."* 13: 220.
188.19. *everybody else.)* 2: 6.
189.19. *Cretaceous sandstone.* 2: 6–8.
189.33. *fourth dimension.* 2: 8.
189.39. *static art."* 12: 12.
190.3. *four-dimensional art."* 12: 15.
190.26. *I feel!"* 13: 230.
190.36. *flowering everywhere.* 2: 90.
191.4. *of strength."* 6: 370.
191.11. *of November."* 11: 7.
192.4. *architect, Surdatta.* 12: 304.
192.18. *misshapen utopia."* 11: 389.

192.32. *ultimate happiness.* 13: 453–54.
193.32. *will record.* 6: 144.
194.24. *white shape.* 3: 542.
196.35. *their luck?* 6: 160–61.
197.34. *the way.* 12: 9.
198.43. *and trousers.* 2: 211–12.
199.28. *the clouds"* 12: 13.
199.33. *or false."* 12: 13.
200.8. *and plains.* 11: 87.
200.35. *oozing up?* 12: 242.
201.15. *like this?* 6: 843; 12: 457–58.
201.28. *lying still?* 6: 320.
202.18. *pine grove* 12: 531.
202.37. *the field.* 5: 458.
203.12. *the field.* 5: 458.

203.20. *the field.* 6: 564.
204.25. *particular time."* 5: 455.
205.24. *a completion."* 12: 16.
206.3. *"beauty" perishes.* 12: 10–11.
206.31. *and productive)."* 14: 781.
207.13. *the world."* 12: 13.
207.23. *old-fashioned faith)* 2: 12.
208.10. *four-dimensional art."* 12: 15.
209.30. *to take.* Cf. 6: 207–12, 778–85.
210.8. *degraded itself."* 12: 10.
211.9. *of you.* 4: 267–68.
211.22. *one's labor."* 14: 781.
211.25. *deepen it."* 12: 10–11.
212.6. *that course."* 13: 453.
212.23. *the east.* 4: 52.
213.30. *a man.* 6: 353–54.
214.30. *love itself?* 4: 514–15.
215.16. *out automatically."* 14: 771.
216.10. *children's drama."* 13: 238.
216.28. *the wind.* 11: 304–5.
217.32. *small lily.* 1: 130.
217.36. *my wife. Ishikawa Takuboku zenshū,* 1: 23.

218.13. *my forehead.* 1: 155.
218.17. *my eyebrows. Ishikawa Takuboku zenshū,* 1: 41.
221.3. *sounds rough.* 14: 781.
221.6. *and "u."* 14: 781.
221.11. *or "h."* 13: 402.
221.16. *a windflower.* 8: 179.
221.29. *pet name."* 6: 583–84.
222.23. *white splashes.* 4: 19.
222.35. *faintly extend.* 5: 46.
223.24. *4. Rhyme.* 12: 617.
225.8. *my doubts.* 1: 190.
225.12. *the woods.* 11: 199.
225.20. *hope for."* 13: 402.
226.7. *conscious effort.* Cf. 14: 536.
226.10. *his notebooks,* 12: 72.
226.11. *is religion."* 13: 215.
226.32. *so on."* 3: 9.
227.38. *to pieces!"* 6: 569–70.
228.37. *that furrow.* 4: 166–67.
229.17. *a pheasant?* 4: 28.
229.37. *the clouds.* 12: 13.
230.3. *happy creation.* 12: 10.
230.7. *into pain."* 12: 19.

CHAPTER SIX. TAKAMURA KŌTARŌ

Volume and page numbers are those of *Takamura Kōtarō zenshū,* 18 vols. (Tokyo: Chikuma Shobō, 1957–58), unless otherwise noted.

232.22. *my Japanese.* 3: 342.
233.19. *for me.* 3: 298.
234.13. *and education.* 9: 137–38.
234.24. *artist's creation.* 5: 106.
235.3. *real person.* 5: 335.
235.9. *does itself."* 10: 198.
235.13. *and wasteful."* 5: 335.
235.28. *his model.* 10: 42.
236.10. *Japanese model.* 10: 245, 312.
236.30. *grotesque face.* 2: 163.
237.31. *safety valve."* 8: 90.
238.3. *produce sculpture."* Kitagawa Taichi, ed., *Kōtarō shiryō,* 3 (1972): 218.
238.22. *that emanation."* 8: 125.

238.26. *seeking release.* 8: 112.
238.29. *carries electricity.* 3: 373.
239.8. *of ways.* 8: 58.
239.17. *for life.* 8: 64.
240.3. *starting point.* 2: 270–71.
240.36. *celestial pole.* 2: 70.
242.23. *of mine.* 1: 253.
243.32. *of thing.* 2: 93–94.
245.29. *quiet love.* 2: 19–21.
248.13. *the source!* 3: 58–59.
249.33. *covering everything.* 3: 381–82.
251.24. *his mind.* 3: 92–94.
252.7. *the event.* In Kitagawa Taichi, ed., *Takamura Kōtarō zen shi kō* (Tokyo, 1967), p. 513.

252.11. *great earth.*" 8: 261.
252.13. *of dawn.*" 14: 328.
252.14. *an inevitability.*" 9: 318;
 11: 233.
252.20. *his product.*" 8: 6.
254.10. *of days.* 12: 165–81.
254.21. *August 23.* 12: 356–68.
255.6. *wretched idea?* 3: 351–52.
256.6. *an aim!* In Kitagawa, ed.,
 Takamura Kōtarō zen shi kō, p.
 272.
256.12. *accompanying letter.* 14:
 130.
256.25. *an aim!* 2: 174–75.
257.22. *my life.* 2: 373.
258.12. *him, too.* 2: 279–81.
260.38. *a sudden.* 4: 45.
261.28. *the soil!*" 5: 239.
261.34. *blue sky.* 1: 277.
262.8. *the spectators.*" 4: 20.
262.11. *read them.*" 8: 158.
262.23. *true life-force.*" 4: 118.
262.26. *nature's force.*" 3: 320.
262.30. *within himself.*" 8: 160.
262.37. *a personality.*" 8: 161.
263.8. *daily life.*" 5: 296.
263.16. *gloomy doubts.* 8: 280–81.
263.31. *of beauty.* 5: 208.
264.24. *Year's greeting.* 3:
 377–78.
264.28. *their world.*" *Kōtarō shiryō*,
 3: 402.
265.4. *Verlaine's diaries.* 8: 12–14.
265.15. *their work.* 8: 25–32.
265.32. *of all.* 9: 188–89.

265.34. *wintry beauty.*" 9: 189.
266.2. *skeleton's beauty.*" 1: 340.
266.8. *has come,*" 1: 231.
266.11. *getting sweaty.*" 9: 248.
266.38. *I will!*" 2: 54–55.
267.8. *and beautiful,*" *Kōtarō shiryō*,
 1 (1972): 136.
267.15. *the heart.*" 8: 134.
267.18. *in advance.*" 8: 6.
268.7. *the soul.*" 8: 310.
269.5. *to happen.*" 15: 33.
269.17. *bought it.*" 15: 117.
270.1. *toward tanka.* 8: 79.
270.16. *Spring rain* . . . 9: 82.
270.26. *smoking cigarettes.* 11: 70.
271.8. *tanka form,*" 8: 81.
271.11. *momentary feelings.*" 8:
 129.
271.26. *the past.*" 8: 78.
271.32. *speak up.* 3: 331.
272.16. *of feeling.* 1: 252.
273.8. *will find.* 2: 128–29.
274.6. *the artist.* 9: 84–85.
274.7. *its maker.* 8: 35.
275.12. *verse expressed.*" 9: 107.
276.5 *to give.* 11: 80–81.
276.26. *in heaven.* 2: 289–90.
279.17. *nonrealistic standpoint.*" 5:
 235.
279.30. *this world.* 2: 224–25.
280.6. *in words.*" 10: 185.
281.6. *before them.* 4: 235.
281.22. *one's environment.*" 6: 298.
282.12. *my countrymen.*" 3: 298.
282.23. *his boat.* 3: 309.

CHAPTER SEVEN. OGIWARA SEISENSUI

No comprehensive collection of Seisensui's works has been published. The place of publication of his works listed below is Tokyo, unless otherwise indicated.

286.25. *a haiku.* Shin haiku kenkyū
 (1926), pp. 332–33.
287.9. *and shape.* Haiku to seinen
 (1943), p. 128.
287.14. *a basket.* Haiku no te
 (1937), pp. 35–36.

287.24. *to moment.* Jiyūritsu haiku
 hyōshaku (1935), pp. 4–5.
288.5. *17-syllable form.*" Kono michi
 rokujū-nen (1978), p. 89.
288.26. *poetic form.* Jiyūritsu haiku
 hyōshaku, pp. 278–79.

289.22. *haiku nonetheless. Haiku suru kokoro* (1941), p. 166.

290.31. *even smaller. Shin haiku kenkyū*, pp. 78–79.

291.10. *the stars. Bashō kanshō* (1966), pp. 16–17.

291.26. *good poems," Haiku to seinen*, p. 102.

292.9. *analyze it. Shin haiku kenkyū*, p. 18.

292.30. *to set. Ibid.*, pp. 62–65.

293.5. *from overcooking.* Kitahara Hakushū, *Hakushū zenshū*, 18 vols. (Tokyo: Arususha, 1930), 16: 366–67.

293.16. *fresh life. Shin haiku kenkyū*, pp. 135–38.

293.28. *brought together. Ibid.*, p. 64.

293.29. *more spatial." Ibid.*, p. 132.

293.34. *of haiku." Ibid.*, p. 17.

293.37. *pointed top. Ibid.*, p. 47.

294.6. *of haiku." Ibid.*, p. 48.

294.40. *full-eared wheat. Haiku bungaku zenshū: Ogiwara Seisensui hen* (1938), pp. 143–45.

295.31. *we are. Haiku teishō* (1917), pp. 55–56.

296.12. *central Japan. Watakushi no rirekisho* (1957), pp. 80–81.

297.21. *other time. Shin haiku nyūmon*, 3d ed. (1979), pp. 45–46.

297.35. *single theme. Haiku no te*, pp. 116–20.

298.7. *into poems. Shin haiku nyūmon*, pp. 47–48.

298.19. *of nature." Ibid.*, p. 39.

298.36. *our hearts. Haiku no tsukurikata to ajiwaikata* (Fujisawa, 1955), pp. 15–16.

300.4. *free-style haiku. Haiku no te*, pp. 220–22.

300.20. *begging bowl. Ibid.*, pp. 233–34.

300.33. *into being. Jiyūritsu haiku hyōshaku*, pp. 277–78.

301.28. *befriend it. Shin haiku nyūmon*, pp. 69–70.

302.19. *own mind." Haiku to seinen*, p. 60.

302.24. *poet's self." Ibid.*, p. 89.

303.3. *is desolate." Shin haiku kenkyū*, p. 7.

303.12. *of glass." Ibid.*, p. 8.

304.1. *nature's life." Haiku no te*, pp. 310–11.

304.9. *verse writing. Ibid.*, pp. 294–95; *Haiku no tsukurikata to ajiwaikata*, p. 113.

305.10. *the scene. Shin haiku kenkyū*, pp. 318–20.

305.33. *the second. Ibid.*, pp. 270–71.

307.2. *emphasizing perception." Ibid.*, p. 326.

307.21. *great favorites. Ibid.*, pp. 320–34.

308.20. *one's life. Haiku suru kokoro*, p. 9.

308.26. *of strength." Haiku teishō*, p. 327.

309.4. *nature's force. Haiku no te*, pp. 131–32.

309.25. *of life." Haiku bungaku zenshū*, p. 244.

310.8. *Seisensui's words. Shin haiku teishō* (1922), pp. 223–24.

310.23. *of dawn. Haiku to seinen*, pp. 48–49.

310.30. *in it. Shin haiku kenkyū*, p. 89.

311.18. *this life-force." Bashō kanshō*, p. 237.

311.27. *in nature." "The Haiku, or the Japanese Poetry in Seventeen Syllables," Cultural Nippon*, 6, no. 2 (1938), p. 76.

311.32. *three matchsticks. Haiku to seinen*, p. 22.

311.34. *few branches. Oku no hosomichi no kokoro* (1956), p. 110.

312.13. *extremely simple. Haiku suru kokoro*, p. 9.

312.33. *harmonious simplicity.*"
"The Haiku," p. 78.
313.21. *such simplification. Jiyūritsu
haiku hyōshaku*, pp. 282–83.
313.31. *other people." Haiku to
seinen*, p. 98.
314.1. *the product." Haiku teishō*, p.
260.
314.3. *haiku themselves. Haiku no
te*, p. 4.
314.11. *a work." Haiku teishō*, p.
260.
314.27. *to follow. Haiku suru kokoro*, pp. 254–60.
314.30. *of art. Shin haiku teishō*, p.
311.
315.30. *meaning instantly." Tanshi
nyūmon* (1973), p. 111.
317.8. *a metaphor. Ibid.*, pp. 116–
20.
318.12. *one breath. Shin haiku nyūmon*, p. 91.
318.18. *seven syllables. Jiyūritsu
haiku hyōshaku*, pp. 281–82.
318.19. *is rare," Ibid.*, p. 282.
318.23. *look crippled." Ibid.*, p. 283.
319.26. *are haiku.* These examples are cited in Ueda Toshi, *Jiyūritsu haiku bungakushi* (Tokyo,
1975), p. 316.
320.29. *haiku rhythm." Shin haiku
nyūmon*, p. 102.
320.31. *of nature." Haiku no te*, p.
34.
321.18. *and "explanatory." Shin
haiku nyūmon*, pp. 108–11.
321.21. *two lines; Shin haiku teishō*,
p. 124.
321.31. *of haiku. Tanshi nyūmon*,
pp. 31–32.
322.10. *of light." Shin haiku teishō*,
p. 123.

322.14. *haiku collection. Ibid.*, p.
134.
322.25. *temporal rhythm." Ibid.*, p.
137.
322.33. *becomes bare. Tanshi
nyūmon*, pp. 61–63.
324.8. *and earth." Shin haiku
nyūmon*, p. 117.
325.6. *the triangle. Ibid.*, pp. 117–
19.
325.16. *a rainshower. Ibid.*, pp.
123–24.
325.22. *of meaning." Shin haiku
teishō*, p. 125.
326.5. *and natural." Haiku to
seinen*, p. 125.
327.5. *the scene. Haiku no te*, pp.
246–50.
327.12. *the west. Ibid.*, pp. 155–
56; *Shin haiku nyūmon*, p. 126.
328.15. *the wind. Haiku no te*, p.
151.
329.34. *practical purpose." Haiku
no tsukurikata to ajiwaikata*, p. 1.
330.6. *the train." Haiku no te*, p. xi.
330.14. *to create. Ibid.*, pp. 7–8.
330.25. *himself thoroughly." Ibid.*,
pp. 276–77.
331.4. *called resonance." Haiku no
tsukurikata to ajiwaikata*, p. 2.
331.22. *social class." Shin haiku
teishō*, p. 254.
332.9. *route: haiku. Haiku no tsukurikata to ajiwaikata*, pp. 3–4.
332.34. *everyday life." Oku no hosomichi no kokoro*, p. 103.
333.19. *alone satisfied Haiku to
seinen*, p. 228.
333.35. *bed too* Itō Shinkichi et
al., eds., "Ogiwara Seisensui,"
in *Nihon no shiika*, 19: 322.

Unless otherwise noted, volume and page numbers refer to *Takahashi Shinkichi zenshū*, 4 vols. (Tokyo: Seidosha, 1982), although it collects only a portion of the poet's voluminous writings. All of his books cited below were published in Tokyo.

336.17. *out cold. Zen ni sanzu* (1980), p. 84.
336.24. *same page.* 4: 188.
337.13. *destroying all."* 4: 58.
338.4. *be asserted?* 1: 50.
341.7. *of Zen."* 4: 197, 204; *Zen ni asobu* (1977), p. 66; *Zen ni sanzu*, p. 85.
341.15. *Buddhist dada." Dada to zen* (1971), p. 130.
341.20. *dadaist phase. Zen ni sanzu*, pp. 83–88.
342.20. *of Zen." Dada to zen*, p. 291.
342.28. *deny poetry." Zen ni asobu*, p. 185.
343.3. *roundabout way."* 3: 393.
343.7. *not truth."* 4: 224.
343.17. *do so." Dada to zen*, p. 125.
343.33. *do so. Ibid.*, p. 126.
344.12. *helps students. Zen ni asobu*, p. 184.
345.1. *ever died.* 1: 423.
345.37. *nonself" exists.* 2: 553.
346.32. *history pass* 1: 612–13.
347.12. died young. *Nihon shijin zenshū*, 34 vols. (Tokyo; Shinchōsha, 1966–69), 26: 221.
348.3. *not exist."* 3: 179.
348.23. *hair's breadth.* 1: 370–71.
348.26. *at peace." Zen ni asobu*, p. 61.
349.10. *a touch.* 1: 387.
349.17. *behind matter."* 3: 342.
350.4. *are footnotes.* 1: 340.
350.11. *general public. Dada to zen*, pp. 129–35.
350.14. *writing poetry.* 4: 508–11.
350.17. *a fire. Zen ni asobu*, pp. 190–92.
351.8. *is valid.* 3: 348–49.

351.34. *man-made environment." Zen to bungaku* (1970), p. 317.
352.7. *poetry germinates." Ibid.*, p. 317.
352.17. *to music. Ibid.*, p. 316.
352.36. *natural growth." Ibid.*, p. 317.
353.2. *of delivery." Ibid.*, p. 316.
353.7. *'draft' method." Ibid.*, p. 317.
353.18. *artless beauty." Zen ni sanzu*, p. 151.
354.17. *and bent. Ibid.*, pp. 155–56.
354.33. *eternal life." Ibid.*, p. 158.
355.2. *much contemplation." Ibid.*, p. 158.
355.34. *fly's shadow." Ibid.*, p. 157.
356.10. *mathematically finite." Ibid.*, p. 159.
356.37. *and bent. Nihon shijin zenshū*, 26: 165.
357.25. *the poem." Zen to bungaku*, p. 350.
357.29. *million years.* 1: 412.
358.4. Hagiwara Sakutarō. *Zen to bungaku*, p. 351.
358.11. *billion years." Ibid.*, p. 350.
358.36. *at midpoint.* 3: 330.
359.3. *the present." Zen ni asobu*, p. 185.
359.14. *'thoughts,' either."* 3: 349.
360.5. *my job." Shi to zen* (1969), p. 233.
360.26. *gentle heart. Hagiwara Sakutarō zenshū*, 1: 198.
361.8. *of emotion.* 4: 509–10.
361.29. *basically wrong." Zen to bungaku*, pp. 116–17.
361.37. *the Himalayas." Dada to zen*, p. 150.
362.9. *primitive country."* 3: 371.

362.18. *the nose.* 3: 379.
362.24. *later years,* 3: 375–76.
362.29. *outer landscape."* 3: 401.
362.33. *to Buddhism.* 3: 393.
363.6. *Sung times.* 4: 435.
363.13. *my opinion."* 4: 427–28.
363.22. *and unartistic,"* Shi to zen, p. 97.
364.3. *his poetry."* Zen to bungaku, p. 168.
364.17. *a Fool."* Dada to zen, p. 269; Zen ni asobu, pp. 110–15.
364.27. *any value."* 4: 438.
365.5. *to say."* In Ebara Taizō, ed., Bashō bunshū (Tokyo, 1955), p. 251.
365.17. *and Hakuin."* 3: 82.
365.28. *we are.* Zen ni sanzu, pp. 94–97.
366.5. *a Buddhist's.* Shi to zen, p. 17.
366.10. *contracting syphilis."* 3: 218.
366.14. *of Zen."* Dada to zen, p. 47.
366.22. *Zen books."* 3: 79.
367.33. *Zen monks,"* Dada to zen, p. 5.
368.14. *write one."* Shi to zen, p. 95.

368.26. *blue sparrow.* Dada to zen, p. 103.
369.7. *of them."* Shi to zen, p. 101.
369.11. *the future."* 3: 76–77.
369.13. *the past."* Dada to zen, p. 130.
370.3. *in delirium.* Shi to zen, pp. 104–5.
370.18. *I think."* Ibid., pp. 105–6.
371.23. *by sunset?* 1: 309–10.
371.27. *in expression."* Zen ni sanzu, p. 142.
372.13. *or form.* 1: 383.
372.30. *at most."* 4: 147.
373.8. *are short."* Zen ni sanzu, p. 151.
373.16. *every day.* 1: 378.
373.19. *and rivers.* 1: 385.
375.28. *and father-killers.* Dada to zen, p. 150.
376.13. *no use.* Gendai Nihon shijin zenshū, 16 vols. (Tokyo: Sōgensha, 1954–55), 12: 132.
376.37. *a retreat.* Takahashi Shinkichi no zen no shi to essē (1973), p. 11.
377.14. *my being."* 4: 300.
377.23. *study Buddhism."* 4: 359.
378.33. *to carve.* 1: 430.

Checklist of Poems Translated into English

In the following list, translations are arranged chronologically by year for each poet. When more than one set of translations has been published in a year, complete books, if any, are given first, followed by shi, haiku, and tanka in that order. Haiku and tanka have no titles, so only the number of poems translated is given in each entry. If the same translation has appeared more than once, the publication most likely to be available is listed.

MASAOKA SHIKI

71 haiku. Tr. Asatarō Miyamori. In his *Anthology of Haiku, Ancient and Modern*. Tokyo, 1932.

13 haiku. Tr. Harold Gould Henderson. In his *The Bamboo Broom*. Boston, 1934.

3 tanka. Tr. Asatarō Miyamori. In his *Masterpieces of Japanese Poetry, Ancient and Modern*. Tokyo, 1936.

16 haiku. Tr. Asatarō Miyamori. In his *Haiku Poems, Ancient and Modern*. Tokyo, 1940.

12 haiku. Tr. Shōson (Kenneth Yasuda). In his *A Pepper Pod*. New York, 1947.

2 haiku. Tr. Lois J. Erickson. In her *Songs from the Land of Dawn*. New York, 1949.

385 haiku. Tr. R. H. Blyth. In his *Haiku*. 4 vols. Tokyo, 1952.

3 tanka. Tr. Kenneth Yasuda. In his *Lacquer Box*. Tokyo, 1952.

15 haiku. Tr. Peter Beilenson. In his *Japanese Haiku*. Mt. Vernon, N.Y., 1955.

25 haiku and 9 tanka. Tr. V. H. Viglielmo. In Yoshie Okazaki, *Japanese Literature in the Meiji Era*. Tokyo, 1955.

5 haiku. Tr. Kenneth Yasuda. In his *The Japanese Haiku*. Rutland, Vt., 1957.

9 tanka. Tr. H. H. Honda. In *The Reeds*, 3 (1957).

44 haiku. Tr. Harold G. Henderson. In his *An Introduction to Haiku*. Garden City, N.Y., 1958.

41 haiku. Tr. The Translation Committee of Japan Society for the Promotion of Scientific Research. In its *Haikai and Haiku*. Tokyo, 1958.

32 haiku. Tr. Peter Beilenson. In his *The Four Seasons*. Mt. Vernon, N.Y., 1958.

42 tanka. Tr. H. H. Honda. In *The Reeds*, 4 (1958).

24 haiku. Tr. anonymously. In *Cherry Blossoms*. Mt. Vernon, N.Y., 1960.

17 haiku. Tr. Harold Stewart. In his *A Net of Fireflies*. Tokyo, 1960.

17 haiku. Tr. Peter Beilenson and Harry Behn. In their *Haiku Harvest*. Mt. Vernon, N.Y., 1962.

69 haiku. Tr. R. H. Blyth. In his *A History of Haiku*, Vol. 2. Tokyo, 1964.

9 haiku. Tr. Harry Behn. In his *Cricket Songs*. New York, 1964.

10 haiku and 2 tanka. Tr. Geoffrey Bownas and Anthony Thwaite. In their *The Penguin Book of Japanese Verse*. Baltimore, 1964.

2 haiku. Tr. Unity Evans. In Roger Bersihand, *Japanese Literature*. New York, 1965.

35 haiku. Tr. Harold Stewart. In his *A Chime of Windbells*. Rutland, Vt., 1969.

14 haiku. Tr. Earl Miner. In his *Japanese Poetic Diaries*. Berkeley, Calif., 1969.

2 haiku. Tr. Harold P. Wright. In his "The Poetry of Japan." *Asia*, no. 16 (Autumn 1969).

4 haiku and 4 tanka. Tr. Donald Keene. In his *Landscapes and Portraits*. Tokyo, 1971.

13 tanka. Tr. Robert H. Brower. In his "Masaoka Shiki and Tanka Reform." Donald H. Shively, ed., *Tradition and Modernization in Japanese Culture*. Princeton, 1971.

309 haiku. Tr. Harold J. Isaacson. In his *Peonies Kana: Haiku by the Upasaka Shiki*. New York, 1972.

14 haiku. Tr. William Howard Cohen. In his *To Walk in Seasons*. Rutland, Vt., 1972.

7 haiku. Tr. Daniel C. Buchanan. In his *One Hundred Famous Haiku*. Tokyo, 1973.

8 haiku. Tr. Kenneth Rexroth. In his *One Hundred More Poems from the Japanese*. New York, 1974.

43 haiku and 34 tanka. Tr. Janine Beichman. In her "Masaoka Shiki: His Life and Works." Ph.D. dissertation, Columbia University, 1974.

8 haiku. Tr. Takamasa Sasaki. In *Eigo seinen*, 120, no. 10 (1975).

5 haiku and 10 tanka. Tr. Janine Beichman-Yamamoto. In her "Masaoka Shiki's *A Drop of Ink*." *Monumenta Nipponica*, 30, no. 3 (Autumn 1975).

20 haiku. Tr. Makoto Ueda. In his *Modern Japanese Haiku: An Anthology*. Toronto, 1976.

18 haiku. Tr. Lucien Stryk and Takashi Ikemoto. In their *The Penguin Book of Zen Poetry*. Chicago, 1977.

6 haiku. Tr. Hiag Akmakjian. In his *Snow Falling from a Bamboo Leaf*. Santa Barbara, Calif., 1979.

5 haiku. Tr. Hiroaki Sato. In his "Translating Hokku and Haiku." *Frogpond*, 4, no. 2 (1981).

39 haiku and 15 tanka. Tr. Burton Watson. In Hiroaki Sato and Burton

Watson, eds., *From the Country of Eight Islands*. Garden City, N.Y.,
1981.

YOSANO AKIKO

30 tanka. Tr. Glenn Hughes and Yōzan T. Iwasaki. In their *Three Women
Poets of Modern Japan*. Seattle, 1927.
122 tanka and "My Songs," "Mother's Soul," "Sunrise," "Willows," "Cool
Evening," "Man and Weeds," "One Night," "Song of an Autumn
Night," "My Guests," "A Man at the Back Door," "My Great Grand-
mother's Prayer Beads," "A Garment," "A Mouse," "Tracks in the
Mud," "The Mother-of-Pearl Shell." Tr. Shio Sakanishi. In her *Tangled Hair*. Boston, 1935.
16 tanka. Tr. Asatarō Miyamori. In his *Masterpieces of Japanese Poetry, Ancient and Modern*. Tokyo, 1936.
3 tanka. Tr. Asatarō Miyamori. In his *Anthology of Japanese Poems*. Tokyo,
1938.
"Heaven Forbid That You Shall Die!" Tr. Shigeshi Nishimura. In *The
Current of the World*, 28, no. 10 (1951).
"The Typhoon." Tr. Shigeshi Nishimura. In *The Current of the World*, 29,
no. 10 (1952).
3 tanka. Tr. Kenneth Yasuda. In his *Lacquer Box*. Tokyo, 1952.
"The Herd of Burden Beasts." Tr. Shigeshi Nishimura. In *The Current
of the World*, 30, no. 2 (1953).
11 tanka. Tr. V. H. Viglielmo. In Yoshie Okazaki, *Japanese Literature in
the Meiji Era*. Tokyo, 1955.
2 tanka. Tr. Kenneth Rexroth. In *The Atlantic Monthly*, January 1955.
100 tanka. Tr. H. H. Honda. In his *The Poetry of Yosano Akiko*. Tokyo,
1957.
7 tanka. Tr. H. H. Honda. In *The Reeds*, 3 (1957).
"Please Do Not Die." Tr. Hisakazu Kaneko. In *Orient/West*, 9, no. 3
(1964).
4 tanka. Tr. Geoffrey Bownas and Anthony Thwaite. In their *The Penguin Book of Japanese Verse*. Baltimore, 1964.
2 tanka. Tr. Unity Evans. In Roger Bersihand, *Japanese Literature*. New
York, 1965.
"A Song of May." Tr. Hisakazu Kaneko. In *London Magazine*, 6, no. 9
(December 1966).
3 tanka. Tr. Armando Martins Janeira. In his *Japanese and Western Literature*. Rutland, Vt., 1970.
165 tanka. Tr. Sanford Goldstein and Seishi Shinoda. In their *Tangled
Hair*. Lafayette, Ind., 1971.
4 tanka. Tr. Mineyo Inai and Marie Philomène. In *Poetry Nippon*, no. 23
(1973).
10 tanka and "You Must Not Die," "Mouse," "Killifish," "Labor Pains,"
"Being Unbearably Sad," "Hair," "Inn at Munich," "Self Declaration,"
"Winter Twilight," "Window," "The Sound of Autumn." Tr. Ikuko

Atsumi and Graeme Wilson. In *Japan Quarterly*, 21, no. 2 (April–June 1974).
16 tanka. Tr. Kenneth Rexroth. In his *One Hundred More Poems from the Japanese*. New York, 1974.
4 tanka. Tr. Mineyo Inai. In *Poetry Nippon*, no. 27 (1974).
4 tanka. Tr. Harumi Sugiyama. In Poetry Nippon, nos. 29 and 30 (1975).
11 tanka and "Labor Pains." Tr. Kenneth Rexroth and Ikuko Atsumi. In their *The Burning Heart*. New York, 1977.
"Never Let Them Kill You, Brother!," "On Love." Tr. James Kirkup. In A. R. Davis, ed., *Modern Japanese Poetry*. St. Lucia, Queensland, 1978).
39 tanka. Tr. Hiroaki Sato. In Hiroaki Sato and Burton Watson, eds., *From the Country of Eight Islands*. Garden City, N.Y., 1981.

ISHIKAWA TAKUBOKU

138 tanka and "Sing Then," "Why?," "My Sister-in-Law," "An Excuse," "Daphne," "Terror of Summer in the City," "To a Crab," "Wake Not," "A Willow Leaf," "A Fist," "Autumn Evening," "Images." Tr. Shio Sakanishi. In her *A Handful of Sand*. Boston, 1934.
13 tanka. Tr. Asatarō Miyamori. In his *Masterpieces of Japanese Poetry, Ancient and Modern*. Tokyo, 1936.
"On the Hill-Top." Tr. Shigeshi Nishimura. In *The Current of the World*, 15, no. 5 (1938).
"The White Bird and the Sea of Blood." Tr. Saburō Katayama. In *English Aoyama*. Tokyo, 1938.
2 tanka. Tr. Asatarō Miyamori. In his *Anthology of Japanese Poems*. Tokyo, 1938.
3 tanka. Tr. Kenneth Yasuda. In his *Lacquer Box*. Tokyo, 1952.
7 tanka. Tr. V. H. Viglielmo. In Yoshie Okazaki, *Japanese Literature in the Meiji Era*. Tokyo, 1955.
3 tanka. Tr. Donald Keene. In his *Modern Japanese Literature*. New York, 1956.
3 tanka. Tr. Kenneth Rexroth. In his *In Defense of the Earth*. New York, 1956.
"An Old Man," "A Clenched Fist," "Better Than Crying." Tr. Ichiro Kōno and Rikutaro Fukuda. In their *An Anthology of Modern Japanese Poetry*. Tokyo, 1957.
6 tanka. Tr. H. H. Honda. In *The Reeds*, 3 (1957).
100 tanka. Tr. H. H. Honda. In his *The Poetry of Ishikawa Takuboku*. Tokyo, 1959.
177 tanka and "To the Crab." Tr. Hiroshi Takamine. In his *A Sad Toy: Takuboku's Life and Poems*. Tokyo, 1962.
13 tanka and "After a Fruitless Argument," "Rather Than Cry." Tr. Geoffrey Bownas and Anthony Thwaite. In their *The Penguin Book of Japanese Verse*. Baltimore, 1964.

"Family." Tr. Harold P. Wright. In *Poetry Northwest*, 4, nos. 3 and 4 (Autumn–Winter 1963–64).

"Sick Face at the Base of the Earth." Tr. Geoffrey Bownas and Anthony Thwaite. In their *The Penguin Book of Japanese Verse*. Baltimore, 1964.

"Bamboo." Tr. Harold P. Wright. In *Western Humanities Review*, 19, no. 3 (Summer 1965).

"Grass Stem," "Night in the Tavern," "Solitude," "The White Moon," "A Sad Moon," "The Death of a Frog." Tr. Samuel Grolmes and Yumiko Tsumura. In *The East-West Review*, 2, no. 3 (Spring–Summer 1966).

"I Fire a Cannon," "The World of Fantasy Buddha Saw." Tr. Makoto Ueda. In *The East-West Review*, 2, no. 3 (Spring–Summer 1966).

"Night in Spring," "Suicide by Hanging in Heaven," "Winter," "Sadness of a Distant Landscape." Tr. Harold P. Wright. In *The East-West Review*, 2, no. 3 (Spring–Summer 1966).

"These Animals Are Dangerous." Tr. Graeme Wilson. In *Japan Quarterly*, 13, no. 4 (1966).

"Toad." Tr. Graeme Wilson. In *Japan Quarterly*, 13, no. 1 (1966).

"Goldfish," "Domestic Animals," "Seedling." Tr. Graeme Wilson. In *Japan Quarterly*, 14, no. 3 (1967).

"Person Who Digs the Ground," "Divine Wisdom," "Chair." Tr. Graeme Wilson. In *Japan Quarterly*, 14, no. 4 (1967).

"Barking at the Moon." Tr. Graeme Wilson. In *Encounter*, December 1968.

"Being Afraid of the Country," "Seed in the Palm," "Birds." Tr. Graeme Wilson. In *Japan Quarterly*, 15, no. 2 (1968).

"Dead Man in May." Tr. Graeme Wilson. In *Japan Quarterly*, 15, no. 3 (1968).

"Heavenly Suicide by Hanging," "Portrait of a Hand," "Hunting Fireflies." Tr. Graeme Wilson. In *Japan Quarterly*, 15, no. 4 (1968).

"White Night." Tr. Graeme Wilson. In *Encounter*, November 1968.

"Ai Ren," "Green Flute," "Duel," "In the Bar at Night," "Woman," "Rotten Clam," "To Dream of a Butterfly," "Portrait," "Winter," "Spring Night," "Dawn," "Bamboos," "Person Who Loves Love," "Harmful Animals," "White Moon," "Sad Moonlit Night," "Seaside Hotel," "Fieldmouse," "Death of an Alcoholic," "With a Gift," "Eggs," "Elegant Appetite," "Enchanted Graveyard," "Turtle," "Skyscape," "Face at the Bottom of the World," "Blue Flame," "New Road at Koide," "Moonlight and Jellyfish," "Swimmer," "Sea Shell," "Cafe of the Drunken Moon," "Still Life," "Polished Metal Hands," "Dwarf Landscape," "Late Autumn," "Night Train," "Death of a Frog," "Murder Case," "In the Mountains." Tr. Graeme Wilson. In his *Face at the Bottom of the World*. Rutland, Vt., 1969.

"Arm-chair," "Pine," "Double Feature," "At a Corner of the Barley Field." Tr. Graeme Wilson. In *Japan Quarterly*, 16, no. 4 (1969).

3 tanka. Tr. Unity Evans. In Roger Bersihand, *Japanese Literature*. N
York, 1965.

181 tanka. Tr. Carl Sesar. In his *Takuboku: Poems to Eat*. Tokyo, 1966.

2 tanka. Tr. Donald Keene. In his *Landscapes and Portraits*. Tokyo, 197

Sad Toys. Tr. Sanford Goldstein and Seishi Shinoda. West Lafayet
Ind., 1977.

3 tanka and "Fragments," "The Horrors of a Summer Street," "Do N
Get Up," "Fist," "Reading in the Afternoon." Tr. James Kirkup.
A. R. Davis, ed., *Modern Japanese Poetry*. St. Lucia, Queensland, 197

193 tanka and "A Woodpecker," "The Horror of a Town in Summer
"A Spring Twilight When Something Is About to Happen," "Dor
Wake Up!," "A Willow Leaf," "The Fist," "After Endless Discussions
"A Spoonful of Cocoa," "An Afternoon in My Study," "An Airplane
Tr. Yukihito Hijiya. In his *Ishikawa Takuboku*. Boston, 1979.

47 tanka. Tr. Hiroaki Sato. In Hiroaki Sato and Burton Watson, eds
From the Country of Eight Islands. Garden City, N.Y., 1981.

HAGIWARA SAKUTARŌ

Cat Town. Tr. George Saito. Tokyo, 1948.

"The Deathless Octopus," "The Clock in the Country," "The Sea." T
Junsaku Ozawa. In *Eigo kenkyū*, 39, no. 9 (1950).

"Night Train," "Cats," "Harmful Animals," "The Corpse of a Cat," "Th
New Road of Koide." Tr. Donald Keene. In his *Modern Japanese Liter
ature*. New York, 1956.

"Tortoise," "Song Without a Name," "Littoral Zone," "Death of a Frog,
"The White Moon," "A Dish of Skylarks." Tr. Satoru Sato and Con
stance Urdang. In *Poetry*, 88, no. 2 (May 1956).

"Late Autumn," "Night Train," "A Leisurely Indulgence," "Woman!,"
"Tortoise," "A Sick Face below the Surface of the Earth." Tr. Taka
michi Ninomiya and D. J. Enright. In their *The Poetry of Living Japan*.
London, 1957.

"An Octopus Which Did Not Die," "Is Thought Just a Pattern?," "At a
Post-Office Window," "A Journey," "The Sick Face in the Bowels of
the Earth." Tr. Ichiro Kōno and Rikutarō Fukuda. In their *An Anthol
ogy of Modern Japanese Poetry*. Tokyo, 1957.

"A Ballooner's Dream," "Black Bat," "I Dream of a Butterfly." Tr.
Makoto Ueda. In *Assay*, 17, no. 2 (Winter 1961).

"From the Inside Shell of a Scene," "The Feeling of Spring." Tr. Makoto
Ueda. In *The Sewanee Review*, 69, no. 2 (Spring 1961).

"The Path of Peach and Damson Blossoms." Tr. Makoto Ueda. In *Chi
cago Review*, 15, no. 3 (Winter–Spring 1962).

"Polished Metal Hands," "Moonlight and Jellyfish," "Melancholy Riverside," "The Essence of Spring," "Dawn." Tr. Makoto Ueda. In *Poetry
Northwest*, 3, no. 2 (Summer 1962).

"Cock." Tr. Makoto Ueda. In *The Beloit Poetry Journal*, 13, no. 2 (Winter
1962–63).

"Death," "Dangerous Walk." Tr. Harold P. Wright. In *Poetry Nippon*, nos. 5 and 6 (1969).

"Diseased Fish and Shellfish," "Penitentiary," "Terrible Mountain," "Dinner at the Empty House." Tr. Graeme Wilson. In *Japan Quarterly*, 16, no. 3 (1969).

"Heart," "The Soured Chrysanthemum," "The Voluptuous Soul," "A Dream," "A Farewell." Tr. Reiko Tsukimura. In *Literature East and West*, 13, nos. 3 and 4 (1969).

"Insects." Tr. James H. Sanford. In *Japan Quarterly*, 16, no. 3 (1969).

"Minimal Spring," "Grass Stem," "Flute." Tr. Graeme Wilson. In *Japan Quarterly*, 16, no. 2 (1969).

"The Ninth Small Poem," "Field Landscape," "Will with Teeth," "Nature Study," "Crime That I Committed." Tr. Graeme Wilson. In *Japan Quarterly*, 16, no. 1 (1969).

"Blue Snow," "Ancestors," "Disturbed Person," "To Drown in the Mountains." Tr. Graeme Wilson. In *The Malahat Review*, no. 14 (April 1970).

"Death of an Alcoholic." Tr. Harold P. Wright. In *Poetry Nippon*, nos. 9 and 10 (1970).

"Hand Turning Ghost." Tr. Graeme Wilson. In *Quadrant*, November–December, 1970.

"Home," "Barleys," "At Market." Tr. Graeme Wilson. In *Japan Quarterly*, 17, no. 2 (1970).

"Loneliness," "Toy Box—Evening," "Near Mount Futago," "Angler." Tr. Graeme Wilson. In *Japan Quarterly*, 17, no. 1 (1970).

"Toy Box—Morning," "The Third Patient," "Corpse and Bamboo," "Moonlit Night," "Ultramarine," "Toothache." Tr. Graeme Wilson. In *Japan Quarterly*, 17, no. 3 (1970).

"Water Rite," "Autumn Cricket," "Amakusa," "Ghosts," "Hirose River," "Mountain Top." Tr. Graeme Wilson. In *Japan Quarterly*, 17, no. 4 (1970).

"Zoo," "Shadow of My Former Self," "Hagitei Inn," "Early Summer." Tr. Graeme Wilson. In *Poetry*, 116, nos. 5 and 6 (August–September 1970).

"Bamboos." Tr. Ko Won. In *Comparative Literature Studies*, 8, no. 3 (September 1971).

"Blue Sky," "Suddenly," "Grass Nerve," "The Most Primitive Feeling," "Shining in the Sky," "Sea Spa in Late Autumn," "Face," "A Dish of Skylarks," "Senescence," "Shining Road of Disease." Tr. Graeme Wilson. In *Japan Quarterly*, 18, no. 4 (1971).

"Bottles." Tr. Graeme Wilson. In *Japan Quarterly*, 18, no. 2 (1971).

"Miracle," "Viewpoint," "Death Wish." Tr. Graeme Wilson. In *Japan Quarterly*, 18, no. 1 (1971).

"Autumn," "Cherry Blossoms," "Sunset," "Howling at the Moon," "Sparrows," "Idealism," "Small Town Geisha," "Shining Hand." Tr. Graeme Wilson. In *Japan Quarterly*, 19, no. 1 (1972).

"Group of Three Persons," "Village Where the Flute Is Playing," "Pine-field by the River Tone," "Garden of the Dreamt Empty House," "Bal-loonist's Dream," "Club Nogisaka," "Night," "Tiger," "Useless Book," "Home-Coming," "New Maebashi Railway Station." Tr. Graeme Wil-son. In *Japan Quarterly*, 19, no. 2 (1972).

"The Swimmer," "Death of a Frog," "You Frogs," "Wanting to Be Walk-ing among Crowds," "Buddha." Tr. Edith Marcombe Shiffert and Yūki Sawa. In their *Anthology of Modern Japanese Poetry*. Rutland, Vt., 1972.

"Under the Peach Blossoms." Tr. Hideo Yamaguchi. In *Kobe jogakuin daigaku ronshū*, 18, no. 3 (1972).

"White Cock," "Water Weed," "House," "On the Bridge at Maebashi," "Human Body." Tr. Graeme Wilson. In *Japan Quarterly*, 19, no. 3 (1972).

"Chrysanthemum Gone Sour," "Frog's Death," "The Reason the Person Inside Looks like a Deformed Invalid," "The Chair," "Spring Night," "The World of Bacteria," "The Swimmer," "Daybreak," "Sunny Spring," "Afraid of the Countryside." Tr. Hiroaki Sato. In his *Ten Jap-anese Poets*. Hanover, N.H., 1973.

"The Cockerel," "Lady of Raven-Plumage." Tr. Reiko Tsukimura. In *Journal of Comparative Literature*, 16 (1973).

"Cracksman." Tr. Graeme Wilson. In *Japan Quarterly*, 20, no. 3 (1973).

"In the Dreadfully Gloomy Woods," "Climbing a Mountain." Tr. Graeme Wilson. In *Japan Quarterly*, 20, no. 1 (1973).

"Small Boat," "Whose House." Tr. Graeme Wilson. In *Japan Quarterly*, 20, no. 4 (1973).

"Turtle." Tr. Jim Cogswell. In *Poetry Nippon*, no. 22 (1973).

"Under Green Shadow," "Mountain Pilgrims," "When I Awoke." Tr. Graeme Wilson. In *Japan Quarterly*, 20, no. 2 (1973).

"Blue Cat and Stone Bamboo," "Decomposing Body," "Dog." Tr. Graeme Wilson. In *Japan Quarterly*, 21, no. 3 (1974).

"Landscape with Disgusting Objects," "That Nape's a Fish." Tr. Graeme Wilson. In *Japan Quarterly*, 21, no. 2 (1974).

"Sick Room," "Garden," "Descent of Man," "By the River Tone." Tr. Graeme Wilson. In *Japan Quarterly*, 21, no. 1 (1974).

"In Dreams." Tr. Graeme Wilson. In *Japan Quarterly*, 22, no. 2 (1975).

"Withering Crime." Tr. Graeme Wilson. In *Japan Quarterly*, 22, no. 1 (1975).

8 tanka. Tr. Reiko Tsukimura. In *Journal of the Association of Teachers of Japanese*, 11, no. 1 (January 1976).

Blue Cat. Tr. Hiroaki Sato. In his *Howling at the Moon*. Tokyo, 1978.

Howling at the Moon. Tr. Hiroaki Sato. In his *Howling at the Moon*. Tokyo, 1978.

"Ascending a Mountain," "Inside a Carriage," "Death of a Frog." Tr. Edith Marcombe Shiffert and Yūki Sawa. In *Loon*, nos. 10 and 11 (December 1978).

"Death," "Impatience." Tr. Stephen Wolfe. In *Loon*, nos. 10 and 11 (December 1978).

"Drunken Death," "Dried Up Crime." Tr. Stephen Wolfe. In *Poetry Nippon*, nos. 43 and 44 (1978).

"The Frog's Death." Tr. Greg Campbell. In *Loon*, nos. 10 and 11 (December 1978).

"Mid-Spring." Tr. Takeyuki Osada. In *Loon*, nos. 10 and 11 (December 1978).

"The Stem," "Bamboo." Tr. Stephen Wolfe. In *Poetry Nippon*, nos. 41 and 42 (1978).

"Tender Love," "Buddha." Tr. James Kirkup. In A. R. Davis, ed., *Modern Japanese Poetry*. St. Lucia, Queensland, 1978.

"Night Train," "Cherry," "On a Trip," "An Impression of Early Summer," "Bamboo," "Sickly Face at the Bottom of the Ground," "Spring Night," "Sunny Spring," "Lover of Love," "White Public Benches," "The Hand Is a Cake," "Twilight Room," "The Army," "In the Horse Carriage," "A Barren Area," "Out of the Inner Shell of a Certain Landscape," "Pinks and a Blue Cat," "The Corpse of a Cat," "The Octopus That Does Not Die," "Yoshiwara." Tr. Hiroaki Sato. In Hiroaki Sato and Burton Watson, eds., *From the Country of Eight Islands*. Garden City, N.Y., 1981.

MIYAZAWA KENJI

"Never Marred by Rain." Tr. Shigeshi Nishimura. In *Eigo seinen*, 101, no. 12 (1955).

"Composition 1063." Tr. Donald Keene. In his *Modern Japanese Literature*. New York, 1957.

"Refractive Index," "The Snow on Saddle Mountain," "Spring and the Ashura," "Cloud Semaphore," "The Scene," "A Break," "Dawn," "Some Views Concerning the Proposed Site of a National Park," "Cow," "Floating World Picture," "Spring in the Kitagami Mountains," "Orders," "Distant Labor," "The Politicians," "Moon, Son of Heaven," "Daydreaming on the Trail," "The Great Power Line Pole," "Pine Needles," "Thief." Tr. Gary Snyder. In his *The Back Country*. New York, 1957.

"Sapporo City," "Orchard," "Fantasia under the Clear Sky," "Silent Wail." Tr. Takamichi Ninomiya and D. J. Enright. In their *The Poetry of Living Japan*. London, 1957.

"Unyielding to Rain." Tr. Ichiro Kōno and Rikutaro Fukuda. In their *An Anthology of Modern Japanese Poetry*. Tokyo, 1957.

"Shadow from a Future Sphere," "Petals of Karma," "The Dance of a Snake." Tr. J. G. Mills and Rikutaro Fukuda. In *Japan Quarterly*, 5, no. 1 (1958).

"November Third." Tr. Geoffrey Bownas and Anthony Thwaite. In their *The Penguin Book of Japanese Verse*. Baltimore, 1964.

"Spring," "The Carbide Warehouse," "A Young Land Cultivation De-

partment Technician's Recitative on Irises," "The Last Farewell,"
"The Master of the Field," "The Prefectural Engineer's Statement
Regarding Clouds." Tr. Hiroaki Sato. In his *Ten Japanese Poets.* Hanover, N.H., 1973.
"Spring & Asura," "The Thief," "An Impression," "Report," "Proem,"
"A Mountain Cop," "Massaniello," "Pine Needles," "Voiceless Grief,"
"White Birds," "Okhotsk Elegy," "Volcano Bay: A Nocturne," "Spring,"
"Reservoir Note," "Mountain Fire," "The Sea-Eroded Tableland,"
"The Crow," "The Weather Bureau," "Rest," "Bamboo & Oak," "Untitled (14)," "The Light and the Wound," "A Letter," "Single Tree
Field," "Commandments Forbidding Greed & Desire," "Past Desire,"
"'The hard keyura jewels . . . ,'" "Spring," "Mr. Pamirs the Scholar
Takes a Walk," "The Bull," "The Horse," "Untitled (99)," "An Opinion Concerning a Proposed National Park Site," "Wind & Resentments," "A Valediction," "Drought & Zazen," "Shadow from the
Future," "Fantasy During a Journey," "Flower Petals of Karma," "Excursion Permit," "Praying for the Good Devil's Absolution," "Harvesting the Earless Millet," "Cloud," "The Highway," "The Snake
Dance," "Field," "Flood," "Work," "Hospital," "Untitled (1015)," "Sapporo City," "Ambiguous Argument about a Spring Cloud," "The Unruly Horse," "Untitled (1071)," "Colleagues," "Rice-Growing," "The
Breeze Comes Filling the Valley," "Member of a Committee to Inspect Free-Style Paintings," "Flowers & Birds: November," "Untitled
(1087)," "'The man I parted from, below,'" "The Landowner," "The
Hateful Kuma Eats His Lunch," "'A few more times,'" "'In the
leaden moonlight,'" "'Since the doctor is still young,'" "Pictures of
the Floating World," "October 20th," "Talking with Your Eyes." Tr.
Hiroaki Sato. In his *Spring & Asura.* Chicago, 1973.
"The Sword-Dancers' Troupe of Haratai—a Mental Picture." Tr. Hideo
Yamaguchi. In *Kobe jogakuin daigaku ronshū,* 18, no. 3 (1973).
"Politicians," "Ukiyo-e," "Spring in Kitagami Mountains, Part 1." Tr.
Joshua Goldberg. In *Poetry Nippon,* nos. 29 and 30 (1975).
"Dawn." Tr. Joshua Goldberg. In *Poetry Nippon,* nos. 35 and 36 (1976).
"Daydreams of a Lakeside Exile." Tr. Fumio Morizuka. In *The Reeds,* 14
(1976).
"The Morning I Said Farewell to My Sister," "Farewell." Tr. James
Kirkup. In A. R. Davis, ed., *Modern Japanese Poetry.* St. Lucia,
Queensland, 1978.
"That Very Dark, Large Object." Tr. Stephen Wolfe. In *Loon,* nos. 10
and 11 (December 1978).
"Spring & Asura," "The Landscape Inspector," "Traveler," "Bamboo &
Oak," "The Last Farewell," "Okhotsk Elegy," "'Spring' Variation,"
"The Prefectural Engineer's Statement Regarding Clouds," "The
Breeze Comes Filling the Valley," "Night," "Rest," "November 3rd."
Tr. Hiroaki Sato. In Hiroaki Sato and Burton Watson, eds., *From the
Country of Eight Islands.* Garden City, N.Y., 1981.

TAKAMURA KŌTARŌ

2 tanka. Tr. Asataro Miyamori. In his *Masterpieces of Japanese Poetry, Ancient and Modern.* Tokyo, 1936.
"A Young Girl." Tr. Shigeshi Nishimura. In *The Current of the World*, 29, no. 7 (1952).
3 tanka. Tr. V. H. Viglielmo. In Yoshie Okazaki, *Japanese Literature in the Meiji Era.* Tokyo, 1955.
"The Land of Netsuke," "Winter Has Come." Tr. Donald Keene. In his *Modern Japanese Literature.* New York, 1956.
"Winter Has Come." Tr. Satoru Sato and Constance Urdang. In *Poetry*, 88, no. 2 (May 1956).
"My Poetry," "Taciturn Sea Captain," "The Rain-Beaten Cathedral." Tr. Takamichi Ninomiya and D. J. Enright. In their *The Poetry of Living Japan.* London, 1957.
"A Night at Atelier." Tr. Ichiro Kono and Rikutaro Fukuda. In their *An Anthology of Modern Japanese Poetry.* Tokyo, 1957.
"A Cock Horse," "Pearl Harbor Day," "Paris." Tr. Ryōzō Matsumoto. In his *Japanese Literature, New and Old.* Tokyo, 1961.
"Bedraggled Ostrich," "Artless Talk," "Chieko Mounting on the Wind." Tr. Geoffrey Bownas and Anthony Thwaite. In their *The Penguin Book of Japanese Verse.* Baltimore, 1964.
"My Father's Face." Tr. Makoto Ueda. In *The East-West Review*, 2, no. 3 (Spring–Summer 1966).
"A Ragged Ostrich." Tr. William L. Clark. In *Jiji eigo kenkyū* 21, no. 6 (1966).
"December 8th." Tr. Donald Keene. In his *Landscapes and Portraits.* Tokyo, 1971.
"A Lonely Road," "The Mountain," "Chieko and the Plovers." Tr. Hideo Yamaguchi. In *Kobe jogakuin daigaku ronshū*, 18, no. 3 (1972).
"A Man Sharpening a Knife," "Mars Is Out," "Plum Wine," "Another Rotating Thing," "The Itinerary," "Winter Has Come," "Difficult Chieko." Tr. Edith Marcombe Shiffert and Yūki Sawa. In their *Anthology of Modern Japanese Poetry.* Rutland, Vt., 1972.
"The Bath Is Brimful," "Winter Comes." Tr. Takurō Ikeda, John Needham, and Keiko Kikuchi. In *Poetry Nippon*, no. 25 (1973).
"Cathedral Beaten by Rain." Tr. Takurō Ikeda and John Needham. In *Poetry Nippon*, no. 24 (1973).
"Father's Face," "Rodin in the Railway Carriage," "Chieko Climbs the Wind," "Jottings," "Winter Has Come," "A Long Bead Drawn on Life," "Lemon Elegy," "At a Cafe," "You Grow More Beautiful," "Chieko Who No Longer Fits," "Person Who Delivers Beauty to Imprisonment," "The Day of Pearl Harbor," "Six Edgy Epigrams," "Central Park Zoo," "Seven Impromptu Pieces." Tr. Ikuko Atsumi and Graeme Wilson. In *Japan Quarterly*, 20, no. 3 (1973).
"To Someone," "Late Night Snow," "Dinner," "Two under the Tree,"

"Cattle on a Mad Run," "Two at Night," "Child's Talk," "Chieko Riding the Wind," "Chieko Playing with Plover," "Invaluable Chieko," "Two at the Foot of the Mountain," "Lemon Elegy," "Barren Homecoming," "Metropolis," "Dream," "Soliloquy on a Night of Blizzard." Tr. Hiroaki Sato. In his *Ten Japanese Poets*. Hanover, N.H., 1973.

Chieko-sho. Tr. Soichi Furuta. New York, 1974.

"Chieko Soaring on the Wind," "Autumn Prayer." Tr. Kyōko Yamasaki and Keiko Kikuchi. In *Poetry Nippon*, no. 28 (1974).

"An Innocent Story of the Sky," "Two People at Night," "Chieko Playing with Chidori," "Chieko Flying in the Wind," "A Homecoming That Is Hopeless," "Lemon Elegy," "Snow Late at Night," "Chiselling Out a Carp," "Carving a Locust," "Ode to the Nude Statues at Lake Towada." Tr. Edith Shiffert and Yūki Sawa. In their *Chieko*. Memphis, 1974.

"Long Journey." Tr. Naoshi Kōriyama. In *Poetry Nippon*, no. 28 (1974).

"A Sultry Day." Tr. Keiko Kikuchi. In *Poetry Nippon*, no. 27 (1974).

"You and I." Tr. Kyōko Yamasaki. In *Poetry Nippon*, no. 26 (1974).

"Night in a Studio," "Wind," "Summer," "Winter Comes," "Night," "Mountain," "Winter Has Come," "The Soil in May," "You and I under a Tree," "You Are Becoming Increasingly Lovelier," "Chieko Plays with Plovers," "Unattainable Chieko," "Alone with You at the Mountain," "An Elegy on Lemons," "A Lost Homecoming." Tr. Keiko Kikuchi and Kyōko Yukawa. In Marie Philomène, ed., *Japanese Songs of Innocence and Experience*. Tokyo, 1975.

"You and I under a Tree," "Night in a Studio," "Winter Poem." Tr. Kyōko Yukawa, Keiko Kikuchi, Takurō Ikeda, and John Needham. In *Poetry Nippon*, nos. 29 and 30 (1975).

3 tanka. Tr. Keiko Kikuchi. In *Poetry Nippon*, nos. 35 and 36 (1976).

Chieko's Sky. Tr. Soichi Furuta. Tokyo, 1978.

"Autumn Prayer," "Two at the Foot of a Mountain," "Specimen." Tr. James Kirkup. In A. R. Davis, ed., *Modern Japanese Poetry*. St. Lucia, Queensland, 1978.

"The Country of Netsuke," "Night in a Studio," "Desolation," "My Father's Face," "Italian Pilgrimage," "Complaint," "Winter Has Come," "Clay," "The Journey," "Autumn Prayer," "Clearing Sky," "Cat," "Melon," "Cathedral in the Thrashing Rain," "Wooden Clogs," "From the Workshop: II," "Integrity," "Polar Bears," "Head-Hunting," "Onions," "Harsh Insight," "Comic Verse," "Gratitude," "Thunder Beast," "Waiting for Autumn," "Big Sneeze," "Late Night," "Mars Is Out," "Winter, My Friend," "What's Great," "Daybreak," "Thinking of Mother," "15 Occasional Pieces," "Peaceful Time," "Tattered Ostrich," "The Natural Thing," "Alone Absorbing Oxygen," "Falling Ill on a Journey," "Kitajima Setsuzan," "Knife Whetter," "The Lanky Fellow Keeps Silent," "Portrait," "Haunted House," "Making a Carp," "Shark," "Baboon," "Unprecedented Time," "The History of Making the Statue of Danjūrō," "Sitting Alone," "Night in the Haunted

House," "Carving a Cicada," "Setting Sun," "Living and Cooking by Myself," "Beautiful Dead Leaf," "To General Kuribayashi," "The Snow Has Piled White," "Hunger for the Human Body," "Hands Wet with Moon," "Fear," "To Someone in the Suburbs," "To Someone," "Fountain of Mankind," "In Adoration of Love," "Catfish," "Life in Perspective," "To One Who Died," "Plum Wine," "Shōan Temple," "Kowtow," "Topknot," "First Lieutenant Gunji," "Sino-Japanese War," "Sculpting in the Imperial Presence," "Funds for Building Warships," "The Statue of Lord Kusunoki," "Sculpting Only," "Paris," "Unfilial," "Decadence," "Living in Beauty," "Terrifying Emptiness," "Cooperative Council," "The Day of Pearl Harbor," "Romain Rolland," "Imbecility," "End of the War," "Report," "Mountain Woods." Tr. Hiroaki Sato. In his *Chieko and Other Poems of Takamura Kōtarō*. Honolulu, 1980.

"To Someone," "In Adoration of Love," "Cathedral in the Thrashing Rain," "Comic Verse," "Knife Whetter," "Spouting Whale," "Lemon Elegy," "Beautiful Dead Leaf," "Shōan Temple," "Sculpting in the Imperial Presence," "Cooperative Council," "The Day of Pearl Harbor." Tr. Hiroaki Sato. In Hiroaki Sato and Burton Watson, eds., *From the Country of Eight Islands*. Garden City, N.Y., 1981.

OGIWARA SEISENSUI

5 haiku. Tr. Asatarō Miyamori. In his *Anthology of Haiku, Ancient and Modern*. Tokyo, 1932.

2 haiku. Tr. Asatarō Miyamori. In his *Haiku Poems, Ancient and Modern*. Tokyo, 1940.

3 haiku. Tr. V. H. Viglielmo. In Yoshie Okazaki, *Japanese Literature in the Meiji Era*. Tokyo, 1955.

2 haiku. Tr. R. H. Blyth. In his *Haiku*, Vol. 1. Tokyo, 1956.

20 haiku. Tr. R. H. Blyth. In his *A History of Haiku*, Vol. 2. Tokyo, 1964.

4 haiku. Tr. Edith Marcombe Shiffert and Yūki Sawa. In their *Anthology of Modern Japanese Poetry*. Rutland, Vt., 1972.

20 haiku. Tr. Makoto Ueda. In his *Modern Japanese Haiku: An Anthology*. Toronto, 1976.

3 haiku. Tr. Hiroaki Sato. In *Frogpond*, 4, no. 2 (1981).

TAKAHASHI SHINKICHI

"Birth." Tr. Satoru Sato and Constance Urdang. In *Poetry*, 88, no. 2 (May 1956).

"Rainbow on the Seashore," "The Ache of Life," "A Butterfly," "The Eastern Sky," "Endless," "Dishes," "Fish." Tr. Ichiro Kōno and Rikutaro Fukuda. In their *An Anthology of Modern Japanese Poetry*. Tokyo, 1957.

"The Raven," "The Fine Rain." Tr. Takamichi Ninomiya and D. J. Enright. In their *The Poetry of Living Japan*. London, 1957.

"Beach Rainbow," "Birth." Tr. Geoffrey Bownas and Anthony Thwaite. In their *The Penguin Book of Japanese Verse*. Baltimore, 1964.
"Strange Thing." Tr. Makoto Ueda. In *The East-West Review*, 2, no. 1 (Spring–Summer 1965).
"Calm." Tr. Graeme Wilson. In *Japan Quarterly*, 14, no. 1 (1967).
"Dreams," "Bottom of the Sea." Tr. Graeme Wilson. In *Japan Quarterly*, 14, no. 2 (1967).
"Dishes." Tr. Harold P. Wright. In *The Malahat Review*, no. 6 (April 1968).
"Wind I," "Wind II." Tr. Lucien Stryk and Takashi Ikemoto. In *Literature East and West*, 13, nos. 3 and 4 (1969).
"Broken Glasses," "The Fly," "The Ocean." Tr. Edith Marcombe Shiffert and Yūki Sawa. In their *Anthology of Modern Japanese Poetry*. Rutland, Vt., 1972.
"A Wood in Sound," "Aching of Life," "Snow Wind," "Canna," "Time," "The Pink Sun," "Thistles," "Rat on Mount Ishizuchi," "Burning Oneself to Death," "Nehru," "Strawberry," "Ox and Sleet," "Cock," "Back Yard," "The Pipe," "Crow," "White Flower," "A Spray of Hot Air," "City," "Murmuring of the Water," "Pigeon," "Mummy," "Red Waves," "Sparrow in Winter," "The Martian Rock," "Destruction," "Disclosure," "The Hare," "Duck," "What Is Moving," "Autumn Flowers," "The Peach," "One Hundred Billionth of a Second," "Quails," "Flower," "Stillness," "Horse," "Misty Rain," "Collapse," "Sun," "Words," "Rain," "Chidori Pool," "Bream," "Time," "Cat," "The Position of the Sparrow," "Life Infinite," "Paper Door," "Deck," "Spring Snow," "The Cloud and the Butterfly," "On a Day of Continuous Rain," "Black Smoke," "Evening Clouds," "Mascot," "Wind," "Wind among the Pines," "Stitches," "Sun and Flowers," "Comet," "Immutability," "Snail," "Here," "If I Am Flowers," "Man," "Statue of Kudara-Avalokitesvara," "Fish," "Cock," "Crab," "Ants," "Sun," "Sun Through the Leaves," "Magpie," "A Richer Ground," "Penguins," "Ivies," "Sparrow," "Apricot," "White Paper," "On the Wind," "Like Dewdrops," "Apex of the Universe," "Ice," "What Dashes?," "Wild Camomiles," "The Solid Season," "Lovebird," "Rat and Woman," "Body," "Afterimages." Tr. Lucien Stryk and Takashi Ikemoto. In their *Afterimages*. Garden City, N.Y., 1972.
"After I Was Born," "Butterfly," "Eastern Sky." Tr. Harold P. Wright. In Dorothy B. Shimer, ed., *Voices of Modern Asia*. New York, 1973.
"White Cloud." Tr. Harold P. Wright. In Jackson Bailey, ed., *Listening to Japan*. New York, 1973.
"Assertion Is Dadaist," "Dish," "A Deaf Man," "A Blind Man," "A Mute," "Nocturnal Emission," "I Am Not I," "Absence," "1911 Poems (Nos. 3, 4, 5, 7, 17, 22, 26, 31, 41, 46, 57, 62)." Tr. Ko Won. In his *Buddhist Elements in Dada*. New York, 1977.
"Shell," "Mushroom," "Flight of the Sparrow," "Sky," "Sparrow in Withered Field," "Afternoon," "Hand," "Sweet Potato," "Camel," "Raw

Fish and Vegetables," "Downy Hair," "Toad," "Drizzle," "Sea of Oblivion," "Cloud," "Mother and I," "Sheep," "Eternity," "Sparrow and Bird-Net Building," "Clay Image," "Gods," "Braggart Duck," "Stone Wall," "Beach," "Moon and Hare," "Lap Dog," "Moon," "Vimalakirti," "Snowy Sky," "Near Shinobazu Pond," "Let's Live Cheerfully," "Rocks," "Urn," "Spring," "Peach Blossom and Pigeon," "Spinning Dharma Wheel," "Four Divine Animals," "A Little Sunlight," "Explosion," "Railroad Station," "Absence." Tr. Lucien Stryk and Takashi Ikemoto. In their *The Penguin Book of Zen Poetry*. Chicago, 1977.

"No Meaning," "My Body," "Afterimage." Tr. James Kirkup. In A.R. Davis, ed., *Modern Japanese Poetry*. St. Lucia, Queensland, 1978.

Selected Bibliography

I. IN ENGLISH

Masaoka Shiki

Beichman, Janine. "Masaoka Shiki: His Life and Works." Ph.D. diss., Columbia Univ., 1974.
———. "Masaoka Shiki—The First Modern Haiku Poet." In Thomas J. Harper et al., eds., *An Invitation to Japan's Literature*. Tokyo, 1974.
Beichman-Yamamoto, Janine. "Masaoka Shiki's *A Drop of Ink*." *Monumenta Nipponica*, 30, no. 3 (Autumn 1975).
Blyth, R. H. "Shiki." In his *Haiku*, Vol. 1. Tokyo, 1952.
———. "Shiki: The Critic," "Shiki: On Furu-ike-ya," and "Shiki: The Haiku Poet." In his *A History of Haiku*, Vol. 2. Tokyo, 1964.
Brower, Robert H. "Masaoka Shiki and Tanka Reform." In Donald H. Shively, ed., *Tradition and Modernization in Japanese Culture*. Princeton, 1971.
Henderson, Harold Gould. "Masaoka Shiki." In his *The Bamboo Broom*. Boston, 1934.
———. "Shiki." In his *An Introduction to Haiku*. Garden City, N.Y., 1958.
Keene, Donald. "Masaoka Shiki." In his *Some Japanese Portraits*. Tokyo, 1978.
———. "Shiki and Takuboku." In his *Landscapes and Portraits*. Tokyo, 1971.
Miner, Earl. "The Verse Record of My Peonies." In his *Japanese Poetic Diaries*. Berkeley, Calif., 1969.

Yosano Akiko

Atsumi, Ikuko, and Graeme Wilson. "The Poetry of Yosano Akiko." In *Japan Quarterly*, 21, no. 2 (April–June 1974).
Honda, H. H. "The Poetry of Yosano Akiko." In his *The Poetry of Yosano Akiko*. Tokyo, 1957.
Sakanishi, Shio. "Introduction." In her *Tangled Hair*. Boston, 1935.
Shinoda, Seishi, and Sanford Goldstein. "Introduction." In their *Tangled Hair*. Lafayette, Ind., 1971.

Ishikawa Takuboku

Goldstein, Sanford, and Seishi Shinoda. "Introduction." In their *Sad Toys*. West Lafayette, Ind., 1977.

Hijiya, Yukihito. *Ishikawa Takuboku*. Boston, 1979.

Keene, Donald. "Shiki and Takuboku." In his *Landscapes and Portraits*. Tokyo, 1971.

Linhart, Ruth. "Ishikawa Takuboku—Poetry: A Winter's 'Sad Toys.'" In Thomas J. Harper et al., eds., *An Invitation to Japan's Literature*. Tokyo, 1974.

Sakanishi, Shio. "Introduction." In her *A Handful of Sand*. Boston, 1934.

Sesar, Carl. "Introduction." In his *Takuboku: Poems to Eat*. Tokyo, 1966.

Takamine, Horoshi. *A Sad Toy: Takuboku's Life and Poems*. Tokyo, 1962.

Hagiwara Sakutarō

Sato, Hiroaki. "Introduction." In his *Howling at the Moon*. Tokyo, 1978.

Tsukimura, Reiko. "Hagiwara Sakutarō and the Japanese Lyric Tradition." *Journal of the Association of Teachers of Japanese*, 11, no. 1 (January 1976).

———. "A Japanese Adaptation of 'The Raven': Hagiwara and Poe." *Journal of Comparative Literature*, 16 (1973).

———. "The Language of Symbolism in Yeats and Hagiwara." Ph.D. diss., Indiana Univ., 1967.

Wilson, Graeme. "Introduction." In his *Face at the Bottom of the World*. Rutland, Vt., 1969.

———. "Some Longer Poems of Hagiwara Sakutarō." *Japan Quarterly*, 19, no. 2 (April–June 1972).

Miyazawa Kenji

Bester, John. "Foreword." In Kenji Miyazawa, *Winds from Afar*. Tokyo, 1972.

———. "To the Reader." In Kenji Miyazawa, *Winds and Wildcat Places*. Tokyo, 1967.

Nakajima, Kenzō. "Miyazawa Kenji, the Man and His Works." *Japan Quarterly*, 5, no. 1 (January–March 1958).

Sato, Hiroaki. "Introduction." In his *Spring & Asura*. Chicago, 1973.

Takamura Kōtarō

Atsumi, Ikuko, and Graeme Wilson. "The Poetry of Takamura Kōtarō." *Japan Quarterly*, 20, no. 3 (July–September 1973).

Furuta, Soichi. "Translator's Preface." In his *Chieko's Sky*. Tokyo, 1978.

Sato, Hiroaki. "Introduction." In his *Chieko and Other Poems of Takamura Kōtarō*. Honolulu, 1980.

434 Bibliography

Ogiwara Seisensui

Blyth, R. H. "The New Haiku." In his *A History of Haiku*, Vol. 2. Tokyo, 1964.

Takahashi Shinkichi

Ko Sung-Won. "Dada and Buddhist Thought: Takahashi Shinkichi as a Dada Poet Compared to Tristan Tzara." Ph.D. diss., New York Univ., 1974.
Ko Won. *Buddhist Elements in Dada.* New York, 1977.
Stryk, Lucien. "Shinkichi Takahashi: Contemporary Zen Poet." *The Malahat Review*, no. 18 (1971).

II. IN JAPANESE

Primary sources can be found in the preceding section entitled "Source Notes." The place of publication for the works below is Tokyo unless otherwise indicated.

Masaoka Shiki

Fujikawa Chūji. *Masaoka Shiki.* 1933.
Itō Shinkichi et al., eds. "Masaoka Shiki" (selected poems with commentaries by Katō Shūson). In their *Nihon no shiika*, Vol. 3. 1969.
Kubota Masafumi. *Masaoka Shiki.* 1967.
Kusumoto Kenkichi. *Masaoka Shiki.* 1966.
Matsui Toshihiko. *Masaoka Shiki no kenkyū.* 2 vols. 1976.
Murooka Kazuko. *Shiki bungakuron no kenkyū.* 1978.
Takahama Kyoshi. *Masaoka Shiki.* 1943.

Yosano Akiko

Hirano Banri. *Akiko kanshō.* 1949.
Itō Shinkichi et al., eds., "Yosano Akiko" (selected poems with commentaries by Shinma Shin'ichi). In their *Nihon no shiika*, Vol. 4. 1968.
Itsumi Kumi. *Midaregami zenshaku.* 1978.
Kubota Utsubo. *Yosano Akiko.* 1950.
Matsuda Yoshio. *Midaregami kenkyū.* 1952.
Satake Toshihiko. *Zenshaku midaregami kenkyū.* 1957.
Satō Sukeo. *Midaregami kō.* 1956.

Ishikawa Takuboku

Itō Shinkichi et al., eds., *Ishikawa Takuboku* (selected poems with commentaries by Yamamoto Kenkichi). *Nihon no shiika*, Vol. 5. 1967.
Iwaki Yukinori. *Ishikawa Takuboku den.* 1955.
Katsura Kōji. *Takuboku tanka no kenkyū.* 1968.
Kindaichi Kyōsuke et al., eds. *Takuboku kenkyū. Ishikawa Takuboku zenshū*, Vol. 8. 1979.

Kunisaki Mokutarō. *Takuboku ron josetsu.* 1960.
Nakano Shigeharu and Kubokawa Tsurujirō, eds. *Ishikawa Takuboku. Kindai bungaku kanshō kōza*, Vol. 8. 1960.
Nihon Bungaku Kenkyū Shiryō Kankōkai, ed. *Ishikawa Takuboku.* 1970.

Hagiwara Sakutarō

Fujiwara Sadamu. *Genshisha Hagiwara Sakutarō.* 1977.
Itō Sei, ed. *Hagiwara Sakutarō. Kindai bungaku kanshō kōza*, Vol. 15. 1960.
Itō Shinkichi et al., eds. *Hagiwara Sakutarō* (selected poems with commentaries by Itō Shinkichi). *Nihon no shiika*, Vol. 14. 1968.
Miyoshi Tatsuji. *Hagiwara Sakutarō.* 1963.
Naka Tarō, ed. *Hagiwara Sakutarō kenkyū.* 1974.
Nihon Bungaku Kenkyū Shiryō Kankōkai, ed. *Hagiwara Sakutarō.* 1971.
Takada Mizuho, ed. *Hagiwara Sakutarō kenkyū.* 1973.

Miyazawa Kenji

Amazawa Taijirō. *Miyazawa Kenji ron.* 1976.
Itō Shinkichi et al., eds. *Miyazawa Kenji* (selected poems with commentaries by Nakamura Minoru). *Nihon no shiika*, Vol. 18. 1968.
Miyazawa Kenji Kenkyūkai, ed. *Miyazawa Kenji ronshū*, Vol. 1. 1971.
Nakamura Minoru. *Miyazawa Kenji.* 1972.
Nihon Bungaku Kenkyū Shiryō Kankōkai, ed. *Takamura Kōtarō: Miyazawa Kenji.* 1973.
Sakai Tadaichi. *Hyōden Miyazawa Kenji.* 1975.
Tanikawa Tetsuzō. *Miyazawa Kenji no sekai.* 1963.

Takamura Kōtarō

Itō Shinkichi. *Takamura Kōtarō kenkyū.* 1966.
———— et al., eds. *Takamura Kōtarō* (selected poems with commentaries by Itō Shinkichi). *Nihon no shiika*, Vol. 10. 1967.
Kitagawa Taichi. *Takamura Kōtarō.* 1965.
Kusano Shinpei, ed. *Takamura Kōtarō kenkyū.* 1959.
Ukegawa Toshio. *Takamura Kōtarō ron.* 1969.
Yoshida Seiichi, ed. *Takamura Kōtarō no ningen to geijutsu.* 1972.
Yoshimoto Takaaki. *Takamura Kōtarō.* 1957.

Ogiwara Seisensui

Itō Shinkichi et al., eds. "Ogiwara Seisensui" (selected poems with commentaries by Murano Shirō). In their *Nihon no shiika*, Vol. 19. 1969.
Izawa Motoyoshi. "Ogiwara Seisensui." In his *Gendai haiku no nagare.* 1956.
Murano Shirō. "Ogiwara Seisensui." In Yoshida Seiichi and Kusumoto Kenkichi, eds., *Gendai haiku hyōshaku.* 1969.
"Ogiwara Seisensui tsuitō tokushū." In *Haiku*, 25, no. 8 (1976).
"Ogiwara Seisensui tsuitō tokushū." In *Haiku kenkyū*, 43, no. 11 (1976).

Ōno Rinka. "Ogiwara Seisensui." In his *Kindai haiku no kanshō to hihyō.* 1967.

Ueda Toshi. *Jiyūritsu haiku bungaku shi.* 1975.

Takahashi Shinkichi

Aida Tsunao. "Takahashi Shinkichi: hito to sakuhin" and "Kaisetsu." In *Nihon shijin zenshū*, Vol. 26. 1968.

Ikemoto Takashi. "Kaisetsu." In Takahashi Shinkichi, *Takahashi Shinkichi no zen no shi to essei.* 1973.

Itō Shinkichi et al., eds. "Takahashi Shinkichi" (selected poems with commentaries by Iijima Kōichi). In their *Nihon no shiika*, Vol. 20. 1969.

Kamei Katsuichirō. "Takahashi Shinkichi oboegaki." In *Takahashi Shinkichi shishū* (Kadokawa bunko). 1957.

Satō Haruo. "Takahashi Shinkichi no koto." In Tsuji Jun, ed., *Dadaisuto Shinkichi no shi.* 1923.

Shimizu Yasuo. "Kaisetsu." In Shimizu Yasuo, ed., *Takahashi Shinkichi shishū.* 1972.

Yamanoguchi Baku. "Takahashi Shinkichi oboegaki." In *Shinchō*, 53, no. 2 (1956).

Index

Takahashi Shinkichi

Miyazawa Kenji

Hagiwara Sakutarō

Yosano Akiko